Lecture Notes in Computer Science 5430

Commenced Publication in 1973
Founding and Former Series Editors:
Gerhard Goos, Juris Hartmanis, and Jan van Leeuwen

T0216671

Marina L. Gavrilova   C.J. Kenneth Tan
Edward David Moreno (Eds.)

Transactions on Computational Science IV

Special Issue on Security in Computing

 Springer

Editors-in-Chief

Marina L. Gavrilova
University of Calgary
Department of Computer Science
2500 University Drive N.W.
Calgary, AB, T2N 1N4, Canada
E-mail: marina@cpsc.ucalgary.ca

C.J. Kenneth Tan
OptimaNumerics Ltd.
Cathedral House
23-31 Waring Street
Belfast BT1 2DX, UK
E-mail: cjtan@optimanumerics.com

Guest Editor

Edward David Moreno
University of Amazonas State - UEA
Manaus, AM, Brazil
E-mail: edwdavid@gmail.com

Library of Congress Control Number: Applied for

CR Subject Classification (1998): D.4.6, C.2-4, F.2, E.1-4, K.4.4, K.6.5

ISSN 0302-9743 (Lecture Notes in Computer Science)
ISSN 1866-4733 (Transaction on Computational Science)

ISBN 978-3-642-01003-3 Springer Berlin Heidelberg New York

springer.com

© Springer-Verlag Berlin Heidelberg 2009

Typesetting: Camera-ready by author, data conversion by Scientific Publishing Services, Chennai, India
Printed on acid-free paper   SPIN: 12649952   06/3180   5 4 3 2 1 0

LNCS Transactions on Computational Science

Computational science, an emerging and increasingly vital field, is now widely recognized as an integral part of scientific and technical investigations, affecting researchers and practitioners in areas ranging from aerospace and automotive research to biochemistry, electronics, geosciences, mathematics, and physics. Computer systems research and the exploitation of applied research naturally complement each other. The increased complexity of many challenges in computational science demands the use of supercomputing, parallel processing, sophisticated algorithms, and advanced system software and architecture. It is therefore invaluable to have input by systems research experts in applied computational science research.

Transactions on Computational Science focuses on original high-quality research in the realm of computational science in parallel and distributed environments, also encompassing the underlying theoretical foundations and the applications of large-scale computation. The journal offers practitioners and researchers the opportunity to share computational techniques and solutions in this area, to identify new issues, and to shape future directions for research, and it enables industrial users to apply leading-edge, large-scale, high-performance computational methods.

In addition to addressing various research and application issues, the journal aims to present material that is validated – crucial to the application and advancement of the research conducted in academic and industrial settings. In this spirit, the journal focuses on publications that present results and computational techniques that are verifiable.

Scope

The scope of the journal includes, but is not limited to, the following computational methods and applications:

- Aeronautics and Aerospace
- Astrophysics
- Bioinformatics
- Climate and Weather Modeling
- Communication and Data Networks
- Compilers and Operating Systems
- Computer Graphics
- Computational Biology
- Computational Chemistry
- Computational Finance and Econometrics
- Computational Fluid Dynamics
- Computational Geometry

- Computational Number Theory
- Computational Physics
- Data Storage and Information Retrieval
- Data Mining and Data Warehousing
- Grid Computing
- Hardware/Software Co-design
- High-Energy Physics
- High-Performance Computing
- Numerical and Scientific Computing
- Parallel and Distributed Computing
- Reconfigurable Hardware
- Scientific Visualization
- Supercomputing
- System-on-Chip Design and Engineering

Security in Computing: Trends and Challenges

Guest Editor s Foreword

In an increasingly connected world, security has become an essential component of modern information systems. Our ever-increasing dependence on information implies that the importance of information security is growing. Several examples of security applications are present in everyday life such as mobile phone communication, secure e-mail, internet banking, data encryption, etc.

The thrust of embedded computing has both diversified and intensified in recent years as the focus on mobile computing, ubiquitous computing, and traditional embedded applications has begun to converge. A side effect of this intensity is the desire to support sophisticated applications such as speech recognition, visual feature recognition, and secure wireless networking in a mobile, battery-powered platform. Unfortunately these applications are currently intractable for the embedded space.

Another consideration is related to mobile computing, and, especially, security in these environments. The first step in developing new architectures and systems which can adequately support these applications is a precise understanding of the techniques and methods that comes close to meeting the needs of security, performance, and energy requirements.

This special issue brings together high-quality and state-of-the-art contributions on "Security in Computing." The papers included in this issue deal with some hot topics in the security research sphere: new architectures, novel hardware implementations, cryptographic algorithms and security protocols, and new tools and applications. Concretely, the special issue contains 14 selected papers that represent the diverse applications and designs being addressed today by the security and cryptographic research community.

As a whole, this special issue provides a perspective on trends and challenges in security research. With authors from around the world, these articles bring us an international sampling of significant work.

The title of the first paper is "Hardware Mechanisms for Memory Authentication: A Survey of Existing Techniques and Engines," by Reouven Elbaz, David Champagne, Catherine Gebotys, Ruby B. Lee, Nachiketh Potlapally and Lionel Torres. This paper describes tree hardware mechanisms (Merkle Tree, PAT and TEC-Tree) that provide memory authentication and the architectural features proposed in the literature to efficiently implement those trees in computing platforms. The authors also discuss the impact of operating system compromise on the integrity verification engine and present an existing solution for secure and efficient application memory authentication despite an untrusted operating system. Finally, they show which additional security issues should be considered for data authentication at runtime in symmetric multi-processors platforms and how they differ from memory authentication in uniprocessor systems.

In the second contribution, entitled "Behavioral Characterization for Network Anomaly Detection," Victor P. Roche and Unai Arronategui propose a methodology for detecting abnormal traffic on the net, such as worm attacks, based on the observation of the behavior of different elements at the network edges. This methodology means an advance in the detection of a new infection in the backbone of the network, but also in the identification of the infected hosts of a specific network. The authors try to detect network anomalies by tracking the behavior of different network levels. This proposed method is not based on intrinsic characteristics of the worm but on their manner of acting. This methodology has proved its effectiveness in real infections caused by viruses such as SpyBot and Agobot in accordance with experimental tests.

In the third contribution, which is entitled "The Power of Anonymous Veto in Public Discussion," Feng Hao and Piotr Zielinski propose an exceptional solution—Anonymous Veto Network (or AV-net)—to allow a group of participants to compute a boolean-OR function securely. This protocol is provably secure under the Decision Diffie-Hellman (DDH) and random oracle assumptions. When compared with other related works, this solution does not require any private channels or third parties; it has no message collisions, hence requires no retransmissions; being semantically secure, it provides the strongest protection of a vetoer's anonymity until all the other participants are compromised; it resists robustly against jamming, hence ensures each participant's veto power; it requires only two rounds of broadcast. Finally, the computational load, the bandwidth usage, and the cost of verifying zero-knowledge proofs are also interesting.

The fourth contribution, which is entitled "Collusion-Resistant Message Authentication in Overlay Multicast Communication," by Emad Eldin Mohamed and Hussein Abdel-Wahab, introduces a new technique for collusion-resistant message authentication in overlay multicast. A basic feature of overlay multicast is that the receivers may also take over the responsibility of delivering the multicast traffic from the source to other group members. The proposed technique minimizes the computational cost through signature amortization. In order to evaluate their technique, the authors conducted a simulation study to compare the proposed technique against previous ones. Results obtained from the study show that the proposed technique is more suitable for overlay multicast than those developed for IP multicast. More specifically, the proposed technique has better communication and better receiver computation overheads (especially when forged messages are considered) than earlier ones.

In the fifth contribution, entitled "A Model for Authentication Credentials Translation in Service-Oriented Architecture," Emerson Ribeiro de Mello, Michelle S. Wangham, Joni da Silva Fraga, Edson T. de Camargo, and Davi da Silva Böger describe a model that enables authentication with SSO (single sign on), which was developed to simplify the interactions among clients and different service providers. This paper deals with interoperability between heterogeneous security technologies. The proposed model is based on the credential translation service that allows SSO, and even heterogeneous security technologies are considered. In the entire system, access authorizations to resources depend on this authentication, which sensibly diminishes the data flux between the domains and the management of these data in the system as a whole. Therefore, the proposed model provides authentication credential translation and attribute transposition and, as a consequence, provides authorization involving different kinds of credentials and permissions in the federation environment.

By making use of Web Services, this study is strongly based on concepts introduced in the SAML, WS-Trust, and WS-Federation specifications.

In the sixth paper, which is entitled "Secure and Efficient Group Key Agreements for Cluster Based Networks," Ratna Dutta and Tom Dowling consider that ad hoc networks may be logically represented as a set of clusters; they then present two dynamically efficient authenticated group key agreement protocols by reflecting ad hoc networks in a topology composed of a set of clusters. The protocols support dynamic membership events and their communication and computation efficiencies are favorably compared with a previous group of key agreement protocols in a cluster-based structure. The proposed protocols avoid the use of a trusted third party (TTP) or a central authority, eliminating a single point attack. They allow easy addition an removal of nodes, and achieve better performance in comparison with the existing cluster-based key agreement protocols. Additionally, their proposed schemes are supported by sound security analysis in formal security models under standard cryptographic assumptions. The authors have distinguished between the two approaches from a performance point of view and have shown that the second scheme is the better one in the context of wireless ad hoc networks.

In the seventh paper, entitled "An Integrated ECC-MAC Based on RS Code," Jaydeb Bhaumik and Dipanwita Roy Chowdhury propose a new integrated scheme for message authentication (MAC algorithm) based on RS code having t-symbol error correcting capability. In their proposed MAC generation algorithm, the authors used a function Nmix for mixing the sequence with the error-correcting check symbols. The proposed scheme is secured even if the same pad is used for more than one MAC generation. The proposed function reduces the bias of linear approximations exponentially. In addition, the proposed MAC is found to be a good choice for the keyed-hash technique and evaluated successfully for bit-variance and entropy test. The proposed function can be used effectively as a key mixing function in hardware-based block ciphers.

In the eighth paper, which is entitled "Optimizing Pseudonym Updation in Vehicular Ad-hoc Network," Brijesh Kumar Chaurasia, Shekhar Verma, G. S. Tomar, and Ajith Abraham focus on the problem of diminishing the possibility of forging a relationship between vehicle identity and its transmissions by determining the conditions that maximize anonymity during an identity switch. A vehicle can be tracked through its transmission. The broadcast by a source contains its current identity and also allows estimation of its location by receivers. This mapping between the physical entity and the estimated location through the communication broadcast is a threat to privacy. Therefore, this paper addresses the challenges in providing anonymity to a moving vehicle that uses a temporary identity for transmission and continually changes this pseudonym. The authors propose a heuristic that allows a vehicle to switch its pseudonym at a time and place where the anonymity can be maximized. Results indicate that updating pseudonyms in accordance with the heuristic maximizes the entropy and, through it, the anonymity of a vehicle.

The paper "Security Analysis of Role-Based Access Control Models Using Colored Petri Nets and CPNtools" authored by Hind Rakkay and Hanifa Boucheneb presents a formal technique to model and analyze role based access control models (RBAC) using colored Petri nets (CP-nets) and CPN-tools for editing and analyzing CP-nets which describes generic access control structures based on an RBAC policy that can then be composed with different context-specific aspects depending on the application. In this way, RBAC aspects can be reused across different applications with similar access control requirements. The authors propose an analysis framework that can be used by security administrators to generate correct specification iteratively. A significant benefit of CP-nets and, particularly, CPN-tools is to provide a more intuitive way for system developers to model and analyze complex systems.

The paper "Role-Based Access Control with Spatiotemporal Context for Mobile Applications," by Subhendu Aich, Samrat Mondal, Shamik Sural, and Arun Kumar Majumder, proposes a complete RBAC model in a spatiotemporal domain based on the idea of spatiotemporal extent. The concept of a spatiotemporal role extent and spatiotemporal permission extent introduced here enables the model to specify granular spatiotemporal access control policies not specifiable in the existing approaches. In a typical access request, a user activates a suitable role where the required permission to access the requested object is available. Thus in classical RBAC, role and permission are important logical entities through which a user ultimately gains the access to an object. The concept of spatiotemporal access is introduced in the form of role extent, and permission extent, which is simple to understand and expressive in terms of specifying combined space time-based security policy. As a proof of concept, the authors have implemented the proposed spatiotemporal access control method in a mobile telemedicine system.

The paper "A Method for Estimation of the Success Probability of an Intrusion Process by Considering the Time Aspects of the Attacker Behavior" authored by Jaafar Almasizadeh and Mohammad Abdollahi Azgomi proposes a generic and new method for modeling and quantifying the security of computer systems. The authors utilize stochastic modeling techniques for quantitative assessment of security measures for computer systems. In the proposed method, intrusion process is divided into its principal phases. At each phase, the probability of attacker success is computed. It is assumed that the attacker will finally succeed if he can pass all steps successfully. The interaction between the attacker and the system is displayed by a semi-Markov chain (SMC). Intrusion process modeling is done by an SMC. Distribution functions assigned to SMC transitions are uniform distributions. Uniform distributions represent the sojourn time of the attacker or the system in the transient states. This probability is a numerical measure for the security level provided by the system. Then the SMC is converted into a discrete-time Markov chain (DTMC). The DTMC is analyzed and the probability of attacker success is then computed based on mathematical theorems. Thus the security measure can be obtained.

The paper "A Hardware Architecture for Integrated-Security Services," authored by Fabio Dacêncio Pereira and Edward David Moreno, proposes a special architecture and describes the functionalities of an embedded system of SSI (integration of the security services), which prevents malicious attacks on systems and networks. It was implemented in an embedded security system (into a SoC system). The different modules dedicated to security such as AES, RSA, HASH, among others, were implemented. It is important to note that the performance statistics (runtime related to circuit delays) and physical area of implementation in hardware are presented and discussed. It reaches an improved performance and the SoC prioritizes the implementation of dedicated functions in hardware such as cryptographic algorithms, communication interfaces, among others. In their prototype, initially, the flow control functions and settings are running in software. This article shows the architecture, functionality, and performance of the system developed, and the authors discuss a real implementation in FPGA.

The paper "Evaluating Resistance of MCML Technology to Power Analysis Attacks Using a Simulation-Based Methodology" authored by Francesco Regazzoni et al. presents a simulation-based methodology for evaluating the resistance of cryptographic circuits to power analysis attacks. The authors used a special methodology to evaluate the MCML technology as a possible counter-measure against side channel attacks based on power analysis, and demonstrated the robustness of MCML against the SPA and against the powerful variant of DPA based on correlation. To achieve this result, they developed a design flow and a SPICE-level simulation environment. Their results show that the power traces obtained by simulating two full cores, implementing the AES algorithm and realized in MCML, are very difficult to attack, as opposed to an CMOS implementation for which the same attacks were always successful.

The last paper in this special issue, "Putting Trojans on the Horns of a Dilemma: Redundancy for Information Theft Detection" by Jedidiah R. Crandall, John Brevik, Shaozhi Ye, Gary Wassermann, Daniela A.S. de Oliveira, Zhendong Su, S. Felix Wu, and Frederic T. Wong, presents an approach that detects information theft by measuring explicitly everything that could have happened. The authors propose a technique based on repeated deterministic replays in a virtual machine to detect the theft of private information. The authors prove upper bounds on the average amount of information an attacker can steal without being detected, even if they are allowed an arbitrary distribution of visible output states.

To conclude, we sincerely hope that this special issue stimulates your interest in the many issues surrounding the area of security. The topics covered in the papers are timely and important, and the authors have done an excellent job of presenting their different approaches. Regarding the reviewing process, our referees (integrated by recognized researches from the international community) made a great effort to evaluate the papers. We would like to acknowledge their effort in providing us with the excellent feedback at the right time. Therfore, we wish to thank all the authors and reviewers. Finally, we would also like to express our gratitude to the Editor-in-Chief of TCS, Marina L. Gravilova, for her advice, vision and support.

January 2009   Edward David Moreno

LNCS Transactions on Computational Science – Editorial Board

Reviewers

Konstantinou Elisavet	Department of Information and Communication Systems Engineering, University of the Aegean, Samos, Greece
Leonardo Augusto Ribeiro	University of Pernambuco, UFPE, Brazil
Luiza de Macedo Mourelle	State University of Rio de Janeiro, Brazil
Maria Luisa Damiani	University of Milan, Italy
Martin Drahansky	Brno University of Technology, Faculty of Information Technology, Czech Republic
Martin Rehak	Czech Technical University in Prague, Czech Republic
Mehran Misaghi	SOCIESC (Sociedade Educacional de Santa Catarina), Brazil
Meuse Nogueira de Oliveira Júnior	Federal Center of Technological Education of Pernambuco State, Brazil
Michael Kirkpatrick	Purdue University, USA
Michelle Silva Wangham	University of Vale do Itajaí (UNIVALI), Brazil
Mikaël Ates	Université de Lyon – University Jean Monnet of Saint-Etienne
Milena Milenkovic	IBM
Mohsen Toorani	Iran University of Science and Technology, Iran
Nachiketh Potlapally	Intel Corporation
Nadia Nedjah	State University of Rio de Janeiro, Brazil
Naixue Xiong	Department of Computer Science, Georgia State University, USA
Neil Vachharajani	Google
Nur Zincir-Heywood	Dalhousie University, Canada
Paolo Perlasca	University of Milan, Italy
Phongsak Keeratiwintakorn	King Mongkut's University of Technology North Bangkok, Thailand
Raimundo da Silva Barreto	Federal Universitiy of Amazonas, Brazil
Rami Yared	JAIST – Japan Advanced Institute of Science and Technology, Japan
Ratna Dutta	Claude Shannon Institute, NUIM, Maynooth, Ireland
Ren-Chiun Wang	Department of Electrical Engineering, National Taiwan University, Taiwan
Reouven Elbaz	University of Waterloo, Canada
Ruy de Queiroz	University of Pernambuco, UFPE, Brazil
Shamik Sural	School of Information Technology, Indian Institute of Technology, India
Siddhartha Chhabra	NC State University, USA
Steven Galbraith	Mathematics Department at Auckland University, New Zealand
Tai-hoon Kim	Hannam University, Korea
Tamás Holczer	BME, Budapest, Hungary

Table of Contents

Hardware Mechanisms for Memory Authentication: A Survey of Existing Techniques and Engines

Reouven Elbaz[1,2], David Champagne[2], Catherine Gebotys[1], Ruby B. Lee[2], Nachiketh Potlapally[3], and Lionel Torres[4]

[1] Department of Computer and Electrical Engineering, University of Waterloo
Waterloo, Canada
{reouven,cgebotys}@uwaterloo.ca
[2] Department of Electrical Engineering, Princeton University
Princeton, USA
{relbaz,dav,rblee}@princeton.edu
[3] Security Center of Excellence (SeCoE), Intel Corporation
Hillsboro, USA
nachiketh.potlapally@intel.com
[4] Department of Microelectronics, LIRMM, University of Montpellier
Montpellier, France
torres@lirmm.fr

Abstract. Trusted computing platforms aim to provide trust in computations performed by sensitive applications. Verifying the integrity of memory contents is a crucial security service that these platforms must provide since an adversary able to corrupt the memory space can affect the computations performed by the platform. After a description of the active attacks that threaten memory integrity, this paper surveys existing cryptographic techniques – namely integrity trees – allowing for memory authentication. The strategies proposed in the literature for implementing such trees on general-purpose computing platforms are presented, along with their complexity. This paper also discusses the effect of a potentially compromised Operating System (OS) on computing platforms requiring memory authentication and describes an architecture recently proposed to provide this security service despite an untrusted OS. Existing techniques for memory authentication that are not based on trees are described and their performance/security trade-off is discussed. While this paper focuses on memory authentication for uniprocessor platforms, we also discuss the security issues that arise when considering data authentication in symmetric multiprocessor (shared memory) systems.

Keywords: Security, Trusted Computing, Memory Authentication, Integrity Trees, Active attacks, Board level attacks.

1 Introduction

The increasing connectivity of computing devices coupled with rapid growth in number of services these devices offer, has resulted in more and more end users deploying computing platforms for a wide variety of tasks including those which handle

M.L. Gavrilova et al. (Eds.): Trans. on Comput. Sci. IV, LNCS 5430, pp. 1–22, 2009.

sensitive data. Examples of sensitive data include bank account number, passwords, social security number, health information etc. A typical user logs into online accounts using secret passwords almost every day, and procuring services requires the user to create new accounts (for instance, subscribing to a cable service, and creating an online account to manage it), and consequently create and store additional passwords. Even asking for an online insurance quote might require the user to give out personal information such as his or her social security number. Thus, going by these trends, we can say that the amount of sensitive information processed by and stored on the computing devices is projected to further increase with time. In such online transactions, users expect their sensitive data to be properly stored and handled by trusted computer systems of the service provider at the receiving end. However, if this trust assumption proves to be wrong, then the breach in user confidence can severely undermine the reputation and profits of the service provider, as was the case in a recent scandal where a computer previously owned by a bank and containing information on several million bank customers was sold on eBay [20]. On first glance, this appears solely to be an issue of data confidentiality and access control. However, when an attacker gets control of a computing system on which data is encrypted, the attacker can still compromise security of user transactions by appropriately manipulating the encrypted data. This was illustrated in an attack carried out on a crypto-processor where an adversary could alter the execution flow of software by corrupting encrypted code and data in memory to reveal confidential information [5]. Thus, it is not sufficient to just enforce data confidentiality and access controls, but, it is imperative to also take data integrity into account. Data integrity refers to ability to detect any adversarial corruption or tampering of data.

Several recent research efforts in academia [1, 2, 3] and industry [4] aim to provide trust in the computations performed by sensitive applications—e.g., Digital Rights Management (DRM) client, personal banking application, distributed computing client—on general-purpose computing platforms. Protecting confidentiality of private data and detecting any tampering are important features of trusted computing. Since an adversary corrupting the memory space of an application (through software [21] or physical attacks [5]) can affect the outcome of its computations, these computing platforms must provide memory authentication for sensitive applications. Memory authentication is defined as the ability to verify that the data read from memory by the processor (or by a specific application) at a given address is the data it last wrote at this address.

In past work on memory authentication, the main assumption of the trust model is that only the processor chip is trusted i.e., the trust boundary includes the computing and storage elements within the processor. A naïve approach to memory authentication would be to compute a cryptographic digest of contents of the entire external memory, store it on the trusted area (i.e., the processor chip) and use that digest to check the integrity of every block read from off-chip memory. Since the digest is inaccessible to the adversary, any malicious modification of the memory can be easily detected. However, this solution requires fetching on-chip all external memory contents on every read operation to check the digest, and on every write operation, to update it; clearly, this generates an unacceptable overhead in memory bandwidth. Another simple solution (based on the same trust model mentioned above) would be to keep on-chip a cryptographic digest of every memory block (e.g., cache block) written to off-chip memory. Although this strategy greatly reduces memory bandwidth overhead compared to the previous solution, it imposes an unacceptable cost in terms of the amount of on-chip memory required for storing all the digests. To improve on these two extreme solutions (i.e., to reduce memory bandwidth overhead to a small number of metadata blocks and the on-chip memory cost to a few bytes), researchers [6, 7, 8] have proposed tree-based structures whose leaves are the memory blocks to be protected, and the value of the root is computed by successively applying an authentication primitive to tree nodes starting from the leaves. Thus, the root node captures the current state of the memory blocks, and it is made tamper-resistant by being stored on-chip. When the processor reads a datum from external memory, a dedicated on-chip memory authentication engine computes the root node hash value by using values stored in internal nodes lying on the path from the leaf (corresponding to the memory block read) to the root. If the memory block was not tampered, then the computed root value matches the one stored on-chip else they would differ. On a write, the authentication engine updates the root hash value to reflect the change in state of memory due to the newly written value.

This paper surveys tree-based memory authentication techniques. We discuss various implementation-based issues raised by the integration of these trees into general-purpose computing platforms, namely: How can the processor address tree nodes in memory? Can integrity tree nodes be cached? Do the security properties of the integrity tree hold under Operating System (OS) compromise? To the best of our knowledge, we are not aware of any other work which offers a similar comprehensive analysis of architectural issues and trade-offs arising from implementing existing tree-based memory authentication schemes. By connecting theory to implementation, our work provides insights which will prove useful in designing more efficient memory authentication schemes, and we consider this to be an important contribution of this paper. For the sake of completeness, we also describe techniques proposed in literature that employ non-tree based techniques for verifying memory integrity, and show how they achieve improved performance at the cost of decrease in system security. Finally we briefly discuss the issues raised by data authentication in multiprocessor systems by highlighting the difference with a uniprocessor platform.

The paper is organized as follows. Section 2 describes the active attacks threatening the integrity of the memory contents. Then Section 3 presents the existing techniques providing memory authentication, namely integrity trees; in particular, we show why all existing memory authentication solutions defending against the attacks in Section 2 are based on tree structures. Section 4 presents the architectural features proposed in the literature to efficiently integrate those integrity trees to general-purpose computing platforms. Section 5 discusses the security of the integrity tree under operating system compromise and describes an architecture proposed recently to efficiently deploy an integrity tree on a computing platform running an untrusted OS. Section 6 describes techniques proposed in the literature to verify memory integrity and not based on tree structures. While this paper focuses on memory integrity for uniprocessor platforms, we present in Section 7 the additional security issues to consider for data authentication in symmetric multiprocessor (shared memory) systems. Section 8 concludes the paper.

2 Threat Model

This section describes the attacks challenging the integrity of data stored in the off-chip memory of computer systems. Section 2.1 describes the model we consider for active attacks in the context of physical adversaries. Section 2.2 widens the discussion by including the cases where these attacks are carried out through a malicious operating system; we conclude the section by defining two threat models upon which existing solutions for memory integrity are built.

2.1 Hardware Attacks

The common threat model considered for memory authentication assumes the protected system is exposed to a hostile environment in which physical attacks are feasible. The main assumption of this threat model is that the processor chip is resistant to all physical attacks, including invasive ones, and is thus trusted. Side-channel attacks are not considered.

The common objective of memory authentication techniques is to thwart active attackers tampering with memory contents. In an active attack, the adversary corrupts the data residing in memory or transiting over the bus; this corruption may be seen as data injection since a new value is created. Figure 1 depicts the example of a device under attack, where an adversary connects its own (malicious) memory to the targeted platform via the off-chip bus. We distinguish between three classes of active attacks, defined with respect to how the adversary chooses the inserted data. Figure 2 depicts the three active attacks; below, we provide a detailed description of each one by relying on the attack framework in Figure 1:

1) *Spoofing* attacks: the adversary exchanges an existing memory block with an arbitrary fake one (Figure 2-a, the block defined by the adversary is stored in the malicious memory, the adversary activates the switch command when he wants to force the processor chip to use the spoofed memory block).

2) *Splicing* or *relocation* attacks: the attacker replaces a memory block at address A with a block at address B, where A≠B. Such an attack may be viewed as a spatial permutation of memory blocks (Figure 2-b: the adversary stores at address 5 in the malicious memory the content of the block at address 1 from the genuine memory. When the processor requests the data at address 5, the adversary activates the switch command so the processor reads the malicious memory. As a result, the processor reads the data at address 1).

3) *Replay* attacks: a memory block located at a given address is recorded and inserted at the same address at a later point in time; by doing so, the current block's value is replaced by an older one. Such an attack may be viewed as a temporal permutation of a memory block, for a specific memory location (Figure 2-c: at time t1, the adversary stores at address 6 in the malicious memory the content of the block at address 6 from the genuine memory. At time t2, the memory location at address 6 has been updated in the genuine memory but the adversary does not perform this update in the malicious memory. The adversary activates the malicious memory when the processor requests the data at address 6, thus forcing it to read the old value stored at address 6).

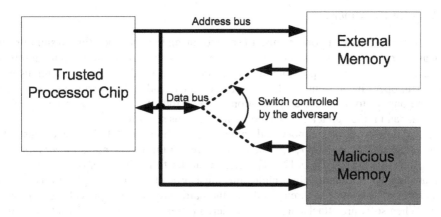

Fig. 1. An Example of Framework of Attack Targeting the External Memory of a Computing Platform

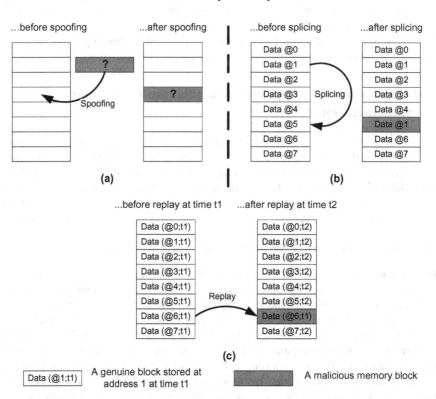

Fig. 2. Three Kinds of Active Attacks: (a) Spoofing, (b) Splicing and (c) Replay

2.2 Software Attacks

In a software attack, a compromised (or outright malicious) operating system or application tries to corrupt the memory space of a sensitive application. To model these attacks, we subsume all possible attack vectors into a single threat: a malicious, all-powerful operating system. Such an OS can directly read and write any memory location belonging to a sensitive application and can thus carry out any of the splicing, spoofing and replay attacks presented in the previous section.

In existing work on memory authentication, the threat model either excludes software attacks [2, 8, 9, 10, 11, 12, 13, 14] (referred in the following as *threat model 1*) or includes software attacks [2, 21] (referred in the following as *threat model 2*). In threat model 1, the hardware architecture must protect sensitive applications against attacks from software; in threat model 2, the hardware does not provide such protection. When software attacks are not considered (threat model 1), the operating system (OS) or at least the OS kernel must thus be trusted to isolate sensitive applications from malicious software. In the other case, the OS can contain untrusted code since the hardware protects sensitive applications against malicious software.

Conceptually, integrity trees are built and maintained in the same way regardless of the considered threat model. Section 3 describes existing integrity trees without specifying the threat model. Section 4 presents the strategies allowing efficient integration to computing platforms when threat model 1 is considered. Section 5 shows that threat model 2 requires trees built over the virtual (rather than physical) address space or, as recently proposed in [21], over a compact version of it.

3 Integrity Trees: Cryptographic Schemes for Memory Authentication

We consider there are three distinct strategies to thwart the active attacks described in our threat model. Each strategy is based on different authentication primitives, namely cryptographic hash function, Message Authentication Code (MAC) function and block-level Added Redundancy Explicit Authentication (AREA). In this section, we first describe how those primitives allow for memory authentication and how they must be integrated into tree structures in order to avoid excessive overheads in on-chip memory.

3.1 Authentication Primitives for Memory Authentication

Hash Functions. The first strategy (Figure 3-a) allowing to perform memory authentication consists in storing on-chip a hash value for each memory block stored off-chip (*write operations*). The integrity checking is done on *read operations* by recomputing a hash over the loaded block and by then comparing the resulting hash with the on-chip hash fingerprinting the off-chip memory location. The on-chip hash is stored on the tamper-resistant area, i.e., the processor chip and is thus inaccessible to adversaries. Therefore, spoofing, splicing and replay are detected if a mismatch occurs in the hash comparison. However, this solution has an unaffordable on-chip memory cost: by considering the common strategy [2, 3, 9, 13] of computing a fingerprint per cache line and assuming 128-bit hashes and 512-bit cache lines, the overhead is of 25% of the memory space to protect.

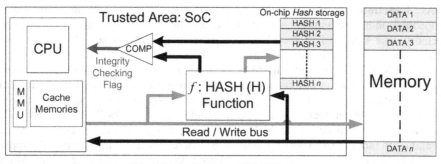

(a) Hash functions: Hash$n$ = H(DATA n)

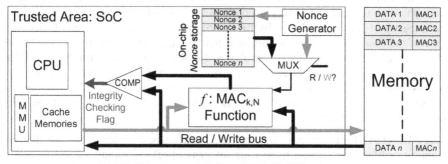

(b) MAC functions: MACn = MAC$_k$(DATA n)

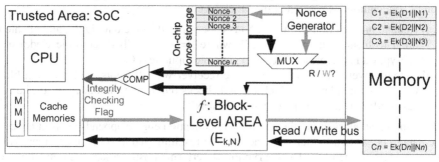

(c) Block-Level AREA: Cn = E$_k$(Dn||Nn)

→ Write Operation Signals

← Read Operation Signals

|| : Concatenation Operator

$E_{k,N}$: Block Encryption under key K and using a Nonce N ($E_{k,N}(D)= E_k(D||N)$)

$MAC_{k,N}$: Message Authentication Code Function under key K and using a Nonce N ($MAC_{k,N}(D)= MAC_k(D||N)$)

H : Hash Function

C : Ciphertext

D : Data

N : Nonce

Fig. 3. Authentication Primitives for Memory Integrity Checking

MAC Functions: In the second approach (Figure 3-b), the authentication engine embedded on-chip computes a MAC for every data block it *writes* in the physical memory. The key used in the MAC computation is securely stored on the trusted processor chip such that only the on-chip authentication engine itself is able to compute valid MACs. As a result, the MACs can be stored in untrusted memory because the attacker is unable to compute a valid MAC over a corrupted data block. In addition to the data contained by the block, the pre-image of the MAC function contains a nonce. This allows protection against splicing and replay attacks. The nonce precludes an attacker from passing a data block at address A, along with the associated MAC, as a valid (data block, MAC) pair for address B, where $A \neq B$. It also prevents the replay of a (data block, MAC) pair by distinguishing two pairs related to the same address, but written in memory at different points in time. On *read operations*, the processor loads the data to read and its corresponding MAC from physical memory. It checks the integrity of the loaded block by first re-computing a MAC over this block and a copy of the nonce used upon writing, and then it compares the result with the fetched MAC. To ensure the resistance to replay and splicing, the nonce used for MAC re-computation must be genuine. A naïve solution to meet this requirement is to store the nonces on the trusted and tamper-evident area, the processor chip. The related on-chip memory overhead is 12.5% if we consider computing a MAC per 512-bit cache line and that we use 64-bit nonces.

Block-Level AREA: The last strategy [13, 14] (Figure 3-c) leverages the diffusion property of block encryption to add the integrity-checking capability to this type of encryption algorithm. To do so, the AREA (Added Redundancy Explicit Authentication [22]) technique is applied at the block level:

i) Redundant data (a n-bit nonce N) is concatenated to the data D to authenticate in order to form a plaintext block P (where P=D||N); ECB (Electronic CodeBook) encryption is performed over P to generate ciphertext C.

ii) Integrity verification is done by the receiver who decrypts the ciphertext block C' to generate plaintext block P', and checks the n-bit redundancy in P', i.e., assuming P'=(D'||N'), verifies whether N=N'.

Thus, upon a *memory write*, the on-chip authentication engine appends an n-bit nonce to the data to be written to memory, encrypts the resulting plaintext block and then writes the ciphertext to memory. The encryption is performed using a key securely stored on the processor chip. On *read operations*, the authentication engine decrypts the block it fetches from memory and checks its integrity by verifying that the last n bits of the resulting plaintext block are equal to the nonce that was inserted upon encryption (on the write of the corresponding data). [13, 14] propose a System-on-Chip (SoC) implementation of this technique for embedded systems. They show that this engine is efficient to protect the Read-Only (RO) data of an application (e.g., its code) because RO data are not sensitive to replay attacks; therefore the address of each memory block can be efficiently used as a nonce[1]. However, for Read/Write (RW) data (e.g., stack data), the address is not sufficient to distinguish two data writes at the same address carried out at two different points in time: the nonce must change on each write. To recover such a changing nonce on a read operation while ensuring its integrity, [13, 14] propose

---

[1] Note that the choice of the data address as nonce also prevent spoofing and splicing attacks of RO data when MAC functions are used as authentication primitives.

storing the nonce on-chip. They evaluate the corresponding overhead between 25% and 50% depending on the block encryption algorithm implemented.

3.2 Integrity Trees

The previous section presented three authentication primitives preventing the active attacks described in our threat model. Those primitives require the storage of reference values – i.e., hashes or nonces – on-chip to thwart replay attacks. They do provide memory authentication but only at a high cost in terms of on-chip memory. If we consider a realistic case of 1GB of RAM memory, the hash, MAC (with nonce) and the block-level AREA solutions require respectively at least 256MB, 128MB and 256 MB of on-chip memory. Those on-chip memory requirements clearly are unaffordable, even for high-end processors. It is thus necessary to "securely" store these reference values off-chip. By securely, we mean that we must be able to ensure their integrity to preclude attacks on the reference values themselves.

Several research efforts suggest applying the authentication primitives recursively on the references. By doing so, a tree structure is formed and only the root of the tree—the reference value obtained in the last iteration of the recursion—needs to be stored on the processor chip, the trusted area. There are three existing tree techniques:

i) Merkle Tree [6] uses hash functions,
ii) PAT (Parallelizable Authentication Tree) [7] uses MAC functions with nonces,
iii) TEC-Tree (Tamper-Evident Counter Tree) [8] uses the block-level AREA primitive.

In this section, we first present a generic model for the integrity tree, then we describe the specific characteristics of each existing integrity tree; we finally compare their intrinsic properties.

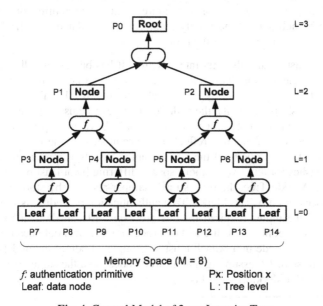

Fig. 4. General Model of 2-ary Integrity Tree

General Model of Integrity Tree. The common philosophy behind integrity trees is to split the memory space to protect into M equal size blocks which are the leaf nodes of the balanced A-ary integrity tree (Figure 4). The remaining tree levels are created by recursively applying the authentication primitive f over A-sized groups of memory blocks, until the procedure yields a single node called the root of the tree. The arity of the constructed tree is thus defined by the number of children A a tree node has. The root reflects the current state of the entire memory space; making the root tamper-resistant thus ensures tampering with the memory space can be detected. How the root is made tamper-resistant depends on the nature of f and is detailed next. Note that the number of checks required to verify the integrity of a leaf node depends on the number of iterations of f and thus on the number of blocks M in the memory space. The number of check corresponds to the number of tree levels N_L defined by: $N_L = \log_A(M)$.

Tree Authentication Procedure. For each memory block B (i.e., leaf node), there exists a branch[2] – starting at B and ending at the root – composed of the tree nodes obtained by recursive applications of f on B. For instance in Figure 4 for the leaf node at position P8, the branch is composed of the nodes at positions P3, P1 and the root P0. Thus, when B is fetched from untrusted memory, its integrity is verified by re-computing the tree root using the fetched B and the nodes – obtained from external memory – along the branch from B to the root (i.e., the branch nodes and their siblings; so for the leaf node at position P8, the nodes that need to be fetched are at position P7, P3, P4, P1 and P2). We confirm B has not been tampered with during the last step of the authentication process when the re-computed root is identical to the root (which has been made tamper-resistant).

Tree Update Procedure. When a legitimate modification is carried out over a memory block B, the corresponding branch – including the tree root – is updated to reflect the new value of B. This is done by first authenticating the branch B belongs to by applying the previous tree authentication procedure, then by computing on-chip the new values for the branch nodes, and finally by storing the updated branch off-chip – except for the on-chip component of the root.

Merkle Tree is historically the first integrity tree. It has been originally introduced by Merkle [6] for efficient computations in public key cryptosystems and adapted for integrity checking of memory content by Blum et al. [15]. In a Merkle Tree (Figure 5-a), f is a cryptographic hash function H(); the nodes of the tree are thus simple hash values. The generic verification and update procedures described above are applied in a straightforward manner. The root of this tree reflects the current state of the memory space since the collision resistance property of the cryptographic hash function ensures that in practice, the root hashes for any two memory spaces differing by at least one bit will not be the same. With Merkle Tree, the root is made tamper-resistant by storing it entirely on the trusted processor chip. The Merkle Tree authentication procedure is fully parallelizable because all the inputs required for this process can be made available before the start of this procedure; however, the update procedure is sequential because the computation of a new hash node in a branch must be completed before the update to the next branch node can start. By assuming that all tree nodes have the same size, the memory overhead MO_{MT} of a Merkle Tree [9] is of:

---

[2] This branch is also called in the following the authentication branch.

$$MO_{MT} = \frac{1}{(A-1)}.$$

The Parallelizable Authentication Tree (PAT) [7] overcomes the issue of non-parallelizability of the tree update procedure by using a MAC function (with nonces N) $M_{K,N}()$ as authentication primitive f where K and N are the key and nonce, respectively (Figure 5-b). The memory space is first divided into M memory blocks (in Figure 5-b, M=4). We begin by applying the MAC function to A memory blocks (in Figure 5-b, we have A=2) using an on-chip key K and a freshly generated nonce N, i.e., $MAC_{K,N}(d_1 \| \ldots \| d_A)$ where d_i is a memory block. Next, the MAC is recursively applied to A-sized groups formed with the nonces generated during the last iteration of the recursion. For every step of the recursion but the last, both the nonce and the MAC values are sent to external memory. The last iteration generates a MAC and a nonce that form the root of the tree. The root MAC is sent to external memory but the nonce N is stored on-chip; this way the tree root is made tamper-resistant since an adversary cannot generate a new MAC without the secret key K stored on-chip or replay an old MAC since it will not have been generated with the current root nonce. Verifying a memory block D in a PAT requires recomputing D's branch on-chip and verifying that the top-level MAC can indeed be obtained using the on-chip nonce.

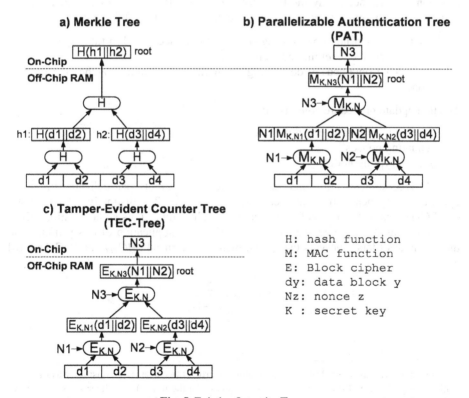

a) Merkle Tree

b) Parallelizable Authentication Tree (PAT)

c) Tamper-Evident Counter Tree (TEC-Tree)

H: hash function
M: MAC function
E: Block cipher
dy: data block y
Nz: nonce z
K : secret key

Fig. 5. Existing Integrity Trees

Whenever a block D is legitimately modified, the CPU re-computes D's branch using fresh nonces. The tree authentication procedure is parallelizable since all inputs (data and nonces) are available for all branch node verifications. The tree update procedure is also parallelizable because each branch tree node is computed from independently generated inputs: the nonces. In [7] the authors highlight that the birthday paradox implies the nonce does not need to be longer that $h/2$, with h the MAC-size. Thus, the memory overhead MO_{PAT} of PAT is of:

$$MO_{PAT} = \frac{1}{A-1} + \frac{1}{2}\frac{1}{A-1} = \frac{3}{2(A-1)}$$

The Tamper-Evident Counter Tree (TEC-Tree). In TEC-Tree [8], the authentication primitive f is the Block-level AREA. Thus, such authentication primitive tags its input (dy in Figure 5-c) with a nonce N before ciphering it with a block encryption algorithm in ECB mode and a secret key K kept on-chip. The block-level AREA is first applied to the memory blocks to be stored off-chip, and then recursively over A-sized groups of nonces used in the last iteration of the recursion. The resulting ciphered blocks are stored in external memory and the nonce used in the ciphering of the last block created – i.e., the root of the TEC-Tree – is kept on-chip making the root tamper-resistant. Indeed, an adversary without the key cannot create a tree node and without the on-chip root nonce he cannot replay the tree root. During verification of a data block D, D's branch is brought on-chip and decrypted. The integrity of D is validated if:

i) each decrypted node bears a tag equal to the nonce found in the payload of the node in the tree level immediately above;
ii) the nonce obtained by decrypting the highest level node matches the on-chip nonce.

The tree update procedure consists in:

i) loading D's branch decrypting nodes,
ii) updating nonces
iii) re-encrypting nodes.

TEC-Tree authentication and update procedures are both parallelizable because f operates on independently generated inputs: the nonces. The distinctive characteristic of TEC-Tree is that it allows for data confidentiality. Indeed, its authentication primitive being based on a block encryption function, the application of this primitive on the leaf nodes (data) encrypts them. The memory overhead[3] MO_{TEC} of TEC-Tree [8] is of :

$$MO_{TEC} = \frac{2}{(A-1)}$$

---

[3] [8] gives a different formula for their memory overhead because they consider ways to optimize it (e.g. the use of the address in the construction of the nonce). For the sake of clarity, we give a simplified formula of the TEC-Tree memory overhead by considering that the nonce consists only in a counter value.

Comparison. Table 1 sums up the properties of the existing integrity trees. PAT and TEC-Tree are both parallelizable for the tree authentication and update procedure while preventing all the attacks described in the state of the art. Parallelizability of the tree update process is an important feature when the write buffer is small (e.g., in embedded systems) to prevent bus contention due to write operation requests that may pile up. TEC-Tree additionally provides data confidentiality. However, TEC-Tree and PAT also have a higher off-chip memory overhead when compared to Merkle Tree, in particular because they require storage for additional metadata, the nonces.

Table 1. Summary of Existing Integrity Trees Properties

	Merkle Tree	**PAT** (Paralleliz-able Authentica-tion Tree)	**TEC-Tree** (Tam-per-Evident Counter Tree)
Splicing, Spoofing, Replay resistance	Yes	Yes	Yes
Parallelizability	Tree Authentica-tion only	Tree Authentica-tion **and** Update	Tree Authentica-tion **and** Update
Data Confidential-ity	No	No	Yes
Memory Overhead	1/(A-1)	3/2(A-1)	2/(A-1)

4   Integration of Integrity Trees in Computing Platforms

In this section we survey the implementation strategies proposed in the literature to efficiently integrate integrity trees in computing platforms when threat model 1 is considered (i.e., active physical attacks and trusted OS kernel). We first describe the tree traversal technique allowing for node addressing in memory. Then, a scheme leveraging caching to improve tree performance is detailed. Finally, the Bonsai Merkle Tree concept is described.

4.1   Tree Traversal Technique

One of the issues arising when integrating an integrity tree into a computing platform is making it possible for the processor to retrieve tree nodes in memory. [9] proposes a method for doing so with Merkle trees, while [8] adapts it for TEC-Tree. The principle of this method is to first associate a numerical position (P_x in Figure 3) to each tree node, starting at 0 for the root and incrementally up to the leaves. The position of a parent node P^l (at level l in the tree) can be easily found by subtracting one from its child at position P^{l-1} (on level l-1), by dividing the result by the tree arity A and by rounding down:

$$P^l = \left\lfloor \frac{P^{l-1} - 1}{A} \right\rfloor \quad \text{(eq. 1)}$$

Now that we know how to find a parent node position from a child position, the issue is to retrieve a position number from the address of a child or parent node. To solve this issue, [9] proposes a simplified layout of the memory region to authenticate: the tree nodes are stored starting from the top of the tree (P1 in Figure 4) down to the leaves, with respect to the order given by positions. By having all tree nodes be the same size, the translation from position to address or from address to position can be easily done by respectively multiplying or dividing the quantity to be translated by the node size.

This method imposes that the arity be a power of 2 to efficiently implement the division of eq.1 in hardware. Moreover, all data to authenticate must be contained in a contiguous memory region to allow for the children to parent position and address retrieval scheme to work.

4.2 Cached Trees

The direct implementation of integrity trees can generate a high overhead in terms of execution time due to the $\log_A(M)$ checks required on each load from the external memory. In [9], Gassend et al. show that the performance slowdown can reach a factor of 10 with a Merkle Tree. To decrease this overhead, they propose to cache tree nodes. When a hash is requested in the tree authentication procedure, it is brought on-chip with its siblings in the tree that belong to the same cache block. This way, those siblings usually required for the next check in the authentication procedure are already loaded. However, the main improvement comes from the fact that once checked and stored in the on-chip cache, a tree node is trusted and can be considered as a local tree root. As a result, the tree authentication and update procedures are terminated as soon as a cached hash (or the root) is encountered. With this cached tree solution, Gassend et al. decreased the performance overhead of a Merkle Tree to less than 25%. By changing the hash function – from SHA-1[16] to the GCM[17] – [11] even claims to keep the performance overhead under 5%.

4.3 The Bonsai Merkle Tree

Memory authentication engines based on integrity trees should be designed for efficient integration into computing platforms. The last engine proposed toward this objective has been presented in [12] and is based on a concept called Bonsai Merkle Tree.

The idea behind the Bonsai Merkle Tree (BMT) is to reduce the amount of data to authenticate with a Merkle Tree in order to decrease its height, i.e., reduce the number of tree levels to obtain a smaller tree that can be quickly traversed (Figure 6). To do so, [12] proposes to compute a MAC M over every memory block C (i.e., every cache block) with a nonce, i.e., a counter ctr concatenated with the data address, as extra input of the MAC function MAC_K: $M = MAC_K (C, addr, ctr)$[4]. The counter ctr consists of a local counter $Lctr$ concatenated with a global counter $Gctr$. Each memory block is associated with a local counter while each memory page is associated with a global counter. Each time a given memory block is updated off-chip, the corresponding $Lctr$

---

[4] The authentication primitive used in [12] is basically the MAC function with nonces presented in section 3.

is incremented. When *Lctr* rolls over, *Gctr* is incremented. In [12], the authors proposed the use of a 7-bit long *Lctr* and of a 64-bit long *Gctr*; this way *ctr* never rolls over in practice. *ctr* counter values are made tamper-evident while stored off-chip using a Merkle tree, thus making the memory space protected by the MAC-with-nonce scheme also tamper-evident.

On average, an 8-bit counter is required for 4KB memory pages and 64B cache blocks. The amount of memory to authenticate with the Bonsai Merkle tree is thus decreased of a ratio 1:64 when compared to a regular Merkle tree applied directly to the memory blocks. However, the shortcoming of this scheme is that a full page needs to be cryptographically processed every time a local counter rolls over. In other words, in this case the MACs of all memory blocks belonging to the page having *Gctr* updated must be recomputed as well as the tree branches corresponding to the tree leaves containing the updated *Gctr* and *Lctr*. Despite this, according to [12], this approach decreases the execution time overhead of integrity trees from 12.1% to 1.8% and reduces external memory overhead for node storage from 33.5% to 21.5%.

Duc et al. proposed a similar architecture in [25] except that instead of using a nonce in the MAC computation, they include a random number; therefore, their architecture, called CryptoPage, is sensitive to replay with a success probability proportional to the size of the random value.

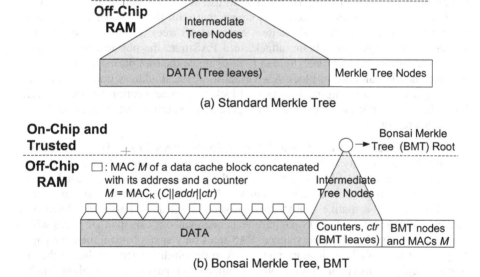

Fig. 6. Bonsai Merkle Tree Principle

5   Memory Authentication with an Untrusted Operating System

In many scenarios, the security policy of a computing platform must exclude the operating system from the trusted computing base. With modern commodity operating systems in particular, it is practically impossible to verify that no exploitable software vulnerability exists in such a large, complex and extendable software system. As a result, the OS cannot be trusted to isolate a sensitive application from malicious software, hence it needs to be considered as untrusted in the threat model (as in our threat model 2).

The first step towards protecting the memory of a sensitive application running on an untrusted OS is to build an integrity tree which covers only pages belonging to the application and which can only be updated when the application itself is running. This precludes the OS, with certain well-defined exceptions for communication, from effecting modifications to the application's memory space that cause the tree to be updated, i.e., any OS write to the application's memory is considered as corruption. Although this approach prevents the OS from carrying out splicing, spoofing and replay attacks through direct writes to the application's memory (because such corruptions would be detected by the integrity tree scheme), [21] shows that the OS can still perform splicing attacks indirectly, by corrupting the application's page table.

The Branch Splicing Attack. The page table is a data structure maintained by the OS, which maps a page's virtual address to its physical address. On a read operation, when a virtual-to-physical address translation is required by the processor, the page table is looked up[5] using the virtual address provided by the running process to obtain the corresponding physical address. The *branch splicing attack* presented in [21] corrupts the physical address corresponding to the virtual address of a given memory block. This causes the on-chip integrity verification engine not only to fetch the wrong block in physical memory, but also to use the wrong tree branch in verifying the integrity of the block fetched. [21] shows that with threat model 2, building an integrity tree over the Physical Address Space (PAS tree) is insecure because it is vulnerable to the branch splicing attack. In a PAS tree, the physical address determines the authentication branch to load to re-compute the root during verification. As a result, the OS can corrupt block A's virtual-to-physical address translation to trick the integrity checking engine into using block B's authentication branch to verify block B, hence substituting B for A (In Figure 7, substituting data at address @0 for data at address @4).

Building a Tree over the Virtual Address Space (VAS-Tree). To defend against this attack, the integrity tree can be built over the Virtual Address Space (VAS tree). In this case, the virtual address generated by the protected application is used to traverse the tree so page table corruption has no effect on the integrity verification process. The VAS tree, unlike a PAS tree, protects application pages that have been swapped out to disk by the OS paging mechanism since it can span all pages within the application's virtual memory space. PAS trees only span physical memory pages: they do not keep track of memory pages sent to the on-disk page file, hence they require a separate mechanism to protect swapped out pages [12]. Without such a mechanism, a PAS tree scheme cannot detect corruption of data that might occur during paging—i.e. between the time a page is moved from its physical page frame to the on-disk page file and the time that page is fetched again by the OS, from disk back into a physical page frame.

---

[5] In modern processor, the page table is cached on-chip in a Translation Lookaside Buffer. This does not affect the feasibility of the attack described here.

The VAS tree is not a panacea however, as it presents two major shortcomings: it must span a huge region of memory and it requires one full-blown tree for each application requiring protection, rather than a single tree protecting all software in physical memory. In addition, this solution requires extra tag storage for the virtual address [2] in the last level of cache (when implemented) which is usually physically tagged and indexed. Indeed, on cache evictions, the virtual address is required to traverse and update the integrity tree.

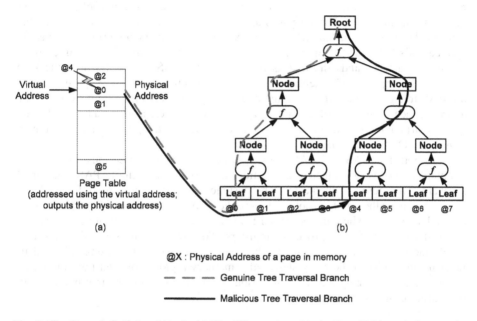

(a)   (b)

@X : Physical Address of a page in memory

— — — Genuine Tree Traversal Branch

————— Malicious Tree Traversal Branch

Fig. 7. The Branch Splicing Attack. (a) The OS tampers with the Page Table and changes the second entry from physical address @0 to @4. (b) data at @4 are verified instead of data at @0; however, since the physical address – which is corrupted – is used to retrieved the branch nodes required to verify the data read, the attack is undetected and data at @4 are considered genuine.

Impractical VAS-Tree Overheads. The extra security afforded by the VAS tree over the PAS tree comes at the cost of very large memory capacity and initialization overheads. Application code and data segments are usually laid out very far apart from one another in order to avoid having dynamically growing segments (e.g., the heap and stack) overwrite other application segments. The VAS tree must thus span a very large fraction of the virtual address space in order to cover both the lowest and highest virtual addresses that may be accessed by the application during its execution. The span of the tree is then several orders of magnitude larger than the cumulative sum of all code and data segments that require protection. In the case of a VAS tree protecting a 64-bit address space, the tree span can be so enormous as to make VAS tree impractical, i.e., VAS tree is not scalable. Indeed, it not only requires allocating physical page frames for the 2^{64} bytes of leaf nodes that are defined during initialization, but also requires allocating memory for the non-leaf tree nodes, which represent 20% to 100% of the leaf space size depending on the memory overhead of the underlying integrity tree [7, 8, 9]. The CPU time required to initialize such a tree is clearly unacceptable in practice.

The Reduced Address Space. To overcome these problems, [21] introduces a new processor hardware unit which builds and maintains an integrity tree over a *Reduced Address Space* (RAS). At any point in time, the RAS contains only those pages needed for the application's execution; it grows dynamically as this application memory footprint increases. Virtual pages are mapped into the RAS using an index that follows the page's translation. The new hardware builds an integrity tree over the application's RAS (a RAS tree), carries out the integrity verification and tree update procedures and expands the tree as the underlying RAS grows. Because the RAS contains the application's memory footprint in a contiguous address space segment, the RAS tree does not suffer from the overheads of the VAS tree, built over a sparse address space. The value of tree nodes along a block's verification path is tied to the block's virtual address so corruption of the RAS index or the physical address translation by the OS is detected.

With both the VAS and RAS trees, a full-blown integrity tree must be built and maintained for every protected application, as opposed to a single PAS tree for all software. Therefore, a scheme must be designed to manage tree roots for a Merkle Tree scheme, or the on-chip roots and secret keys for PAT and TEC-Tree. [2] presents an implementation where the processor hardware manages the roots of several Merkle Trees stored in dedicated processor registers. To provide some scalability despite a fixed amount of hardware resources, the authors suggest implementing spill and fill mechanisms between these registers and a memory region protected by a master integrity tree. Minimizing the hardware resources required to operate multiple integrity trees is an open research area.

6 Memory Authentication without a Tree Structure

Several engines that are not based on tree schemes have been proposed in the literature to ensure memory authentication. In most cases however, these techniques intentionally decrease the security of the computing platforms to cope with the overhead they generate. This section surveys these techniques.

Lhash. The researchers who proposed the cached tree principle also designed a memory authentication technique not based on a tree and called Log hash (Lhash [23]). Lhash has been designed for applications requiring integrity checking after a sequence of memory operations (as opposed to checking off-chip operations on every memory access as in tree schemes). Lhash relies on an incremental multiset hash function (called Mset-Add-Hash) described by the authors in [24]). This family of hash takes as an input a message of an arbitrary size and outputs a fixed size hash as a regular hash function, but the ordering of the chunks constituting the message is not important. The Lhash scheme has been named after the fact that a write and a read log of the memory locations to be checked are maintained at runtime using an incremental multiset hash function and stored on-chip. The write and read logs are respectively called ReadHash and WriteHash.

The Lhash scheme works as follows for a given sequence of operations. At initialization WriteHash is computed over the memory chunks belonging to the memory region that needs to be authenticated; WriteHash is then updated at runtime when an off-chip write is performed or when a dirty cache block is evicted from cache. This way, WriteHash reflects the off-chip memory state (and content) at anytime. ReadHash is computed the first time a chunk is brought in cache and updated on each subsequent off-chip read operations. When checking the integrity of the sequence of operations, all the blocks belonging to the memory region to authenticate and not present in cache are read to make even the number of chunks added to the read log and those added to the write log. If ReadHash happens to be different from WriteHash, it means that the memory has been tampered with at runtime. Re-ordering attacks are prevented by including a nonce in each hash computation. Authors performed a comparison of Lhash with a cached hash tree (4-ary). They showed that overhead can be decreased from 33% to 6.25% in term of off-chip memory and from 20-30% to 5-15% at runtime. However, the scheme does not suit threat models such as the ones defined in this paper since an adversary is able to perform an active attack before the integrity checking takes place.

PE-ICE. A Parallelized Encryption and Integrity Checking Engine, PE-ICE, based on the block-level AREA technique was proposed in [13] and [14] to encrypt and authenticate off-chip memory. However, to avoid re-encryption of the whole memory when the nonce reaches its limit (e.g., a counter that rolls over), the authors propose to replace it with the chunk address concatenated with a random number. For each memory block processed by PE-ICE, a copy of the random value enrolled is kept on-chip to make it tamper-resistant and secret. The drawback of using a random number is that a replay attack can be performed with a probability p of success inversely proportional to the bit length r of the random number ($p = 1/2^r$). Since a small random number is advised [14] to keep the on-chip memory overhead reasonable, the scheme is likely to be insecure with respect to replay attacks.[6]

7 Data Authentication in Symmetric Multi-Processors (SMP)

High-end computing platforms are more and more based on multi-processor technology. In this section, we highlight the new security challenges related to runtime data authentication that arise on such shared memory platforms.

We have defined memory authentication as "verifying that data read from memory by the processor at a given address is the data it last wrote at this address". However, in a multiprocessor system with shared memory, the definition of data authentication cannot be restricted to that of memory authentication: additional security issues must be considered. First, every processor core of a SMP platform may legitimately update data in memory; thus each processor must be able to differentiate a legitimate write

---

[6] Note that in [14], the author proposes to build a tree – called PRV-Tree, for PE-ICE protected Random Value Tree – similar to TEC-Tree except that it uses random numbers instead of nonces. The purpose of PRV-Tree is to decrease the probability of an adversary succeeding with a replay attack by increasing the length of the random number, while limiting the on-chip memory overhead to the storage of a single random number (the root of PRV-Tree).

operation done by a core of the system from malicious data corruption. Moreover, in addition to the traditional memory authentication, the data authentication issue in a SMP platform must also consider bus transaction authentication on cache-to-cache transfers required in cache coherency protocols (Figure 8). [18] notes that to take into consideration bus transaction authentication, an additional active attack must be considered: message dropping. In SMP platforms, when a processor sends a data to another core, it broadcasts the same data to all other SMP's cores to maintain cache coherency. Thus, message dropping takes place upon those broadcasting cache-to-cache communications and consists in blocking a message destined to one of the processor cores (In Figure 8, CPU2 is temporarily disconnected from the bus to perform a message dropping).

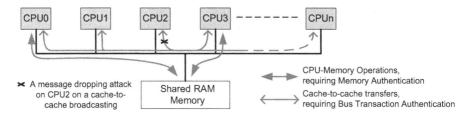

Fig. 8. Data Authentication Requirements in a Symmetric Multi-Processors (SMP) Platform

[18] and [19] propose solutions for data authentication in SMP platforms. However, as highlighted in [18], [19] is sensitive to message dropping. Moreover, [18] and [19] focus on SMP systems with a small number of processors and do not evaluate the scalability of their solutions. Thus, data authentication at runtime in SMP platforms is still an open research topic.

Active research efforts [26, 27, 28] are also being carried out in the field of data authentication in multiprocessor systems with Distributed Shared Memory (DSM). Data authentication issues in these systems are similar to those mentioned for SMP platforms, except that designers of security solutions have to deal with additional difficulties due to the intrinsic characteristics of the DSM processor. First, a typical DSM system does not include a shared bus that could help synchronization of metadata (e.g., counter values) between the processors participating in a given memory authentication scheme. Also, as mention in [28], the interconnection network that enables processor-to-memory communications is usually exposed at the back of server racks, providing an adversary with an easier way to physically connect to the targeted system compared to a motherboard in an SMP platform

8 Conclusion

In this paper we described the hardware mechanisms to provide memory authentication, namely integrity trees. We presented a generic integrity tree model, the intrinsic properties of each existing integrity tree (Merkle Tree, PAT and TEC-Tree) and the architectural features proposed in the literature to efficiently implement those trees in computing platforms. We also discussed the impact of operating system compromise on hardware integrity verification engine and presented an existing solution for secure and efficient application memory authentication despite an untrusted OS. Finally, we showed the additional security issues to consider for data authentication at runtime in symmetric multi-processors platforms and how they differ from memory authentication in uniprocessor systems.

References

1. Lie, D., Thekkath, C., Mitchell, M., Lincoln, P., Boneh, D., Mitchell, J., Horowitz, M.: Architectural Support for Copy and Tamper Resistant Software. In: Int'l. Conf. on Architectural Support for Programming Languages and OS (ASPLOS-IX), pp. 168–177 (2000)
2. Suh, G.E., Clarke, D., Gassend, B., van Dijk, M., Devadas, S.: AEGIS: Architecture for Tamper-Evident and Tamper-Resistant Processing. In: Proc. of the 17th Int'l. Conf. on Supercomputing (ICS) (2003)
3. Lee, R.B., Kwan, P.C.S., McGregor, J.P., Dwoskin, J., Wang, Z.: Architecture for Protecting Critical Secrets in Microprocessors. In: Int'l. Symp. on Computer Architecture (ISCA-32), pp. 2–13 (June 2005)
4. IBM Extends Enhanced Data Security to Consumer Electronics Products, IBM (April 2006), http://www-03.ibm.com/press/us/en/pressrelease/19527.wss
5. Kuhn, M.G.: Cipher Instruction Search Attack on the Bus-Encryption Security Microcontroller DS5002FP. IEEE Trans. Comput. 47, 1153–1157 (1998)
6. Merkle, R.C.: Protocols for Public Key Cryptography. In: IEEE Symp. on Security and Privacy, pp. 122–134 (1980)
7. Hall, W.E., Jutla, C.S.: Parallelizable authentication trees. In: Preneel, B., Tavares, S. (eds.) SAC 2005. LNCS, vol. 3897, pp. 95–109. Springer, Heidelberg (2006)
8. Elbaz, R., Champagne, D., Lee, R.B., Torres, L., Sassatelli, G., Guillemin, P.: EC-Tree: A Low Cost and Parallelizable Tree for Efficient Defense against Memory Replay Attacks. In: Cryptographic Hardware and embedded systems (CHES), pp. 289–302 (2007)
9. Gassend, B., Suh, G.E., Clarke, D., van Dijk, M., Devadas, S.: Caches and Merkle Trees for Efficient Memory Integrity Verification. In: Proceedings of Ninth International Symposium on High Performance Computer Architecture (February 2003)
10. Suh, G.E.: AEGIS: A Single-Chip Secure Processor, PhD thesis, Massachusetts Institute of Technology (September 2005)
11. Yan, C., Rogers, B., Englender, D., Solihin, Y., Prvulovic, M.: Improving Cost, Performance, and Security of Memory Encryption and Authentication. In: Proc. of the International Symposium on Computer Architecture (2006)
12. Rogers, B., Chhabra, S., Solihin, Y., Prvulovic, M.: Using Address Independent Seed Encryption and Bonsai Merkle Trees to Make Secure Processors OS– and Performance–Friendly. In: Proc. of the 40th IEEE/ACM Symposium on Microarchitecture (MICRO) (December 2007)
13. Elbaz, R., Torres, L., Sassatelli, G., Guillemin, P., Bardouillet, M., Martinez, A.: A Parallelized Way to Provide Data Encryption and Integrity Checking on a Processor-Memory Bus. In: Proceedings of the 43rd Design Automation Conference DAC (July 2006)
14. Elbaz, R.: Hardware Mechanisms for Secured Processor Memory Transactions in Embedded Systems, PhD Thesis, University of Montpellier (December 2006)
15. Blum, M., Evans, W., Gemmell, P., Kannan, S., Naor, M.: Checking the correctness of memories. In: Proc. 32nd IEEE Symposium on Foundations of Computer Science, pp. 90–99 (1991)

16. National Institute of Science and Technology (NIST), FIPS PUB 180-2: Secure Hash Standard (August 2002)
17. NIST Special Publication SP800-38D: Recommendation for Block Cipher Modes of Operation: Galois/Counter Mode (GCM) and GMAC (November 2007)
18. Zhang, Y., Gao, L., Yang, J., Zhang, X., Gupta, R.: SENSS: Security Enhancement to Symmetric Shared Memory Multiprocessors. In: Proc. of the 11th International Symposium on High-Performance Computer Architecture (2005)
19. Shi, W., Lee, H.-H., Ghosh, M., Lu, C.: Architectural Support for High Speed Protection of Memory Integrity and Confidentiality in Multiprocessor Systems. In: Proc. of the 13th International Conference on Parallel Architectures and Compilation Techniques (2004)
20. http://news.bbc.co.uk/2/hi/uk_news/7581540.stm
21. Champagne, D., Elbaz, R., Lee, R.B.: The Reduced Address Space (RAS) for Application Memory Authentication. In: Wu, T.-C., Lei, C.-L., Rijmen, V., Lee, D.-T. (eds.) ISC 2008. LNCS, vol. 5222, pp. 47–63. Springer, Heidelberg (2008)
22. Fruhwirth, C.: New Methods in Hard Disk Encryption, Institute for Computer Languages, Theory and Logic Group, Vienna University of Technology (2005)
23. Suh, G.E., Clarke, D., Gassend, B., van Dijk, M., Devadas, S.: Efficient Memory Integrity Verification and Encryption for Secure Processors. In: Proceedings of the 36th Annual International Symposium on Microarchitecture (MICRO 36), San Diego, CA, pp. 339–350 (December 2003)
24. Clarke, D., Devadas, S., van Dijk, M., Gassend, B., Suh, G.E.: Incremental multiset hash functions and their application to memory integrity checking. In: Laih, C.-S. (ed.) ASIACRYPT 2003. LNCS, vol. 2894, pp. 188–207. Springer, Heidelberg (2003)
25. Duc, G., Keryell, R.: CryptoPage: An Efficient Secure Architecture with Memory Encryption, Integrity and Information Leakage Protection. In: Jesshope, C., Egan, C. (eds.) ACSAC 2006. LNCS, vol. 4186, pp. 483–492. Springer, Heidelberg (2006)
26. Rogers, B., Prvulovic, M., Solihin, Y.: Effective Data Protection for Distributed Shared Memory Multiprocessors. In: Proc. of International Conference of Parallel Architecture and Compilation Techniques (PACT) (September 2006)
27. Lee, M., Ahn, M., Kim, E.J.: I2SEMS: Interconnects-Independent Security Enhanced Shared Memory Multiprocessor Systems. In: Malyshkin, V.E. (ed.) PaCT 2007. LNCS, vol. 4671, pp. 94–103. Springer, Heidelberg (2007)
28. Rogers, B., Yan, C., Chhabra, S., Prvulovic, M., Solihin, Y.: Single-Level Integrity and Confidentiality Protection for Distributed Shared Memory Multiprocessors. In: Proc. of the 14th International Symposium on High Performance Computer Architecture (HPCA) (2008)

Behavioural Characterization for Network Anomaly Detection

Victor P. Roche and Unai Arronategui

University of Zaragoza, Spain
vroche@unizar.es,
unai@unizar.es

Abstract. In this paper we propose a methodology for detecting abnormal traffic on the net, such as worm attacks, based on the observation of the behaviours of different elements at the network edges. In order to achieve this, we suggest a set of critical features and we judge normal site status based on these standards. For our goal this characterization must be free of virus traffic. Once this has been set, we would be able to find abnormal situations when the observed behaviour, set against the same features, is significantly different from the previous model. We have based our work on NetFlow information generated by the main routers in the University of Zaragoza network, with more than 12,000 hosts. The proposed model helps to characterize the whole corporate network, sub-nets and the individual hosts. This methodology has proved its effectiveness in real infections caused by viruses such as SpyBot, Agobot, etc in accordance with our experimental tests. This system would allow to detect new kind of worms, independently from the vulnerabilities or methods used for their propagation.

1 Introduction

The use of the Internet has greatly risen in the last fifteen years. This increase has not always been with security measures to guarantee that connected computers were not able to suffer from attacks that could virtually endanger them. Nowadays there is an enormous number of computers in the network which are either infected by a worm or are able to; in fact if we connect a computer with Windows XP/2000 OS without any upgrade, it will just take ten minutes [24] to be infected by one or more worms. These use for their propagation well known vulnerabilities, nevertheless, there are continuous new infections on the Net.

Against this threat the "silver bullet" type solutions are not valid. Neither firewalls nor network antivirus can fight in an effective way against this kind of infection because the attacks do not proceed from outside. The threat usually proceeds from our own intranet.

If we observe the traffic generated by an infected host, we will soon see that it shows several characteristics which are greatly different from habitual traffic in a user machine. On many occasions this traffic is relevant in the network in a violent way, by increasing explosively the number of connection attempts to

M.L. Gavrilova et al. (Eds.): Trans. on Comput. Sci. IV, LNCS 5430, pp. 23–40, 2009.
© Springer-Verlag Berlin Heidelberg 2009

other machines in an effort to spread the infection. Nevertheless, this does not always happen, some worms can present a slow behaviour on infection spreading [26] or even potentially there might be worms that detain attempts to infect [17] after a period of propagation. These new propagation models hinder classic detection based on observations of a traffic graphics by a human being.

Other important characteristic of worms spreading is that their infection attempts are directed mainly to other computers located in the same network segment. Infection signs are more present in local area networks traffic rather than in backbone. This is the reason why we have focused our investigations in one Internet edge.

In this paper we propose a methodology that means an advance in the detection of a new infection in the backbone of the network, but also in the identification of the infected hosts of our network. We try to detect network anomalies by tracking behaviour of different network levels. This proposed method is not based on intrinsic characteristics of the worm but in their manner of acting.

We use NetFlow data, the de facto standard from Cisco for network accounting, as information base for our system. This real traffic data is harvested from main routers on the University of Zaragoza. This network has over 12,000 hosts that generate over 350 million of flows per day.

At first we will define a set of critical features including number of attempts of connection to specific ports per unit of time, number of different computers that a suspicious host is trying to talk with, etc. The objective is to characterize a normal situation of a network level with these defined features. This methodology is valid to characterize the whole network, a segment of it or a concrete host. The second step would base on the endless observations of that network layer, evaluating it in similar intervals of time. When this evaluation results exceed specific margins we would assure that malicious traffic, caused by the activity of infected hosts, is present in our net.

Apart from these objectives that we could name locals, we are able to extract important information about infected hosts activity and involved outer hosts. This knowledge could be shared with other organizations having similar elements of control. As we will see, collaboration between network edges is essential for detection and containment of the worm.

The organization of this paper is as follows: After a survey of related work in Section 2 we will pass to describe our method in Section 3 and present the features used for the characterization in Section 4. In Section 5 we show a description of the Experimental System Architecture fed by real traffic from University of Zaragoza network, and present the Experimental Results in subsection 5.1. Finally we will include our conclusions and future work in Section 6 and 7 respectively.

2   Related Work

The field of the worm detection and anomaly based intrusion detection has been studied in a special way in the last seven years. Initiatives like the Internet Storm

Center [14], CAIDA [1] or DDoSVax [23] are good examples of it. These systems search for infection signals on large scale networks. These projects work with information volume extremely huge, which makes it difficult to carry out host level processing.

Barford et al. [3] present interesting conclusions about the detection of abnormal behaviours in traffic signals, characterized by the number of packets and amount of transferred data by using signal processing techniques. This methodology allows detecting abnormal situations quickly on a large scale, but does not bring a real information about the infected machines.

Ellis et al. [9] defines a series of models of behaviour used by virus to spread their infection, for example the sending of similar information from an infected host to its victims, the propagation in tree or the change from client to server that happens when a host is successfully compromised. This approximation presents the difficult of exponential computation complexity in number of hosts, which practically makes real-time response impossible. Besides, the patterns or models of behaviour are defined by the human being, which would bring forth difficulties to succeed in this methodology for new behaviour models, like a host would have in an ad-hoc network.

Gates and Becknel [12] presents an approximation of the detection of anomalies in a class B network characterizing a normal behaviour of the whole network by evaluating the traffic amount per host and per destination port in a first phase of system training. Subsequently if there are hosts-ports that increase their traffic notably the system quantifies the increase and consequently it sends an alert to the administrator of the network. This model presents computation difficulties due to large quantity of memory required to store data structures and the time used on searching.

Works like those of Noh et al. [21] or Wagner et al. [27] characterize a state of normality based on its entropy and detect abnormal situations on entropy variations in a suddenly way. This approximation is very interesting but it presents difficulties due to the way traffic is analyzed over a wide network segment.

In MINDS project Ertoz et al. [11] try to score every connection to express how anomalous it is in comparison to the normal network traffic. In order to do that they define a set of characteristics based on the relations between IP directions and the implicated ports. They evaluate the situation not only in time but also throughout a concrete number of connections, what according to the authors, would help to detect low activity worms. The only drawback of this method is the amount of alarms generated, due to it evaluates every connection as unit of data for intrusion detection.

It is important to highlight Singh et al. [25] work with their EarlyBird System. They present three characteristics to observe. A significant increase in the sending of similar packets, a variation in the number of hosts that send packets in an interval of traffic and a third parameter based on the quantity of hosts getting this traffic. Certainly the most interesting contribution of this paper is the use of Rabin fingerprints over segments of packet payload for the search of similar packets. This is a really good approximation but limited by the requirement of process huge payload data for use Rabin fingerprints over it.

Dübendorfer et al. works result especially interesting. In their article about Blaster and Sobig worms [8], based on stored traffic by the DDoSVax project [23] since 2003, they offer an analysis by speaking about how important is to model the worm infection steps as well as the monitoring of specific sensitive ports (135/TCP, 69/UDP, 4444/TCP or SMTP in the case of Sobig). They evaluate parameters like the number of packets, bytes towards those ports and size of the sent packets in the backbone of the SWITCH, the Swiss Education & Research Network. Nevertheless, in the conclusions of this article they recognize that the vast majority of the generated traffic by the infected hosts remains inside the intranet. This usually happens because the ports like 135/TCP or 445/TCP, commonly used in the infections of windows boxes, are filtered in the border routers or because worms usually try to spread towards the local network.

In another of their articles [7] Dübendorfer et al. characterize every host individually according to some behaviour parameters like the input and output traffic ratio or number of connections. Tracking the quantity of hosts that there are in each class they will be able to detect new virus outbreaks. One more time this approximation is focuses on the backbone traffic. In case of detection of a new massive infection it would be necessary to carry out an investigation to know the characteristics, the origin and which hosts are infected.

Brauckhoff et al. present a set of articles ([4],[5],[6]) related with the detection of anomalies based on NetFlow information, but centered in the generation of syntethic anomaly present NetFlow information. This is not our problem cause we work directly with real traffic with real anomalies.

Lakhina et al. [16] aproximation use the entropy of the IP addresses and ports distribution and clustering techniques to detect the presence of known anomalies or even to define new kinds of them.

Finally Münz and Carle [19] present a promising framework, TOPAS, that perform a real-time detection of anomalies based on NetFlow information. According with the results of the tests with real traffic presented by the autors, this project will be able to include different kinds of detection methods by the use of pluggable modules. This solution focuses on single hosts interactions more than whole network or subnetwork behaviour. The drawback of the cutting edge real-time detection is that some underground behaviours could result unnoticed by the system.

3   Model

As we have explained, it is in the intranets where most infections happen. In Blaster analysis done by Thomas Dübendorfer et al. [8], they discover that only a minimum percent of the successful infections traffic cross the backbone. This fact is empirically proved due to next reasons:

- Corporate networks are usually protected by firewalls which filter the traffic directed to critical ports like 135/TCP, 445/TCP, 1433/TCP, etc... but intranet traffic directed to these ports are normally free. As we can see in Fig. 1, the infected computer placed in the Corporate Network is able to send attack attempts to 445/TCP port of the computers located in the same network area, but the same traffic directed to the Wide Area Network is filtered by the corporate firewall.

– Most intranets use private addressing and NAT to access the Internet. This normally avoids outer computers connections directed to local area network hosts. In the Fig. 1, an infected external host tries to send 445/TCP port traffic to the corporate network. In this case, the traffic is discarded by the corporate firewall that could be working just as a NAT Server or as a firewall filtering the 445/TCP port traffic. In both cases the result will be the same.

– Empirically, we have detected that viruses try to infect mainly in the subnet where they are sited more than to distant hosts.

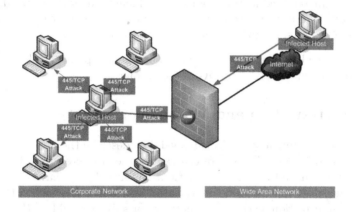

Fig. 1. Network scenario with the presence of an infected host

For these reasons, we conclude that most of malicious traffic happens in our own intranet. The proposed model is divided in four levels of characterization and analysis of the behaviour based on:

– Entire corporate network traffic.
– Each one of the subnets traffic.
– Individual host traffic.
– Threat features examination.

This top-down model would be valid to achieve a double objective: high level malicious traffic detection and reliable compromised hosts location.

Once we know which ones of the hosts are compromised, we are going to be able to discover specific characteristics of this concrete threat. As our main target is to detect, announce and try to block new attacks is essential to share this knowledge to the rest of the community. Our method focuses the detection of new threats in the local area network but if we want to fight against worm threat we must think in a globally way.

There are some incipient projects to share basic information about worm threats, especially command and control servers information and other related issues, all of them in order to defeat the worm activity. Most of those initiatives are quick start solutions, but we will need more complex information structures to ensure the success:

- Robust detection methodology: Corporations must have automatic detection methods that provide high accuracy. As we have seen there are several approximations that may be valid.
- Small reaction time: As Moore et al. explain [18] containment systems require automated methods to detect and react to worm threat, human being based solutions are absolutely ineffective.
- High cooperation and cooperation: If worms are everywhere we must act from everywhere. Protect the Internet from worms is a challenge where all sites (commercial, educational and governmental) must be implied.
- Common countermeasures tactics: Isolation, content filtering or other ways to obstruct the spreading of new worms must be agreed.

In this article we have developed a solution of the first point, a robust detection methodology, future works will solve the next ones.

4   Characterization and Methodology

We are going to define a set of features valid to describe the behaviour in every proposed network levels. These are critical features to determine the difference between a normal and abnormal situation. Empirically we have demonstrated that these features suffer significant variations on worm presence in the net.

The characterization at corporate network or subnet would be the same, and the unique restriction is that the evaluated segment must have a significant number of hosts. We have noticed that in networks with less than 50 hosts, legitimate but particular behaviour of one or two hosts can considerably disturb the entire network characterization. We define two features at this characterization level, first one related with destination port information and the second one with the different IP numbers that act in this evaluation period.

- *Network-Feature 1* - Number of flows per destination port for the entire network: This feature shows when there is excessive number of flows to a define destination port. This is a basic indicator that usually present huge disturbance on the presence of aggressive worms with high number of connections per unit of time.
- *Network-Feature 2* - Ratio between different source-IP addresses and different destination-IP addresses. This indicator evaluates the number of connections attempts that are not answered. This situation appears when the destination computer that source host is trying to establish connection with does not exist or destination computer is alive but by one or another reason drops received packets and does not reply. In absence of anomalous traffic, this feature takes values in a range near 1.

These features are evaluated for a precise time interval. In this level of characterization, we do not propose complex features, due the large quantity of information to process. We use the mean and standard deviation of every feature in a free of worm status of the network to define a warning and alert level.

The possibility of evaluation these feature at a lower level than corporate network (i.e. VLAN level) may result useful because of the organization of users. Normally computer users are grouped by professional profile and this usually means different network behaviours of the implied hosts. Experimental tests have shown that Computer Science Department has not the same traffic outline than Nursing School or the School of Social Studies. For example, in Table 1 we present the number of active hosts in the networks of these three cases, and the number of internet hosts they are communicating with.

Table 1. Reation between internal and external hosts in different environments

Network	Number of active hosts	Number of internet hosts	Ratio
Computer Science Department	119	9588	1:88
Nursing School	50	2749	1:54
School of Social Studies	62	1200	1:19

Once we have define network level features, we continue describing these features at host level. This will help us to detect the machines who are the origin of the anomaly. In order to achieve this we define the following features:

- *Host-Feature 1* - Traffic structure in accordance with destination port: This feature let us to take a snapshot of the traffic layout of a host. Host abnormal behaviour is detected due significant number of flows to the same destination port. This situation is labelled as abnormal if exceed normal number of flows per unit of time characterization for this destination port.
- *Host-Feature 2* - Percentage of hosts towards suspicious machine sends traffic and receives no answer: This is an *Network-Feature 2* extension at host level. Too many output flows with no answer is a very suspicious situation. A high value in this feature is important for decide if a host is infected or not, but the conclusions obtained by this feature are not definitive. Hosts using P2P technology usually try to establish connections to over hundreds or thousands of different computers and not always get response from them. In order to differentiate these two situations we will use next *Host-Feature 3*.
- *Host-Feature 3* - Derivative of source port values from the start time of the flow: Empirically we have detected a pseudo constant increment in used source port value of the infected hosts. This indicator is useful to differentiate between malicious traffic and P2P traffic. In both cases there are large number of connections to different hosts, but in P2P case these connections are grouped in one or two different source ports. Unlike this, infected hosts use consecutive and incremental source port numbers for infection attempts. This feature is based on observed worms behaviour, but it is not impossible that there would be other worms that use random source ports or just one source port for their activities.

All these features are defined for a generic host employed by a standard user, and normal characterizations would be valid for most of the cases, but there would be some problems with concrete hosts i.e. server machines. A short-term solution would be to develop a particular characterization for every network server.

Until this moment we have treated only existing traffic in the intranet, without worrying excessively of outer world. Once we have descended to host level, we will be able to extract useful information referring to the infection. The objective of this task is to export this knowledge to other corporate networks or authorities in a superior level. In particular, we will remark the following items:

- Characterization of the traffic generated by the infected hosts: Source and destination port(s) involved, number of bytes and packets used in infection attempts, etc. Belligerence level in terms of number of connections per unit of time would be interesting too.
- Detection of outer hosts that all our infected hosts or some of them are trying to connect with. This is essential in the case of botnets with their command & control servers. These hosts are neuralgic centres of the infected machines networks.
- Outer hosts abnormal behaviour detection: We could be able to detect anomalies on the basis of the received traffic from a host located out of our intranet, and even try to characterize outer machines traffic, but this idea is so far infeasible because of two reasons: first one is that we probably are receiving only a part of the traffic generated by this host, and the second one is that as well as we work with over 8,000 different active host in the intranet in quarter hour, we would register over 800,000 different outer IP numbers in the same time period.

5   Experimental System Architecture

We have chosen to make use of flow-level information rather than packet-level due to the huge quantity of traffic generated by the network hosts. It would be about 8,000 active hosts in diurnal hours in the University of Zaragoza intranet. These hosts generate about 4,500 flows per second in the main backbone switch, a 6500 Cisco. The chosen flow format is NetFlow v7. The generated information by this means is processed and stored in a relational database gathered in segments of 15 minutes. In 24 hours we usually store about 350 millions of flows.

The hosts taking part in the network consist of investigators, personnel management and students machines connected in the University or remotely from their houses. This variety of examined population, especially concerning the students group, guarantees a good variety of different behaviours in the network.

As we have explained before we have based our flow storage system in a relational database. There are some publications around this idea like the paper from Nickless et al. [20]. Now we are working with a MySQL v5.1 slightly tuned to increase memory cache for keys. At present we are saving 24 hours of NetFlow data, divided in 15 minutes blocks that are cyclical filled. We also have defined indexes based on the IP source address and source port, and IP destination address and destination port to speed up the queries.

The database is composed by 96 tables were are stored 24 hours of net-flow information (each table contains 15 minutes). Every table has the same set of fields defined in Table 2. The tables have indexes over source IP (ipSrcX fields), destination IP (ipDstX fields), source and destination port. The number of flows stored in a table depends on the period of time this table is refeering to. For example in the 12:45 to 13:00 quarter of a usual working day over 4 millions flows could be generated, while 6:00 to 6:15 a.m. quarter it will store just 2 millions. A normal working day will generate over 21 Gb of NetFlow data plus 13 Gb of indexes information.

Table 2. Table definition

FIELD	DESCRIPTION
flowsSeen	Number of flows exported in this flow frame
engineID	ID of the engine that has generated the NetFlow information
ipSrc1	First byte of the IP source of the TCP transaction
ipSrc2	Second byte of the IP source of the TCP transaction
ipSrc3	Third byte of the IP source of the TCP transaction
ipSrc4	Fourth byte of the IP source of the TCP transaction
ipDst1	First byte of the IP destination of the TCP transaction
ipDst2	Second byte of the IP destination of the TCP transaction
ipDst3	Third byte of the IP destination of the TCP transaction
ipDst4	Fourth byte of the IP destination of the TCP transaction
nextHop1	First byte of the next Router
nextHop2	Second byte of the next Router
nextHop3	Third byte of the next Router
nextHop4	Fourth byte of the next Router
inboundSnmpIfIndex	Index of the Switch's interface that receibe the packets from the source IP
outboundSnmpIfIndex	Index of the Switch's interface that send the packets to the destination IP
packetCount	Number of packets in the NetFlow
byteCount	Number of bytes in the NetFlow
startTime	SysUptime, in seconds, at start of flow.
endTime	SysUptime, in seconds, at the time the last packet of the flow was received.
sourcePort	TCP/UDP source port number
destinationPort	TCP/UDP destination port number
flagsV7	Flags indicating, among other things, what flow fields are invalid.
tcpFlags	TCP flags
layer4Protocol	Protocol type (TCP=6, UDP=7,)
typeOfService	IP type of service (ToS)
sourceAutonomousSysId	Autonomous system number of the source, either origin or peer
destinationAutonomousSysId	Autonomous system number of the destination, either origin or peer
sourceMaskBitsCount	Source address prefix mask
destinationMaskBitsCount	Destination address prefix mask

Store NetFlow data in a relational database have the drawback of spend over four times (seven times with table index data) more disk space than save it inf binary format use for example in flow-tools [2], but queries in database are over 300 times faster than using flat files systems.

The use of SQL language for queries is specially interesting. It is extremely easy to accomplish every aggregation of data, or any kind of query. For the insertion we use INSERT DELAYED method to avoid loss of NetFlow data by concurrent queries and insertions.

Physically we use two servers to perform every task in our system as it is shown in the Fig. 2. This is not due CPU requirements but for monitoring purposes. *Balaitous* receives the UDP flow data and pre-processes it to create the SQL statements. *Vignemale* receives the SQL statements and does the rest of the work, it manage SQL tables and process of characterization and detection. This scheme is scalable up to 32,000 flows per second with a generic Pentium IV for *Balaitous* server, and a dual Xeon with 2 Gbytes of ram for *Vignemale* server. We are using actually Fecora Core 8 linux in both severs.

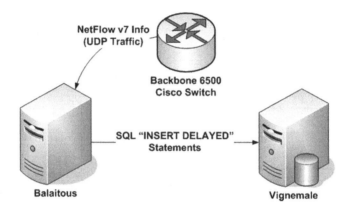

Fig. 2. Implied systems schema

We have observed during the preliminary test time of the project (from September 2005 to February 2006) that the features profile present three defined periods associated to the workers and students of the University presence and activity. From 08:00 to 15:00 there is a big activity caused by the main working time of the day. From 15:00 to 22:00 most of the workers and students leave the University so the activity is substantially reduced. Finally from 22:00 to 08:00 in the next day, most of the network traffic is generated by computers without human interaction. We have noticed that this division is much more better approach than evaluate all day quarters by equal. The evaluation happens at the end of each quarter hour interval. An extensive and deep evaluation spends 2 minutes at most.

5.1   Experimental Results

As we have explained before, we have used real traffic from the University of Zaragoza network for method validation. The suspicious sample of traffic has been collected in April 2006. During this month there have been no massive infections but we have detected some malicious activity caused by one or more species of bot-worms family.

We begin with the *Network-Feature 1* normal characterization. A complete description of it would define warning and alert levels based on the mean and the standard deviation of every possible destination port. To characterize this feature for our three daytime periods and for each one of the 65536 TCP and UDP ports is not very practical. We will characterize by this way only that ports that present a significant activity.

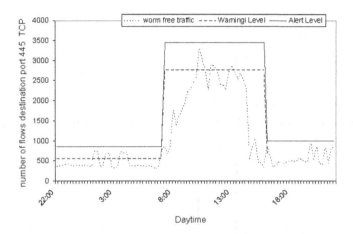

Fig. 3. Normalized flow levels to 445/TCP destination port in worm free status

The graph in Fig. 3 shows normal characterization of 445/TCP port along 24 hours. We define a warning level, until we consider that activity to this port is in normalized margins and an alarm level. Upper activity to this level is an abnormal indicator that alerts us about the presence of worms in the net. In a worm free network the feature evaluation result must keep under alarm levels, as the example shows.

The Fig. 4 is an example of *Network-Feature 1* evaluation with worm presence in the network. As we can see traffic directed to 445/TCP largely exceeds both levels. Infected machines get to generate up to 30,000 flows to this destination port. To locate problem origin we query the traffic amount to this port by VLAN, as Fig. 5 shows. In this figure we notice that malicious traffic comes out from three VLANs.

Network-Feature 2 tries to detect if there are infected hosts scanning the network. It computes different source-IP and destination-IP addresses relation. In this analysis it does not heed traffic from and to outer LAN hosts. The evaluation formula is:

$$ratio = \frac{uniqueDestinationIp}{uniqueSourceIp}$$

In absence of anomalous traffic, this ratio value would have to be around 1. Higher values for this feature indicate the presence of traffic directed to hosts that

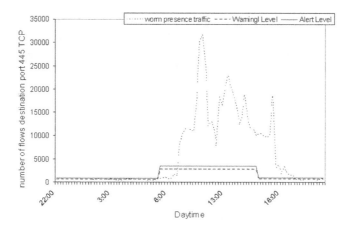

Fig. 4. Normalized 445 port flow number levels with worm infected hosts presence

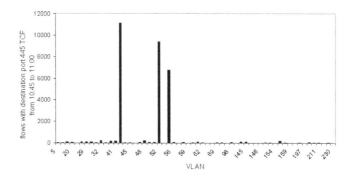

Fig. 5. Number of flows with destination port 445/TCP by VLAN from 10:45 to 11:00 on worm presence

generate no traffic as reply. This anomalous traffic would reveal worm infected hosts in searching of new victims. The graph in Fig. 6 shows *Network-Feature 2* evaluation in a worm free environment in comparison to upper signal, which alerts about scans from infected hosts located in our network.

Once we have notice about anomalies caused by infected hosts, and we know in which VLAN they are located, we are going to search suspicious hosts in this segment on the basis of the data obtained until now. In Fig. 4 we have warned about abnormal traffic between 10:45 and 11:00 a.m. to 445/TCP port. This traffic is coming from VLAN 42, 52 and 55. Evaluating *Host-Feature 1* (number of flows by destination port) of 42 VLAN hosts with 445/TCP we notice that host 10.33.42.34 has 12,544 flows in this quarter as Table 3 shows. This is very suspicious, specially when the second host in rank has 22 flows and the normal characterization of this daytime period for a generic host is 11,65.

Evaluating the *Host-Feature 2* we show the number of different IP that have received connections attempts from VLAN 42 hosts in this quarter, and the

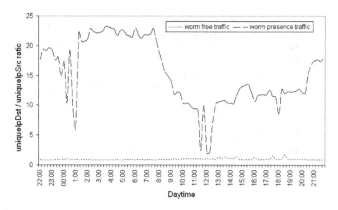

Fig. 6. Ratio of uniqueDestinationIp / uniqueSourceIp

Table 3. Number of flows per IP to port 445 in VLAN 42

IP	Flows
10.33.42.34	12544
10.33.42.110	22
10.33.42.41	18
10.33.42.71	16
10.33.42.115	13
10.33.42.73	13
10.33.42.103	12
10.33.42.74	11
10.33.42.38	9
10.33.42.83	8
10.33.42.158	1
10.33.42.163	1
10.33.42.95	1

number of different IP that answer. This evaluation is presented in Table 4. In this rank appears other hosts with a high number of different destinations in addition to our well know 10.33.42.34. In the same period of time we obtain that it has tried to establish communication with 11,443 different hosts, and has received answers from only 735, so most of the 90% of IP which it tries to connect to does not reply. We have to highlight those situations where appears some answer IP that it's not asked. These flows are attempts of connections from other hosts that are dropped by evaluated machine, like infection tries for example.

It is necessary to clarify that when we talk about hosts that reply to suspicious host requests we do not refer to a standard TCP handshake, where destination port and IP is transformed in source port and IP of the reply. We are talking about communication in a higher abstraction level, using all kinds of communication (TCP or UDP at every port) as a reply signal.

Table 4. Percent of no answer IP

IP	UnqIpDst	UnqIpResponse	Percent
10.33.42.34	11445	735	93,57%
10.33.42.41	5638	2232	60,41%
10.33.42.249	1376	37	97,31%
10.33.42.38	625	532	14,88%
10.33.42.195	449	530	0%
10.33.42.115	58	57	1,72%
10.33.42.103	52	56	0%
10.33.42.196	45	46	0%
...	...	...	...

In *Host-Feature 2* evaluation, appears other hosts, for example 10.33.42.41 or 10.33.42.249, with a high value in their evaluation. Both IP present an alarm level in *Host-Feature 2*, but it is not by itself an evidence of infection. In fact, this apparently suspicious behaviour is caused by the use of P2P software, but we something that help us to differentiate between non-infected hosts running P2P software and infected hosts. We will use the *Host-Feature 3* evaluation to accomplish this task. Empirically it is observed that scanning hosts use correlative source ports throughout the time, whereas these hosts that use P2P mainly concentrate their traffic in one or two source ports.

The Fig. 7 shows source port numbers of the two first hosts in the Table 4. There we can see how the source port number of host 10.33.42.34 increase along time. In the same period of time the host 10.33.42.41 groups his traffic in port 3253, and occasionally uses other source ports.

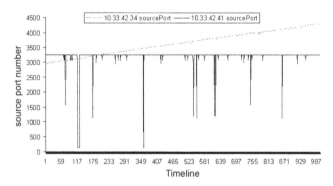

Fig. 7. Source Port organization in timeline

Once we have caught worm infected host, we will trye to extract as much information as we can from network traffic. To accomplish a deeper analysis we would inspect the infected host incoming and outgoing packets payload.

Table 5 shows destination ports our 10.33.42.34 host is trying to connect with. In addition to usual connections (ICMP, DNS, HTTP, ...) we can see malicious

Table 5. Suspicious host destination ports

Dst.Port	Flows to	Explanation
0	6	ICMP attempts
53	3	DNS requests
80	14	Web traffic
135	428	Microsoft's DCOM RPC
137	4	Netbios Name Service
138	1	Netbios Datagram Service
139	45	Netbios Session Service
445	12544	Win2k+ SMB
5226	8	HP Status ???
6667	3	ircu ???

traffic grouped at 135/TCP and 445/TCP and at last a small percent not so well known ports: 5226/TCP and 6667/TCP.

This list of implied ports, as well as a possible concentration of traffic from a same source port would serve to make a basic characterization of this worm behaviour. These connections to no well characterized ports are specially interesting. If we make a query to know which hosts are behind these ports we will discover two outer machines. These ones have much to do with the abnormal traffic detected in our network, in fact in 211.227.236.143 port 5226/TCP and in 206.53.56.16 port 6667/TCP are running two botnet command and control IRC servers. It is sure that there will be more machines along the Internet controlled by these same servers, so an early alert to the rest of the community is essential by two reasons: ISP that manages this servers IP numbers must block them and corporations that have infected hosts in their networks could locate them with this information.

6   Conclusions

We have presented a successful approximation for worm detection based on a normal status characterization and a subsequent detection of deviations from it. As we have demonstrated this deviations are caused by abnormal behaviour presence in the local area network traffic. Suspicious traffic sample is compared with the assigned normal characterization of the network segment in the same daytime period. Dividing the evaluation of anomalies in at least two or three levels is a useful way to accomplish the worm detection. Also we are able to locate the malicious traffic origins and extract useful information about the threat from the activity of the infected hosts. This knowledge could be of vital importance to other corporations that are suffering the same threat.

Our model has been proved with real traffic from the University of Zaragoza network. Within the diversity of detections that this method can accomplish it has been able to alert about malicious traffic in the University network, it has located the origin at one VLAN and finally it has identified several infected hosts with a bot-worm and has extracted useful information related with this threat too.

7   Future Work

In the short term, our objectives are to reduce the initial quarter-hour evaluation period to less than 5 minutes. By this way we would improve the system response time in order to active countermeasures that could minimize the threat damage as far as possible. In addition to this we keep on working in the definition of new and better features and characterizations that could enhance the network anomaly detection with more preciseness.

We have begun to work with traffic classification at application level to complement our NetFlow information. This kind of classification will allow us to identify traces of a concrete protocol (i.e. IRC) independently of the source and destination ports involved in. There are quite a number of works related with this topic. Karagiannis et al. [15] and Erman et al. [10] or more recently [13] and [22] are good examples of this investigation line.

A natural evolution of the host generic characterization would be to define several profiles that express more accurately individual host behaviour. An extreme model would define a normal characterization for each one of the hosts connected to our network. This proposition has serious difficulties in terms of scalability, but we do not discard it. Anyway this particular characterization is a good scheme for special machines as servers.

As we have explained along this paper, the target of our efforts must be the global defense of the Internet against massive infections threat. Next step in this path is to define in a precise way what kind of information must be exchanged by the nodes of a worm detection/containment future network, and how could be its structure.

Acknowledgements

We wish thank University of Zaragoza's network administrators and the rest of the communications area by their support and collaboration in NetFlow data harvesting. Specially thanks to Manuel Jimenez, Jose Manuel Güemes, Jose Antonio Valero and David Romero.

References

1. Caida: Cooperative association for internet data analysis, http://www.caida.org
2. Flow-tools: Tool set for working with netflow data,
   http://www.splintered.net/sw/flow-tools
3. Barford, P., Kline, J., Plonka, D., Ron, A.: A signal analysis of network traffic anomalies. In: ACM SIGCOMM Internet Measurement Workshop (2002)
4. Brauckhoff, D., Fiedler, U., Plattner, B.: Towards systematically evaluating flow-level anomaly detection mechanisms. In: Workshop on Monitoring, Attack Detection and Mitigation (MonAM 2006), Tübingen, Germany (September 2006)
5. Brauckhoff, D., May, M., Plattner, B.: Flow-level anomaly detection - blessing or curse? In: IEEE INFOCOM 2007, Student Workshop, Anchorage, Alaska, USA (May 2007)

6. Brauckhoff, D., Wagner, A., May, M.: Flame: A flow-level anomaly modeling engine. In: Proceedings of CSET 2008 workshop, Usenix, San Jose, CA, USA (July 2008)
7. Dübendorfer, T., Plattner, B.: Host behaviour based early detection of worm outbreaks in internet backbones. In: WETICE - Security Technologies (STCA) Workshop (2005)
8. Dübendorfer, T., Wagner, A., Hossmann, T., Plattner, B.: Flow-level traffic analysis of the blaster and sobig worm outbreaks in an internet backbone. In: Julisch, K., Krügel, C. (eds.) DIMVA 2005. LNCS, vol. 3548, pp. 103–122. Springer, Heidelberg (2005)
9. Ellis, D.R., Aiken, J.G., Attwood, K.S., Tenaglia, S.D.: A behavioral approach to worm detection. In: ACM Workshop on Rapid Malcode WORM (2005)
10. Erman, J., Arlitt, M., Mahanti, A.: Traffic classification using clustering algorithms. In: MineNet 2006: Proceedings of the 2006 SIGCOMM workshop on Mining network data, pp. 281–286. ACM, New York (2006)
11. Ertoz, L., Eilertson, E., Lazarevic, A., Tan, P.-N., Dokas, P., Kumar, V., Srivastava, J.: Minds,detection of novel network attacks using data mining. In: ICDM Workshop on Data Mining for Computer Security (DMSEC) (2003)
12. Gates, C., Becknel, D.: Host anomalies from network data. In: IEEE SMC Information Assurance Workshop (2005)
13. Gu, R., Hong, M., Wang, H., Ji, Y.: Fast traffic classification in high speed networks. In: Ma, Y., Choi, D., Ata, S. (eds.) APNOMS 2008. LNCS, vol. 5297, pp. 429–432. Springer, Heidelberg (2008)
14. S. Institute. Internet storm center, http://isc.sans.org/, http://www.dshield.org/
15. Karagiannis, T., Papagiannaki, K., Faloutsos, M.: Blinc: Multilevel traffic classification in the dark. In: Proceedings of ACM SIGCOMM, pp. 229–240 (2005)
16. Lakhina, A., Crovella, M., Diot, C.: Mining anomalies using traffic feature distributions. SIGCOMM Comput. Commun. Rev. 35(4), 217–228 (2005)
17. Ma, J., Voelker, G.M., Savage, S.: Self-stopping worms. In: ACM Workshop on Rapid Malcode WORM (2005)
18. Moore, D., Shannon, C., Voelker, G.M., Savage, S.: Internet quarantine: Requirements for containing self-propagating code. In: INFOCOM (2003)
19. Münz, G., Carle, G.: Real-time analysis of flow data for network attack detection. In: Proceedings of IFIP/IEEE Symposium on Integrated Management (IM2007), Munich, Germany (May 2007)
20. Nickless, B., Navarro, J., Winkler, L.: Combining cisco netflow exports with relational database technology for usage statistics, intrusion detection, and network forensics. In: Proceedings of the Fourteenth Systems Administration Conference (LISA 2000), Berkeley, CA, December 3-8 2000, pp. 285–290. The USENIX Association (2000)
21. Noh, S., Lee, C., Ryu, K., Choi, K., Jung, G.: Detecting worm propagation using traffic concentration analysis and inductive learning. In: Yang, Z.R., Yin, H., Everson, R.M. (eds.) IDEAL 2004. LNCS, vol. 3177, pp. 402–408. Springer, Heidelberg (2004)
22. Park, B., Won, Y.J., Choi, M.-J., Kim, M.-S., Hong, J.W.: Empirical analysis of application-level traffic classification using supervised machine learning. In: Ma, Y., Choi, D., Ata, S. (eds.) APNOMS 2008. LNCS, vol. 5297, pp. 474–477. Springer, Heidelberg (2008)

23. Plattner, B., Wagner, A., Dübendorfer, T.: In search of a vaccine against distributed denial of service attacks (ddosvax) (2003)
24. Project, T.H.: The honeynet project & research alliance: Know your enemy: Tracking botnets. Technical report (March 13, 2004)
25. Singh, S., Estan, C., Varghese, G., Savage, S.: The earlybird system for real-time detection of unknown worms. In: ACM - Workshop on Hot Topics in Networks (HOTNETS) (2003)
26. Staniford, S., Paxson, V., Weaver, N.: How to 0wn the internet in your spare time (May 14, 2002)
27. Wagner, A., Plattner, B.: Entropy based worm and anomaly detection in fast ip networks. In: WETICE - Security Technologies (STCA) Workshop (2005)

The Power of Anonymous Veto in Public Discussion

Feng Hao[1] and Piotr Zieliński[2],*

[1] Thales Information Systems Security, nCipher product line
[2] Google Inc.
feng.hao@thales-esecurity.com, piotrzielinski@google.com

Abstract. The Dining Cryptographers problem studies how to securely compute the boolean-OR function while preserving the privacy of each input bit. Since its first introduction by Chaum in 1988, it has attracted a number of solutions over the past twenty years.

In this paper, we propose an exceptionally efficient solution: Anonymous Veto Network (or AV-net). Our protocol is provably secure under the Decision Diffie-Hellman (DDH) and random oracle assumptions, and is better than past work in the following ways. It provides the strongest protection of each input's privacy against collusion attacks; it requires only two rounds of broadcast, fewer than any other solution; the computational load and bandwidth usage are the least among the available techniques; and the efficiency of our protocol is achieved without relying on any private channels or trusted third parties. Overall, the efficiency of our protocol seems as good as one may hope for.

Keywords: Dining Cryptographers problem; DC-net; anonymous veto; secure multiparty computation.

1 Introduction

In a galaxy far far away ...

During an open meeting, the Galactic Security Council must decide whether to invade an enemy planet. One delegate wishes to veto the measure, but worries that such a move might jeopardize the relations with some other member states. How can he veto the proposal without revealing his identity?

The above shows a picture of the council delegates – with mutual suspicion – discussing a decision in public. There are no private channels. The only way to communicate between each other is through public announcement; and during announcement, every word uttered or message sent can be traced back to its sender. There is no external help either, as trusted third parties do not exist.

---

* The work was done when both authors were at the Computer Laboratory, University of Cambridge. This is an extended version of an earlier conference paper [1].

M.L. Gavrilova et al. (Eds.): Trans. on Comput. Sci. IV, LNCS 5430, pp. 41–52, 2009.
© Springer-Verlag Berlin Heidelberg 2009

In essence, this problem requires a secure computation of the boolean-OR function, while preserving the privacy of each input bit. It was coined by Chaum as the Dining Cryptographers problem [5]; however, the "unconditional secrecy channels" assumed in [5] are no longer readily available in our case, which makes the delegate's task harder.

There have been a number of solutions in past work, ranging from circuit evaluation [20,10] and Dining Cryptographers Network (or DC-net) [5] proposed nearly twenty years ago, to several anonymous veto protocols [15,11,4] published in recent years. However, these techniques all have various limitations, as we discuss now.

The DC-net protocol was proposed by Chaum in 1988, and has long been considered a classic privacy-preserving technique [12]. This protocol has two stages. First, n participants set up pairwise shared secrets through secret channels. Next, each participant P_i broadcasts a one bit message a_i, which is the XOR of all the shared one-bit secrets that P_i holds if he has no message (i.e., no veto) to send, or the opposite bit otherwise. After the broadcast round, the sent message is decoded by all participants through computing the XOR of the broadcast bits. More details can be found in [5].

However, deploying DC-nets is hampered for several reasons. First, the "unconditional secrecy channels" are assumed in the protocol, but difficult to achieve in practice. This problem is further compounded by the rapid increase of the total number of such channels (i.e., $O(n^2)$) when there are more participants. Second, message collisions are problematic too. Even when all participants are honest, an even number of messages will still cancel each other out, forcing retransmissions. Third, a DC-net is vulnerable to malicious jamming. For example, the last participant P_n may send $\oplus_{i=1}^{n-1} a_i$, so that the final outcome will always be '0' (i.e., non-veto). Countermeasures include setting up "traps" to catch misbehaviors probabilistically, but make the system more complex (see [5,12,18]).

While a DC-net is "unconditionally secure", all the other solutions are built upon public key cryptography, and are thus computationally secure. These include the circuit evaluation technique [10] and several anonymous veto protocols [15,11,4]. A lack of efficiency is their common problem. We will explain this in more detail in Section 4.

Despite the problems in a DC-net, we still find it, among all the past solutions, most attractive for its simplicity and elegance. It combines all others' secret keys to encrypt data, but requires no secret keys to decrypt it. This idea is seminal, but undeservedly, has rarely been exploited in secure multiparty computations for the past twenty years.

By contrast, the mix-net protocol – a twin technique introduced by Chaum to protect anonymity – has been extensively studied and applied in the field [6]. It encrypts messages in multiple layers using public key cryptography, and usually requires a chain of proxy servers to perform secure decryption. In comparison, a DC-net is more lightweight; it sends anonymous data by a one-round broadcast and allows rapid decryption with no servers needed.

Our solution, Anonymous Veto Network (or AV-net), captures the essence of the original DC-net design [5] – it combines everyone else's public key to encrypt data, but requires no private keys to decrypt it. This, as we will show in Section 4, leads to the optimal efficiency of our protocol in many aspects. However, despite the similarity in the underlying design principles, the technical developments for the DC-net and AV-net protocols are completely different. In the following section, we will explain how an AV-net works.

2   Protocol

2.1   Model

We assume an authenticated public channel available for every participant. This assumption is made in all the past work in this line of research [5, 15, 11, 4]; in fact, an authenticated public channel is an essential requirement for general multi-party secure computations [10, 3]. This requirement basically ensures that the published votes come from the legitimate or registered voters; otherwise, voting would be meaningless. There are several ways to realize such a channel: by using physical means or a public bulletin board [15]. Apart from this basic requirement, we do not assume any secret channels or trusted third parties.

In the threat model, we consider two types of attackers: a passive one who merely eavesdrops on the communication, and an active one who takes part in the voting. Active attackers may collude in an effort to uncover others' votes or manipulate the voting result. The *full collusion* against a participant involves all the other participants in the network. Any anonymous veto protocol, by nature, cannot preserve the vetoer's anonymity under this circumstance. However, as explained in [5], it is practically impossible to have all participants – who mistrust each other – colluding against just one; there would be no point for that person to stay in the network. Hence, in this paper, we only consider *partial collusion*, which involves only some participants, but not all.

Under the threat model of partial collusion, an anonymous veto protocol should satisfy the following three requirements.

- *Veto Privacy* – If one vetoes, the rest of the participants cannot tell who has vetoed.
- *Veto Completeness* – If one vetoes, all participants accept the veto outcome.
- *Veto Soundness* – If the outcome is veto, all participants accept that someone has vetoed.

Clearly, a DC-net does not satisfy the second requirement, because of the collision problem. More requirements are defined in [15, 11] to reflect the trustworthiness of the third parties involved, but are not needed in our model.

2.2   Two-Round Broadcast

Let G denote a finite cyclic group of prime order q in which the Decision Diffie-Hellman (DDH) problem is intractable [2]. Let g be a generator in G. There are n participants, and they all agree on (G, g). Each participant P_i selects a random value as the secret: $x_i \in_R \mathbb{Z}_q$.

Round 1. *Every participant P_i publishes g^{x_i} and a knowledge proof for x_i.*

When this round finishes, each participant P_i computes

$$g^{y_i} = \prod_{j=1}^{i-1} g^{x_j} \Big/ \prod_{j=i+1}^{n} g^{x_j}$$

Round 2. *Every participant publishes a value $g^{c_i y_i}$ and a knowledge proof for c_i, where c_i is either x_i or a random value $r_i \in_R \mathbb{Z}_q$, depending on whether participant P_i vetoes or not.*

$$g^{c_i y_i} = \begin{cases} g^{r_i y_i} & \text{if } P_i \text{ sends '1' (veto)}, \\ g^{x_i y_i} & \text{if } P_i \text{ sends '0' (no veto).} \end{cases}$$

To check the final message, each participant computes $\prod_i g^{c_i y_i}$. If no one vetoes, we have $\prod_i g^{c_i y_i} = \prod_i g^{x_i y_i} = 1$. This is because $\sum_i x_i y_i = 0$ (Proposition 1). Hence, $\prod_i g^{x_i y_i} = g^{\sum_i x_i y_i} = 1$.

On the other hand, if one or more participants send the message '1', we have $\prod_i g^{c_i y_i} \neq 1$. Thus, the one-bit message has been sent anonymously.

Proposition 1 (Soundness). *For the x_i and y_i defined in an AV-net, $\sum_i x_i y_i = 0$.*

Proof. By definition $y_i = \sum_{j<i} x_j - \sum_{j>i} x_j$, hence

$$\sum_i x_i y_i = \sum_i \sum_{j<i} x_i x_j - \sum_i \sum_{j>i} x_i x_j$$

$$= \sum_{j<i} \sum x_i x_j - \sum_{i<j} \sum x_i x_j$$

$$= \sum_{j<i} \sum x_i x_j - \sum_{j<i} \sum x_j x_i$$

$$= 0.$$

Table 1 illustrates this equality in a more intuitive way.

The above proposition shows that if no one has vetoed, the outcome will be non-veto. Equivalently, if the outcome is veto, someone must have vetoed. This shows that the protocol fulfills the "veto soundness" requirement defined in Section 2.1.

In the protocol, senders must demonstrate their knowledge of the discrete logarithms, namely the secrets x_i and c_i, without revealing them. This can be realized by using a Zero-Knowledge Proof (ZKP), a well-established primitive in cryptography [7, 8, 16, 9].

As an example, we could use Schnorr's signature, for it is non-interactive, and reveals nothing except the one bit information about the truth of the statement:

Table 1. A simple illustration of $\sum_{i=1}^{n} x_i y_i = 0$ for $n = 5$. The sum $\sum_{i=1}^{n} x_i \left(\sum_{j=1}^{i-1} x_j - \sum_{j=i+1}^{n} x_j \right)$ is the addition of all the cells, where $+$, $-$ represent the sign. They cancel each other out.

	x_1	x_2	x_3	x_4	x_5
x_1		$-$	$-$	$-$	$-$
x_2	$+$		$-$	$-$	$-$
x_3	$+$	$+$		$-$	$-$
x_4	$+$	$+$	$+$		$-$
x_5	$+$	$+$	$+$	$+$	

"the sender knows the discrete logarithm" [16]. Note that Schnorr's signature is provably secure under the random oracle model, so our scheme would also work in the random oracle model – that is requiring a secure hash hash function. Let H be such a secure hash function. To prove the knowledge of the exponent for g^{x_i}, one can send $\{g^v, r = v - x_i h\}$ where $v \in_R \mathbb{Z}_q$ and $h = H(g, g^v, g^{x_i}, i)$. This signature can be verified by anyone through checking whether g^v and $g^r g^{x_i h}$ are equal. Note that here the participant index i is unique and known to all. Adding i inside the hash function can effectively prevent a replay of this signature by other participants. Other ZKP techniques can be found in [9].

3 Security Analysis

Simplicity is the main goal in our protocol design. The construct of AV-net is quite straightforward, in fact much simpler than the related works [15, 11, 4]. In addition, we built the protocol upon the well-established technique such as Schnorr's signature whose zero-knowledge property has been well-understood. This greatly simplifies the task of security analysis. Therefore, in this section, we shall aim to provide intuitive (yet rigorous) security analysis without having to go through the lengthy formalism (though formal models can be instantiated).

In the AV-net construct, each participant sends out ephemeral public keys in the first round, and then encrypts his vote by combining the public keys in the second round. To breach the anonymity of a participant, an observer – anyone within the broadcast range – may try to uncover the one-bit message from the announced ciphertext. In the following, we will prove that, under the DDH assumption, the proposed cryptosystem achieves *semantic security* [13]. This is equivalent to showing that under the hard-problem assumption, ciphertext is indistinguishable to observers [13].

In an AV-net, the value of y_i is determined by the private keys of all participants except P_i. The following lemma shows its security property.

Lemma 2. *In an AV-net, y_i is a secret random value to attackers in partial collusion against the participant P_i.*

Proof. Consider the worst case where only P_k $(k \neq i)$ is not involved in the collusion. Hence x_k is uniformly distributed over $\mathbb{Z}_q$ and unknown to colluders.

The knowledge proofs required in the protocol show that all participants know their private keys. Since y_i is computed from x_j ($j \neq i, k$) known to colluders plus (or minus) a random number x_k, y_i must be uniformly distributed over $\mathbb{Z}_q$. Colluders cannot learn y_i even in this worst case.

Theorem 3 (Privacy). *Under the Decision Diffie-Hellman assumption, attackers in partial collusion against P_i cannot distinguish the two ciphertexts $g^{x_i y_i}$ and $g^{r_i y_i}$.*

Proof. Besides the sent ciphertext, the data available to attackers concerning P_i include: g^{x_i}, g^{y_i} and Zero-Knowledge Proofs for the proof of the exponents x_i, y_i. The secret x_i is chosen randomly by P_i. Lemma 2 shows that y_i is a random value, unknown to the attacker. The ZKP only reveal one bit: whether the sender knows the discrete logarithm[1]; it is provable that it does not leak anything more than that [16]. Therefore, according to the Decision Diffie-Hellman assumption, one cannot distinguish between $g^{x_i y_i}$ and a random value in the group such as $g^{r_i y_i}$ [2].

The above theorem states that the individual published ciphertext does not leak any useful information. It is the multiplication of all ciphertexts that tells the outcome. For each participant, the learned information from the protocol is strictly confined to the multiplied result plus his own input. If a participant vetoes, the rest of the participants cannot track down the vetoer without full collusion. This shows that the protocol fulfills the "veto privacy" requirement defined in Section 2.1.

An anonymous veto protocol must resist jamming, to which a DC-net is vulnerable. Apparently, in the second round of broadcast, we need g^{y_i} be a generator for the group, so that participant P_i can produce a valid signature. Because the group G has prime order, any non-identity element is a generator. From Lemma 2, the value y_i is random over $\mathbb{Z}_q$ even in the face of active attacks (partial collusion). Thus, given that q is a large number, say 160-bit [2], the chance that $y_i \neq 0$ is overwhelming: $1 - 2^{-160}$. Only in the full collusion case can attackers manipulate $y_i = 0$, which then makes full collusion immediately evident. The resistance to jamming in an AV-net is formally proved below.

Theorem 4 (Completeness). *Under the Discrete Logarithm assumption, if P_i vetoes, provided that g^{y_i} is not the identity element in the group, P_i's veto cannot be suppressed.*

Proof. Assume P_i's veto can be suppressed, and we will show that one can then solve the Discrete Logarithm problem. Given g^{r_i}, where r_i is a random value, one can compute r_i by simulating the protocol with jamming: participant P_i announces $g^{r_i y_i} = (g^{r_i})^{y_i}$, but his veto is suppressed by others. The simulator generates all other secrets, except $c_i = r_i$. By definition we have $\prod g^{c_i y_i} = 1$.

---

[1] It should be noted that if we choose Schnorr's signature to realize ZKPs, we implicitly assume a random oracle (i.e., a secure hash function), since Schnorr's signature is provably secure under the random oracle model [16].

Table 2. Comparison to the past work

related work	pub year	rnd no	know proof	pvt ch	colli- sion	3rd pty	collu- sion	security reliance	system compl
GMW [10]	1987	3	$O(n)$	yes	no	no	half	trapdoor	$O(n^2)$
Chaum [5]	1988	2+		yes	yes	no	full	uncond	$O(n^2)$
KY [15]	2003	3	$O(n)$	no	no	yes	full	DDH	$O(n^2)$
Groth [11]	2004	$n+1$	2	no	no	yes	full	DDH	$O(n)$
Brandt [4]	2005	4	4	no	no	no	full	DDH	$O(n)$
AV-net		2	2	**no**	**no**	**no**	**full**	**DDH**	$O(n)$

That is $g^{r_i y_i} = \prod_{j=i} g^{-c_j y_j}$. The knowledge proofs required in the protocol show that the simulator knows the values x_j ($1 \leq j \leq n$) and c_j ($1 \leq j \leq n$ and $j \neq i$). Also note that g^{y_i} is not an identity element, so $y_i \neq 0$. Hence, the simulator can easily compute $r_i = y_i^{-1} \sum_{j=i} -c_j y_j$, where $y_i = \sum_{j<i} x_j - \sum_{j>i} x_j$. With the obtained knowledge of the r_i value, the simulation is complete. Thus, one solves the discrete logarithm of g^{r_i} by simulating the protocol with jamming. This, however, contradicts the Discrete Logarithm assumption.

The above theorem states that jamming the protocol implies solving the Discrete Logarithm problem, which is believed to be intractable. In other words, the protocol ensures that when a participant vetoes, his veto message will be received by all. This makes the protocol fulfill the "veto completeness" requirement defined in Section 2.1.

Overall, the zero-knowledge proof, as a crypto primitive, is important in our security analysis. Without it, several attacks would be possible. If there were no knowledge proofs in the first round, participant P_n could manipulate the value of y_1 by announcing $1/\prod_{i=2}^{n-1} g^{x_i}$, so that $y_1 = 0$. Similarly, if there were no knowledge proofs in the second round, the last participant P_n could jam the protocol by announcing $1/\prod_{i=1}^{n-1} g^{c_i y_i}$. Hence, the zero-knowledge proof is the technique to make the protocol self-enforcing – ensuring that participants do perform the asymmetric operations (e.g., exponentiation) as stated, rather than give out random data. With the exception of the DC-net protocol, it is required in all the other solutions based on public key cryptography.

4   Efficiency

For the past twenty years, there have been a few techniques available to compute the boolean-OR function securely. They are summarized in Table 2.

Among all solutions, an AV-net stands out for its optimal efficiency in many aspects. First, it needs only two rounds, fewer than any others. In fact, two is the best round-efficiency achievable (see Appendix A). Second, it takes only a single exponentiation to encrypt data, no matter how many participants there are. Third, the size of the broadcast ciphertext $g^{c_i y_i}$ is only half of that using the standard ElGamal encryption (see [4]). It seems unlikely to be reduced further.

The AV-net protocol adopts the ZKP primitive, which may require additional computation in verification. The exact computational cost depends on the choice of the specific ZKP technique, whether the outcome is in doubt and the trust relationships between participants. It is also significant that since all communication is public in our protocol, any invalid ZKPs would present themselves as publicly verifiable evidence on misbehavior. With the exception of the DC-net protocol, all other solutions require verifying the ZKPs as well. As shown in Table 2, an AV-net has the fewest zero-knowledge proofs per participant: a constant two (i.e., one for each round). Hence, under the same evaluation conditions, the verification cost in an AV-net is the smallest among the related techniques. In the following, we will compare an AV-net with each of the past solutions in detail.

Let us first compare an AV-net with a DC-net. The DC-net protocol could be implemented with different topological designs. A fully-connected DC-net is "unconditionally secure", but suffers from the scalability problem when applied to a large system. For this reason, Chaum suggests a ring-based DC-net in [5], which presents a trade-off between security and system complexity. Recently, Wright, Adler, Levine and Shield showed that the ring-based DC-net described by Chaum (also by Schneier [17]) is easily attacked [19]. They compared different topologies of a DC-net and concluded that the fully-connected one is most resilient to attacks [19]. Hence, we compare an AV-net with the most secure form of a DC-net, i.e., a fully-connected DC-net.

As explained earlier, one of the most problematic parts in a DC-net is its key setup, which produces $O(n^2)$ keys. In the original description of the DC-net protocol, shared keys are established by *secretly* tossing coins behind menus. However, this requires multiple rounds of interaction between pairs of participants. It is slow and tedious, especially when there are many people involved. Other means to establish keys, as suggested by Chaum, include using optical disks or a pseudo-random sequence generator based on short keys [5]. However, such methods are acknowledged by Chaum as being either expensive or not very secure [5].

Our protocol replaces the key-setup phase in a DC-net with a simple one-round broadcast. This is achieved via public key cryptography. Although a DC-net can adopt a similar technique – the Diffie-Hellman key exchange protocol – to distribute keys, its use of the underlying technology is quite different from ours. Suppose a DC-net uses Diffie-Hellman to establish keys[2]. Each participant must perform $O(n)$ exponentiations in order to compute the shared keys with the remaining $n-1$ participants. (A DC-net has the desirable feature that once pairwise keys are established, the protocol can be run continuously [5]. But it might be a question how useful that feature is in practice given the collision and jamming problems.) However, our protocol requires only one exponentiation for each of the two rounds, no matter how many participants in the network (the cost of multiplication is negligible as compared to that of exponentiation).

---

[2] Note that in this case, a DC-net is no longer unconditionally secure, as the Diffie-Hellman key exchange essentially rests on the Decision Diffie-Hellman assumption [2].

Secure circuit evaluation is an important technique for secure Multi-Party Computation (MPC) applications. It evaluates a given function f on the private inputs $x_1, \ldots, x_n$ from n participants. In other words, it computes $y = f(x_1, \ldots, x_n)$, while maintaining the privacy of individual inputs. At first glance, it appears trivial to apply this technique to build a veto-protocol – one only needs to define f as the boolean-OR function. However, this general technique proves to be unnecessarily complex and expensive in solving specific functions [4].

Yao [20] first proposed a general solution for the secure circuit evaluation for the two-party case. Later, Goldreich, Micali, and Wigderson extended Yao's protocol for the multiparty case, and demonstrated that any polynomial-time function can be evaluated securely in polynomial time provided the majority of the players are honest [10]. This conclusion is drawn based on the general assumption of the existence of a trap-door permutation function. Although the general solution proposed in [10] uses an unbounded number of rounds, it was later shown that such an evaluation can be done using only a constant number of rounds of interaction [3]. Recently, Gennaro, Ishai, Kushilevitz, and Rabin showed that three rounds are sufficient for arbitrary secure computation tasks [14].

Although the general GMW solution is versatile, it suffers from the way this technique is evolved – by extending the general solution in the two party case to pairs in the multiparty case. This leads to the $O(n^2)$ system complexity. First, it requires pairwise private channels among participants [10], which could prove problematic especially when there are many participants. Second, it requires a large amount of traffic. Although the protocol could be completed with only three rounds [14], note that each round includes not only the broadcast of public messages, but also the transmission of private messages to everyone else through the pairwise secret channels [14]. The total amount of sent data is $O(n^2)$. Third, it is no longer resistant to collusion when more than half of the participants are compromised. In such a case, the colluders can easily breach the privacy of other inputs.

Our work shows the benefits of designing a protocol directly in the multiparty context. It has the linear complexity, requires no pairwise secret channels, and provides full protection against collusion instead of half. How to apply the underlying design principle in the AV-net protocol to compute more general functions is worth exploring in future research.

All the other techniques in Table 2 are based on the Decision Diffie-Hellman assumption [15, 11, 4]. The first rounds of those protocols are the same as in an AV-net: broadcasting ephemeral public keys. This allows more direct comparisons with an AV-net, as shown below.

Kiayias and Yung investigated the Distributed Decision Making problem, and proposed a 3-round veto protocol [15]. They used a third party – a bulletin board server – to administer the process. The bulletin board server is a common way to realize a reliable broadcast channel. However, the server is needed for some other reasons. In the Kiayias-Yung protocol, each participant publishes $O(n)$ data. The final result on the veto decision is computed from $O(n^2)$ data. In large networks, it would be too demanding for individuals to store and compute such data. The server is a natural choice to perform the intermediary processing.

Groth modified the Kiayias-Yung veto protocol in order to reduce the system complexity [11]. His approach is to trade off round-efficiency for less traffic and computation. As a result, Groth's veto protocol allows each participant to publish a smaller amount of data, but requires participants to send their messages one after another, as one's computation depends on the result sent by the previous participant. Hence, instead of finishing the protocol in 3 rounds as in [15], Groth's veto protocol requires $n + 1$ rounds, where n is the number of participants.

Brandt studied the use of ElGamal encryption techniques for multiparty computation applications, and gave a 4-round veto protocol [4]. The performance of his solution, among others, is the closest match to ours. Its main disadvantage, however, is that it requires four rounds while ours only needs two. The difference in rounds lies in the way the veto messages are encrypted.

In Brandt's veto protocol, the first round is the same as in an AV-net: all participants broadcast ephemeral public keys. It requires one exponentiation to compute a public key. In the second round, each participant applies the standard ElGamal encryption algorithm to encrypt an explicit message: "veto" or "non-veto". Such an encryption requires two exponentiations. The third and fourth rounds are arranged to decrypt the messages, while preserving the privacy of individual inputs. It requires two and one exponentiations in each round respectively. In addition, each round requires a zero-knowledge proof per participant, which amounts to four in total. Without taking the knowledge proofs into consideration, each participant needs to performs six exponentiations in Brandt's protocol.

The novelty of our protocol is that the veto message is encrypted in a very implicit way (i.e., by raising a base to one of two different powers). As a result, the veto decision can be immediately decoded after the second broadcast. It requires only two exponentiations in total, as compared to six in Brandt's protocol. Besides computational load, the traffic generated is also far less in our protocol, due to fewer rounds.

5   Conclusion

In this paper, we propose Anonymous Veto Network (or AV-net) to allow a group of participants to compute a boolean-OR function securely. Our technique is not only provably secure, but also exceptionally efficient. Compared with past work, our solution does not require any private channels or trusted third parties; it has no message collisions, hence requires no retransmissions; being semantically secure, it provides the strongest protection of vetoer's anonymity until all the other participants are compromised; it resists robustly against jamming, hence ensures each participant's veto power; the execution of the protocol requires only two rounds, fewer than any other solutions; and finally, the computational load, the bandwidth usage, and the cost of verifying zero-knowledge proofs are also the least among the related techniques.

Acknowledgments

We thank Markus Kuhn, Ross Anderson, George Danezis, Mike Bond, Saar Drimer, Tyler Moore and other members in the Security Group, Computer laboratory, University of Cambridge, for providing helpful comments and feedbacks. Special thanks go to Lihong Yang, Nick Wolfgang and Rachel Wolfgang for helping improve the readability of this paper.

References

1. Hao, F., Zieliński, P.: A 2-round anonymous veto protocol. In: Proceedings of the 14th International Workshop on Security Protocols, Cambridge, UK (2006)
2. Boneh, D.: The Decision Diffie-Hellman Problem. In: Buhler, J.P. (ed.) ANTS 1998. LNCS, vol. 1423, pp. 48–63. Springer, Heidelberg (1998)
3. Beaver, D., Micali, S., Rogaway, P.: The round complexity of secure protocols. In: Proceedings of the twenty-second annual ACM Symposium on Theory of Computing, pp. 503–513 (1990)
4. Brandt, F.: Efficient cryptographic protocol design based on distributed El Gamal encryption. In: Won, D.H., Kim, S. (eds.) ICISC 2005. LNCS, vol. 3935, pp. 32–47. Springer, Heidelberg (2006)
5. Chaum, D.: The dining cryptographers problem: unconditional sender and recipient untraceability. Journal of Cryptology 1(1), 65–67 (1988)
6. Chaum, D.: Untraceable electronic email, return addresses, and digital pseudonyms. Communications of the ACM 24(2), 84–88 (1981)
7. Chaum, D., Evertse, J.H., van de Graaf, J., Peralta, R.: Demonstrating possession of a discrete logarithm without revealing it. In: Odlyzko, A.M. (ed.) CRYPTO 1986. LNCS, vol. 263, pp. 200–212. Springer, Heidelberg (1987)
8. Chaum, D., Evertse, J.H., van de Graaf, J.: An Improved Protocol for Demonstrating Possession of Discrete Logarithms and Some Generalizations. In: Price, W.L., Chaum, D. (eds.) EUROCRYPT 1987. LNCS, vol. 304, pp. 127–141. Springer, Heidelberg (1988)
9. Camenisch, J., Stadler, M.: Proof systems for general statements about discrete logarithms. Technical report TR 260, Department of Computer Science, ETH Zürich (March 1997)
10. Goldreich, O., Micali, S., Wigderson, A.: How to play any mental game or a completeness theorem for protocols with honest majority. In: Proceedings of the nineteenth annual ACM Conference on Theory of Computing, pp. 218–229 (1987)
11. Groth, J.: Efficient maximal privacy in boardroom voting and anonymous broadcast. In: Juels, A. (ed.) FC 2004. LNCS, vol. 3110, pp. 90–104. Springer, Heidelberg (2004)
12. Golle, P., Juels, A.: Dining Cryptographers Revisited. In: Cachin, C., Camenisch, J.L. (eds.) EUROCRYPT 2004. LNCS, vol. 3027, pp. 456–473. Springer, Heidelberg (2004)
13. Goldwasser, S., Micali, S.: Probabilistic encryption. Journal of Computer and System Sciences 28, 270–299 (1984)
14. Gennaro, R., Ishai, Y., Kushilevitz, E., Rabin, T.: On 2-round secure multiparty computation. In: Yung, M. (ed.) CRYPTO 2002. LNCS, vol. 2442, p. 178. Springer, Heidelberg (2002)

15. Kiayias, A., Yung, M.: Non-interactive zero-sharing with applications to private distributed decision making. In: Wright, R.N. (ed.) FC 2003. LNCS, vol. 2742, pp. 303–320. Springer, Heidelberg (2003)
16. Schnorr, C.P.: Efficient signature generation by smart cards. Journal of Cryptology 4(3), 161–174 (1991)
17. Schneier, B.: Applied Cryptography. J. Wiley and Sons, Chichester (1996)
18. Waidner, M., Pfitzmann, B.: The Dining Cryptographers in the Disco: Unconditional Sender and Recipient Untraceability with Computationally Secure Serviceability. In: Quisquater, J.-J., Vandewalle, J. (eds.) EUROCRYPT 1989. LNCS, vol. 434, pp. 690–690. Springer, Heidelberg (1990)
19. Wright, M., Adler, M., Levine, B.N., Shields, C.: The predecessor attack: an analysis of a threat to anonymous communications systems. ACM Transactions on Information and Systems Security (TISSEC) 7(4) (2004)
20. Yao, A.: How to generate and exchange secrets. In: Proceedings of the twenty-seventh annual IEEE Symposium on Foundations of Computer Science, pp. 162–167 (1986)

A   Lower Bound for Round Efficiency

Theorem 5. *Without shared symmetric or asymmetric secrets between participants, any anonymous veto protocol relying on authenticated broadcast only must require at least two rounds.*

Proof. To obtain a contradiction, we assume a one-round anonymous veto protocol. Each participant holds a secret vote $v_i \in \{0, 1\}$, and has no shared secrets with others. In one round, every participant P_i broadcasts $f_i(v_i)$, where f_i is a publicly known function.

Note that the function definition f_i cannot be secret (known to P_i only). Otherwise, the value of $f_i(v_i)$ would contain no useful information to the rest of participants, and could be equivalently replaced by an arbitary value. This contradicts the veto power that P_i has on the decision making. So f_i must be a publicly known function.

The protocol allows participants to determine the Boolean-OR of all votes. Suppose every participant P_i can do so by applying a function g_i to all data available: $g_i(f_i(v_i), \dots, f_n(v_n)) = v_1 \vee \dots \vee v_n$. Thus participant P_i can trivially reveal the vote of another participant, say P_k, through simulating other participant's inputs as 0: $g_i(f_i(0), \dots, f_k(v_k), \dots f_n(0)) = 0 \vee \dots \vee v_k \vee \dots \vee 0 = v_k$. This contradicts the secrecy of the vote v_k, which shows that any such anonymous veto protocol requires at least two rounds.

Collusion-Resistant Message Authentication in Overlay Multicast Communication

Emad Eldin Mohamed[1] and Hussein Abdel-Wahab[2]

[1] College of Information Technology, United Arab Emirates University,
Al-Ain, United Arab Emirates
[2] Computer Science Department, Old Dominion University,
Norfolk, Virginia 23529, USA
emohamed@uaeu.ac.ae, wahab@cs.odu.edu

Abstract. This paper aims at providing message authentication service in overlay multicast. Previous work has mostly focused on the network layer IP multicast and not as much work has been done on the application layer overlay multicast. A main feature of overlay multicast is that end systems carry on the responsibility of delivering the multicast traffic. Taking advantage of this feature, this paper presents a new collusion resistant technique, which is based on digital signature, for overlay multicast message authentication. The proposed technique minimizes both the computational cost (through signature amortization) and the communication overhead (using retransmissions and utilizing multiple multicast groups in handling message loss). In addition, it resists denial of service attacks via early dropping of forged messages. A simulation study is conducted to evaluate our proposed technique. Results of the study show that the proposed technique outperforms earlier ones.

Keywords: Multicast communication; Overlay multicast; Multicast security; Message authentication.

1 Introduction

Multicast communication concerns the transfer of data from one user (the source) to more than one user (the receivers). Multicast communication has attracted the attention of many researchers since it is involved in a wide range of applications. Examples of such applications are distance learning, teleconferencing, multiplayer games, real time delivery of stock quotes, distributed simulation, distribution of software updates, and distributed radar tracking; just to name a few. The multicast service can be provided either at the network layer or at the application layer. A well known example of the network layer multicast is the IP multicast which follows the host group model [7]. In this model, receivers within a multicast session are organized into a group. End systems have to explicitly join and become members of a group before they can receive data oriented to that group. End systems, however, need not be members of the group in order to send data to it.

The host group model has the advantages of flexibility and scalability. However, many security concerns—among many other difficulties such as billing—have limited

M.L. Gavrilova et al. (Eds.): Trans. on Comput. Sci. IV, LNCS 5430, pp. 53–67, 2009.

its success. Examples of security issues in this model are access control and authentication. Many service providers were hesitant in delivering packets to unknown set of receivers. A more recent approach of multicast is performed at the application level; also known as overlay multicast [1], [4]. In this approach, an overlay network of the multicast end systems (nodes) is built atop the network layer and data is routed to the receivers at the application level. This approach enables nodes self-organize and manage multicast sessions independent of the network conditions. In addition, it offers better access control and authentication services since intermediate nodes can take part in providing these services. Many techniques for overlay multicast have been proposed. Examples are Narada [5] and ALMI [16]. An important issue in overlay multicast is secure routing, which cannot be achieved without message authentication, however.

Message authentication can be defined as the assurance that the received message is from the alleged source without alteration. A simple solution to this problem in unicast communication is having the two communicating parties encrypt messages with a shared secret key. Another solution is to use message authentication codes (MACs). These two solutions, however, are inadequate in multicast communication. Sharing a key among all group members only provides group authentication—the assurance that the message originates from a member of the group—but does not provide source (data origin) authentication. In order to provide data origin authentication in multicast communication, other asymmetric mechanisms such as public key encryption should be employed.

An important concern in multicast message authentication is collusion attacks: a group of receivers collude to forge messages on behalf of a source. It has been shown on the study by Boneh et al. [3] that digital signature is a necessity in building collusion resistant multicast message authentication. However, digital signature operations (message signing and verifying) are computationally expensive. This raises the need for efficient solutions to handle this problem.

Early solutions in multicast message authentication mainly have targeted the network layer IP multicast. Many of these solutions have relied on the reliable delivery of authentication information from the source to the receivers. To provide reliability in delivering the authentication information, forward error correction (FEC) has been used [11], [14], [15]. A main difficulty in using FEC, however, is that it is not known in advance how many messages will be lost.

This paper investigates message authentication in overlay multicast communication. A new collusion resistant authentication technique is introduced. The proposed technique minimizes the computational cost through signature amortization. Based on a previous study [12], we provide the reliable delivery of crucial authentication messages to receivers by retransmissions and we utilize multiple multicast groups to minimize the communication overhead. To reduce the effect of denial of service attacks, intermediate nodes of the multicast delivery structure are required to verify messages before forwarding them to other nodes; that is intermediate nodes deliver verified messages only and drop those failed the verification. To evaluate our technique we have conducted a simulation study to compare the proposed technique against previous ones. Results obtained from the study show that the proposed technique is more suitable for overlay multicast than those developed for IP multicast. More specifically, the proposed technique gives better receiver computational cost and better communication overhead.

The rest of this paper is organized as follows. Section 2 gives related work. Section 3 introduces our new technique. Performance evaluation is presented in Section 4. Section 5 is the conclusion and future work.

2 Related Work

As it is has been stated earlier, digital signature is a main building block in collusion resistant multicast message authentication [3]. Signing every message, however, is not practical, since digital signature is computationally an expensive operation. Two approaches have been taken to deal with this problem. The first is to devise more efficient signing schemes to sign each message independent of other messages. Instances of this approach are [9], [19], which use one time signature. A main advantage of one time signing is low computational requirement. Its disadvantage, however, is high communication overhead in distributing large keys. The second approach is to amortize the signature among several messages. Many techniques have been introduced following this approach. Examples are Tesla [28], hash chaining [8], [9], EMSS [17], and hash tree [20].

In Tesla [18], the source initially generates a key K_n at random. From K_n, the source, using a one way function f, generates a key chain as follows:

$$K_{n-1} = f(K_n), K_{n-2} = f(K_{n-1}), \ldots, K_1 = f(K_2).$$

The source uses K_1 to generate MACs for a specific duration of time and reveals it after its lifetime expires. Then, the source uses K_2 and the procedure is repeated until K_n is revealed. The source digitally signs K_n and sends it to all receivers. In other words, the source sends the following to the set of receivers:

$$S \rightarrow \{R\}: \begin{cases} \left\| _{i=1}^{i=x_1} M_i \, \| \, MAC(K_1, M_i), t_0 \quad t < t_1 \\ K_1 \, \| \, \left\| _{i=x_1+1}^{i=x_2} M_i \, \| \, MAC(K_2, M_i), t_1 \quad t < t_2, K_1 = f(K_2) \\ \quad \vdots \\ K_{n-1} \, \| \, \left\| _{i=x_{n-1}+1}^{i=x_n} M_i \, \| \, MAC(K_n, M_i), t_{n-1} \quad t < t_n, K_{n-1} = f(K_n) \\ K_n \, \| \, \sigma(K_n), t \quad t_n \end{cases}$$

Where the function $\left\| _{i=1}^{i=n} Z_i$ is the concatenation of Z_i for $1 \leq i \leq n$, t is the time, and $\sigma(K_n)$ is the digital signature of K_n. The first line in the expression gives the messages sent from the source S to the set of receivers $\{R\}$ during the period t_0 to t_1, the second line gives the messages sent during the period t_1 to t_2, and so on.

At the receiving end, the receiver buffers all messages and all keys until the key K_n is revealed. The receiver then can verify all keys using the one way function f used by the source, and only then can verify messages. Receivers accept messages that are authenticated by a key during its lifetime and reject those that use the key after its lifetime. Tesla suffers from high buffering and delay requirements on the receivers and it requires synchronization between the source and the receivers.

In hash chaining [8], [9], a stream of n messages M_1, M_2, ..., M_n forms a block. The source computes the hash $H_n = h(M_n)$ of the last message M_n in the block and appends H_n to its predecessor M_{n-1} to form a new message $M'_{n-1} = M_{n-1} \| H_n$. This new message M'_{n-1} is in turn hashed and the hash value H'_{n-1} is appended to its predecessor M_{n-2} to form a new message $M'_{n-2} = M_{n-2} \| H'_{n-1}$. The procedure is continued downward to the first message in the block so as to have $M'_1 = M_1 \| H'_2$, which is signed using one of the digital signature schemes. This can be expressed as follows:

$$S \rightarrow \{R\}: \quad M_1 \| \sigma(h(M_1')) \| M_2 \| h(M_2') \| ... \| M_n \| h(M_n)$$

At the receiver, the same procedure is performed but backward: verify the first message using its signature and extract the hash of the second message. The second message is verified using the hash extracted from the first message and the hash of the third message is extracted from the second message. The procedure continues up to the last message in the block. The computation effort in this approach is one hash per message and one signature per n messages at both the source and the receiver. Increasing the number of messages n in the stream decreases the signature overhead. However, this increases the buffering requirements at the source and hence increases the delay. Moreover, a lost message may break the chain of the hashes.

In EMSS [17], the hash of each message is randomly augmented to several messages. At the source, whenever a message is ready, hashes of some other messages are augmented to the current message and the hash of the augmented message is computed. This hash is then inserted randomly in other subsequent messages in the stream. In essence, this technique decreases the affect of message loss encountered in the hash chaining described above. The main advantage of EMSS is its high verification rate (the number of the verifiable messages in a block divided by the number of the block received messages). This, however, comes at the cost of a relatively high computation and communication overhead.

Wong et al. proposed the use of a hash tree to amortize the signature of n messages [20]. In their work, a stream of n messages M_1, M_2, ..., M_n forms a block. The hashes H_1, H_2, ..., H_n of the block messages are computed and a tree is built on top of these hashes. The leaf nodes of the tree are the computed message hashes. Each intermediate node of the tree is the hash of its children. The root of the tree is the hash of all messages' hashes. On sending a message, the source sends some authentication information particular to this message along with it. This authentication information includes the block signature (the hash of all messages within the block signed by the source), the position of the message in the block, and the hashes of the siblings of each node in the message path to the root. For a block of n messages, this can be expressed as follows:

$$S \rightarrow \{R\}: \quad M_i \| \sigma(H_{1n}) \| i \| (H_j \| H_{ab} ... \| H_{xy})$$

Where M_i is the message, $\sigma(H_{18})$ is the signature of the hash root, i is the message position in the block, and H_j through H_{xy} are the hashes of the siblings of each nodes in the message path to the root.

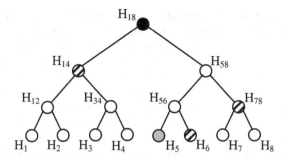

Fig. 1. Tree chaining signature amortization

The receiver uses the authentication information to authenticate each message independent of other messages. Fig. 1 demonstrates this technique for a block size of eight messages M_1, M_2, ..., M_8. The hashes of these messages H_1, H_2, ..., H_8 are computed and placed at the leaves of the tree. The intermediate nodes are the hashes of their children. For example, H_{12} is computed as $h(H_1 \parallel H_2)$ and H_{58} is computed as $h(H_{56} \parallel H_{78})$, where $h(x)$ is the hash of x. The authentication information of message M_5 is given as the triplet $\{\sigma(H_{18}), 5, (H_6, H_{78}, H_{14})\}$, where $\sigma(H_{18})$ is the signature of H_{18} (the block signature), 5 is the position of the message in the block, and (H_6, H_{78}, H_{14}) are the hashes of the siblings of each node in the message path to the root. On verifying message M_5, the receiver computes the following: the hash H_5 of the message, the hash $H_{56} = h(H_5 \parallel H_6)$, the hash $H_{58} = h(H_{56} \parallel H_{78})$, the hash $H_{18} = h(H_{14} \parallel H_{58})$, and verifies against the received signature $\sigma(H_{18})$.

This scheme has three main drawbacks. First, it involves a high communication overhead, since a large amount of authentication information is sent along with each message, which is of the order of $\log_d n$, where d is the tree order and n is the number of messages in the block. In the example given above, the block signature and the three hashes are sent along with every message. Second, the computation overhead at the source and receiver is also high and it is of the order of $\log_d n$. Third, buffering is required at the source. The main advantage is that a message loss has no affect on the authentication of other messages, since receivers authenticate each message independent of other messages.

3 New Technique

In this paper, we present a collusion resistant message authentication technique for overlay multicast. Normally, multicast communication is a best effort service in which messages may get lost. Thus, solutions targeting message authentication in such setting should tolerate message loss. In addition, we aim at efficient solutions that provide a complete verification rate and resist denial of service attacks. This work is based on the assumption that sources' public keys are already known to all end systems.

Several solutions have targeted IP multicast. These solutions, however, may not fit well in overlay multicast. For example, Tesla faces many difficulties such as high delay, high buffering requirement, and clock synchronization between the end systems.

Hash chaining and EMSS do not provide complete verification rate (a receiver may not be able to verify some of the received messages). The main approach that can provide the required service is hash tree. Hash trees are collusion-resistant, give full verification rate, and have low computation overhead. However, the communication overhead is high. The technique proposed in this paper is a more efficient variation of hash trees, which in addition resists denial of service attacks, as will be discussed later.

In our technique, we use a star topology (a hash tree that has only one level) and we provide a reliable mechanism to deliver the authentication information. The proposed technique consists of four elements: signing multicast messages, error control, early dropping of forged messages, and verification. In the following, we introduce these elements, after which we demonstrate them through examples.

The signing element proposed in this paper generates a signature for a block of n messages and works as follows. A stream of n messages M_1, M_2, ..., M_n forms a block. Hashes H_1, H_2, ..., H_n of the block messages are calculated (using for example MD5). These hashes are concatenated to each other, forming $H_{1-n} = H_1 \| H_2 \| ... \| H_n$. The hash of H_{1-n} is calculated resulting in the block hash H_{1n}. The block hash is signed (using RSA for example) to get the block signature $\sigma(H_{1n})$. The source reliably sends all message hashes along with the block signature $\{H_{1-n}, \sigma(H_{1n})\}$ to the receivers. The block signature and the message hashes must be sent reliably, since the authenticities of all block messages depend on this authentication information. However, all block messages can be sent using a best effort service as they do not affect the authenticity of each other. This can be expressed as follows (assuming a block of n messages):

$$S \rightarrow \{R\}: \quad \begin{cases} M_1, M_2, ..., M_n \\ H_1 \| H_2 \| ... \| H_n \| \sigma(H_{1n}) \end{cases}$$

Where M_1, M_2, ..., M_n are the messages of the block and they may be sent using a best effort service, and H_1, H_2, ..H_n, $\sigma(H_{1n})$ are the message hashes and block signature and they are sent reliably one time per block.

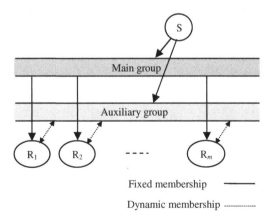

Fig. 2. Error control using two multicast groups

The second element in our proposal is error control. To provide the reliable delivery of the authentication information we adapt an earlier solution in multicast error control schemes [10], [13] that utilizes multiple multicast groups to efficiently deliver the authentication information to interested receivers. In our approach, we have two multicast groups as shown in Fig. 2. The first group—which we call the *main* group—carries the regular multicast traffic along with authentication information. All receivers (R_1, R_2, ..., R_m) must join this group. The other multicast group—called the *auxiliary* group—carries error control messages. Members of this group are the source (S in the figure), all intermediate nodes, and end systems experiencing the message loss. A receiver joins the auxiliary group when it experiences a message loss and remains a member as long as it encounters losses.

The error control unit works as follows. Messages are assigned sequence numbers. A receiver detects a message loss when there is a gap in the sequence numbers of the received messages. On detecting a gap in the messages' sequence numbers, the receiver waits for a specific duration of time (in case the message is just delayed), and if not received within this duration, the receiver assumes a message loss. When detecting a lost message, the receiver joins the auxiliary group. To prevent oscillation (frequent join/leave), the receiver joins the group for a minimum amount of time before leaving. After joining the auxiliary group, the receiver multicasts a retransmit request of the specific message to the auxiliary group. Any member of the auxiliary group having the message sends the message to the group. To prevent multiple retransmit requests of the same message sent by different receivers, a receiver waits a random time before sending its request. During this time, it listens to the auxiliary group to see if the request is already sent by another receiver. If the request is not sent by another receiver, the receiver can send its request. Same procedure is used in retransmitting the message.

The Third element in our proposal is early dropping of forged messages. In overlay multicast, intermediate nodes within the delivery structure serve as end systems and routers at the same time. Based on this fact, our technique requires intermediate nodes to verify messages before further delivery. A message can be forwarded to other nodes if it passes the verification process, otherwise it is dropped. This way, forged messages are dropped as early they are discovered saving communication and computational resources of the system.

The verification element verifies messages and works as follows. On receiving the authentication information $\{H_1 \| H_2 \| ... \| H_n \| \sigma(H_{1n})\}$, the receiver calculates the block hash H_{1n} and verifies it against the received signature $\sigma(H_{1n})$. The receiver buffers the hashes H_1, H_2, ..., H_n for later use. On receiving a message M_i, the receiver calculates its hash H_i and compares it against the buffered hash.

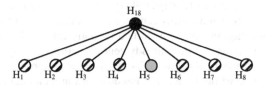

Fig. 3. Star chaining signature amortization

For example, suppose we have a block of eight messages M_1, M_2, ..., M_8. The hashes of these messages H_1, H_2, ..., H_8 are computed and placed as the nodes of the star (Fig. 3). The center of the star has the hash H_{18}, which is computed as $h(H_1 \parallel H_2, ..., \parallel H_8)$, where $h(x)$ is the hash of x. The authentication information of all messages is given as the pair $\{(H_1, H_2, H_3, H_4, H_5, H_6, H_7, H_8), \sigma(H_{18})\}$, where $\sigma(H_{18})$ is the signature of H_{18} (the block signature). This authentication information is sent only once for all messages. Its transmission, however, is performed reliably using the error control scheme described above. When the authentication information is received, the receiver verifies the hashes $H_1 \parallel H_2$, ..., $\parallel H_8$ using the signature $\sigma(H_{18})$. On verifying a message, M_5 for an instance, the receiver computes the hash (H_5 in this case) of the message. The receiver compares the calculated hash against the received hash for verification.

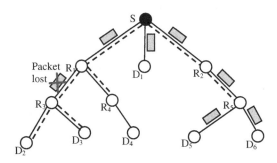

Fig. 4. Lost message retransmission over auxiliary tree

The reliable delivery of the authentication is efficiently provided through the use of the auxiliary channel to direct retransmissions to receivers having message loss and at the same time to reduce the effect of these retransmissions on receivers that do not experience message loss (not all receivers experience the same error pattern). As Fig. 4 shows, a message is lost during its delivery from R_1 to R_3. Retransmitting this message to all receivers using the main tree (the continuous lines in the figure) may waste communication bandwidth and end system resources. To better deal with this situation, an auxiliary tree (the dashed lines in the figure) is formed as a subset of the main tree to retransmit the message to affected receivers only. In the example, there are three end systems (R_3, D_2, and D_3) that experience the message loss. Every end system of them starts a random timer. On the timer expiration, the end system checks if there is any retransmission sent over the auxiliary group. If it finds a retransmission request already sent, it refrains from sending its request. Otherwise, it sends the request over the auxiliary group. On receiving a retransmission request, an end system (receiver or router) that has the authentication information starts a random timer. When the timer expires, it checks whether the retransmission already sent by another end system before multicasting the retransmission to the group. The reason why some routers are included within the auxiliary tree while there is no message loss in their side is that maintaining the auxiliary tree is an expensive operation—joining and leaving the tree adds a large delay to the error control procedure.

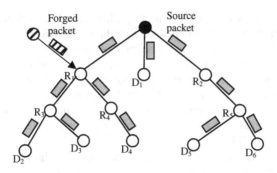

Fig. 5. Dropping forged messages in overlay multicast

Fig. 5. demonstrates the effect of early dropping of forged messages in our technique. As the figure shows, when the source S sends a message, all routers (R_1 through R_5) verify the message before delivery. Since the message is truly originated from the source, it will be delivered to all receivers (R_1 through R_5 and D_1 through D_6). When a forged message is inserted into the network, the first router detects it (router R_1 in the figure) drops it. This saves the communication overhead in delivering the message along the path from R_1 to all its children down to the leaf nodes. In addition, this saves the computation overhead involved in verifying this message by other receivers. Recalling that routers are themselves end systems, requiring them to verify messages before sending is a reasonable procedure.

Our proposed technique is different from tree chaining scheme in two important aspects. The first difference, in our technique the authentication information is sent reliably only one time per block, whereas in the tree chaining scheme the source sends the full authentication information for every message. This subtle difference has a big impact on the communication overhead and receiver computation effort. The second difference is that in our technique, forged messages are dropped by the routing entities. This procedure is facilitated in overlay multicast since end systems take over the routing functionalities. This difference dramatically reduces the effect of forged messages on receivers' computation effort and network resources.

4   Performance Evaluation

In this paper, a simulation study is used to evaluate the proposed technique. We compare our technique, which is based on star topology against the tree topology if deployed in overlay multicast. Other techniques such as hash chaining and EMSS do not provide the required services (they do not provide full verification rate) and they are not included in our comparisons.

We model the overlay multicast network as a directed graph in which nodes are hosts in the networks and edges are connection between the hosts. A multicast delivery tree is built as a subset of this graph. The root of the tree is the source. The intermediate nodes and the leaves are the receivers. The multicast traffic is modeled as a continuous stream of messages. Messages are organized into blocks of equal size and the authentication information is calculated for every block. Every edge (communication link) in the tree is characterized by its message loss rate. We assume a burst message loss [2], [21], which happens when the throughput approaches the link bandwidth (typical in many situations such as multimedia applications).

Naturally, whenever a loss occurs at a receiver it affects all of its children. Forged messages are assumed to be inserted by an adversary to any receiver (randomly selected). In our study, we assume RSA for digital signature where the signing process is more expensive than the verification process. We assume a signing rate of 0.7 operations per millisecond and a verification rate of 14 operations per milliseconds. In addition, we assume MD5 to hash messages with a hashing rate of 258 Mbytes per second and a hash size of 128 bits. These numbers are based on the Crypto++ benchmark [6]. The performance indexes that have been used are the computation overhead (expressed as the processing time at the source and the receivers) and the communication overhead.

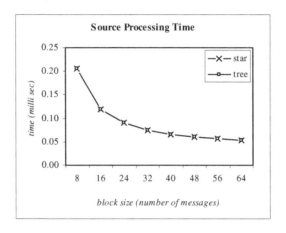

Fig. 6. Source processing time

Equations 1 and 2 give the source processing time for the star and tree topologies:

$$t_{star} = \frac{\sum_{i=1}^{n} t_{hi} + t_{h_{1n}} + t_s}{n} \tag{1}$$

$$t_{tree} = \frac{\sum_{i=1}^{n} t_{hi} + \sum_{j=1}^{n-1} t_{hj} + t_s}{n} \tag{2}$$

Where n is the number of messages in a block, t_{hi} is the time required to hash message M_i, t_{h1n} is the time to calculate H_{1n} (the hash of H_{1-n}), t_{hj} is the time to calculate the intermediate hashes, and t_s is the time to sign the block hash H_{1n}. Since the signing time t_s is the dominant factor in both equations (digital signature is very expensive when compared with hashing), the processing times in both the star and the tree topologies are almost identical (there is a slight improvement for the star topology over the tree). This is apparent in Fig. 6, which gives the results of the simulation when varying the block size. Forging and message loss have no effect on the source processing time as it has no contribution on the source's computational cost.

Equations 3 and 4 give the receiver processing times per message for the star and tree topologies as follows:

$$t_{star} = \frac{\sum_{i=1}^{n} t_{hi} + t_{h} + t_{v}}{n} \cdot (1 + P_{f}) \qquad (3)$$

$$t_{tree} = \frac{\sum_{i=1}^{n} (t_{hi} + \log_{2} t_{h}) + t_{v}}{n} \cdot (1 + P_{f} + P_{fp}) \qquad (4)$$

Where n is the number of messages in the block, t_{hi} is the processing time required to hash a message M_i, t_h is the time to calculate H_{1n} (the hash of H_{1-n}), t_v is the time to verify the messages' hashes, P_f is the direct forging factor, P_{fp} is the propagated forging factor due to forged messages received from the receiver's parent.

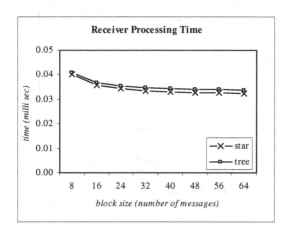

Fig. 7. Receiver processing time without forging

The simulation study shows that most of the processing time is due to hashing rather than the amortized verification. Figure 7 gives the processing times for both the star and tree topologies when there are no forged messages in the system. As the figure shows, both are of almost the same performance, with a slight improvement for the proposed star topology (as it requires less hashing) over the tree. However, when forging is considered, the early dropping technique employed in the star topology has a great impact on the performance as demonstrated by the simulation results shown in Fig. 8.

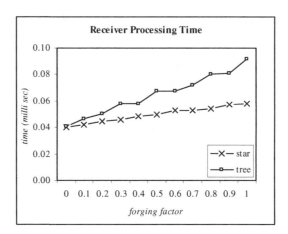

Fig. 8. Receiver processing time with forging

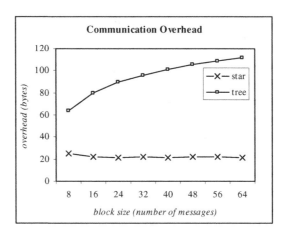

Fig. 9. Communication overhead
(no forging, maximum error probability = 0.5, and average error probability = 0.3)

Equations 5 and 6 give the communication overhead per message for the star and tree topologies:

$$c_{star} = \frac{(n \cdot s_h + s_s)}{n} \cdot (1 + f \cdot P_1) \tag{5}$$

$$c_{tree} = \log_2 n \cdot s_h + s_s \cdot (1 + P_{fp}) \tag{6}$$

Where n is the number of messages, s_h is the size of message hash, s_s is the size of the signature, P_1 is the probability of message loss, f is the fraction of the network affected by the loss (some nodes may experience message loss while others may not), and P_{fp} is the propagated forging factor. Note that the authentication information must be sent reliably in the star topology—retransmissions will be performed to those nodes affected by message loss.

In the star chaining, retransmission has a minor affect on the communication overhead as only one message (the authentication message) per block has to be sent reliably. If the authentication information message is lost, it will be sent only to those receivers who experience the loss. This greatly lessens the effect of message loss over the communication overhead. On the other hand, increasing the block size in the tree topology increases the size of the authentication information to be transmitted. This is demonstrated in Fig. 9, which shows that star chaining gives a better performance than tree chaining, especially for large block sizes. When forged messages are injected in the network, using the early dropping greatly improves the communication overhead as shown in Fig. 10.

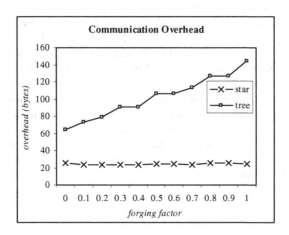

Fig. 10. Communication overhead with forging
(maximum error probability = 0.5, and average error probability = 0.3)

Table 1. Performance comparison between star chaining and tree chaining

Comparison criteria	Star chaining	Tree chaining
Computation overhead at the source	Similar to tree chaining.	Similar to star chaining.
Computation overhead at the receivers (without forging)	Slight improvement than tree chaining.	Little higher than star chaining.
Computation overhead at the receivers (with forging)	Better than tree chaining.	Higher than star chaining.
Communication overhead (with and without forging)	Better than tree chaining.	Higher than star chaining.

From the above discussion, source and receiver computation overheads in both star and tree topologies are almost the same. However, the star chaining technique given in this paper has the advantage of better communication overhead especially for large block sizes than the tree chaining. In addition, using the early dropping of forged message significantly decreases the communication and receiver computation overhead. These results are summarized in Table 1.

5 Conclusion

In this paper we have introduced a new technique for collusion resistant message authentication in overlay multicast. A basic feature of overlay multicast is that the receivers may also take over the responsibility of delivering the multicast traffic from the source to other group members. Based on this feature, we have proposed a digital signature-based authentication technique in which a star topology is built over the hashes of the messages. In addition, forged messages are dropped as early as they are detected; since the routing entities are themselves group members in overlay multicast. In our technique, the authentication information is sent reliably. We have presented a scheme that deploys retransmission over multiple multicast groups to resend lost authentication information. We have conducted a simulation study to evaluate the performance of our work. Results of the study show that our technique has better communication and better receiver computation (especially when forged messages are considered) overheads than earlier ones.

References

1. Banerjee, S., Kommareddy, C., Kar, K., Bhattacharjee, B., Khuller, S.: OMNI: An Efficient Overlay Multicast Infrastructure for Real-Time Applications. Computer Networks 50(6), 826–841 (2006)
2. Bolot, J.-C.: End-To-End Packet Delay and Loss Behavior in the Internet. In: Proc. Sigcomm 1993, San Francisco, CA (1993)
3. Boneh, D., Durfee, G., Franklin, M.: Lower Bounds for Multicast Message Authentication. In: Pfitzmann, B. (ed.) EUROCRYPT 2001. LNCS, vol. 2045, pp. 437–452. Springer, Heidelberg (2001)
4. Chu, Y., Rao, S., Seshan, S., Zhang, H.: Enabling Conferencing Applications on the Internet using an Overlay Multicast Architecture. In: Proc. of the 2001 Conference on Applications, Technologies, Architectures, and Protocols for Computer Communications, San Diego, CA, pp. 55–67 (2001)
5. Chu, Y., Rao, S., Seshan, S., Zhang, H.: A Case for End System Multicast. IEEE Journal on Selected Areas in Communications 20(8), 1456–1471 (2002)
6. Dai, W.: Crypto++ 5.5 Benchmarks (2007),
   http://www.cryptopp.com/benchmarks.html
7. Deering, S.: Host Extensions for IP Multicast, Internet RFC 1112 (1989)
8. Even, S., Goldreich, O., Micali, S.: On-line/Off-line digital signatures. In: Brassard, G. (ed.) CRYPTO 1989. LNCS, vol. 435, pp. 263–275. Springer, Heidelberg (1990)
9. Gennaro, R., Rohatgi, P.: How to Sign Digital Streams. In: Kaliski Jr., B.S. (ed.) CRYPTO 1997. LNCS, vol. 1294, pp. 180–197. Springer, Heidelberg (1997)

10. Kasera, S., Kurose, J., Towsley, D.: Scalable Reliable Multicast using Multiple Multicast Groups. In: Proc. ACM Sigmetrics 1997, Seattle, WA, pp. 64–74 (1997)
11. Lysyanskaya, A., Tamassia, R., Triandopoulos, N.: Multicast Authentication in Fully Adversarial Networks. In: Proc. IEEE Symposium on Security and Privacy, pp. 241–253 (2004)
12. Mohamed, E., Abdel-Wahab, H.: Multicast for Multimedia Collaborative Applications: Services and Mechanisms. International Journal of Advanced Media and Communication (IJAMC) 1(3), 224–236 (2007)
13. Mohamed, E., Abdel-Wahab, H.: Multicast Error Control for Multimedia Collaborative Applications. In: The 9th IEEE Symposium on Computers and Communications (ISCC 2004), Alexandria, Egypt (2004)
14. Pannetrat, A., Molva, R.: Efficient Multicast Packet Authentication. In: The 10th Annual Network and Distributed System Security Symposium (NDSS 2003), San Diego, CA (2003)
15. Park, J., Chong, E., Siegel, H.: Efficient Multicast Packet Authentication using Erasure Codes. ACM Transactions on Information and System Security 6(2), 258–285 (2003)
16. Pendarakis, D., Shi, S., Verma, D., Waldvogel, M.: ALMI: An Application Level Multicast Infrastructure. In: Proc. of the 3rd Usenix Symposium on Internet Technologies and Systems (2001)
17. Perrig, A.: The BiBa One-Time Signature and Broadcast Authentication Protocol. In: Proc. of the 8th ACM Conference on Computer and Communications Security, Philadelphia, PA (2001)
18. Perrig, A., Canetti, R., Tygar, J., Song, D.: The Tesla Broadcast Authentication Protocol. CryptoBytes 5(2), 2–13 (2002)
19. Rohatgi, P.: A Compact and Fast Hybrid Signature Scheme for Multicast Packet Authentication. In: 6th ACM Conference of Computing and Communication Security CCS 1999, Singapore (1999)
20. Wong, C., Lam, S.: Digital Signatures for Flows and Multicasts. IEEE/ACM Transactions on Networking 7(4), 502–513 (1999)
21. Yajnik, M., Kurose, J., Towsley, D.: Packet Loss Correlation in the Mbone Multicast Network: Experimental Measurements and Markov Chain Models. In: Proc. IEEE Globecom, pp. 94–99 (1996)

A Model for Authentication Credentials Translation in Service Oriented Architecture*

Emerson Ribeiro de Mello[1,2,**], Michelle S. Wangham[3,**],
Joni da Silva Fraga[1,**], Edson T. de Camargo[1], and Davi da Silva Böger[1]

[1] Department of Automation and Systems
Federal University of Santa Catarina
Florianópolis, SC, Brazil
[2] Federal Institute of Santa Catarina
São José, SC, Brazil
[3] Embedded and Distributed Systems Group
Univali - São José, SC, Brazil
{emerson,fraga,camargo,dsborger}@das.ufsc.br,wangham@univali.br

Abstract. Due to the increasing number of service providers, the grouping of these providers following the federation concept and the use of the Single Sign On (SSO) concept are helping users to gain a transparent access to resources, without worrying about their locations. However, current industry and academic production only provide SSO in cases with homogeneous underlying security technology. This paper deals with interoperability between heterogeneous security technologies. The proposed model is based on the Credential Translation Service that allows SSO authentication even heterogeneous security technologies are considered. Therefore, the proposed model provides authentication credentials translation and attribute transposition and, as a consequence, provides authorization involving different kinds of credentials and permissions in the federation environment. By making use of Web Services, this study is strongly based on concepts introduced in the SAML, WS-Trust and WS-Federation specifications.

Keywords: Web Services, Security, Single Sign-on.

1 Introduction

The demand for sharing information among different administrative domains in a transparent and secure manner and the need for establishing trust relationships are both up-to-date requirements mainly within the Internet context. Clients and service providers are entities that are present in this domain and that seek some kind of interaction. In this scenario, there are three barriers to overcome: (1) the heterogeneity of the security infrastructures, present in the many corporate

---

* This work has been developed within the scope of the "Security Mechanisms for Business Processes in Collaborative Networks" project (CNPq 484740/2007-5).
** Supported by CNPq - Brazil.

domains, (2) the establishment of trust relationships among unknown entities, and (3) the management of identities carried out not only by service providers but also by clients.

In distributed systems, traditional authorization models are based upon an authentication authority to mediate the trust among unknown parties (Trusted Third Party). Therefore, the interactions among distinct parties are done through the presentation of credentials issued by an authentication authority known by the parties involved. In more complex environments such as the Internet, this model of simple interaction is limited, since each domain has its own policies, security infrastructures, and also a particular way of managing the principals'[1] identities. In other words, each domain runs its authorization controls according to its local policies, without considering the attributes of other domains, and thus previous authentication is usually required in the domain itself.

Single Sign On (SSO) was developed to simplify the interactions among clients and different service providers. Under this approach, the client authenticates only once and makes use of this authentication in the interactions with other service providers. In open systems, it is desirable that each domain have the freedom to choose and adopt an authentication mechanism. However, the difficulty lies in assuring the SSO's interoperability among these domains, since the authentication information is no longer understood by all the entities present in the domains with different technologies. This problem motivated the present work.

This work aims to describe a model that enables the authentication with SSO, that is, the translation of authentication credentials, even when dealing with administrative domains with different security technologies. In this model, a principal can access resources in domains with security technologies, which are different from those in its source domain, by using the credentials provided in its own domain. In the entire system, access authorizations to resources depend on this authentication, which sensibly diminishes the data flux between the domains and the management of these data in the system as a whole.

According to [1], in the management of federated entities, each company builds a domain, in which its service, identity and credential providers are present. The deals established among domains can allow local identities of a domain to be accepted in the other domains participating in the agreement. Hence, a user with an identity registered in its domain can access resources in other domains of the federation without opening a new register or identity. In this study, the management of federated identities significantly contributes to the translation of the principals' authentication credential.

The Web Services technology, based on Service Oriented Architecture (SOA), is one of the promising solutions to the integration of administrative domains in distributed systems [2]. Although this technology contributes to overcome the challenges involving authentication and authorization in distributed applications, the large number of specifications and standards aiming at security not only imposes a certain level of complexity but also hinders its wide adoption [3].

---

[1] Users, processes or machines authorized by the systems policy.

With the support of Web Services security technologies, this article introduces a model to authentication and authorization in service oriented distributed systems. Based on the concept of federated identities, this model performs the translation of a principal's authentication credential among administrative domains with different security technologies (e.g. X.509, SPKI/SDSI) in a transparent manner. The model also supports the transposition of client attributes. In order to prove the applicability of the model, a prototype was implemented and integrated into a distributed application - an information portal in the area of entertainment.

2   Security in Web Services

The Web Services architecture is linked to XML and to the security extensions of this standard, defined by W3C, such as **XML-Signature**[4] and **XML-Encryption**[5]. These specifications allow for the representation of digital signatures and data encryption in the XML format, while the signed and/or encrypted data may be XML documents or not. These mechanisms make end-to-end security possible for Web Services using XML for data exchange and storage.

The **XACML** (eXtensible Access Control Markup Language) specification [6] describes both a language to express policy rules and a request/response protocol for decisions on access control. This specification uses two elements to implement the access control in distributed environments: PEP (Policy Enforcement Point, responsible for mediating and performing the access, and PDP (Policy Decision Point), which is called by the PEP to perform the policy processing and to decide, based on subject and resource information, whether or not access will be granted. Two more entities defined in this specification are PIP (Policy Information Point) and PAP(Policy Access Point). The former is responsible for retrieving information on the subject, environment and resource, while the latter is in charge of the access to the policy resource.

The **SAML** (Secure Assertion Markup Language) specification[7] is a security infrastructure projected to express information[2] about authentication, authorization and attributes of a given subject. Also, it allows for the exchange of this information among business partners. The SAML does not provide the authentication itself, but ways to express authentication information. The client can authenticate only once and use this same authentication in the other affiliated domains (Single Sign On). These characteristics make the SAML standard an important foundation to the management of federated identities in the proposed model.

WS-Security [8], the main security specification to Web Services, is based on XML-Signature[4] and XML-Encryption standards[5] to provide safe message exchanges. The specification aims at flexibility, and thus enables the use of a variety of security mechanisms. More specifically, this technology provides support to different kinds of security credentials[3], which enables a client to use multiple

---

[2] With the objective of being interoperable, the information is expressed in security assertions.

[3] Other security credential formats are UserNameToken, X.509, Kerberos and SAML.

credential formats for authentication and authorization, multiple formats for signature and multiple technologies for data encryption. These characteristics are very important in order for interoperability between security technologies of different administrative domains to be reached.

The **WS-Policy** [9] specification provides an extensible and flexible grammar, which allows for the expression of competencies, requirements and general characteristics of Web Services. It defines a framework and a model to represent these properties as policies[4]. The structure of policy assertions, such as the kinds of credentials required and the encryption algorithms supported, are defined in the WS-SecurityPolicy specification [10]. The WS-Policy does not describe how these policies are published or how they are attached to a Web Service. The mechanisms to attach the policies to XML, WSDL and UDDI elements are defined in the WS-PolicyAttachement specification [11].

The **WS-Trust** specification [12] defines services and protocols and aims at the exchange of security attributes (e.g. SAML assertions), in order to allow for the communication between different administrative and security domains. The WS-Trust defines a trust model in which a client without the credentials requested by the service provider can request the credentials to an authority which owns them. This authority is named Security Token Services (STS). This service forms the foundation for the establishment of trust relationships and is responsible for issuing, exchanging and validating the credentials. Nevertheless, this specification does not tackle how to translate the information contained in the principal's security credentials, when dealing with domains with different technologies.

The WS-Security, WS-Trust and WS-Policy specifications provide a foundation to the **WS-Federation** specification, which describes how these specifications are combined in order to allow for the construction of domains of trust. The foundation for the establishment of trust in the WS-Federation is the STS Service. However, the WS-Federation adds to this service the Identity Provider (IdP) and the Attribute/Pseudonym service functionalities, combined or not in a single entity. An identity provider functions as an authentication service, in which the domain members authenticate and make use of that authentication. The Attribute/Pseudonym service enables the protection of the user's privacy, through pseudonyms[5].

The WS-Federation fits into the centralized model for the management of federated identities, whereby only one identity and credential provider is used by all the service providers of the federation. In this model, a user can access all the services present in the federation through the use of a single identifier. The model resembles the federated identity model; however, unlike its counterpart, it dispenses with credential mapping [1]. This constraint ties the client to a single identity provider in the federation. In a fashion similar to WS-Trust, the WS-Federation does not signal how the information within the original credential can be translated in the presence of different security technologies.

---

[4] It introduces ways to express quality of service policies related to security and confiability.

[5] A random opaque identifier, which is not discernible by another entity.

3   A Model for Translation of Authentication Credentials

After having defined the concepts of domain and federated identities, this section introduces the model in a general sense at first, based upon an IETF proposition [13] and upon an SAML specification proposition. Next, it describes the model in a more concrete manner, assuming Web Services specifications. The challenge of the proposed model is to handle a large set of security specifications for Web Services, which are still under development, for the most part, or have recently been launched.

3.1   Security Domains and Federated Identities in the Proposed Model

In the proposed model, each administrative domain groups clients and service providers according to their underlying security infrastructures. Domains based upon different technologies determine different security controls for the protection of their resources. The premise assumed in the model is that, in the security controls for the domains clients must prove their identities before an authentication authority and, based on this authentication, a verification is made of the associated rights to access the system resources.

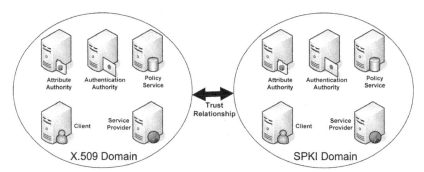

Fig. 1. Security Domains

In a security domain, the authentication and attribute authorities and the policy service are autonomous entities that manage their respective database for queries performed during authentication and authorization operations (see Figure 1). The authentication authority contains information on registers of clients and domain service providers. The attribute authority is responsible for managing the attributes informed by the users during the registration process in the domain; for instance, email, credit card, ZIP code, etc. The policy service centers the authorization policies for the domain, and thus functions only as a repository.

Trust relationships are the basis so the identities and the credential attributes can be recognized in the different participating domains, and thus allow for the translation of authentication credentials when facing different security technologies, concept introduced in this propose.

Within the context of federated identities, a client may be affiliated to more than one domain, with distinct accounts and different attributes spread over different domains. As in studies that implement the concept of federated identities, such as WS-Federation [14], Shibboleth [15] and Liberty Alliance [16], in the proposed model, the service provider is also the one responsible for retrieving the user's information. The client provides only its identity or pseudonym and the service provider is the one who searches, among its federation partners, for the client attributes.

3.2   Model Overview

The authorization model discussed in this article is based on the model proposed by IETF [13], which describes two fundamental elements for policy management: **PEP (Policy Enforcement Point)** and **PDP (Policy Decision Point)**. PEP is an element, which controls the access to a resource, and its function is to apply policy decisions, whereas PDP is an entity, which defines the policy to be applied to the required service requisition. Fig. 2 shows the proposed model and highlights the steps of the authorization process.

Other entities were added to the IETF propositions as a starting point to the model, the **attribute** and **authentication authorities** that are called before the authorization process. As authorization verifications in the model are assumed to be local for service providers, then both PEP and PDP are supposed to have their implementations in the service providers that control the requests to those services.

Initially, the model is considered that domain clients have already been registered and that information on their attributes is available to service providers, in the attribute authority of the domain, according to a privacy policy defined by the user itself. This policy determines which attributes the user wishes to inform the providers of its domain and also providers of other domains. The client authenticates to its authentication authority and receives an authentication credential with information related to the issuing authority, the client's identity, the expiration date, etc. This credential must then be presented whenever the client wishes to access resources in the service providers located at the domains with which the client's domain has trust relationships.

As the proposed model is based on the security standards of the Web Service technology, it assumes a service-oriented format. The attribute and authentication authorities are the Security Token Service/ Identity Provider (STS/IdP) and the Attribute and Pseudonym Service (APS), respectively (see Fig. 2). This proposal combines Security Token Service (STS) and IdP (Identity Provider) into a single entity, known as STS/IdP that is responsible to issue, validates and exchanges identity and authentication credentials. Both user's privacy and attribute provide are functions performed by Attribute and Pseudonym Service (APS), which works together with STS/IdP. The credentials issued by STS/IdP are **SAML authentication assertions** and the attributes retrieved from APS are **SAML attribute assertions**.

The security of SOAP messages is ensured through the *WS-Security* specification, which provides end-to-end security and avoids attacks such as replay and man-in-the-middle, using encryption and digital signature mechanisms in compliance with the requirements defined in the quality of protection policy expressed in compliance with the WS-Policy specification[6].

In a policy server, the authorization policies that protects the resource are expressed in XACML and the messages exchange between PEP and PDP follow the XACML specification. XACML was chosen since this de facto standard was specifically designed to represent access control policies. When PDP queries the authentication authority, the STS/IdP, to validate an authentication assertion received, it does so through the protocol defined in the WS-Trust specification. PDP's interactions with the STS/IdP of its domain are justified by the fact that the service provider may not support the format of the received credential and might need this credential to be translated into the technology it supports. It should be highlighted that, in the proposed model, STS/IdP acts in a similar manner as the PIP (Policy Information Point) of the XACML standard.

The challenges of the model appear when an access request involves different security domains, that is, the model must ensure interoperability among different administrative domains.The integration of different underlying technologies requires a standard language to represent security attributes, either authentication or authorization ones. As aforementioned The WS-Trust and WS-Federation specifications do not tackle how to translate the information contained in the principal's security credentials, when dealing with different technologies.

In this study, we chose to describe a case composed by two security domains, both based upon PKIs. Besides, clients and service providers were considered to be able to work only with the security technology employed in their domain, as the client domain is based on SPKI, and the service provider domain is based on X.509. However, the model is generic enough to allow for the use of other technologies.

In the proposed model, the translation of authentication credentials and the attribute transposition to different security domains is based on the Attribute/ Pseudonym Service (APS), on the Security Token Service (STS/IdP), and also on a new service, the Credential Translation Service (CTS), introduced in this article.

The Attribute/Pseudonym Service (APS) is directly linked to the STS/IdP and has two purposes: providing attributes associated with a principal[7] and managing a pseudonym system, which allows a principal to authenticate and to use this authentication in the remaining domain entities without having its real identity revealed. For the proposed model, the STS/IdP of the domains establishes trust relationships, and thus forms "federations". Then, in this environment, there is a need for the standardization of the attributes provided by each Attribute/Pseudonym service. In the literature, many studies have been

---

[6] It should be noted that the security of sensitive information stored in the clients is beyond the scope of this article.

[7] Respecting the privacy policy of this principal.

concerned with defining a standard set of attributes needed for a federated environment [17,18,19]. Among them, approximately 40 attributes have been defined as *common identity attributes*[20]; 6 of which are highly recommended, 10 are suggested, and 25 are optional. In this proposal, we adopted a standard set of attributes composed of 6 highly recommended attributes and of 10 suggested attributes, as shown in the [20] document. This set is enough to allow credentials of an SPKI domain to be converted into X.509 certificates. Nevertheless, it can also be expanded in order to accommodate other security technologies, such as Kerberos tickets and biometric credentials.

All the entities of the domain trust their STS/IdP and thus a client identification in the presence of a service provider will be attested through an SAML authentication assertion issued by the STS/IdP. In the model, we consider the existence of trust relationships between STSs of different domains, given that these relationships allow the assertions issued in a domain to be valid in the remaining domains. In order to accomplish so, as an STS receives an SAML authentication assertion, it can ask the authentication authority that issued the assertion (the STS of the client domain) to provide additional information about this authentication so that it can assess the level of trust of the assertion.

The specification [21] defines an XML Schema for the creation of authentication context declarations - XML documents that allow the authentication authority to provide the relying party with this additional information. This information could include: the initial user's identification mechanisms (e.g. face-to-face, online, shared secret), the mechanisms for storing and protecting credentials (e.g. smartcard, password rules) and the authentication mechanism or method (e.g. password, certificate-based SSL, digital signatures). Additionally, this specification defines a number of authentication context[8] classes. Each class defines a proper subset of the full set of authentication contexts. For the purposes of the model, the X.509 and SPKI authentication context classes were used. The former indicates that the principal authenticated by means of a digital signature where the key was validated as part of an X.509 PKI, and the latter indicates that the principal authenticated by means of a digital signature where the key was validated via an SPKI Infrastructure.

3.3   Dynamics for Translation of Authentication Credentials

Fig. 2 shows all the steps taken in order for a client in an domain to access resources in a service provider present in another domain, and also shows the interactions among the STS, APS and CTS (Credential Translation Service) services introduced below. To a better comprehension, consider a scenario where the client's domain is based on SPKI and the service provider's domain uses X.509.

Before a client can call the service provider, it needs to authenticate to its STS (Step 1, Fig. 2), and it may request a pseudonym to associate the authentication credential (Step 2). In Step 3, the client receives an SAML authentication

---

[8] Authentication context is defined as the information, additional to the authentication assertion itself, which the relying party may require before it makes an entitlement decision with respect to an authentication assertion [21].

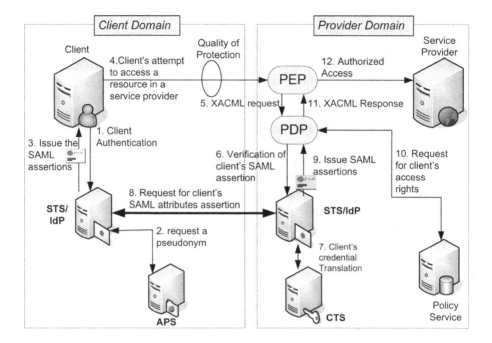

Fig. 2. Dynamics for Translation of Authentication Credentials

assertion based on the security attributes provided by SPKI. In this case, the assertion only carries the client SPKI public key. In Step 4, the client calls the service provider and provides, together with the request, the previously received SAML assertion. The enforcement of an authorization policy starts at the service provider with the provider's PEP.

When PEP intercepts a client's request, it issues a XACML request with a policy decision request to PDP (Step 5). PEP's request to PDP defines one or more policy elements, as well as information on the desired access. In order to make the decision concerning the request, PDP may query authentication and attribute authorities, the STS/IdP and the APS, to validate the SAML authentication assertion received and to obtain the client attributes.

It is known that the service provider is only apt to work with X.509 credentials. Consequently, the SAML assertion received from the client is forwarded to its STS (Step 6), which is in charge of assessing the trust in the SAML assertion received and translating the assertion into an X.509 certificate. In Step 7, the STS calls the Credential Translation Service (CTS) (see Fig. 3) so that the CTS extracts, from the SAML assertion and authentication context, the necessary fields to compose an X.509 certificate. In this case, the SAML assertion does not show all the necessary attributes. Therefore, the CTS requests its STS/IdP to call the client's STS/IdP (which, in turn, calls its respective APS) in order to obtain the missing attributes (Step 8). Finally, the STS/IdP of the X.509 domain issues, to the service provider, (1) an X.509 certificate composed of information

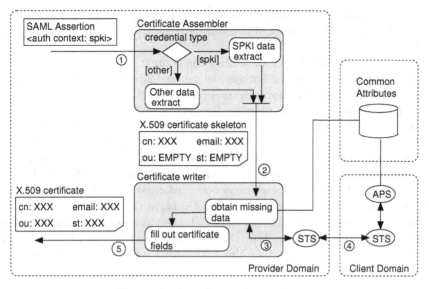

Fig. 3. Credential Translation Service

provided by the client's SAML authentication assertion, and (2) the attributes
gathered in the client's STS/IdP (Step 9). At this point, the client is identified
through a credential which the service provider understands and whose issuer
(the STS) the service provider trusts. Therefore, it is the service provider's duty
to ensure whether or not the client will have access to the service, based on its
access control policies. Next (Step 10), PDP receives the authorization policy
that protects the resource. After these queries, in Step 11, PDP returns the
policy decision and PEP applies it, accepting or denying access (Step 12).

3.4   Credential Translation Service

The use of SAML assertions in tandem with trust relationships allows for the
translation of authentication credentials, that is, a client that has authenticated
to domain A can use this authentication information to access resources of a
service provider present in domain B. However, as aforementioned, clients and
service providers are only able to operate with the underlying security technology of the domain and, in case the client and service providers use different
technologies, there appears the need for a way of mapping the authentication
information from one domain to another.

A solution to this problem lies in the use of the Credential Translation Service
(CTS), which aims at the extraction of SAML authentication assertion information in order to compose a new authentication credential so that it can be
understood by the domain entities (step 1 in Fig. 3). Therefore, a client making
use of the SPKI technology will have its authentication attributes converted into
SAML assertions which, when received by a service provider using X.509, will
be converted again into this provider security technology (step 2 in Fig. 3). This

functioning ensures that clients and service providers keep their security features and thus let the CTS in charge of translating the attributes of a technology into another.

The use of X.509 and SPKI authentication context classes, as defined in [21], aids the translation process of authentication credentials, since the CTS makes use of this information to perform the mapping of the SAML assertion received at the credential required by the provider (for instance, X.509 or SPKI). Nevertheless, information present at authentication assertions may still not suffice to the credential's translation. For instance, in a service provider in the X.509 domain, a client authentication is carried out by means of digital signatures, whereby the key was validated as part of an X.509 PKI. Additionally to the client public key, it is known that X.509 certificates carry other information such as organizational unit, city, etc. Also, it is common knowledge that, in the SPKI, this information is absent and thus the conversion of an SAML assertion issued in a SPKI domain into an X.509 certificate depends on the presence of all the necessary certificate's attributes. It is at this point that the Attribute/Pseudonym Service is needed (step 3 and step 4 in Fig. 3).

4   Implementation

In this section, we discuss the implementation of the proposed model prototype. In addition, we address the performance of our prototype implementation. Finally, we describe the integration of the prototype into a entertainment portal.

4.1   Implementation Details

A prototype was implemented in order to attest the flexibility of the proposed model and also the feasibility of its use in distributed applications based on a service-oriented architecture. Figure 4 shows the prototype's architecture. For the implementation Java was the programming language used and as an application server Apache Tomcat. Apache Axis 1.4 was used as implementation SOAP. Other open source libraries were adopted to compose the prototype, they are: WSS4J library[9], XML-Security library[10], SunXACML[11], OpenSAML [12] and SDSI1.2 library [22].

The prototype implemented consists of two security domains: one based on X.509 PKI, and other based on SPKI. One of the reasons these PKIs were chosen was that the XML Signature specification provides support for both. However, OpenSAML, XMLSecurity e WSS4J libraries provide support only to X509. The WSS4J library had its STS extended, having the capability to issue authentication credentials by using the SPKI infrastructure. The OpenSAML library was extended in order to sign SAMLTokens [23] with SPKI keys, because the current

---

[9] http://ws.apache.org/wss4j
[10] http://xml.apache.org/security
[11] http://sunxacml.sourceforge.net
[12] http://www.opensaml.org

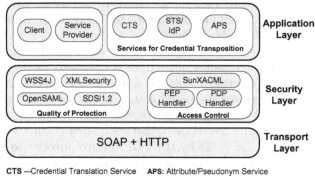

CTS —Credential Translation Service   APS: Attribute/Pseudonym Service
STS/IdP —Security Token Service/Identity Provider

Fig. 4. Prototype Architecture

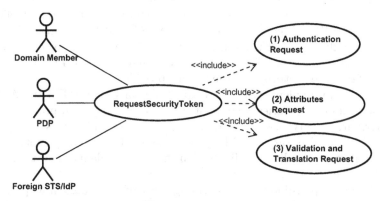

Fig. 5. Requests Handled by STS/IdP

version of OpenSAML only supports X.509 keys. Finally, some extensions were implemented in the XML Security library, in compliance with the recommendations for extensions defined by Apache Foundation, in order to define which SPKI/SDSI elements can be inserted into an XML signature.

Each STS/IdP deals with security technology of its domain, as a consequence, for each technology was necessary to define an implementation of STS/IdP. In the prototype, the STS/IdPs must to process three requests types (see Figure 5): (**1**) member's authentication requests; (**2**) attribute requests in the form of SAML assertions; and (**1**)credential validation and translation request.

According to WS-Trust model, all such requests are to issue tokens. Thus, in all requests the element wst:RequestType in RequestSecurityToken (RST) message contains the URI field. The difference among request types is made up analyzing the other fields of the message. The requests of type 1 are made by a client to STS/IdP of its domain when it wants to access a service that requires authentication. An authentication request has the SAML assertions URI, defined in the SAML Token Profile, in the content of the element wst:TokenType.

In those requests, STS/IdP uses the OpenSAML library to issue and to sign a SAML assertion that contains a subject (the requestor), an authentication statement and some other attributes.

The requests of type 2 also have the SAML assertions URI as the element content wst:TokenType, however differ from the requests of type 1 since they have the element wst:Claims, it contains a list of non-empty attribute names. When the STS/IdP receives such a request, it reads the list of attributes and accesses the APS to obtain required attributes. Then it uses the library Open-SAML to issue and sign a SAML assertion containing client's attributes. The requests of the type 3 are made by the PDP service provider to the STS/IdP of its domain when it wants to validate the authentication token received from the client. In those requests, the element wst:TokenType contains the URI indicating the type of credential-specific domain. When the STS / IdP receives a request of this type, it uses the library OpenSAML to validate the SAML assertion received in accordance with its trust over the issuer (STS/IdP). Then, it invokes CTS to know if is necessary to get more attributes of the client. If yes, then STS/IdP will request attributes of the STS/IdP that issued the SAML assertion. Finally, the CTS is required to translate the assertion to a credential in the domain technology. The credential generated by the CTS and signed by the STS/IdP is then returned to the service provider.

The services for implementation of credential translations (CTS and APS) are not implemented at libraries used, so it was fully developed in prototype. APS is an attributes repository of the domain's members and it was implemented as a STS/IdP local library. APS has two tasks in the current prototype: it retrieves attributes according to a list of identifiers; and it defines how to transport identifier inside of wst:Claims field.

The CTS is responsible for transforming a list of attributes in a specific credential of it domain. In the prototype, the CTS was developed as a STS/IdP local library and has two operations: one to obtain a list of attributes necessary to generate the credential; and another to carry out the translation. For each security technology supported by the prototype, the list of attributes needed and how those attributes will be processed on the credentials are different. For example, in X.509 domain, the attributes needed are the fields of a X.509 certificate, as the subject's X.500 name, the subject's public key, etc.

To facilitate the development of client applications, a library was implemented to aid the interaction between a client and the STS/IdP of its domain. A general PEP was implemented to help on the creation of new services. This PEP is able (1) to intercept client's messages, (2) to interact with PDP and (3) to enforce the PDP decision. SunXACML library was extended to carry out communication with the STS/IdP of service provider domain.

4.2   Performance

This section presents some results of tests applied with the purpose of evaluating the performance (processing time) of the prototype in three representative usage scenarios. That is, we intend to evaluate additional costs introduced by the credentials translation process and the use of security mechanism in compliance with WS-Security. We did 50 experiments using two computers with identical configuration – a 3.0GHz Pentium 4 with 1 GB RAM running Linux (kernel 2.6.24). Both computers had the Java 2 Software Development Kit (J2SDK), version 1.6.0.

In the first scenario, client and service provider are in the same domain that does not provide security mechanisms. Client sends a simple resource request to service provider. This scenario was ran across the department's network at midday and we found that, on average, it executed in 8.18 ms with a standard deviation of 3.02ms.

In the second scenario, client and service provider are in the same security domain (X.509). In this experiment, client does authentication process with its STS/IdP (steps 1 to 3 in Figure 2) and receives a respective SAML authentication assertion. In the next step, client invokes the service provider and at this point occours the enforcement of authorization policy. In this scenario, basic security properties of all SOAP messages are ensured by WSS4J library that implements WS-Security specification. On average, this scenario executed in 53.12ms over the same network with a standard deviation of 8.18ms.

In the third scenario we consider that the client's security domain is based on SPKI and the service provider's security domain is based on X.509. Client receives a SAML authentication assertion based on its SPKI's security attributes and than client involkes service provider. PEP entity intercepts client's request and it issues a XACML request to PDP entity. PDP queries the STS/Idp and the APS to validate the SAML authentication assertion and to obtain client's attributes. Finally, SAML assertion has to be translated into a X.509 certificate because the service provider only work with this security mechanism. On average, this scenario executed in 410.74ms over the same network with a standard deviation of 28.07 seconds.

The difference in processing time between the first and second scenarios expresses the computational cost of digital signatures of asymmetric cryptography. Clearly, executing the authentication credentials translation process (third scenario) takes longer than using a more traditional means of SSO in homogenous security domain (e.g., based on X.509). The difference occurs, mainly due to the greater number of message exchanges. They are, overall, four invocations where all messages are signed with asymmetric cryptography. This cost is justified when the SSO authentication in heterogenous domains is desired front of different technologies that the third case provides. Additionally, the credentials translation process need to be executed only one time in a conversation, so this overhead is eliminate in the next invocations between these client and provider. Further, the prototype has not been optimized for performance. In future research is feasible implements a solution with much better performance.

4.3   Integrating the Prototype into a Distributed Application

An entertainment portal was integrated into the implemented prototype. The goal of the portal is to gather within a single interface several service providers that aim at personal entertainment - for example, movie theaters, amusement parks, video stores, theaters, etc. The open source portal used was *Stringbeans*[13]. he services offered via the Portal were implemented by providers in different domains and trust relationships among the portal domain and the service provides were established. When a client subscribes itself on the portal, this can customize their access defining what and how services are provided. Moreover, the client informs the portal his personal data. The portal register the data in the APS to permit that foreign STS/IdP access the attributes necessary to generate the credentials of this client.

In order to access the services offered via the Portal, a client must authenticate through valid login and password, over an SSL session, as shown in Fig. 6[14]. That portal, in the name of the client, asks the STS for an SAML authentication assertion. It should be noted that SPKI is the security technology supported in the portal. From this point onwards, all of this client's requests will be added to the SAML authentication assertion issued by the portal's STS, so that the client can access all the resources offered by the service providers that can be within an X.509 or an SPKI domain (see Fig. 6).

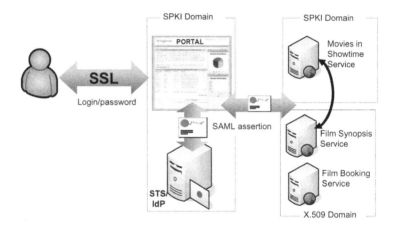

Fig. 6. Entertainment Portal

In Figure 7, the UML communication diagram illustrates the messages exchanged among the services (in the portal and service provider domains) to enforce the authentication credentials translation, according to what was implemented. It should be noted that while receiving the SAML assertion, the service provider requests its STS to translate the assertion into an X.509 certificate. Hence, the portal is responsible for mediate the access among the clients and the service providers and the client can make use of a SSO authentication.

---

[13] http://www.nabh.com/projects/sbportal

[14] This occurs because the clients access the portal through common browsers and, in general, it did not supported SOAP messages.

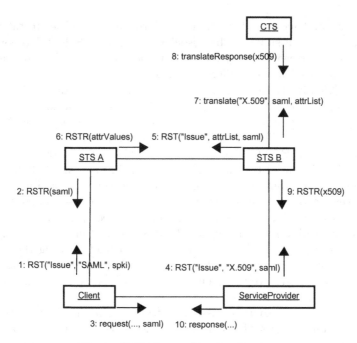

Fig. 7. UML Communication Diagram

5 Related Work

In the literature, some studies have struggled to gather a set of *Web* Service-related specifications to carry out authentication credentials translation. Most of these studies take the concept of federated identities through *Web* Services into account, but only consider the use of X.509 as security infrastructure [24,15,25]. An issue that still needs clarification is the nature of the interaction among domains with different security technologies.

CredEx [24] enables the safe storage of credentials and the dynamic exchange of different kinds of credentials, by using the protocol defined in the WS-Trust specification. However, the implementation only considers the previous association of a username and a password with an X.509 proxy certificate or vice-versa. Thus, the model neither encompasses different security technologies, such as SPKI or Kerberos, nor enables dynamic credential translation.

The Shibboleth framework [15] is an implementation of the browser profiles from the OASIS SAML specification, which provides a SSO service and attribute exchange from the user's home site to the site he is accessing. This framework is based on the concept of federations and also enables authentication credentials translation. Most organizations, which adopt Shibboleth use the X.509 standard for server authentication and password-based authentication for client authentication. The model proposed in this article differs from Shibboleth as it gives more flexibility to the members of the federation, which do not need to use a web browser when interacting with services. The proposed model also enables direct communication among service providers, that is, provider to provider. Service providers do not have to follow strict standardization in order to take part in the federation; it will suffice to be associated with a STS/IdP. Moreover, they can also keep their own security technology and use the Credential Translation when they need to deal with different technologies.

ShibGrid [26] and SHEBANGS [27] projects aim to provide Shibboleth based authentication for grid infrastructures, especially the UK National Grid Service (NGS). The authentication infrastructure behind NGS is based on X.509 certificates and proxies[15] This infrastructure is known as the Grid Security Infrastructure (GSI). SHEBANGS has adopted a proxied push model, wherein users first contact a credential translation service, which, after Shibboleth-based authentication and attribute retrieval, generates a credential stored in a MyProxy server. Access to that credential is then achieved by the user logging on to the NGS portal with details returned to them from the credential translation service. On the other hand, ShibGrid uses MyProxy servers to link two user identities (Shibboleth identity and X.509 certificate DN) instead of using the credential translation service. In both projects, the authentication credentials translation occurs only when there are two security domains (Shibboleth/SAML and Grid Security Infrastructure/X.509).

Cardea [25] makes a dynamic assessment of the authorization requests, taking into account features of the resource and of the request instead of only assessing local identities. Users are identified by proxy X.509 certificates. Unlike what is proposed in the present study, Cardea builds the federation through the SAML standard, that is, SAML authorities, rather than through WS-Trust and WS-Federation specifications; besides, Cardea does not take into consideration different security technologies involved in the authentication process.

The TrustBuilder project[16] is investigating trust negotiation, an attribute-based access control (ABAC) model in which parties conduct bilateral and iterative exchanges of policies and certified attributes to negotiate for access to system resources. In the architecture proposed in this project, a policy compliance checker translates the attribute credentials from X509 certificate or a neutral format, such as XML, into statements in the policy language [29]. However, the Trust Builder approach does not deal with SSO's interoperability among heterogeneous security technologies.

In [30,31], a Credential Conversion Service (CCS) is proposed to integrate authorization schemes. This service is responsible by translate non SAML-based credentials, such as X.509 attribute certificates into SAML Attribute Statements. In this approach, whole security domains need supported a authentication mechanism based on SAML assertions.

6   Conclusion

The concept of federated identities, which forms the basis of this research, (1) favors an effective and independent translation, (2) enables the client to use the

---

[15] NGS portals use MyProxy servers [28] as the means by which grid credentials are obtained.

[16] http://dais.cs.uiuc.edu/dais/security/trustb.php

resources of the federation through authentication carried out in its domain and (3) potentially increases the number of prospective clients for service providers.

Through the definitions proposed in the model, a client that is unknown to the service provider may undergo identity authentication thanks to the trust established among the domains. The provider does not need to know its prospective clients in advance, which thus makes it easier for clients to use the service and enhances business opportunities among service providers.

The model has overcome translation drawbacks by proposing the Credential Translation Service to translate the credentials that service providers failed to understand. Moreover, in the proposed solution, the model has gathered several security specifications in Web Services, which is not a simple task, given the large number of specifications and their complexity. In the future, by means of the Credential Translation Service, it will be also possible to translate not only X.509 and SPKI/SDSI but also authentication credentials in compliance with the Kerberos format (tickets) and according to biometrical profiles (e.g. digital fingerprinting). This will enable communication with providers and clients that support those technologies.

As regards the scalability of the proposed model, communication among domains should suffice to make credential exchange possible, as each domain has its own credential provider. Certainly, this dynamics does not pose scale problems, since this is what happens in current Internet applications. In other words, in the proposed model there is no centralizing entity in charge of mapping the credentials. Each domain is responsible for the required mapping and, thus, the system scale is assured; it will suffice that well requested domains provide solutions for load distribution through, for example, the grouping of machines.

References

1. J sang, A., Pope, S.: User centric identity management. In: AusCERT Asia Pacific Information Technology Security Conference 2005 (May 2005)
2. W3C: Web Services Architecture. W3C Working Group (February 2004), http://www.w3.org/TR/2004/NOTE-ws-arch-20040211
3. Vogels, W.: Web services are not distributed objects. Internet Computing 7(6), 59–66 (2003)
4. Bartel, M., Boyer, J., Fox, B.: XML-Signature Syntax and Processing. W3C (February 2002), http://www.w3.org/TR/xmldsig-core
5. Imamura, T., Dillaway, B., Simon, E.: XML Encryption Syntax and Processing. W3C (December 2002), http://www.w3.org/TR/xmlenc-core
6. OASIS: eXtensible Access Control Markup Language (XACML) version 2.0. Organization for the Advancement of Structured Information Standards (February 2005)
7. OASIS: Security Assertion Markup Language (SAML) 2.0 Technical Overview. Organization for the Advancement of Structured Information Standards (June 2005)
8. OASIS: Web Services Security: SOAP Message Security 1.0. OASIS. (March 2004), http://docs.oasis-open.org/wss/2004/01/oasis-200401-wss-soap-message-security-1.0.pdf
9. WS-Policy: Web Services Policy 1.5 (March 2007)

10. WS-SecurityPolicy: Web Services Security Policy Language (July 2005)
11. WS-PolicyAttachment: Web Services Policy Attachment (March 2006)
12. WS-Trust: Web Services Trust Language (WS-Trust) (February 2005), `http://msdn.microsoft.com/library/en-us/dnglobspec/html/WS-Trust.asp`
13. Yavatkar, R., Pendarakis, D., Guerin, R.: A Framework for Policy-based Admission Control. IETF RFC 2753 (January 2000)
14. WS-Federation: Web Services Federation Language (July 2003), `http://msdn.microsoft.com/ws/2003/07/ws-federation`
15. Shibboleth: Shibboleth Architecture (June 2005), `http://shibboleth.internet2.edu/docs/draft-mace-shibboleth-tech-overview-latest.pdf`
16. Liberty: Introduction to the Liberty Alliance Identity Architecture. Liberty Alliance (March 2003)
17. Internet2, EduCause: eduperson, `http://www.educause.edu/eduperson`
18. Wahl, M.: A Summary of the X.500(96) User Schema for use with LDAPv3. IETF RFC 2256 (December 1997)
19. Smith, M.: Definition of the inetOrgPerson LDAP Object Class. IETF RFC 2798 (April 2000)
20. InComm: Incomm federation: Common identity attributes, `http://www.incommonfederation.org/docs/policies/federatedattributes.pdf`
21. OASIS: Authentication Context for the OASIS Security Assertion Markup Language (SAML) v2.0. Organization for the Advancement of Structured Information Standards (March 2005)
22. Morcos, A.: A Java implementation of Simple Distributed Security Infrastructure. Master's thesis, MIT (May 1998)
23. OASIS: Web Services Security: SAML Token Profile. Organization for the Advancement of Structured Information Standards (December 2004)
24. Vecchio, D.D., Basney, J., Nagaratnam, N.: Credex: User-centric credential management for grid and web services. In: International Conference on Web Services, Orlando, Florida - EUA, pp. 149–156 (2005)
25. Lorch, M., Proctor, S., Lepro, R., Kafura, D., Shah, S.: First experiences using xacml for access control in distributed systems. In: ACM Workshop on XML Security (October 2003)
26. Spence, D., Geddes, N., Jensen, J., Richards, A., Viljoen, M., Martin, A., Dovey, M., Norman, M., Tang, K., Trefethen, A., Wallom, D., Allan, R., Meredith, D.: Shibgrid: Shibboleth access for the uk national grid service. In: Proceedings of the Second IEEE International Conference on e-Science and Grid Computing (e-Science 2006), p. 75. IEEE Computer Society, Los Alamitos (2006)
27. Jones, M., Pickles, S.: Shebangs final report. Technical report, University of Manchester (2007)
28. Basney, J., Humphrey, M., Von Welch: The myproxy online credential repository: Research articles. Softw. Pract. Exper. 35(9), 801–816 (2005)
29. Winslett, M., Yu, T., Seamons, K.E., Hess, A., Jacobson, J., Jarvis, R., Smith, B., Yu, L.: Negotiating trust on the web. IEEE Internet Computing 06(6), 30–37 (2002)
30. Canovas, O., Lopez, G., Gomez-Skarmeta, A.F.: A credential conversion service for SAML-based scenarios. In: Katsikas, S.K., Gritzalis, S., López, J. (eds.) EuroPKI 2004. LNCS, vol. 3093, pp. 297–305. Springer, Heidelberg (2004)
31. Lopez, G., Canovas, O., Gomez-Skarmeta, A.F., Otenko, S., Chadwick, D.: A heterogeneous network access service based on PERMIS and SAML. In: Chadwick, D., Zhao, G. (eds.) EuroPKI 2005. LNCS, vol. 3545, pp. 55–72. Springer, Heidelberg (2005)

Secure and Efficient Group Key Agreements for Cluster Based Networks

Ratna Dutta and Tom Dowling

Claude Shannon Institute*
Computer Science Department
NUI Maynooth, Co. Kildare, Ireland
{rdutta,tdowling}@cs.nuim.ie

Abstract. Ad hoc wireless networks offer anytime-anywhere networking services for infrastructure-free communication over the shared wireless medium. The proliferation of portable devices and ad hoc networks have led to the need for security services. This is illustrated daily in the media with reports of wireless network vulnerabilities. In this setting, secure group key agreement and efficient group key management are considered challenging tasks from both an algorithmic and computational point of view due to resource constraint in wireless networks. In this article, we present two dynamically efficient authenticated group key agreement protocols by reflecting ad hoc networks in a topology composed by a set of clusters. We analyse the complexity of the schemes and differentiate between the two approaches based on performance in a wireless setting. The proposed protocols avoid the use of a trusted third party (TTP) or a central authority, eliminating a single point attack. They allow easy addition and removal of nodes, and achieve better performance in comparison with the existing cluster based key agreements. Additionally, our proposed schemes are supported by sound security analysis in formal security models under standard cryptographic assumptions.

Keywords: clustering, provable security, wireless networks, group key agreement and key management.

1 Introduction

Wireless ad hoc networks support rapid on-demand and adaptive communication among the nodes due to their self-configurable and autonomous nature and lack of fixed infrastructure. These properties ensure that ad hoc wireless networks are especially suitable for creating instant communication for civilian and mission critical applications such as military, emergency and rescue missions. Security is a crucial factor for such systems. It may not be realistic to assume pre-distributed symmetric keys shared between nodes or the presence of a common reliable public key infrastructure (PKI) supported by all nodes. Since ad

---

* This material is based upon works supported by the Science Foundation Ireland under Grant No. 06/MI/006.

M.L. Gavrilova et al. (Eds.): Trans. on Comput. Sci. IV, LNCS 5430, pp. 87–116, 2009.

hoc networks rely on the collaboration principle, the issue of key distribution in such networks represents an important problem. Secure key agreement and efficient group key management are two of the most important mechanisms to build a secure network. However, traditional cryptographic approaches and assumptions are inappropriate for ad hoc wireless networks as the nodes may be resource-constrained in energy, bandwidth, computational ability and memory.

There are quite a number of group key agreements in literature [15], [26], but all are not applicable in ad hoc networks because of dynamic and multi-hop nature of the mobile nodes. Clustering is a usual solution that splits the problem into pieces. We assume ad hoc networks consist of nodes which have no prior contact, trust or authority relation and which may move freely and communicate with other nodes via wireless links. One may logically represent an ad hoc network as a set of clusters. While all nodes are identical in their capabilities, certain nodes are elected to form the sponsors which are vested with the responsibility of routing messages for all the nodes within their clusters. Sponsors typically communicate with sponsors of other clusters. The election of sponsors has been a topic of many papers as documented in [2], [3], [17]. There are several mission critical applications (such as in military, emergency, rescue missions), scientific explorations (such as in environmental monitoring and disaster response), civilians (such as in law enforcement, building automation) and other collaborative applications for commercial uses where sponsors have a powerful radio which other nodes in the cluster do not have so that sponsors can communicate among themselves. For example, military networks consists of mobile devices carried by soldiers, automatic weapons, sensing devices etc. In this setup, a platoon commander may play the role of sponsor and may be able to communicate with platoon commanders of other clusters. On the other hand, soldiers are cluster mobile nodes and may move from one cluster to another.

Clustering method enables nodes to be organised in an hierarchical ad hoc network based on their relative proximity to one another, thereby weakening the one-hop assumption in common group key agreement protocols. Contributory group key agreement and key management are easier to handle inside each cluster compared to the entire ad hoc network. This is because of the fact that clusters have more stable internal connections due to the larger amount of links between nodes within the same cluster. Besides, inter-cluster key agreement is more sensible as clusters are assumed to stay together longer than the nodes do in average for wireless ad hoc networks. Clustering may thus bring the necessary scalability into key establishment in very large networks. Designing provably secure key agreement protocols in such clustered environments is always a challenging task. Li *et al.* [24] propose a communication efficient hybrid key agreement using the concept of connected dominating set. However, the protocol is inefficient in handling dynamic events. Based on this work, Yao *et al.* [36] propose a hierarchical key agreement protocol which is communication efficient in handling dynamic events. Both the protocols of [24] and [36] employ some existed group key agreement protocol such as GDH [35] and are unauthenticated with no security analysis against active adversary. The existing group key agreement protocols that use clusters and pairings are [34], [1], [23].

Our Contribution. Being inspired with these works, we propose two dynamically efficient authenticated group key agreement protocols, namely AP $-$ 1 and AP $-$ 2 for clustered wireless ad hoc networks. AP $-$ 1 is designed without pairings and is proven to be secure under Decision Diffie-Hellman (DDH) assumption. AP $-$ 2 is pairing-based and is proven to be secure under DDH and Decision Hash Bilinear Diffie-Hellman (DHBDH) assumption.

The basic idea of our constructions is the following: In a mobile ad hoc environment, the number of nodes could be very large. We divide all the nodes into clusters based on their relative proximity to one another. We differentiate between two types of keys. By cluster key we mean key generated among all the nodes within a cluster and by session key we mean a common network key among all the nodes in the system. All nodes within a cluster dynamically generate their cluster keys *using a scalable constant round dynamic group key agreement protocol.* We choose the constant round multi-party dynamic key agreement protocol of Dutta-Barua DB [14] for this purpose, which is a variant of Burmester-Desmedt protocol BD-I [8] and is very efficient. Each cluster selects a sponsor using a sponsor selection mechanism. Both AP $-$ 1 and AP $-$ 2 consider a network of mobile nodes where all sponsors need to be able to communicate among themselves in a single hop. AP $-$ 1 invokes the DB protocol among the sponsors to agree upon a common session key considering the sponsors as the nodes of a virtual ring. AP $-$ 2 invokes the pairing-based group key agreement protocol DBS of Dutta-Barua-Sarkar [11] among the sponsors to agree upon a common session key considering the sponsors as the leaf nodes of a virtual balanced ternary tree. While agreeing upon a common session key, the sponsors make use of their cluster keys in such a way that the resulting common session key leads to a contributory group key agreed among all the nodes in the system. This shared group key can then be used by all the nodes in the network to perform efficient symmetric encryption such as DES [29] and AES [28] for secure and faster communication among themselves.

We authenticate our protocols using digital signature schemes with appropriate modifications in Katz-Yung [21] compiler as described in [14]. In keeping with the dynamic nature of mobile ad hoc networks, these protocols facilitate efficient handling of elements leaving and joining clusters. Our proposed protocols are highly efficient as compared to the existing cluster based key agreement protocols [1], [19], [23], [24], [34], [36]. In contrast of invoking the DB or DBS protocol from scratch among all the nodes in the system (which may be infeasible in ad hoc environments), we obtain efficiency gain in terms of both communication and computation for most of the nodes in our proposed cluster-based protocols (which are more amenable to wireless ad hoc networks). AP $-$ 1 is communicationally more efficient than AP $-$ 2. But for any dynamic membership change, AP $-$ 2 is more economic in saving most user's computation costs as compared to AP $-$ 1. AP $-$ 2 uses a tree-structure of sponsors which enables efficient handling of member join/leave. For a member join, AP $-$ 1 requires to rearrange the virtual ring of sponsors/clusters while AP − 2 does not need to rearrange its virtual tree of sponsors/clusters. For a member leave, AP − 1 requires the neighboring clusters of the modified cluster (where the leave has occurred) to update their cluster keys (by executing the initial key agreement phase of the DB protocol once again among all the nodes in the respective neighboring clusters). On the contrary, AP − 2 does not require such cluster key updations for neighbouring clusters of the modified cluster (from which a member leaves). Cluster key updation for AP − 2 is done only for the clusters where Join or Leave has occurred and session key updation is done only along the paths from modified leaf nodes (clusters) to root in the tree. This provides gains in communication and computation for most of the nodes in ad hoc networks as compared to group key maintenance phase of AP − 1. To the best of our knowledge, our proposals are the *first* attempt in the context of cluster based key agreement to provide security analysis in formal security model under standard cryptographic assumptions and also handling dynamic membership change efficiently to make these protocols suitable for ad hoc wireless networks. We emphasize our second key agreement protocol AP − 2 from a performance point of view, especially in handling dynamic operations as compared to our first key agreement protocol AP − 1.

Related Works. Shi *et al.* [34] propose a hierarchical key agreement protocol suitable for wireless ad hoc networks as it can handle the dynamic events efficiently. They use an unbalanced ternary tree structure with leaf nodes as users and employ Joux's [20] tripartite protocol and a generalized DH protocol as the basic building blocks. However, this protocol is computationally costly as each user needs to compute h pairings. Here h is the height of the cluster key tree which has order $O(\log_3 n)$, where n is the number of nodes in the system. Also the communication round is linear to n for this protocol, whereas our pairing-based protocol AP − 2 requires $\lceil \log_3 n \rceil$ rounds. The authentication is achieved using an ID-based signature scheme and heuristic arguments are made in support of the security of the protocol. In contrast, AP − 2 uses a most balanced ternary tree with leaf nodes as sponsors and height of the tree is $\lceil \log_3 n \rceil$. Consequently, AP − 2 requires less pairing computation per user as compared to [34]. Moreover, AP − 2 is supported by a concrete security analysis instead of heuristic arguments unlike [34].

Abdel-Hafez *et al.* [1] provide a partial solution to the key management problem in ad hoc wireless networks and propose a protocol that uses clusters of arbitrary size and requires a trusted authority. However, the protocol is not efficient as it requires n rounds and $n − 1$ pairing computations per user, where n denotes the node count in the whole network. Our protocol AP − 2 requires each node $\leq \lceil \log_3 n \rceil$ pairings and $\lceil \log_3 n \rceil$ communication rounds.

Recently, Konstantinou [23] propose two protocols using pairings, one is contributory and another is non-contributory. They use the concept of binary cluster trees with each cluster having 3 (or 2) nodes and incorporate Joux's [20] tripartite protocol to construct the group key. The contributory scheme is similar to [11] with the exception that no mechanism is provided to make the tree structure most balanced. The round complexity of these protocols are $O(h)$, where h is the height of the bigger branch of the tree structure. Each participant broadcasts at most 3 messages, computes at most 2 scalar multiplications, 1 symmetric encryption and 1 symmetric decryption. Additionally, each user computes at most 2 pairings. However, each internal node in the binary tree structure is a user. Consequently, handling dynamic membership change, especially, the leave operation is very difficult. More precisely, there is no clear description on how to manage a leave event in case the tree structure becomes disconnected due to the leave of internal nodes. Also the protocols are not supported by proper security analysis. Thus although initial key agreement phase of the protocols presented in [23] are more efficient as compared to initial key agreement phase in AP − 2, the protocols in [23] do not handle group key maintenance phase efficiently and complexity of these protocols may become huge (may be linear) as there is no mechanism in these protocols to make the binary tree most balanced.

We should mention here another work by Hietalahti [19] who presents a solution that uses BD protocol [8] within each cluster and then invokes AT-GDH protocol [18] by employing a spanning tree of sponsors. Both BD and AT-GDH protocols are static and consequently handling dynamic events are not easy for this scheme. Our tree-based scheme AP − 2 uses DB protocol within each cluster, then DBS protocol among the sponsors and both DB and DBS protocols are dynamic. All (internal as well as leaf) nodes in the spanning tree for AT-GDH are sponsors, whereas sponsors are arranged only as leaf nodes of the tree-structure in DBS protocol. Moreover, Hietalahti [19]'s work does not provide any security analysis whereas our protocols are supported by proper security analysis in formal security model instead of heuristic arguments.

Organization. In section 2 we present the background for the main ideas in the paper. Section 3 introduces our proposed group key agreement protocols and details their components. For the ease of understanding, we first describe the unauthenticated versions of our protocols. We then show how to transform these unauthenticated protocols into authenticated protocols. Section 4 is concerned with the security analysis following standard security framework under standard cryptographic assumptions. Proofs of security for unauthenticated and authenticated versions are dealt with here. This section is the main contribution of the paper. Section 5 considers complexity and efficiency issues. We present conclusions in Section 6.

2   Preliminaries

2.1   Cryptographic Bilinear Maps

Let G_1, G_2 be two groups of the same prime order q. We view G_1 as an additive group and G_2 as a multiplicative group. A mapping $e : G_1 \quad G_1 \rightarrow G_2$ satisfying the following properties is called a cryptographic bilinear map: (*Bilinearity*) $e(aP, bQ) = e(P, Q)^{ab}$ for all $P, Q \in G_1$ and $a, b \in Z_q^*$; (*Non-degeneracy*) if P is a generator of G_1, then $e(P, P)$ is a generator of G_2; and (*Computablity*) there exists an efficient algorithm to compute $e(P, Q)$. Modified Weil Pairing [6] and Tate Pairing [5] are examples of cryptographic bilinear maps.

2.2   Decision Diffie-Hellman (DDH) Problem

Let $G = \langle g \rangle$ be a multiplicative group of some large prime order q. Then Decision Diffie-Hellman (DDH) problem on G is defined as follows (We use the notation $a \longleftarrow S$ to denote that a is chosen randomly from S):

    $Instance$: (g^a, g^b, g^c) for some $a, b, c \in Z_q^*$.

    $Output$: **yes** if $c = ab \bmod q$ and output **no** otherwise.

We consider two distributions as:

$$\Delta_{\mathsf{Real}} = \{a, b \longleftarrow Z_q^*, A = g^a, B = g^b, C = g^{ab} : (A, B, C)\}$$

$$\Delta_{\mathsf{Rand}} = \{a, b, c \longleftarrow Z_q^*, A = g^a, B = g^b, C = g^c : (A, B, C)\}.$$

The advantage of any probabilistic, polynomial-time, 0/1-valued distinguisher $\mathcal{D}$ in solving DDH problem on G is defined to be :

$$\mathsf{Adv}_{\mathcal{D},G}^{\mathsf{DDH}} = |\mathsf{Prob}[(A, B, C) \longleftarrow \Delta_{\mathsf{Real}} : \mathcal{D}(A, B, C) = 1]$$
$$-\mathsf{Prob}[(A, B, C) \longleftarrow \Delta_{\mathsf{Rand}} : \mathcal{D}(A, B, C) = 1]|.$$

The probability is taken over the choice of $\log_g A$, $\log_g B$, $\log_g C$ and $\mathcal{D}$'s coin tosses. $\mathcal{D}$ is said to be a (t, ϵ)-DDH distinguisher for G if $\mathcal{D}$ runs in time at most t such that $\mathsf{Adv}_{\mathcal{D},G}^{\mathsf{DDH}}(t) \geq \epsilon$. We define $\mathsf{Adv}_G^{\mathsf{DDH}}(t) = \max_{\mathcal{D}}\{\mathsf{Adv}_{\mathcal{D},G}^{\mathsf{DDH}}(t)\}$ where the maximum is over all $\mathcal{D}$ with time complexity t.

DDH assumption: There exists no (t, ϵ)-DDH distinguisher for G. In other words, for every probabilistic, polynomial-time, 0/1-valued distinguisher $\mathcal{D}$, $\mathsf{Adv}_{\mathcal{D},G}^{\mathsf{DDH}} \leq \epsilon$ for any sufficiently small $\epsilon > 0$.

2.3   Decision Hash Bilinear Diffie-Hellman (DHBDH) Problem

Let (G_1, G_2, e) be as in Section 2.1. We define the following problem. Given an instance (P, aP, bP, cP, r) for some $a, b, c, r \in_R Z_q^*$ and a one way hash function $H : G_2 \to Z_q^*$, to decide whether $r = H(e(P, P)^{abc}) \bmod q$. This problem is termed Decision Hash Bilinear Diffie-Hellman (DHBDH) problem as defined in [11] and is a combination of the bilinear Diffie-Hellman (BDH) problem and a variation of the hash Diffie-Hellman (HDH) problem. The DHBDH assumption is that there exists no probabilistic, polynomial time, 0/1-valued algorithm which can solve the DHBDH problem with non-negligible advantage.

2.4   Protocol DBS [11]

Suppose a set of n users $\{U_1, U_2, \ldots, U_n\}$ wish to agree upon a secret key. Quite often, we identify a user with its instance during the execution of a protocol. Let US be a subset of users (or instances). In case US is a singleton set, we will identify US with the instance it contains. Each user set US has a representative $\mathsf{Rep}(\mathsf{US})$ and for the sake of concreteness we take $\mathsf{Rep}(\mathsf{US}) = U_j$ where $j = \min\{k : \Pi_{U_k}^{d_k} \in \mathsf{US}\}$, where $\Pi_{U_k}^{d_k}$ denotes the d_k-th instance of user U_k.. We use the notation

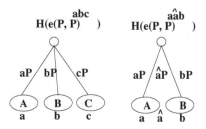

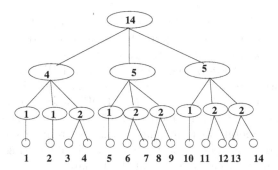

Fig. 1. procedure CombineThree **and procedure** CombineTwo

Fig. 2. procedure KeyAgreement for $n = 14$

$A[1, \ldots, n]$ for an array of n elements $A_1, \ldots, A_n$ and write $A[i]$ or A_i to denote the ith element of array $A[\,]$. We take G_1 to be a cyclic subgroup of an elliptic curve group of some large prime order q and the bilinear map $e : G_1^2 \to G_2$ to be either a modified Weil pairing or a Tate pairing [5], [16]. Let P be an arbitrary generator of G_1. Choose a hash function $H : G_2 \to Z_q^*$. The system parameters for the unauthenticated protocol are $params = \langle G_1, G_2, e, q, P, H \rangle$.

Let $p = \frac{n}{3}$ and $r = n \bmod 3$. The set of users participating in a session is partitioned into three user sets $\mathsf{US}_1, \mathsf{US}_2, \mathsf{US}_3$ with respective cardinality being p, p, p if $r = 0$; $p, p, p + 1$ if $r = 1$; and $p, p + 1, p + 1$ if $r = 2$. This top down recursive procedure is invoked for further partitioning to obtain a ternary tree structure (*cf.* Figure 2). The lowest level 0 consists of singleton users having a private ephemeral key. We invoke CombineTwo, a key agreement protocol for two user sets and CombineThree, a key agreement protocol for three user sets in the key tree thus obtained. We demonstrate these two procedures in Figure 1.

All communications are done by representatives and users in each user set have a common agreed key. In CombineThree, a, b, c respectively are the common agreed key of user sets A, B, C. Representative of user set A sends aP to both the user sets B, C. Similarly, representative of B sends bP to both A, C and representative of C sends cP to both A, B. After these communications, each user can compute the common agreed key $H(e(P, P)^{abc})$. In CombineTwo, users in user set A have common agreed key a, users in user set B have common agreed key b. Representative of A sends aP to user set B and representative of B sends bP to user set A. Moreover, representative of user set A generates

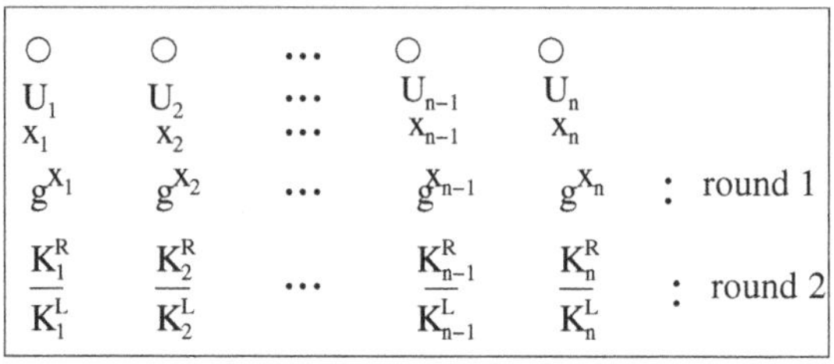

Fig. 3. Constant Round Group Key Agreement

a random key $\hat{a} \in Z_q^*$ and sends $\hat{a}P$ to all the users in both A, B. After these communications, each user can compute the common agreed key $H(e(P, P)^{a\hat{a}b})$.

The protocol is proven to be secure against passive adversary under the assumption that Decision Hash Bilinear Diffie-Hellman (DHBDH) problem is hard. The authors incorporate authentication signature based mechanism and proved its security against active adversary under DHBDH assumption using a modified version of Katz-Yung [21] security model. In [12], the authors extended this protocol by additional operations that handle dynamic group change, *i.e.* addition and deletion of group members. Both events are handled using a sponsor and result in the updated logical tree T' and the updated secret value at the root of T' whereby private ephemeral keys of some users remain unchanged. The authentication is achieved using digital signatures and multi-signatures as in [11]. This dynamic version is also proven to be secure against active adversary under DHBDH assumption using their own modifications in Katz-Yung [21] compiler.

2.5   Protocol DB [13]

Let G be a finite multiplicative group of some large prime order q where the well-known Discrete Logarithm (DL) problem is believed to be intractable and g be a generator of G. Also consider a hash function $\mathcal{H} : \{0,1\}^* \to Z_q^*$. Suppose a set of n users $\{U_1, \ldots, U_n\}$ wish to establish a common session key among themselves. Consider users $U_1, \ldots, U_n$ participating in the protocol are on a *virtual* ring and U_{i-1}, U_{i+1} are respectively left and right neighbours of U_i for $1 \le i \le n$. Here the indices are taken modulo n so that user U_0 is U_n and user U_{n+1} is U_1 (*i.e.* index i stands for $i \bmod n$ and we have $U_0 = U_n$ and $U_{n+1} = U_1$). The protocol consists of three algorithms DB.Setup, DB.Join and DB.Leave for initial setup, user join and user leave respectively. The protocol is executed as follows among n users $U_1, \ldots, U_n$ (*cf.* Figure 3).

(a) **Protocol DB.Setup**
  1. In round 1, each user U_i chooses randomly a private ephemeral key $x_i \in Z_q^*$ and broadcasts $y_i = g^{x_i} \bmod q$.
  2. In round 2, user U_i on receiving y_{i-1} and y_{i+1} computes its left key $K_i^L = y_{i-1}^{x_i} \bmod q$, right key $K_i^R = y_{i+1}^{x_i} \bmod q$, $Y_i = K_i^R / K_i^L \bmod q$ and broadcasts Y_i. Here $K_i^L = K_{i-1}^R$ is a common DH key between users U_i, U_{i-1} and $K_i^R = K_{i+1}^L$ is a common DH key between users U_i, U_{i+1}.

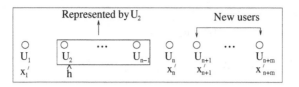

Fig. 4. Join operation

3. Finally, in the key computation phase, U_i computes $\overline{K}^R_{i+1}, \ldots, \overline{K}^R_{i+(n-1)}$ as follows making use of its own right key K^R_i:

$$\overline{K}^R_{i+1} = Y_{i+1} K^R_i \bmod q, \ldots, \overline{K}^R_{i+(n-1)} = Y_{i+(n-1)} \overline{K}^R_{i+(n-2)} \bmod q.$$

Then U_i verifies if $\overline{K}^R_{i+(n-1)}$ is same as that of its own left key $K^L_i (= K^R_{i+(n-1)})$. U_i aborts if verification fails. Otherwise, U_i has correct right keys of all the users. U_i computes the session key $\mathsf{sk} = \overline{K}^R_1 \overline{K}^R_2 \ldots \overline{K}^R_n$ mod q which is equal to $g^{x_1 x_2 + x_2 x_3 + \cdots + x_n x_1}$. U_i also computes and stores $\hat{h} = \mathcal{H}(\mathsf{sk})$ for a possible subsequent join operation and stores its left key and right key K^L_i, K^R_i respectively for a subsequent leave operation.

(b) **Protocol** DB.Join

The key agreement in Join algorithm is done in such a way that new users are unable to know previous session keys. When a set of new users $U[n+1, \ldots, n+m]$ with respective private ephemeral keys $x'[n+1 \ldots, n+m]$ wants to join a group of users $U[1, \ldots, n]$ with respective new randomly chosen private ephemeral keys $x'[1, \ldots, n]$, DB.Setup is invoked among users $U_1, U_2, U[n, n+1, \ldots, n+m]$ with respective private ephemeral keys $x'_1, \hat{h}, x'[n, n+1, \ldots, n+m]$. We consider U_2 as a representative of the set $U[2, 3, \ldots, n-1]$ and execute DB.Setup considering a virtual ring of $m+3$ users, instead of a virtual ring of $n+m$ users (*cf.* Figure 4). Here $\hat{h}$ is the common seed value that users $U[1, 2, \ldots, n]$ agree upon in previous session before users $U[n+1, \ldots, n+m]$ have joined. In addition, from transmitted messages, users $U[3, \ldots, n-1]$ are able to compute the current session key in the same way as U_2 does, as they know the common seed value $\hat{h}$. However, they do not participate in the communication during protocol execution, although they receive all the messages which they are supposed to receive. Here it is assumed that new members have the knowledge of who are in the system, whom to communicate with and who their immediate neighbours are on the virtual ring, *i.e.* they have the knowledge of old partner identity in the previous session before executing the Join algorithm for the current session. To handle join operations efficiently (without restarting the initial protocol), participants use the saved value $\hat{h}$ in the previous session. Thus the proposed join algorithm takes advantage of reusability of users' precomputed values in previous sessions in order to save most users' computations for updating session keys in subsequent session in which users join the group.

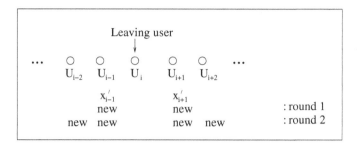

Fig. 5. Leave operation

(c) Protocol DB.Leave

The key update in Leave algorithm is performed to make the set of revoked users in a session unable to know the current and subsequent session keys. The leaving users are dropped from the virtual ring. Left and right neighbours of each leaving user choose new private ephemeral keys. Then the key agreement is done as usual in the resulting ring of users with respective private ephemeral keys by invoking DB.Setup. However, in round 1, only the first closest non-leaving left and right neighbours of a leaving participant choose new private ephemeral keys and broadcast new values, the second closest non-leaving left and right neighbours of a leaving participant broadcast precomputed values, and other users broadcast nothing. On the other hand, in round 2, only the following non-leaving neighbours of a leaving user broadcast the modified new values (*cf.* Figure 5), while the other users broadcast the precomputed values that were saved in previous session:

- the *first* closest non-leaving *left* neighbour of the leaving user computes its new left key and new right key and broadcasts the modified new quotient of new right key and new left key,
- the *first* closest non-leaving *right* neighbour of the leaving user computes its new left key and new right key and broadcasts the modified new quotient of new right key and new left key,
- the *second* closest non-leaving *left* neighbour of the leaving user computes its new right key and broadcasts the modified new quotient of new right key and precomputed left key,
- the *second* closest non-leaving *right* neighbour of the leaving user computes its new left key and broadcasts the modified new quotient of precomputed right key and new left key

Here also, it is assumed that each user knows the positions of its partners on the virtual ring in the current session associated with this Leave operation. To handle leave operations efficiently (without restarting the initial protocol), most of the participants use the saved values of their left keys and right keys precomputed in the previous session, only a limited number of participants compute their new left and right keys as illustrated in Figure 5. Thus the proposed leave algorithm take advantage of reusability of user's precomputed values in previous sessions in order to save most user's computations for updating session keys in subsequent session in which users leave the group.

This unauthenticated protocol can be viewed as a variant of the unauthenticated protocol of Burmester and Desmedt BD-I [8], [9] . However, the session key computation is done differently, although with same complexity as the BD-I protocol. This protocol is proven to be secure against passive adversary assuming the intractability of decision Diffie-Hellman (DDH) problem. Authors incorporate authentication in the above protocol using digital signature with appropriate modifications in Katz-Yung [21] compiler. This authenticated protocol is a simplification of the protocol of [21] in which authors have done away with random nonces and have been able to reduce number of rounds by one. The security proof is actually tighter than that in Katz-Yung [21]. This is due to the fact that authors use a setting of unique instance numbers instead of random nonces and are able to avoid the event Repeat that comes in Katz-Yung security proof, thus reducing complexity of Katz-Yung compiler. They further extend this static authenticated protocol to dynamic setting by introducing algorithms for join and leave as described above. To handle these operations efficiently (without restarting the initial protocol), participants use the saved values $\hat{h} = \mathcal{H}(\mathsf{sk}_{U_i}^{d_i})$, K_i^L and K_i^R to take advantage of reusability of user's precomputed values in previous sessions in order to save most user's computations for updating session keys in subsequent session in which users join and/or leave the group. Thus they gain in computation complexity in their dynamic protocol in contrast to executing the BD-I protocol (which is static) among the new group of users. Besides, the protocol has the ability to detect the presence of a corrupted group member, although it cannot detect who among the group members are behaving improperly. If an invalid message is sent by a corrupted member, then this can be detected by all legitimate members of the group and the protocol execution may be stopped instantly. This feature makes the protocol interesting when the adversarial model no longer assumes that the group members are honest.

2.6 Security Model for Key Agreement

The following security model for key agreement is based on Bresson *et al.*'s [7] formal security model for group key agreement.

Let $\mathcal{P} = \{U_1, \ldots, U_n\}$ be a set of n (fixed) users or participants. At any point of time, any subset of $\mathcal{P}$ may decide to establish a session key. We identify the execution of protocols for key agreement, member(s) join and member(s) leave as different sessions. The adversarial model allows concurrent execution of the protocol and consists of allowing each user an unlimited number of instances where each instance may be used only once, and with which it executes the protocol for key agreement or inclusion or exclusion of a user or a set of users. *We assume adversary has complete control over all communication, but never participates as a user in the protocol.* We will require the following notations.

Π_U^i : i-th instance of user U.

sk_U^i : session key after execution of the protocol by Π_U^i.

sid_U^i : session identity for instance Π_U^i. We set

$\mathsf{sid}_U^i = S = \{(U_1, i_1), \ldots, (U_k, i_k)\}$ such that $(U, i) \in S$ and

$\Pi_{U_1}^{i_1}, \ldots, \Pi_{U_k}^{i_k}$ wish to agree upon a common key.

pid$_U^i$: partner identity for instance Π_U^i, defined by pid$_U^i = \{U_1, \ldots, U_k\}$, such that $(U_j, i_j) \in$ sid$_U^i$ for all $1 \leq j \leq k$.

acc$_U^i$: 0/1-valued variable which is set to be 1 by Π_U^i upon normal termination of the session and 0 otherwise.

The following oracles model an adversary's interaction with the users in the network, where S, S_1, S_2 are three sets such that $S \cap S_1 = \emptyset$ and $S_2 \subseteq S$. More precisely, let $S = \{(U_1, i_1), \ldots, (U_l, i_l)\}, S_1 = \{(U_{l+1}, i_{l+1}), \ldots, (U_{l+k}, i_{l+k})\}, S_2 = \{(U_{j_1}, i_{j_1}), \ldots, (U_{j_k}, i_{j_k})\}$ where $\{U_1, \ldots, U_l\}$ is any non-empty subset of $\mathcal{P}$.

– Send(U, i, m) : The output of the query is the reply (if any) generated by the instance Π_U^i upon receipt of message m. The adversary is allowed to prompt the unused instance Π_U^i to initiate the protocol with partners $U_2, \ldots, U_l, l \leq n$, by invoking Send$(U, i, \langle U_2, \ldots, U_l \rangle)$. This query models an active attack, in which the adversary may intercept a message and then either modify it, create a new one or simply forward it to the intended participant.

– Execute(S) : The output of this query is the transcript of an honest execution of the key agreement protocol among unused instances $\Pi_{U_1}^{i_1}, \ldots, \Pi_{U_l}^{i_l}$. A transcript consists of the messages that were exchanged during the execution of the protocol.

– Join(S, S_1) : The output of this query is the transcript generated by the invocation of algorithm Join for the insertion of user instances $\Pi_{U_{l+1}}^{i_{l+1}}, \ldots, \Pi_{U_{l+k}}^{i_{l+k}}$ in the group $\{\Pi_{U_1}^{i_1}, \ldots, \Pi_{U_l}^{i_l}\}$. If Execute$(S)$ has not taken place, then the adversary is given no output. This query is initiated by a send query.

– Leave(S, S_2) : The adversary is given the transcript generated by the honest execution of procedure Leave for the removal of user instances $\Pi_{U_{j_1}}^{i_{j_1}}, \ldots, \Pi_{U_{j_k}}^{i_{j_k}}$ from the group $\{\Pi_{U_1}^{i_1}, \ldots \Pi_{U_l}^{i_l}\}$. If Execute$(S)$ has not taken place, then the adversary is given no output. This query is also initiated by a send query.

– Reveal(U, i) : This unconditionally outputs session key sk$_U^i$.

– Corrupt(U) : This outputs the long-term secret key (if any) of player U.

– Test(U, i) : A bit $b \in \{0, 1\}$ is chosen uniformly at random. The adversary is given sk$_U^i$ if $b = 1$, and a random session key if $b = 0$.

A *passive* adversary has access to Execute, Join, Leave, Reveal, Corrupt and Test oracles while an *active* adversary is additionally given access to Send oracle. For static case, there are no Join or Leave queries as a group of fixed size is considered. The adversary can ask Send, Execute, Join, Leave, Reveal and Corrupt queries several times, but Test query is asked only once and on a fresh instance as defined below.

We say that an instance Π_U^i is *fresh* unless either the adversary, at some point, queried Reveal(U, i) or Reveal(U', j) with $U' \in$ pid$_U^i$ or the adversary queried Corrupt(V) (with $V \in$ pid$_U^i$) before a query of the form Send$(U, i, *)$ or Send$(U', j, *)$ where $U' \in$ pid$_U^i$.

Finally, the adversary outputs a guess bit b'. Such an adversary is said to win the game if $b = b'$, where b is the hidden bit used by Test oracle. Let Succ denote the event that the adversary $\mathcal{A}$ wins the game for a key agreement protocol XP. We define $\mathsf{Adv}_{\mathcal{A},\mathsf{XP}} := |2\,\mathsf{Prob}[\mathsf{Succ}] - 1|$ to be the advantage of the adversary $\mathcal{A}$ in attacking the protocol XP.

The protocol XP is said to be a secure *unauthenticated key agreement* (KA) protocol if there is no polynomial time *passive* adversary with non-negligible advantage. We say that protocol XP is a secure *authenticated key agreement* (AKA) protocol if there is no polynomial time *active* adversary with non-negligible advantage. In other words, for every probabilistic, polynomial-time, 0/1 valued algorithm $\mathcal{A}$, $\mathsf{Adv}_{\mathcal{A},\mathsf{XP}} < \frac{1}{M^L}$ for every fixed $L > 0$ and sufficiently large integer M For concrete security analysis, we define

$\mathsf{Adv}_{\mathsf{XP}}^{\mathsf{KA}}(t, q_E)$:= the maximum advantage of any passive adversary attacking protocol XP, running in time t and making q_E calls to the Execute.

$\mathsf{Adv}_{\mathsf{XP}}^{\mathsf{AKA}}(t, q_E, q_S)$:= the maximum advantage of any active adversary attacking protocol XP, running in time t and making q_E calls to the Execute and q_S calls to the Send.

3   Proposed Group Key Agreement Protocols

In this section, we propose two cluster-based group key agreement protocols. We first address the clustering technique for organization of the network nodes into clusters and then detail the unauthenticated versions of our protocols $\mathsf{UP} - 1$ and $\mathsf{UP} - 2$. Finally, we will show how to extend these protocols into authenticated protocols $\mathsf{AP} - 1$ and $\mathsf{AP} - 2$ respectively.

3.1   Cluster Formation

Suppose we have a large multi-hop wireless ad hoc network with no fixed infrastructure such as switching centres or base stations. Each mobile node is assumed to have some computational power and an omni-directional antenna. A message sent by a node can be received by all nodes within its transmission range. On the other hand, the nodes that are far apart have to rely on intermediate nodes to relay messages. Clustering is an efficient technique of organizing the nodes in a wireless ad hoc environment. There are large variety of clustering protocols [4], [30], [33]. The overhead involved in a clustering technique comprises of two phases: *cluster initialization phase* and *cluster maintenance phase*. Sucec *et al.* [33] provides a theoretical upper bound (n) (n is the node count) on the communication overhead incurred by a particular clustering algorithm in ad hoc networks. Most of the clustering protocols perform hierarchical routing among the clusters to (i) increase the robustness of routes by providing multiple possibilities for routing among the clusters, (ii) reduce the size of routing tables [4], and (iii) incurs less communication overhead for tracking mobile nodes in large multi-hop mobile wireless network [4], [30].

In our proposed protocols, we use a clustering method based on [24] to (hierarchically) organize the mobile nodes based on their relative proximity to one another. Our clustering algorithm divides nodes into small groups, called clusters. We assume that every node can find a cluster to join, *i.e.* all nodes are reachable by at least one other node. Each cluster elects a cluster head which acts as a backbone node or gateway node or sponsor for cluster interaction. This cluster head election within a cluster can be done according to node connectivity, computational power and/or extra radio facilities. For instance, the node with the highest connectivity in a given area may become the cluster head. We assume that cluster heads have more computation and communication power than the ordinary nodes. More precisely, cluster heads have an additional powerful radio to establish wireless links among themselves. All nodes in a cluster are within direct transmission range of the cluster head and each node pair in the same cluster can also communicate in one-hop. We briefly review below a clustering method based on [24], which consists of two phases: *cluster initialization phase* and *cluster maintenance phase*.

• Cluster Initialization Phase

(*a*) Each node makes its active neighbours aware of its presence by broadcasting an initial IamAlive message and its identity to its one-hop away neighbours.

(*b*) Once the nodes have gathered information about their neighbours, the cluster head within a certain region should broadcast a message IamSponsor to its one-hop away neighbours to confirm its leadership within that cluster.

(*c*) A node receiving IamSponsor message marks itself as an ordinary node and broadcasts IamOrdinary to all its one-hop away neighbours for confirming its inclusion in that cluster.

(*d*) Each node in a cluster knows the identities of all its one-hop away neighbours. The cluster head computes a cluster-identifier, which is concatenation of identities of all the cluster nodes within that cluster.

We assume that a sponsor has the knowledge that it is a designated sponsor. In case a node gets several messages like IamSponsor, it processes only the message that it receives first. So far, each node only has to broadcast twice to its one-hop neighbours – one for telling its identity and one for notifying its sponsor/ordinary status. Wireless nodes are not static and can move around. If the node's movement does not cause the change of the network topology, it is needless to say that no maintenance is necessary. Otherwise, the following steps are executed.

• Cluster Maintenance Phase

Adding Node. (*a*) Suppose a new node falls within the direct transmission range of a cluster, *i.e.* it is able to communicate with all the nodes in the cluster in one-hop. If this new node is willing to join the network, it broadcasts its identity together with a message IamAlive – thereby making aware of its presence to its one-hop away neighbours.

(b) The cluster head broadcasts the cluster-identity and a message IamSponsor to its one-hop away neighbours to confirm its leadership within that cluster.

(c) The new node receiving IamSponsor message marks itself as an ordinary node and broadcasts to its one-hop away neighbours IamOrdinary to confirm its inclusion in that cluster. On receiving the cluster-identity from the cluster head, the new node becomes aware of its neighbours in that cluster.

(d) The cluster head modifies the cluster-identifier by concatenating the identity of the new user with the old cluster-identifier.

Removing Node. (a) Suppose a node has moved out of the range of a cluster. The cluster head would be aware of this variation. Otherwise, when a node wants to get revoked from a cluster, it broadcasts its identity together with a message IamLeaving to all its one-hop away neighbours. The cluster head modifies the cluster-identifier by dropping the identity of the revoked node from the concatenation of the identities (old cluster-identifier).

(b) If the cluster head is revoked, then the cluster should be reconstructed. A new cluster head need to be elected among the nodes of the cluster such that the new cluster head has the highest connectivity with additional power of computation and communication to establish wireless links among the other cluster heads in the network.

3.2   Unauthenticated Protocol UP − 1

We describe UP − 1 in two phases: (a) *Initial Key Agreement (IKA)* phase that establishes the initial group session key, and (b) *Group Key Maintenance (GKM)* phase that handles all dynamic events such as a member join/leave and then refreshes the group session key. Let $\mathcal{H}_0 : G \rightarrow Z_q^*$ be a cryptographically secure public hash function.

Initial Key Agreement. Initially, suppose the entire set of nodes in the network are divided into n clusters $C_1, \ldots, C_n$ following our clustering algorithm as described above. Let S_i be the sponsor node in C_i for $i = 1, \ldots, n$. Our protocol consists of the following steps.

- **Step 1:** (*Cluster Key Agreement*) All clusters execute DB.Setup in parallel and compute their respective cluster keys. Let CK_i be the common cluster key agreed among all the nodes in C_i for $i = 1, \ldots, n$. We call this procedure ClusterKeyAgree. See Algorithm 1.
- **Step 2:** (*Group Key Agreement*) Consider a virtual ring of sponsors $S_1, S_2, \ldots,$ S_n. Alternatively, think each virtual network node in the ring as a cluster headed by the corresponding sponsor. All sponsors execute DB.Setup among themselves using $\mathcal{H}_0(CK_i)$ as the private ephemeral key of S_i for $i = 1, \ldots, n$ to agree upon a common session key. Note that all nodes in a cluster C_i has the same cluster key CK_i and the sponsor S_i of cluster C_i makes use of this cluster key CK_i in agreeing upon the common session key SK. Consequently, this common session key is the group key agreed among all the nodes in the

network. We assume that while executing DB.Setup among the sponsors, each message broadcast by a sponsor is received by other sponsors as well as all the cluster nodes headed by respective sponsors. Thus in agreeing upon the group session key, the sponsors take active participation in the execution of DB.Setup, but the other cluster nodes remain passive, although they do receive all the messages which the sponsor of that cluster is supposed to receive in order to be able to compute the group session key. We call this procedure GroupKeyAgreement − DB. See Algorithm 2.

Algorithm 1. (procedure ClusterKeyAgree) Computation of cluster key CK_i among all the nodes in the cluster C_i for $i = 1, \ldots, n$

1: **for** $i \leftarrow 1$ **to** n **do in parallel**
2:     **call** DB.Setup among all nodes in the cluster C_i
3:     Let CK_i be the common cluster key agreed among all nodes of C_i
4: **end for**

Algorithm 2. (procedure GroupKeyAgree-DB) Agreement of group session key SK among all the nodes in the clusters $(C_1, C_2, \ldots, C_n)$

1: **call** ClusterKeyAgree$(C_1, C_2, \ldots, C_n)$
2: Consider a virtual ring of sponsors $S_1, S_2, \ldots, S_n$
3: **call** DB.Setup among all the sponsors $S_1, S_2, \ldots, S_n$ using $\mathcal{H}_0(CK_1), \ldots, \mathcal{H}_0(CK_n)$
       respectively as the private ephemeral keys
4: Let SK be the common session key agreed among $S_1, S_2, \ldots, S_n$
5: **for** $i \leftarrow 1$ **to** n **do in parallel**
6:     Each cluster node in C_i computes the session key SK in the same way as S_i
       does
7: **end for**

Group Key Maintenance. Wireless nodes are highly mobile in nature and the nodes' movement may cause the change of the network topology frequently. It is therefore important and necessary to update the group session key to ensure security. No maintenance is necessary in case the node's movement do not cause the change of the cluster structure. Otherwise, the following steps are performed.

- **Step 1:** Suppose a set of nodes U wants to join/leave the cluster C_i. Update the cluster key CK_i in C_i by invoking DB.Join among $C_i \cup U$ if U wants to join C_i and DB.Leave among $C_i \setminus U$ if U wants to leave C_i. We call this procedure ClusterKeyUpdate. See Algorithm 3. We update the cluster keys in the clusters where membership changes have occurred by invoking ClusterKeyUpdate.
- **Step 2:** The session key is updated as follows.
   (a) **Case** Join: We rearrange the virtual ring of clusters (or sponsors) and virtually place the modified clusters, where joining of new nodes have occurred, after the other (unchanged) clusters in the virtual ring. This can be done by a group controller and any designated sponsor in the

system may play the role of this group controller. Then DB.Join is executed among all the sponsors using their respective cluster keys as their private ephemeral keys to update the common session key. Here also we assume that other cluster nodes in a particular cluster receive all the messages which the sponsor of that cluster is supposed to receive in order to compute the updated common session key in the same way the sponsor of that cluster does.

(b) **Case Leave**: In the virtual ring of clusters, additionally the first closest unmodified left and right neighboring clusters of a modified cluster (where member leave has occurred) modifies their cluster keys. So we invoke DB.Setup for each of the left and right neighbors of a modified cluster in the virtual ring of clusters. Then DB.Leave is executed among all the sponsors using their respective (modified/updated) cluster keys as their private ephemeral keys to update the common session key. Here also we assume that other cluster nodes in a particular cluster receive all the messages which the sponsor of that cluster is supposed to receive in order to compute the updated common session key in the same way the sponsor of that cluster does.

Algorithm 3. (procedure ClusterKeyUpdate) Cluster key update in the cluster C_i when a set of users U joins/leaves C_i

---

1: **if** U wants to join C_i **then**
2:     **call** DB.Join among the nodes $C_i \cup U$
3: **else if** U wants to leave C_i **then**
4:     **call** DB.Leave among the nodes $C_i \setminus U$
5: **end if**
6: Let CK_i be the updated cluster key in the new cluster

3.3 Unauthenticated Protocol UP − 2

As in UP − 1, protocol UP − 2 also consists of two phases: (a) *Initial Key Agreement (IKA)* phase, and (b) *Group Key Maintenance (GKM)* phase. Let $\mathcal{H}_0 : G \to Z_q^*$ be a cryptographically secure public hash function.

Initial Key Agreement. Initially, all the nodes are divided into n clusters $C_1, \dots, C_n$ with sponsors $S_1, \dots, S_n$ respectively following our clustering algorithm described above. Our protocol consists of the following Steps.

- **Step 1:** (*Cluster Key Agreement*) We invoke procedure ClusterKeyAgree, where all clusters $C_1, \dots, C_n$ execute DB.Setup in parallel and compute their respective cluster keys $\mathsf{CK}_1 \dots, \mathsf{CK}_n$ following Algorithm 1.
- **Step 2:** (*Group Key Agreement*) Consider a most balance ternary virtual tree structure constructed in the same way as in DBS with the sponsors $S_1, S_2, \dots, S_n$ as leaf nodes. Alternatively, think each leaf node in the tree as a cluster headed by the corresponding sponsor and all other nodes in the

tree are virtual. All sponsors execute DBS among themselves with $\mathcal{H}_0(\mathsf{CK}_i)$ as the private ephemeral key of sponsor S_i for $i = 1, \ldots, n$ to agree upon a common session key. Note that all nodes in a cluster C_i has the same cluster key CK_i and the sponsor S_i of cluster C_i makes use of this cluster key CK_i in agreeing upon the common session key SK. Consequently, this common session key SK is the group key agreed among all the nodes in the network. We assume that while executing DBS among the sponsors, each message broadcast by a sponsor is received by other sponsors as well as all the cluster nodes headed by respective sponsors. Thus in agreeing upon the group session key, the sponsors take active participation in the execution of DBS, but the other cluster nodes remain passive, although they do receive all the messages which the sponsor of that cluster is supposed to receive in order to be able to compute the group session key. We call this procedure GroupKeyAgreement − DBS. See Algorithm 4.

Algorithm 4. (procedure GroupKeyAgree-DBS) Agreement of group session key SK among all the nodes in the clusters $(C_1, C_2, \ldots, C_n)$

1: **call** ClusterKeyAgree$(C_1, C_2, \ldots, C_n)$
2: Construct a virtual ternary tree as in DBS with the sponsors $S_1, S_2, \ldots, S_n$ as leaf nodes
3: **call** DBS among all the sponsors $S_1, S_2, \ldots, S_n$ using $\mathcal{H}_0(\mathsf{CK}_1), \ldots, \mathcal{H}_0(\mathsf{CK}_n)$ respectively as the private ephemeral keys
4: Let SK be the common session key agreed among $S_1, S_2, \ldots, S_n$
5: **for** $i \leftarrow 1$ **to** n **do in parallel**
6:     Each cluster node in C_i computes the session key SK in the same way as S_i does
7: **end for**

Group Key Maintenance. The following steps are performed in order to update group session key to handle dynamic membership change.

- **Step 1:** Suppose a set of nodes U wants to join/leave the cluster C_i. Update the cluster keys in the clusters where membership changes have occurred by invoking ClusterKeyUpdate. See Algorithm 3.
- **Step 2:** Now consider the virtual ternary tree as in DBS with leaf nodes as the sponsors (or clusters). We update the common session key (at root level) by updating the keys along the paths from modified clusters to root node in the tree by invoking a procedure UpdateKeyPath as described below.
  Let a membership change (join/leave) has occurred within a cluster. Let path be the path from modified leaf node (cluster) to root in the virtual ternary tree. Let h be the height of the tree and for $1 \leq l \leq h$, i_l be the index of the node at level l whose subtree will contain the modified cluster as a leaf. Parse path $= (i_0, i_1, \ldots, i_h)$. Then path represents the path from modified cluster at the leaf to the root node in the tree, where i_0 is the index of the leaf node (modified cluster). The algorithm UpdateKeyPath works as follows to update keys in level 1 on dynamic membership change due to join/leave.

In the key tree, the number of children of the node i_1 (node at level 1) in the key path is either 1 or 2 or 3. If i_1 has 1 leaf node, then this corresponds to the modified cluster itself. The sponsor corresponding to this leaf node uses the updated cluster key as the new ephemeral private key for the next level. In case i_1 has 2 leaf nodes, the sponsors corresponding to these leaves invoke CombineTwo with their respective cluster keys as their ephemeral private keys to agree upon a common key among them. If i_1 has 3 leaves, then the sponsors corresponding to these leaves invoke CombineThree with their respective cluster keys as their ephemeral private keys to agree upon a common key among them. The subsequent user sets are accordingly changed by algorithm UpdateKeyPath and key updates in level $l + 1$ ($1 \leq l \leq h - 1$) are done by invoking algorithm CombineThree among the three user sets which are subtrees of node i_{l+1}. The modified user set corresponding to the node i_l invokes CombineThree to agree upon a common key with the user sets corresponding to the other two subtrees (siblings of i_l) of node i_{l+1}. We proceed in this way and finally a common key is agreed among all the sponsors. We assume that other cluster nodes in a particular cluster receive all the messages which the sponsor of that cluster is supposed receive in order to compute the updated common session key in the same way as the sponsor of that cluster does.

3.4   Authenticated Protocols AP − 1 and AP − 2

We now describe the idea of transforming our unauthenticated protocols UP − 1 and UP − 2 to secure authenticated protocols AP − 1 and AP − 2 respectively to mount attacks against an active adversary. We adapt the authentication mechanism used by [13], [14] which is an efficient and simplified variant of Katz-Yung [21] generic technique for converting any group key agreement protocol secure against a passive adversary to a group key agreement protocol secure against an active adversary. We use a digital signature scheme DSig = (, $\mathcal{S}, \mathcal{V}$) which is strongly unforgeable under adaptive chosen plaintext attack. Here is key generation algorithm, $\mathcal{S}$ is signature generation algorithm and $\mathcal{V}$ is signature verification algorithm. Let $\mathsf{Adv}_{\mathsf{DSig}}(t)$ denote the maximum advantage of any adversary running in time t in gorging a new message-signature pair. For simplicity, we assume that the signature length is independent of the length of the message signed, which can be achieve in practice by using collision-resistance hash function on the message. We describe briefly the construction of AP − 1 from UP − 1. A similar construction can be given for AP − 2 from UP − 2. From henceforth, $A|B$ stands for concatenation of elements A and B.

1. As part of the signature scheme, each user U_i chooses a signing and a verification key sk_{U_i} and pk_{U_i} respectively by running the key generation algorithm.
2. The users in the network now execute the protocol UP − 1 with the following modifications:
   (a) Quite often, we identify a user U_i with its instance $\Pi_{U_i}^{d_i}$ for some integer d_i that is session specific. Let m be the t-th message broadcast by instance $\Pi_{U_i}^{d_i}$ with identity U_i as part of the protocol UP − 1. Then for the

protocol $\mathsf{AP}-1$, instance $\Pi_{U_i}^{d_i}$ replaces m by $M_i = U_i|t|m|d_i$, computes the signature $\sigma_i = \mathcal{S}(\mathsf{sk}_{U_i}, M_i)$ and broadcasts $M_i|\sigma_i$.

(b) Let instance $\Pi_{U_i}^{d_i}$ receives a message of the form $U_j|t|m|d_j|\sigma_j$ as part of the protocol $\mathsf{AP}-1$. Then $\Pi_{U_i}^{d_i}$ checks that:

- $U_j \in \mathsf{pid}_{U_i}^{d_i}$, $\mathsf{pid}_{U_i}^{d_i}$ being the partner identity for $\Pi_{U_i}^{d_i}$ (see Section 2.6);
- t is the next expected message number for messages from $\Pi_{U_j}^{d_j}$; and
- the validity of the signature σ_j using the verification algorithm $\mathcal{V}$ and respective verification key pk_{U_i}. If verification fails, then $\Pi_{U_i}^{d_i}$ sets $\mathsf{acc}_{U_i}^{d_i} = 0$, $\mathsf{sk}_{U_i}^{d_i} = \mathsf{NULL}$ and aborts. Otherwise, $\Pi_{U_i}^{d_i}$ continues as it would in $\mathsf{UP}-1$ upon receiving t-th message m from instance $\Pi_{U_j}^{d_j}$.

3. Each non-aborted instance computes the session key as in $\mathsf{UP}-1$ and builds up the session identity as the protocol proceeds by extracting the identities and instance numbers of the participants from the publicly transmitted messages. The detail construction of session identity will be described shortly.

We point the following issues related to the above authentication mechanism.

- *Partner identity:* We assume that any instance $\Pi_{U_j}^{d_j}$ knows its partner identity $\mathsf{pid}_{U_j}^{d_j}$, which is essentially the set of users with which it is partnered in the particular session.
- *Numbering of the messages:* Any instance $\Pi_{U_j}^{d_j}$ sends out a finite (two) number of messages, which can be uniquely numbered by $\Pi_{U_j}^{d_j}$ based on their order of occurrence.
- *Session identity:* This is defined in a different way than Katz-Yung and plays an important role in authenticating our protocols. Session identity is required to identify a session uniquely and all participants executing a session should hold the same session identity. Conventionally, session identity sid_U^i for an instance Π_U^i is set to be concatenation of all (broadcast) messages sent and received by Π_U^i during its course of execution. This essentially assumes that all the partners of Π_U^i hold the same concatenation value of sent and received messages which may not be the case in general. Our definition of session identity is different and can be applied for more general protocols. Suppose users $U_{i_1}, \ldots, U_{i_k}$ wish to agree upon a common key in a session using unused instances $\Pi_{U_{i_1}}^{d_1}, \ldots, \Pi_{U_{i_k}}^{d_k}$. According to our definition in Section 2.6, $\mathsf{sid}_{U_{i_j}}^{d_j} = \{(U_{i_1}, d_1), \ldots, (U_{i_k}, d_k)\}$. At the start of the session, $\Pi_{U_{i_j}}^{d_j}$ need not to know the entire set $\mathsf{sid}_{U_{i_j}}^{d_j}$. This set is built up as the protocol proceeds. Of course, we assume that $\Pi_{U_{i_j}}^{d_j}$ knows the pair (U_{i_j}, d_j). Clearly, $\Pi_{U_{i_j}}^{d_j}$ knows U_{i_j}. Knowledge of d_j can be maintained by U_{i_j} by keeping a counter which is incremented when a new instance is created. Each instance keeps the partial information about the session identity in a variable psid_U^i. Before the start of a session an instance $\Pi_{U_{i_j}}^{d_j}$ sets $\mathsf{psid}_{U_{i_j}}^{d_j} = \{(U_{i_j}, d_j)\}$. As the protocol proceeds, $\Pi_{U_{i_j}}^{d_j}$ keeps on extracting identity- instance number

pairs of other instances engaged in that session. Notice that identity- instance number pairs are "patched" with appropriate signatures in the publicly transmitted messages of $\mathsf{AP} - 1$. After completion of the session, $\mathsf{psid}_{U_{i_j}}^{d_j}$ $= \mathsf{sid}_{U_{i_j}}^{d_j} = \{(U_{i_1}, d_1), \ldots, (U_{i_k}, d_k)\}$. We refer to [11], [14] for join and leave algorithms where the detail construction of session identity sid from partial session identity psid is provided.

We will make the assumption that in each session at most one instance of each user participates. Further, an instance of a particular user participates in exactly one session. This is not a very restrictive assumption, since a user can spawn an instance for each session it participates in. On the other hand, there is an important consequence of this assumption. Suppose there are several sessions which are being concurrently executed. Let the session identities be $\mathsf{sid}_1, \ldots, \mathsf{sid}_k$. Then for any instance Π_U^i, there is at most one j such that $(U, i) \in \mathsf{sid}_j$ and for any $j_1 \neq j_2$, we have $\mathsf{sid}_{j_1} \cap \mathsf{sid}_{j_2} = \emptyset$. Thus at any particular point of time, if we consider the collection of all instances of all users, then the relation of being in the same session is an equivalence relation whose equivalence classes are the session identities. Moreover, an instance Π_U^i not only knows U, but also the instance number i – this being achieved by maintaining a counter.

We bind the session identity with the message transmitted during our protocol execution. Since session identities uniquely identifies a session and all users in a particular session hold the same session identity, such an inclusion of session identity in transmitted messages prevents replay attack. In replay attack, adversary uses messages transmitted in a previous session in current session to obtain some information. The use of previously transmitted message in the current session is not valid as session identities are different.

The above variant of Katz-Yung compiler [21] reduces communication rounds by one by avoiding random nonces. Unlike Katz-Yung, we do not need any extra round for communication of random nonces during the initialization phase. A setting of unique instance number is used instead, which additionally avoids the event Repeat that comes in Katz-Yung security proof, thus reducing complexity of Katz-Yung compiler with a tighter security proof.

4 Security Analysis

We consider the security of the initial key agreement (IKA) phase and the group key management (GKM) phase of our proposed protocols separately. Let $\mathsf{UP} -$ 1.IKA and $\mathsf{UP} - 1.\mathsf{GKM}$ respectively denote the IKA and GKM phase of the protocol $\mathsf{UP} - 1$. Similarly, we define $\mathsf{UP} - 2.\mathsf{IKA}$, $\mathsf{UP} - 2.\mathsf{GKM}$ for $\mathsf{UP} - 2$, $\mathsf{AP} - 1.\mathsf{IKA}$, $\mathsf{AP} - 1.\mathsf{GKM}$ for $\mathsf{AP} - 1$, and $\mathsf{AP} - 2.\mathsf{IKA}$, $\mathsf{AP} - 2.\mathsf{GKM}$ for $\mathsf{AP} - 2$.

We first state the security results of $\mathsf{UP} - 2.\mathsf{IKA}$ and $\mathsf{UP} - 1.\mathsf{IKA}$ in Theorem 1 and Theorem 2 respectively and present the proof of Theorem 1 which makes use of Lemma 1 and Lemma 2. A similar proof holds for Theorem 2. Lemma 1 is the security result of DBS protocol against passive adversary and we refer to [11] for its proof. Lemma 2 is the security result of DB protocol against passive adversary and we refer to [13], [14] for its proof.

Lemma 1. *[11] The unauthenticated protocol* DBS *described in Section 2.4 is secure against passive adversary under DHBDH assumption.*

Lemma 2. *[13], [14] The unauthenticated protocol* DB *described in Section 2.5 is secure against passive adversary under DDH assumption, achieves forward secrecy and satisfies the following:* $\mathsf{Adv}_{\mathsf{DB}}^{\mathsf{KA}}(t, q_E) \leq 4 \ \mathsf{Adv}_G^{\mathsf{DDH}}(t') + \frac{4q_E}{|G|}$ *where* $t' = t + O(|\mathcal{P}| \ q_E \ t_{exp})$, t_{exp} *is the time required to perform exponentiation in* G, $|\mathcal{P}|$ *is number of participants in the network (which is a fixed number) and* q_E *is the number of* Execute *queries that an adversary may ask.*

Theorem 1. *The unauthenticated static group key agreement protocol* UP − 2.IKA *described in Section 3.3 is secure against passive adversary under DDH assumption, achieves forward secrecy and satisfies the following:*

$$\mathsf{Adv}_{\mathsf{UP-2.IKA}}^{\mathsf{KA}}(t, q_E) \leq \frac{2 \ \mathsf{Adv}_G^{\mathsf{DDH}}(t')}{n q_E} + \frac{2}{|G|} + \mathsf{Adv}_{\mathsf{DBS}}^{\mathsf{KA}}(t, q_E) + \frac{1}{2 n q_E}$$

where $t' = t + O(|\mathcal{P}_{\max}| \ n \ q_E \ t_{exp})$, t_{exp} *is the time required to perform exponentiation in* G, $|\mathcal{P}_{\max}|$ *is maximum number of nodes in a cluster (which is a fixed number), n is the number of clusters in the network, and q_E is the maximum number of* Execute *queries that an adversary may ask.*

Proof : The proof considers a passive adversary $\mathcal{A}$ who defeats the security of our unauthenticated static group key agreement protocol UP − 2.IKA. Given $\mathcal{A}$, we construct a passive adversary $\mathcal{B}$ attacking the unauthenticated protocol DBS. Relating the success probability of $\mathcal{A}$ and $\mathcal{B}$ gives the stated result of the Theorem. Before describing $\mathcal{B}$, we first define event Bad and bound its probability.

Let Bad be the event that $\mathcal{A}$ is able to distinguish a cluster key (which is a key agreed by DB protocol) from a random value at any point during its execution. Let Prob[Bad] stands for $\mathsf{Prob}_{\mathcal{A},\mathsf{UP-2.IKA}}[\mathsf{Bad}]$. Let Succ denote the event that $\mathcal{A}$ wins the game as described in the security model in Section 2.6 for key agreement protocol DB. Notice that with n clusters in the network, each execution of UP − 2.IKA invokes DB protocol n times to form the cluster keys and DBS protocol only once to form the group session key. The adversary $\mathcal{A}$ makes q_E Execute queries and consequently performs nq_E execution of DB protocol and q_E execution of DBS protocol. Consequently, $\mathsf{Prob}[\mathsf{Bad}] \leq \frac{\mathsf{Prob}[\mathsf{Succ}]}{n q_E}$. Now by definition in Section 2.6, $\mathsf{Adv}_{\mathsf{DB},\mathcal{A}}^{\mathsf{KA}} = |2 \ \mathsf{Prob}[\mathsf{Succ}] - 1|$, which implies $\mathsf{Prob}[\mathsf{Succ}] \leq \frac{\mathsf{Adv}_{\mathsf{DB},\mathcal{A}}^{\mathsf{KA}} + 1}{2}$.

$\mathcal{B}$ simulates all oracle queries of $\mathcal{A}$ by executing the protocol UP − 2.IKA itself. Then $\mathcal{B}$ provides a perfect simulation for $\mathcal{A}$ as long as the event Bad does not occur. If ever the event Bad occurs, $\mathcal{B}$ aborts and outputs a random bit. Otherwise, $\mathcal{B}$ outputs whatever bit is eventually output by $\mathcal{A}$. So $\mathsf{Prob}_{\mathcal{A},\mathsf{UP-2.IKA}}[\mathsf{Succ}|\mathsf{Bad}] = \frac{1}{2}$. Now

$$\mathsf{Adv}_{\mathcal{B},\mathsf{DBS}} := 2 \; |\mathsf{Prob}_{\mathcal{B},\mathsf{DBS}}[\mathsf{Succ}] - 1/2|$$

$$= 2 \; |\mathsf{Prob}_{\mathcal{A},\mathsf{UP-2.IKA}}[\mathsf{Succ} \wedge \overline{\mathsf{Bad}}] + \mathsf{Prob}_{\mathcal{A},\mathsf{UP-2.IKA}}[\mathsf{Succ} \wedge \mathsf{Bad}] - 1/2|$$

$$= 2 \; |\mathsf{Prob}_{\mathcal{A},\mathsf{UP-2.IKA}}[\mathsf{Succ} \wedge \overline{\mathsf{Bad}}] + (1/2)\mathsf{Prob}_{\mathcal{A},\mathsf{UP-2.IKA}}[\mathsf{Bad}] - 1/2|$$

$$= 2 \; |\mathsf{Prob}_{\mathcal{A},\mathsf{UP-2.IKA}}[\mathsf{Succ}] - \mathsf{Prob}_{\mathcal{A},\mathsf{UP-2.IKA}}[\mathsf{Succ} \wedge \mathsf{Bad}]$$
$$+ (1/2)\mathsf{Prob}_{\mathcal{A},\mathsf{UP-2.IKA}}[\mathsf{Bad}] - 1/2|$$

$$\geq |2 \; \mathsf{Prob}_{\mathcal{A},\mathsf{UP-2.IKA}}[\mathsf{Succ}] - 1| - |\mathsf{Prob}_{\mathcal{A},\mathsf{UP-2.IKA}}[\mathsf{Bad}]$$
$$- 2 \; \mathsf{Prob}_{\mathcal{A},\mathsf{UP-2.IKA}}[\mathsf{Succ} \wedge \mathsf{Bad}]|$$

$$\geq \mathsf{Adv}_{\mathcal{A},\mathsf{UP-2.IKA}} - \mathsf{Prob}[\mathsf{Bad}]$$

Also since $\mathsf{Adv}_{\mathcal{B},\mathsf{DBS}} \leq \mathsf{Adv}_{\mathsf{DBS}}(t, q_E)$ by assumption, we obtain

$$\mathsf{Adv}_{\mathsf{UP-2.IKA}}(t, q_E) \leq \mathsf{Adv}_{\mathsf{DBS}}(t, q_E) + \mathsf{Prob}[\mathsf{Bad}]$$

$$\leq \mathsf{Adv}_{\mathsf{DBS}}(t, q_E) + \frac{\mathsf{Adv}_{\mathsf{DB},\mathcal{A}}^{\mathsf{KA}}(t, nq_E) + 1}{2nq_E}$$

$$\leq \mathsf{Adv}_{\mathsf{DBS}}(t, q_E) + \frac{2 \; \mathsf{Adv}_G^{\mathsf{DDH}}(t')}{nq_E} + \frac{2}{|G|} + \frac{1}{2nq_E}$$

by Lemma 1 and Lemma 2 where t' is as in the Theorem. Hence we obtain the statement of the theorem.

Theorem 2. *The unauthenticated static group key agreement protocol* UP − 1.IKA *described in Section 3.2 is secure against passive adversary under DDH assumption, achieves forward secrecy and satisfies the following:*

$$\mathsf{Adv}_{\mathsf{UP-1.IKA}}^{\mathsf{KA}}(t, q_E) \leq \frac{2\mathsf{Adv}_G^{\mathsf{DDH}}(t')}{(n+1)q_E} + \frac{2}{|G|} + \frac{1}{2(n+1)q_E}$$

where $t' = t + O(|\mathcal{P}_{\max}| \, n \, q_E \, t_{exp})$, t_{exp} *is the time required to perform exponentiation in* G, $|\mathcal{P}_{\max}|$ *is maximum number of nodes in a cluster (which is a fixed number),* n *is the number of clusters in the network, and* q_E *is the maximum number of* Execute *queries that an adversary may ask.*

Next we consider the security of the static authenticated protocols AP − 1.IKA and AP − 2.IKA and security of dynamic authenticated protocols AP − 1.GKM and AP − 2.GKM and state the respective results in Theorem 3, Theorem 4, Theorem 5 and Theorem 6. The security of all these authenticated protocols rely on that of unauthenticated UP − 1.IKA and UP − 2.IKA protocols assuming that the signature scheme DSig is secure. Since we use the authentication mechanism of [13], [14], the proofs of these theorems are exactly similar to the reduction proof technique used by [13], [14].

Theorem 3. *The authenticated protocol* AP − 1.IKA *described in section 3.4 is secure against active adversary under DDH assumption, achieves forward secrecy and satisfies the following:*

$$\mathsf{Adv}_{\mathsf{AP-1.IKA}}^{\mathsf{AKA}}(t, q_E, q_S) \leq \mathsf{Adv}_{\mathsf{UP-1.IKA}}^{\mathsf{KA}}(t', q_E + \frac{q_S}{2}) + |\mathcal{P}| \; \mathsf{Adv}_{\mathsf{DSig}}(t')$$

where $t' \leq t + (|\mathcal{P}|q_E + q_S)t_{\mathsf{AP}-1.\mathsf{IKA}}$, with $t_{\mathsf{AP}-1.\mathsf{IKA}}$ is the time required for execution of $\mathsf{AP} - 1.\mathsf{IKA}$ by any party, q_E and q_S are respectively the maximum number of Execute and Send query an adversary may ask.

Theorem 4. *The authenticated protocol* $\mathsf{AP} - 2.\mathsf{IKA}$ *described in section 3.4 is secure against active adversary under DDH assumption, achieves forward secrecy and satisfies the following:*

$$\mathsf{Adv}^{\mathsf{AKA}}_{\mathsf{AP}-2.\mathsf{IKA}}(t, q_E, q_S) \leq \mathsf{Adv}^{\mathsf{KA}}_{\mathsf{UP}-2.\mathsf{IKA}}(t', q_E + \frac{q_S}{2}) + |\mathcal{P}| \, \mathsf{Adv}_{\mathsf{DSig}}(t')$$

where $t' \leq t + (|\mathcal{P}|q_E + q_S)t_{\mathsf{AP}-2.\mathsf{IKA}}$, with $t_{\mathsf{AP}-2.\mathsf{IKA}}$ is the time required for execution of $\mathsf{AP} - 2.\mathsf{IKA}$ by any party, q_E and q_S are respectively the maximum number of Execute and Send query an adversary may ask.

Theorem 5. *The dynamic authenticated key agreement protocol* $\mathsf{AP} - 1.\mathsf{GKM}$ *described in Section 3.4 satisfies the following:*

$$\mathsf{Adv}^{\mathsf{AKA}}_{\mathsf{AP}-1.\mathsf{GKM}}(t, q_E, q_J, q_L, q_S) \leq \mathsf{Adv}^{\mathsf{KA}}_{\mathsf{UP}-1.\mathsf{IKA}}(t', q_E + \frac{q_J + q_L + q_S}{2}) + |\mathcal{P}| \, \mathsf{Adv}_{\mathsf{DSig}}(t')$$

where $t' \leq t + (|\mathcal{P}|q_E + q_J + q_L + q_S)t_{\mathsf{AP}-1.\mathsf{GKM}}$, with $t_{\mathsf{AP}-1.\mathsf{GKM}}$ is the time required for execution of $\mathsf{AP} - 1.\mathsf{GKM}$ by any party, q_E, q_S, q_J and q_L are respectively the maximum number of Execute, Send, Join and Leave query an adversary may ask.

Theorem 6. *The dynamic authenticated key agreement protocol* $\mathsf{AP} - 2.\mathsf{GKM}$ *described in Section 3.4 satisfies the following:*

$$\mathsf{Adv}^{\mathsf{AKA}}_{\mathsf{AP}-2.\mathsf{GKM}}(t, q_E, q_J, q_L, q_S) \leq \mathsf{Adv}^{\mathsf{KA}}_{\mathsf{UP}-2.\mathsf{IKA}}(t', q_E + \frac{q_J + q_L + q_S}{2}) + |\mathcal{P}| \, \mathsf{Adv}_{\mathsf{DSig}}(t')$$

where $t' \leq t + (|\mathcal{P}|q_E + q_J + q_L + q_S)t_{\mathsf{AP}-2.\mathsf{GKM}}$, with $t_{\mathsf{AP}-2.\mathsf{GKM}}$ is the time required for execution of $\mathsf{AP} - 2.\mathsf{GKM}$ by any party, q_E, q_S, q_J and q_L are respectively the maximum number of Execute, Send, Join and Leave query an adversary may ask.

A brief sketch of how the proofs are achieved is the following: We transform an active adversary $\mathcal{A}'$ attacking authenticated protocol P' into a passive adversary $\mathcal{A}$ attacking the underlying unauthenticated protocol P. Adversary $\mathcal{A}$ generates the verification/signing keys pk_U, sk_U for each user $U \in \mathcal{P}$ and gives the verification keys to $\mathcal{A}'$. We define event Forge to be the event that a signature of DSig is forged by $\mathcal{A}'$ and bound its probability following [21] by $\mathsf{Prob}[\mathsf{Forge}] \leq |\mathcal{P}| \, \mathsf{Adv}_{\mathsf{DSig}}(t')$. If ever the event Forge occurs, adversary $\mathcal{A}$ aborts and outputs a random bit. Otherwise, $\mathcal{A}$ outputs whatever bit is eventually output by $\mathcal{A}'$. Note that since the signing and verification keys are generated by $\mathcal{A}$, it can detect occurrence of the event Forge.

$\mathcal{A}$ simulates the oracle queries of $\mathcal{A}'$ using its own queries to the Execute oracle. The idea is that the adversary $\mathcal{A}$ queried its Execute oracle to obtain a transcript T of P for each Execute query of $\mathcal{A}'$ and also for each initial send query $\mathsf{Send}_0(U, i, *)$ of $\mathcal{A}'$. For dynamic case also, $\mathcal{A}$ itself simulates all the oracle queries including Join and Leave oracles of $\mathcal{A}'$ using its own Execute and Reveal oracles as in [13], [14]. $\mathcal{A}$ then patches appropriate signatures with the messages in T to obtain a transcript T' of P' and uses T' to answer queries of $\mathcal{A}'$. Since $\mathcal{A}'$ can not forge signatures with respect to any of the users, $\mathcal{A}'$ is 'limited' to send messages already contained in T'. This technique provides a good simulation. Finally, we relate the advantages of $\mathcal{A}'$ and $\mathcal{A}$ as

$$\mathsf{Adv}_{\mathcal{A},P}^{\mathsf{AKA}} \leq \mathsf{Adv}_{\mathcal{A},P}^{\mathsf{KA}}(t', q_E + q_S/2) + \mathsf{Prob}[\mathsf{Forge}]$$

which gives the results stated in the above theorems. We skip the proofs here due to space constraints and refer to [13], [14] for details of oracle simulations.

The way we bind session identity with each message in our protocol run, enables to handle replay attacks without using random nonces as in Katz-Yung [21]. In our unauthenticated protocols, there are no long term secret keys. Thus we can avoid Corrupt oracle queries and the unauthenticated protocols trivially achieve forward secrecy. Then following Katz-Yung [21], we can avoid Corrupt query for our authenticated protocols (both static and dynamic) also, because this query for the authenticated protocols outputs long-term secret key (if any), defined as part of the unauthenticated protocol. Thus we can trivially achieve forward secrecy for the authenticated protocols.

5   Efficiency

Concerning the efficiency, notice that both our proposed protocols make use of multi-party dynamic key agreement protocol DB which is pairing-free and our second protocol uses multi-party dynamic key agreement protocol DBS which is pairing-based. So we first provide the complexity of DB.Setup, DB.Join, DB.Leave and DBS.Setup in Tables 1, 2, 3 and 4. Then we discuss a comparative summary of the performance analysis of our two protocols $\mathsf{AP}-1$ and $\mathsf{AP}-2$ and mention how an improvement over our pairing-based protocol $\mathsf{AP}-2$ can be achieved by using pairing-less TGDH [22] protocol instead of pairing-based DBS protocol and thus avoiding use of computation-intensive pairings. Table 1 provides the complexity of TGDH.Setup which is initial key agreement phase of TGDH.

In the tables, R stands for total number of rounds, B is the maximum number of broadcast communications per user, Exp is the maximum number of modular exponentiation computed per user, Mul is the maximum number of modular multiplication computed per user, Hash is the maximum number of hash functions $(H, \mathcal{H}, \mathcal{H}_0)$ computed per user, Div is the maximum number of division computed per user, P is the maximum number of pairings computed per user, SM is the maximum number of scalar multiplication in G_1 computed per user, Sig is the maximum number of signature generated per user, and Ver is the maximum number of signature verification per user.

Note that for initial key agreement (IKA) phase in $\mathsf{AP}-1$, we invoke DB.Setup twice - once among the cluster nodes in each cluster and once among the ring of sponsors. So complexity of each sponsor node is just twice the complexity of DB.Setup together with one $\mathcal{H}_0$ evaluation. On the other hand, each cluster

Table 1. Complexity of n-party TGDH.Setup and DB.Setup

Protocol	Communication		Computation					
	R	B	Exp	Mul	Div	Sig	Ver	Hash
TGDH.Setup	$\lceil \log_2 n \rceil$	$\leq \lceil \log_2 n \rceil$	$\lceil \log_2 n \rceil$	0	0	$\lceil \log_2 n \rceil$	$\lceil \log_2 n \rceil$	$\lceil \log_2 n \rceil$
DB.Setup	2	2	3	$2n-2$	1	2	$n+1$	1

Table 2. DB.Join - a set of users $U[n+1, \ldots, n+m]$ joins the set of users $U[1, \ldots, n]$, resulting a user set of size $n+m$

DB.Join	Communication		Computation					
	R	B	Exp	Mul	Div	Sig	Ver	Hash
$U_1, U_2, U[n, \ldots, n+m]$	2	2	3	$2m+4$	1	2	$m+4$	1
$U[3, \ldots, n-1]$		0	2	$2m+4$	0	0	$m+5$	1

Table 3. DB.Leave - users $U_{l_1}, \ldots, U_{l_m}$ leave the set of users $U[1, \ldots, n]$, resulting a new user set of size $n-m$. Users U_{l_i-L}, U_{l_i+R} are respectively the closest non-leaving left and right neighbours of the leaving user U_{l_i} for $1 \leq i \leq m$. 'Rest of the users' in the table means users in $U[1, \ldots, n] \setminus (\{U_{l_1}, \ldots, U_{l_m}\} \cup \{U_{l_i-L-1}, U_{l_i-L}, U_{l_i+R}, U_{l_i+R+1}, 1 \leq i \leq m\})$.

DB.Leave	Communication		Computation					
	R	B	Exp	Mul	Div	Sig	Ver	Hash
$U_{l_i-L}, U_{l_i+R}, 1 \leq i \leq m$	2	2	3	$2(n-m)-2$	1	2	$n-m+1$	1
$U_{l_i-L-1}, U_{l_i+R+1}, 1 \leq i \leq m$		2	1	$2(n-m)-2$	1	2	$n-m+1$	1
Rest of the users		1	0	$2(n-m)-2$	1	1	$n-m+1$	1

Table 4. Complexity of pairing-based n-party DBS.Setup

Protocol	Communication		Computation					
	R	B	Exp in G_2	SM	P	Sig	Ver	Hash
DBS.Setup	$\lceil \log_3 n \rceil$	$\leq \lceil \log_3 n \rceil$	$\lceil \log_3 n \rceil$	$\leq \lceil \log_3 n \rceil$	$\lceil \log_3 n \rceil$	$\leq \lceil \log_3 n \rceil$	$\lceil \log_3 n \rceil$	$\lceil \log_3 n \rceil$

node other than the sponsors does not participate in the communication during execution of DB.Setup among the ring of sponsors, but they perform the same computation as the sponsors to compute the session key. This yields a reduction in the communication cost for most of the nodes in the system.

Similarly, for IKA phase in $AP-2$, we invoke DB.Setup once among the cluster nodes in each cluster and DBS once among the sponsors who are arranged as leaf nodes in a balanced ternary tree. Hence complexity of each node is based on the complexity of these two protocols (see Tables 1,4) together with one $\mathcal{H}_0$ evaluation. We gain a reduction in the communication costs for most of the cluster nodes as they do not participate in the communication during the execution of DBS, however they have the same computation cost as the sponsors to compute the group session key.

Let us now analyse the complexity of each node for group key maintenance (GKM) phase of $AP-1$. For a member join in a cluster, DB.Join is invoked once among all the cluster nodes within that cluster and once again among the ring of sponsors after placing the sponsor corresponding to modified cluster (where member join has occurred) at the end of the ring. For a member leave from a cluster, DB.Leave is invoked once among all the cluster nodes within that cluster, DB.Setup is invoked among the cluster nodes in each of the neighboring clusters of the modified cluster (where member leave has occurred) and DB.Leave is invoked once again among the ring of sponsors. Although second invocation of DB.Leave is only among the sponsors, the other cluster nodes perform the same computation as the sponsors to compute the session key without participating actively in the communication.

Next consider the complexity of each node for GKM phase of AP − 2. For a dynamic membership change in a cluster, DB.Join or DB.Leave is invoked once among all the cluster nodes within that cluster and session key update is done along the path from modified leaf node (*i.e.* the sponsor corresponding to the cluster where membership change has occurred) to the root in the ternary tree of sponsors with communication and computation complexity $\leq \lceil \log_3 n \rceil$ each. This leads to a significant reduction in both communication and computation overhead as compared to GKM phase of AP − 1.

In contrast of invoking the DB or DBS protocol from scratch among all the nodes in the system (which may be infeasible in ad hoc environments), we obtain efficiency gain in terms of both communication and computation for most of the nodes in our proposed cluster-based protocols (which are more amenable to wireless ad hoc networks). Since communication complexity of DB.Setup is less than that of DBS.Setup as evident from Tables 1,4, IKA phase of AP − 1 is communicationally more efficient that the IKA phase of AP − 2. On the other hand, as discussed above, AP − 2 uses a tree structure with leaf nodes as sponsors and consequently handling dynamic events in the clustered network is easier in its GKM phase as compared to GKM phase of AP − 1 which uses a ring structure of sponsors. Moreover, AP − 2 is efficient as compared to the existing contributory group key agreement protocols [1], [19], [23], [34] that use clusters and pairings. Now according to the results in [25], [31], the timing of pairings is more than that of modular exponentiation in RSA [27]. So pairings are not suitable for some time-intensive cases. In such a scenario, AP − 1 may be more efficient than AP − 2. We may replace DBS protocol in designing AP − 2 by TGDH protocol which does not use pairings. Then this yields a protocol, say AP − 3, which is dynamically more efficient than AP − 2 in terms of computation with an increase in the communication overhead, because the tree structure in TGDH protocol is binary whereas that in DBS protocol is ternary. The modular exponentiation and signature computed by each node in AP − 3 is logarithmic to n, the number of nodes in the system whereas that for AP − 1 is constant. However, the modular multiplication, signature verification by each node in AP − 3 is logarithmic to n whereas that for AP − 1 is linear to n and handling dynamic events is easier in AP − 3 is efficient as compared to that in AP − 1.

In summary, AP − 1 is communicationally more efficient that AP − 2 or AP − 3, but computationally AP − 2 or AP − 3 is more efficient than AP − 1. Also group key maintenance for dynamic membership change can be done more efficiently in $AP - 2$ or $AP - 3$ as compared to $AP - 1$. We may use Scott *et al.*'s [32] implementation to accelerate paring computation on smart cards for our protocol $AP - 2$ which may then be computationally comparable with $AP - 3$.

Our proposed protocols are highly efficient as compared to the existing cluster based key agreement protocols [1], [19], [23], [24], [34], [36] which are all tree-based. A detail comparison of these protocols with our tree-based scheme $AP - 2$ is provided in related works of Introduction.

6   Conclusions and Future Work

Ad hoc networks may be logically represented as a set of clusters. We have presented two authenticated and communication efficient group key agreement protocols in the cluster based ad hoc environment. This work is largely based on works previously done by us and existing techniques. The protocols support dynamic membership events and their communication and computation efficiencies are favourably compared to previous group key agreement protocols in a cluster based structure. We have distinguished between the two approaches from a performance point of view and shown that the second scheme is the better scheme in the context of wireless ad hoc networks. While our first scheme is designed without pairings and uses a ring topology of sponsors, our second scheme is pairing-based and uses a tree structure with leaf nodes as sponsors. We have shown that our first scheme is communicationally more efficient than our second scheme whilst our second scheme is computationally more efficient than our first scheme. Moreover, dynamic events such as join/leave are handled more efficiently in our second scheme than our first scheme with reduced communication and computation costs for most of the nodes in the system. We have proved both schemes to be provably secure in the standard model under standard cryptographic assumptions. It may be infeasible in an ad hoc environment with large number of nodes to invoke a group key agreement protocol from scratch among all the nodes in the system. In contrast, our approaches are more amenable to wireless ad hoc networks with huge number of nodes and enable efficiency gain in both communication and computation for most of the users. We have also provided an improvement over our pairing-based scheme by avoiding use of computation-intensive pairings with a trade-off in communication complexity.

As a future work, we plan to implement our key agreement schemes to analyse performance from a practical point of view in the context of Elliptic Curve Cryptography (ECC) as this is most suitable for resource constrained mobile devices that generates the smaller key sizes and provides more efficient computation compared to other public key cryptosystems.

Acknowledgments. Authors would like to thank anonymous reviewers for providing constructive and generous feedback. Despite their invaluable assistance any error remaining in this paper is solely attributed to the author.

References

1. Abdel-Hafez, A., Miri, A., Oronzo-Barbosa, L.: Authenticated Group Key Agreement Protocols for Ad hoc Wireless Networks. Int. Journal of Network Security 4(1), 90–98 (2007)
2. Baker, D.J., Ephremides, A.: The Architectural Organization of a Mobile Radio Network via a Distributed Algorithm. IEEE Transactions on Communications, COM-29(11), 1694–1701 (1981)
3. Baker, D.J., Ephremides, A., Flynn, J.A.: The Design and Simulation of a Mobile Radio Network with Distributed Control. IEEE Journal on Selected Areas in Communications, 226–237 (1984)
4. Belding-Royer, E.M.: Hierarchical Routing in Ad hoc Mobile Networks. Wireless Communication & Mobile Computing 2(5), 515–532 (2002)
5. Barreto, P.S.L.M., Kim, H.Y., Lynn, B., Scott, M.: Efficient algorithms for pairing-based cryptosystems. In: Yung, M. (ed.) CRYPTO 2002. LNCS, vol. 2442, pp. 354–368. Springer, Heidelberg (2002)
6. Boneh, D., Franklin, M.: Identity-Based Encryption from the Weil Pairing. In: Kilian, J. (ed.) CRYPTO 2001. LNCS, vol. 2139, pp. 213–229. Springer, Heidelberg (2001)
7. Bresson, E., Chevassut, O., Pointcheval, D.: Dynamic Group Diffie-Hellman Key Exchange under Standard Assumptions. In: Knudsen, L.R. (ed.) EUROCRYPT 2002. LNCS, vol. 2332, pp. 321–336. Springer, Heidelberg (2002)
8. Burmester, M., Desmedt, Y.: A Secure and Efficient Conference Key Distribution System. In: De Santis, A. (ed.) EUROCRYPT 1994. LNCS, vol. 950, pp. 275–286. Springer, Heidelberg (1995)
9. Burmester, M., Desmedt, Y.: A Secure and Scalable Group Key Exchange System. Information Processing Letters 94(3), 137–143 (2005)
10. Diffie, W., Hellman, M.: New directions in cryptography. IEEE Transaction on Information Theory, IT-22 (6), 644–654 (1976)
11. Dutta, R., Barua, R., Sarkar, P.: Provably Secure Authenticated Tree Based Group Key Agreement. In: López, J., Qing, S., Okamoto, E. (eds.) ICICS 2004. LNCS, vol. 3269, pp. 92–104. Springer, Heidelberg (2004)
12. Dutta, R., Barua, R.: Dynamic Group Key Agreement in Tree-based Setting. In: Boyd, C., González Nieto, J.M. (eds.) ACISP 2005. LNCS, vol. 3574, pp. 101–112. Springer, Heidelberg (2005)
13. Dutta, R., Barua, R.: Constant Round Dynamic Group Key Agreement. In: Zhou, J., López, J., Deng, R.H., Bao, F. (eds.) ISC 2005. LNCS, vol. 3650, pp. 74–88. Springer, Heidelberg (2005)
14. Dutta, R., Barua, R.: Provably Secure Constant Round Contributory Group Key Agreement in Dynamic Setting. IEEE Transactions on Information Theory 54(5), 2007–2025 (2008)
15. Dutta, R., Barua, R.: Overview of Key Agreement Protocols, http://eprint.iacr.org/2005/289
16. Galbraith, S., Harrison, K., Soldera, D.: Implementing the Tate Pairing. In: Fieker, C., Kohel, D.R. (eds.) ANTS 2002. LNCS, vol. 2369, pp. 324–337. Springer, Heidelberg (2002)
17. Gerla, M., Tsai, J.T.-C.: Multicluster, Mobile, Multimedia Radio Network. ACM Baltzer Journal of Wireless Networks 1(3), 255–265 (1995)
18. Hietalahti, M.: Efficient Key Agreement for Ad Hoc Networks. Master's Thesis, Helsinki University of Technology, Department of Computer Science and Engineering, Espoo, Finland (2001)

19. Hietalahti, M.: A Clustering-based Group Key Agreement Protocol for Ad-Hoc Networks. Electronic Notes in Theoretical Computer Science 192, 43–53 (2008)
20. Joux, A.: A One Round Protocol for Tripartite Diffie-Hellman. In: Bosma, W. (ed.) ANTS 2000. LNCS, vol. 1838, pp. 385–394. Springer, Heidelberg (2000)
21. Katz, J., Yung, M.: Scalable Protocols for Authenticated Group Key Exchange. In: Boneh, D. (ed.) CRYPTO 2003. LNCS, vol. 2729, pp. 110–125. Springer, Heidelberg (2003)
22. Kim, Y., Perrig, A., Tsudik, G.: Tree Based Group Key Agreement. ACM Transactions on Information and System Security 7(1), 60–96 (2004)
23. Konstantinou, E.: Cluster-based Group Key Agreement for Wireless Ad Hoc Networks. In: Proc. of IEEE ARES 2008, pp. 550–557 (2008)
24. Li, X., Wang, Y., Frieder, O.: Efficient Hybrid Key Agreement Protocol for Wireless Ad Hoc Networks. In: Proc. of IEEE International Conference on Computer Communications and Networks, pp. 404–409 (2002)
25. Lynn, B., Scott, M., Berreto, P.S.L.M., Lynn, H.Y.: Efficient Algorithms for Pairing-Based Cryptosystems. In: Yung, M. (ed.) CRYPTO 2002. LNCS, vol. 2442, pp. 354–369. Springer, Heidelberg (2002)
26. Manulis, M.: Security-Focused Survey on Group Key Exchange Protocols, http://eprint.iacr.org/2006/395
27. Menezes, A., Van Oorschot, P.C., Vanstone, S.: Handbook of Applied Cryptography. CRC Press, Boca Raton (1997)
28. NIST. AES (December 2000), http://www.nist.gov/aes
29. National Bureau of Standards. Data Encryption Standard, U.S. Department of Commerce, FIPS pub. 46 (1977)
30. Pei, G., Gerla, M., Hong, X., Chiang, C.C.: A Wireless Hierarchical Routing Protocol with Group Mobility. In: Proc. of IEEE WCNC 1999, pp. 1538–1542 (1999)
31. Scott, M.: Computing the Tate Pairing. In: Menezes, A. (ed.) CT-RSA 2005. LNCS, vol. 3376, pp. 293–304. Springer, Heidelberg (2005)
32. Scott, M., Costigan, N., Abdulwahab, W.: Implementing Cryptographic Pairings on Smart Cards, http://www.iacr.org/2006/144
33. Sucec, J., Marsic, I.: Clustering Overhead for Hierarchical Routing in Mobile Adhoc Networks. In: Proc. of IEEE Infocomm 2002, pp. 1698–1706 (2002)
34. Shi, H., He, M., Qin, Z.: Authenticated and Communication Efficient Group Key Agreement for Clustered Ah Hoc Networks. In: Pointcheval, D., Mu, Y., Chen, K. (eds.) CANS 2006. LNCS, vol. 4301, pp. 73–89. Springer, Heidelberg (2006)
35. Steiner, M., Tsudik, G., Waidner, M.: Diffie-Hellman Key Distribution Extended to Group Communication. In: Proc. of ACM CCS 1996, pp. 31–37. ACM Press, New York (1996)
36. Yao, G., Ren, K., Bao, F., Deng, R.H., Feng, D.: Making the Key Agreement Protocol in Mobile Ad Hoc Network More Efficient. In: Zhou, J., Yung, M., Han, Y. (eds.) ACNS 2003. LNCS, vol. 2846, pp. 343–356. Springer, Heidelberg (2003)

An Integrated ECC-MAC Based on RS Code

Jaydeb Bhaumik and Dipanwita Roy Chowdhury

Indian Institute of Technology
Kharagpur-721302, India

Abstract. This paper presents a message authentication code (MAC) with error-correcting capabilities which can be used for wireless transmission. Also the paper introduces a new nonlinear mixing function '*Nmix*' which is cryptographically strong compared to other existing method and secured against linear, differential and other conventional cryptanalysis. This nonlinear function is used to compute proposed MAC from check symbols of Reed-Solomon (RS) code. Our MAC is shown to be secured even if a fixed pad is used in MAC generation.

Keywords: Error correcting code, Message authentication code, Nonlinear mixing, Reed-Solomon code, ECC-MAC.

1 Introduction

A MAC is a symmetric-key method that is used to protect a message from unauthorized alteration. MAC is a function of the message and the secret key that produces a fixed length value, which serves as the authenticator. It is a tag that is appended to the message or encrypted message by the sender. At the receiver the tag is recomputed from the received message and the secret key which is known to both the sender and receiver. Message is accepted, when computed MAC matches with the received one. If the received message is corrupted either by random noise or by intentional forgeries, then the computed MAC does not match the received one and the message is rejected.

For an unreliable and insecure communication channel between a sender and receiver, Error Correcting Codes (ECC) are used to transmit a MAC by first computing the MAC and then error correcting code is added for transmission. However, this increases overhead. An integrated scheme combining MAC and ECC can be a better solution. This combined scheme is appealing, especially in applications where latency is a concern or resources are limited. Thus, it is interesting to construct MAC which can correct a few errors that may occur during transmission.

Applying error correcting codes to construct MAC was first exploited by Krawczyk [6]. Lam *et al.* have proposed error correcting MAC based on BCH and RS code in [12]. A noise tolerant MAC or NTMAC based on cyclic redundancy check (CRC) called CRC-NTMAC has been proposed in [15]. But the tag itself is not error tolerant. BCH-NTMAC for noisy message authentication has been published in [16]. This MAC has much lower false acceptance probability compared to CRC-NTMAC. Both BCH-NTMAC [16] and MAC proposed by Lam *et al.* [12] are error tolerant. Moreover as Lam *et al.*'s MAC generation scheme is a LFSR based, so it is easy to implement. However, Lam *et al.*'s

M.L. Gavrilova et al. (Eds.): Trans. on Comput. Sci. IV, LNCS 5430, pp. 117–135, 2009.

scheme requires truly random pad of size equal to the size of the hash output for each transmitted message. But in most practical applications, the successive pad r is generated using a pseudorandom generator out of a secret seed shared by the parties. In this case the security of the authentication scheme reduces to the security of the pseudorandom generator.

In this paper, we proposed a new integrated scheme for message authentication and error correction using t-symbol error correcting RS code. Also a new nonlinear mixing function called *Nmix* is proposed which is used to produce MAC from check symbols of RS code. The proposed function reduces the bias of linear approximations exponentially. Also differential property of the proposed key mixing is better than other existing methods. The *Nmix* function improves the security against linear, differential cryptanalysis and hence MAC is secured even if, fixed pad with *Nmix* is used.

The rest of this paper is organized as follows. In the next section, a brief overview of Lam *et al.*'s MAC generation scheme is given. Section 3 discusses the proposed ECC-MAC scheme. The new non linear function *Nmix* which is used to construct the proposed MAC is given in section 4. In section 5, security issues are described. Section 6 describes the performance evaluation of the proposed MAC and finally the paper is concluded in section 7.

2   Overview of Lam *et al.*'s Scheme

Lam *et al.* have proposed two schemes for error correcting MAC [12], one of which is based on BCH code while the other is based on RS code. Both the schemes can provide an integrity check for corrupted data and can correct few transmission errors. They have shown that these MACs are secure. It is suggested that the MAC can be applied to less information- sensitive wireless transmission such as voice and image signals. In this section, the MAC generation scheme [12] based on RS code is reproduced.

Authors have considered a typical communication scenario in which two parties communicate over an unreliable channel with a malicious adversary in the middle. The communicating parties share a secret key unknown to the adversary. For simplicity at the beginning it is assumed that the parties exchange only one message M of length m using that secret key. The secret key is used to draw a hash function randomly from the $H_{m,l}$ family of hash functions and a random pad r of length l over Z_2^l. The message M is a vector over Z_2^m and the hash value is a vector over Z_2^l. The message sender sends M together with a tag $= h_g(M) + r$, and is verified at the receiver by recalculating the tag. The hash function h_g is associated with the polynomial g of degree l. The $H_{m,l}$ family of hash functions are defined as

$$h_g(M) = x^l M(x) \mod g(x)$$

$H_{m,l} = \{h_g | \forall \text{ valid generator polynomial } g\}$ Therefore, the MAC of the message M in polynomial form is

$$MAC(x) = x^l M(x) \mod g(x) + r(x) \tag{1}$$

where $g(x)$ is a generator polynomial of degree l and $r(x)$ is the random pad in polynomial form. It is assumed that the adversary knows the family of hash functions, but not the particular value of h_g or the random pad r. In the typical scenario where the parties exchange multiple messages, the hash function h_g can be reused for different messages but for each new message a different random pad will be used for encryption of hash value. Next section introduces our integrated ECC-MAC scheme based on RS code.

3 Proposed Integrated ECC-MAC

In this section, we describe our MAC generation scheme which is based on RS code having t- symbol error correction capability. The message data string is subjected to a padding process both in sender and receiver. The padded string is a bit string of length an integer multiple of n-bit, where n is the length in bits of a symbol of an RS code and the codeword length is $2^n - 1$. RS encoder adds extra $2t$-check symbol with a block of message symbols to correct t-error. Therefore, maximum size of the message block is $2^n - 1 - 2t$ symbols. Our aim is to develop an integrated scheme where this $2t$-check symbol for error correction can also be used to authenticate the message.

The generator polynomial of a t-error correcting RS code [2] is

$$g_k(x) = (x + \alpha^i)(x + \alpha^{i+1})(x + \alpha^{i+2})...(x + \alpha^{i+2t-1})$$

where α is a primitive element of $GF(2^n)$. The generator polynomial depends on primitive element α and the parameter i. In this scheme, both α and i are selected by the secret key k. In GF(2^n), the number of primitive elements is $p = \phi(2^n - 1)$, where ϕ is Euler's totient function. The number of possible generator polynomials that can be formed using a single primitive element for a t-symbol error-correcting code is $q = 2^n - 1$ [4]. Therefore, total number of possible generator polynomials that can be constructed using all primitive elements is given by

$$N = q \cdot p = (2^n - 1) \cdot \phi(2^n - 1) \qquad (2)$$

For $n = 40$ and $t = 4$, the number of possible generator polynomials is given by $N \approx 2^{79}$.

In our scheme, any one of the N generator polynomials is selected by the key to provide security and error correction capability. But the generator polynomial is fixed and known to everybody for a system where RS code is used only for error correction. The selected generator polynomial is used to calculate $2t$-check symbols. Since RS code is linear, the computed bare check symbols are vulnerable to several attacks when it is also used to provide security. Therefore, a sequence is mixed with the check symbols using a non-linear operator. In the proposed algorithm, the secret key of length is four times symbol length. Out of the $4n$ bits, 1^t, 2nd n-bit values are used to select primitive element α, the index i respectively and last $2n$ bits are used as an initial seed of the pseudo random sequence generator. In the following subsection, our integrated scheme for message authentication and error correction is described.

3.1 Algorithm

The algorithm of t-symbol error correcting MAC is as follows.

MACGEN: MAC GENeration Algorithm

1. pad the message to make its length equal to an integer multiple of n bits.
2. partition the padded message into symbols of n-bit each.
3. Select a generator polynomial $g_k(x)$
4. Select $r_k \in Z_2^{2t.n}$; sequence of dimension $2t.n$ over $GF(2)$, the sequence is a function of secret key.
5. Compute the Check symbols using $P(x) = x^{2t} M(x) \ mod \ g_k(x)$
6. Compute MAC using $c = F(P, \ r_k)$, where F is the nonlinear function.
7. Send Message MAC pair (M, c)

MACVEC: MAC Verification and Error Correction Algorithm
Suppose the received message MAC pair is (M', c').

1. Compute $r_k \in Z_2^{2t.n}$; same sequence of dimension $2t.n$ over $GF(2)$.
2. Compute Check symbols using $P' = G(c', r_k)$, where G is the nonlinear function.
3. Compute Syndromes from padded M' and P'.
4. Verify if all syndromes are zero or not. If all are zero, go to step 7.
5. For non-zero syndromes, verify whether the number of errors that have occurred is greater than the error correction capability of the code or not. If yes, reject the message and go to step 8.
6. Correct the errors.
7. Accept the message.
8. Stop.

Next subsection explains the operation of sender and receiver with the help of suitable block diagrams. It also compares the overhead needed for error correcting code (ECC) embedded into the MAC and first MAC then ECC scheme.

3.2   Sender and Receiver

As depicted in Fig.1, sender block diagram consists of an RS encoder, a sequence generator, a nonlinear mixer and an appending block. On the other hand, Fig. 3 shows that the receiver consists of a nonlinear mixer, a sequence generator and an

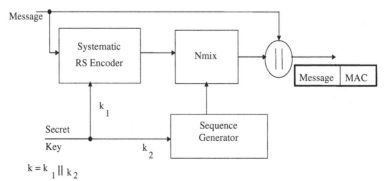

Fig. 1. Sender Block Diagram

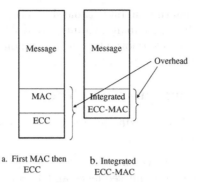

a. First MAC then
   ECC

b. Integrated
   ECC-MAC

Fig. 2. Overhead for Conventional and Integrated Scheme

Table 1. Comparison of Overhead

# of symbol errors to be corrected	Overhead in Bits			
	First MAC then ECC			Integrated ECC-MAC
	For MAC	For ECC	Total	Total
1	320	80	400	320
2	320	160	480	320
3	320	240	560	320
4	320	320	640	320

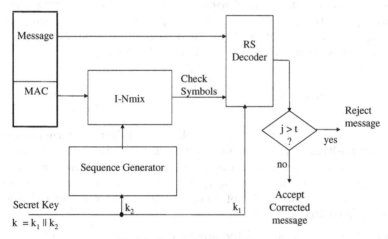

Fig. 3. Receiver Block Diagram

RS decoder. Here j is the number of symbol errors occurred and t is the number of correctable symbol errors. Figure 2 shows that the conventional (first MAC then ECC) scheme needs more over head compared with integrated scheme. A comparison of overhead between the proposed scheme and first MAC then ECC scheme (It is assumed that MAC value computation and error correcting check symbol computation is done in same layer although MAC computation is done in higher layer) is given in Table 1. Here we have considered a MAC length of 320 bits, RS code of symbol length is 40 bits. Table shows that overhead is double for first MAC then ECC scheme compared to integrated ECC-MAC scheme for 4-symbol error correction. Next section introduces new non-linear mixing function *Nmix* which is used to compute the proposed MAC.

4   Nonlinear Mixing Function: *Nmix*

In this section, a new nonlinear mixing function called '*Nmix*' and inverse mixing function '*I-Nmix*' is introduced.

Sequence Mixing (*Nmix*): Assume $X = (x_{n-1} \, x_{n-2} \, ... \, x_0)$ be an $n-$bit data, $R = (r_{n-1} \, r_{n-2} \, ... \, r_0)$ be an $n-$bit sequence and $Y = (y_{n-1} \, y_{n-2} \, ... \, y_0)$ be the $n-$bit output after mixing X with R. Then each output bit is related to the input bits by the following relationship

$$y_i = x_i \oplus r_i \oplus c_{i-1} \; ; \; c_i = \bigoplus_{j=0}^{i} x_j \cdot r_j \oplus x_{i-1}x_i \oplus r_{i-1}r_i \qquad (3)$$

where $0 \leq i < n$, $c_{-1} = 0$, $x_{-1} = 0$, $r_{-1} = 0$ and c_i is the carry term propagating from i^{th} bit position to $(i+1)^{th}$ bit position. The end carry c_{n-1} is neglected. We use the notation $Y = (X \dagger R) \; mod \; 2^n = F(X, R)$, where $\dagger$ is the *Nmix* operator. Each y_i is balanced function for all i ($0 \leq i < n$).

Inverse Sequence Mixing (*I-Nmix*): In inverse sequence mixing, the mixer takes an n-bit data $Y = (y_{n-1} \, y_{n-2} \, . . . \, y_0)$ and an $n-$bit sequence $R = (r_{n-1} \, r_{n-2} \, . . . \, r_0)$ as inputs and produces an $n-$bit output $X = (x_{n-1} \, x_{n-2} \, . . . \, x_0)$. Inverse sequence mixing operation can be defined as

$$x_i = y_i \oplus r_i \oplus d_{i-1} \; ; \; d_i = \bigoplus_{j=0}^{i} x_j \cdot r_j \oplus x_{i-1}x_i \oplus r_{i-1}r_i \qquad (4)$$

where $0 \leq i < n$, $d_{-1} = 0$, $x_{-1} = 0$, $r_{-1} = 0$, and d_i is the carry term propagating from i^{th} bit position to $(i + 1)^{th}$ bit position. The end carry d_{n-1} is neglected. Here we use the notation $X = (Y * R) \; mod \; 2^n = G(Y, R)$, where $*$ is the *I-Nmix* operator. Each x_i is balanced function for all i ($0 \leq i < n$). Next, we summarize the results related to properties of *Nmix* function. The proof of the theorems are given in appendix A.

Theorem 1. The function G is the inverse function of F.

Fact 1. For an n-bit Number X, $F(X, X) \neq 0$.

Fact 2. The function F is commutative, i.e. $F(X, R) = F(R, X)$, where X and R are two n-bit numbers.

Theorem 2. The function F does not hold associative law, i.e. $F(F(X, Y), Z) \neq F(X, F(Y, Z))$, where X, Y and Z are three n-bit numbers.

Theorem 3. Output difference (XOR) of the function F is not equal to input difference (XOR) when single input changes, i.e. $F(X, R) \oplus F(Y, R) \neq X \oplus Y$.

Theorem 4. If X, Y and R are the three n-bit numbers then
$F(F(X, R), F(Y, R)) \neq F(X, Y)$.

Theorem 5. Keeping one input fixed of the two input function F, modulo-2 addition of three outputs for three different inputs is not equal to output of the function F when input is modulo-2 addition of three individual inputs.

i.e. $F(X, R) \oplus F(Y, R) \oplus F(Z, R) \neq F((X \oplus Y \oplus Z), R)$.

Theorem 6. If X, Y, Z and R are the four n-bit numbers then
$F(F(F(X, R), F(Y, R)), F(Z, R)) \neq F(F(F(X, Y), Z), R)$

Next we discuss the hardware requirements for implementing a n-bit key mixer based *Nmix* operator. The logic diagram of *Nmix* and *I-Nmix* are given in appendix B.

4.1 Hardware Requirement

Table 2 shows the gate counts for nonlinear functions addition modulo 2^n, *Slash* modulo 2^n [19] and *Nmix* modulo 2^n for forward as well as reverse transformation. As the linear XOR is mostly used key mixing function, so the Table 2 includes XOR also. It is observed that *Nmix* requires more hardware but provides more security which is discussed in section 5.

Table 2. Comparison of Gate Counts

Transformation	Mixing Function	Number of Logic Gates			
		XOR	OR	AND	NOT
Forward	Bit wise XOR	n			
	Addition modulo2^n	$2n + 1$	$n - 2$	$2(n - 2)$	
	Slash modulo2^n	$3(n - 1)$		$n - 1$	
	Nmix modulo 2^n	$5n - 7$		$3n - 5$	
Reverse	Bit wise XOR	n			
	Subtraction modulo2^n	$2n + 1$	$n - 2$	$2(n - 2)$	$n - 2$
	Reverse Slash modulo2^n	$3(n - 1)$		$2n - 3$	$2(n - 1)$
	I-Nmix modulo 2^n	$5n - 7$		$3n - 5$	

4.2 Logic for Using *Nmix*

In this section, we explain the logic for using *Nmix* instead of XOR. In [12], different random pads are used to compute MAC from check symbols of different messages. But random pad is not practical for real life applications and, on the other hand fixed pads are not secured. So, our aim is to use one nonlinear function in addition with fixed pad to make it secure. It can be shown that if a fixed generator polynomial and fixed pad is used for MAC generation for many messages with XOR as mixing function then the scheme is vulnerable to following two attacks.

Attack-1: Generator Polynomial Recovery

In this attack, it is shown that computation of generator polynomial is possible from few correctly received message-MAC pairs. The generator polynomial $g_k(x)$

and the pad $r_k(x)$ are fixed for a sender and receiver pair because the secret key (k) is fixed. Assume $M_1(x)$ be one message polynomial. Then the corresponding check symbol polynomial $P_1(x)$ for a t-symbol error correcting RS code is given by

$$P_1(x) = x^{2t} M_1(x) \mod g_k(x) \tag{5}$$

If the code polynomial is $d_1(x)$ then

$$d_1(x) = x^{2t} M_1(x) + P_1(x) = q_1(x) \, g_k(x) \tag{6}$$

where $d_1(x)$ is the code polynomial which is multiple of generator polynomial and $q_1(x)$ is a quotient polynomial. The corresponding message-MAC polynomial $C_1(x)$ is as follows

$$C_1(x) = d_1(x) + r_k(x) = q_1(x) \, g_k(x) + r_k(x) \tag{7}$$

Assume $M_2(x)$ be another message polynomial and corresponding message-MAC polynomial $C_2(x)$ is given by

$$C_2(x) = q_2(x) \, g_k(x) + r_k(x) \tag{8}$$

From equations (7) & (8) we get

$$C_1(x) + C_2(x) = [q_1(x) + q_2(x)] \, g_k(x) \tag{9}$$

So attacker can form few equations like equation (9). Then by taking the GCD of few such newly formed equations attacker can determine the generator polynomial.

Attack-2: MAC Forgery

It can be shown that an attacker can calculate the MAC of a message which is combination of three or more odd number of correctly received messages. This attack is possible only when all messages are of equal length. Assume $M_1(x), M_2(x)$ and $M_3(x)$ be the three message polynomials and the corresponding MAC polynomials are $MAC_1(x), MAC_2(x)$ and $MAC_3(x)$ then

$$MAC_1(x) = x^{2t} M_1(x) \mod g_k(x) + r_k(x) \tag{10}$$

$$MAC_2(x) = x^{2t} M_2(x) \mod g_k(x) + r_k(x) \tag{11}$$

$$MAC_3(x) = x^{2t} M_3(x) \mod g_k(x) + r_k(x) \tag{12}$$

From (10),(11) and (12) we get

$$MAC(x) = x^{2t}[M(x)] \mod g_k(x) + r_k(x) \tag{13}$$

where $M_1(x) + M_2(x) + M_3(x) = M(x)$ and $MAC_1(x) + MAC_2(x) + MAC_3(x) = MAC(x)$. So an attacker can produce the MAC of a message (M) which is combination of three messages M_1, M_2 and M_3, provided the original messages are of equal length. This is also valid for more than three odd numbers of messages. But the generated message M may not be a meaningful message always. If it is a garbage message then there is no risk for the sender and receiver. Only adversary can take up the channel by sending such garbage message with a valid

MAC and consumes the computational resources of other node. For preventing these attacks, we proposed a scheme which employs the function $Nmix$. Next we show how it is possible to thwart the above two attacks using $Nmix$.

Nonlinearity has been introduced in our proposed scheme to compute MAC which makes over all scheme nonlinear. So we can not write the message-MAC polynomial as in equation (7). Let $C_1'(x)$ be the message-MAC polynomial in the proposed scheme then

$$C_1'(x) = x^{2t} M_1(x) + F(P_1(x), \ r_k(x)) \tag{14}$$

$$or \ C_1'(x) \neq q_1'(x) \ g_k(x) + r_k(x) \tag{15}$$

Also from Theorem 3 of the nonlinear function $F(X, R) \oplus F(Y, R) \neq X \oplus Y$, where X, Y, and R are three n-bit numbers. Therefore, addition of two message-MAC polynomial is not a multiple of generator polynomial. So, attacker can not find out the generator polynomial by taking GCD.

The new MAC can also resist the attack 2. In our proposed scheme, let any message-MAC polynomial be $C_1'(x)$ then

$$C_1'(x) \neq q_1'(x) \ g_k(x) + r_k(x) \tag{16}$$

Theorem 5 says that $F(X, R) \oplus F(Y, R) \oplus F(Z, R) \neq F(X \oplus Y \oplus Z, R)$, where X, Y, Z and R are four $n-$bit numbers. Since MAC generation scheme is non-linear, so we can conclude using theorem 5 that modulo-2 addition of three correctly received MACs is not equal to the MAC of the message which is modulo-2 addition of these three messages. Therefore an attacker can not produce the MAC of a message which is combination of three messages M_1, M_2 and M_3.

The proposed non-linear function increases the over all nonlinearity of the scheme without affecting the error correcting performance of the integrated scheme. In key mixing by XOR, single bit error in a MAC affects only single bit in the check symbol after inverse operation at the receiver. But in nonlinear mixing error may propagate from LSB to MSB i.e. single bit error in MAC may produce multiple bit errors in the check symbol. In our proposed scheme each check symbol is processed separately i.e. there is no carry propagation from one symbol to the next adjacent symbol. Since RS code can correct symbol errors, so error correcting performance will not be affected by nonlinear mixing.

5   Security Analysis

In this section, we establish that our proposed scheme is secure against some conventional attacks and robustness of the proposed scheme.

Brute force attack: In brute force attack, the level of effort require to attack on a MAC algorithm can be expressed as $\min(2^k, 2^l)$, where k is the key length and l is the MAC length. In our proposed scheme, MAC length is 320 bits and key length is 160 bits. So the level of effort required is 2^{160}, which is computationally infeasible.

Birthday Attack: Our proposed scheme produces 320 bits MAC output, so the effort required for birthday attack is 2^{160}, which is computationally infeasible.

MAC guessing: The attacker selects a message and simply guess the correct MAC value. The probability that the guess will be correct is 2^{-l}, where l is the number of bits in the MAC. In our proposed scheme, the probability that the guess will be correct is 2^{-320}.

Divide and Conquer Attack: In our proposed scheme, we used 80-bit secret information to select a particular $g(x)$ from the set of all possible generator polynomials and another 80-bit as the seed of the sequence generator. So this type of attack is not possible.

Extension Attack: From the definition of F, it can be shown that $F(X, R) \oplus Y \neq F((X \oplus Y), R)$ and $F(F(X, R), Y) \neq F((X \oplus Y), R)$. So we may infer that the proposed construction is robust against extension attack.

Linear Cryptanalysis of *Nmix*: Linear cryptanalysis (LC) tries to take advantage of high probability of occurrences of linear expressions involving message bits, key bits and MAC bits. The approach in LC is to determine linear expressions of the form which have a low or high probability of occurrence. Since the coding scheme is linear, therefore a nonlinear sequence mixing is introduced to resist LC. In this section, we derive the probability that each MAC bit can be expressed linearly in terms of check bits and sequence bits. Assuming that two n-bit inputs are X, R and the corresponding n-bit output is Y, where $Y = F(X, R)$. The following result shows that *Nmix* is a good nonlinear mixing function.

Theorem 7. The bias of best linear approximation of *Nmix* is 2^{-i}, where $2 \leq i < n$

Proof: If two n−bit numbers $X = (x_{n-1} \ldots x_0)$ and $R = (r_{n-1} \ldots r_0)$ generate an n-bit number $Y = (y_{n-1} \ldots y_0)$ such that $Y = F(X, R)$, then one need to prove that the bias of best linear approximation of y_i is 2^{-i}, $where\ 2 \leq i < n$. From the definition of F, it is evident that in the output $y_i = x_i \oplus r_i \oplus c_{i-1}$, where c_{i-1} is the carry input into the ith bit position and is the only nonlinear term of the equation. Therefore, nonlinearity of y_i is same as that of nonlinearity of c_{i-1}, which can be expressed as

$$c_{i-1} = x_0 r_0 \oplus \ \ldots \ \oplus x_{i-1} r_{i-1} \oplus r_{i-1} r_{i-2} \oplus x_{i-1} x_{i-2} \qquad (17)$$

If we assume that $p_j = x_j \oplus r_{j+1}$ and $q_j = r_j \oplus x_{j+1}$ then c_{i-1} can be expressed as

$$c_{i-1} = x_0 r_0 \oplus \ \ldots \ \oplus x_{i-3} r_{i-3} \oplus p_{i-2} q_{i-2} \qquad (18)$$

where p_j and q_j are statistically independent if x_j and r_j are statistically independent and uniformly chosen. Expression of c_{i-1} shows that it is a function of $2(i-1)$ variables and it is in the form of bent function. Therefore, non-linearity of c_{i-1} is $2^{2i-3} - 2^{i-2}$, where $2 \leq i < n$. So, number of matches in the best linear approximation is $2^{2i-2} - 2^{2i-3} + 2^{i-2}$ and hence probability of matches is $\frac{1}{2} + 2^{-i}$. Therefore, bias of best linear approximation is 2^{-i}, where $2 \leq i < n$. Since, $y_0 = x_0 \oplus r_0$, so bias of best linear approximation is $\frac{1}{2}$. For $y_1 = x_1 \oplus r_1 \oplus x_0 r_0$, the bias is $\frac{1}{4}$. Therefore, except the first two bits *Nmix* posses high nonlinearity at all other bits.

Table 3. Comparison of Linear Probability Bias

Mixing by	Bias of best linear Approx. of					
	y_0	y_1	y_2	y_3	y_4	y_5
Addition modulo 2^n	0.50	0.25	0.25	0.25	0.25	0.25
Slash modulo 2^n	0.50	0.25	0.125	0.0625	0.0313	0.0156
Nmix modulo 2^n	0.50	0.25	0.25	0.125	0.0625	0.0313

Table 4. Comparison of Bias of Best Linear Approximation of $y_i \quad y_{i+1}$

Mixing by	Bias of best linear Approx. for				
	$y_0 \quad y_1$	$y_1 \quad y_2$	$y_2 \quad y_3$	$y_3 \quad y_4$	$y_4 \quad y_5$
Addition modulo 2^n	0.25	0.25	0.25	0.25	0.25
Slash modulo 2^n	0.25	0.25	0.25	0.25	0.25
Nmix modulo 2^n	0.25	0.125	0.0625	0.0625	0.0625

Table 3 shows the comparison of bias for best linear approximation for few terms. It is observed that the bias of best linear approximation of y_i decreases exponentially with i. Next we compute the bias value of best linear approximation for $y_i \oplus y_{i+1}$.

It is observed that nonlinearity of $y_i \oplus y_{i+1}$ depends solely on the nonlinearity of $c_i \oplus c_{i-1}$. From the definition, $c_i \oplus c_{i-1}$ can be expressed as

$$c_i \oplus c_{i-1} = x_i r_i \oplus x_{i-1}(x_i \oplus x_{i-2}) \oplus r_{i-1}(r_i \oplus r_{i-2}) \tag{19}$$

where $2 \leq i < n$. If we assume $a_i = x_i \oplus x_{i-2}$ and $b_i = r_i \oplus r_{i-2}$, then $c_i \oplus c_{i-1} = x_i r_i \oplus x_{i-1} a_i \oplus r_{i-1} b_i$. Therefore, $c_i \oplus c_{i-1}$ is a function of six variables and it is in the form of bent function. So, nonlinearity is 28 and bias of best linear approximation is 0.0625, where $2 \leq i < n$. Since $y_0 \oplus y_1 = x_0 \oplus x_1 \oplus r_0 \oplus r_1 \oplus x_0 r_0$, so nonlinearity is 1 and bias is 0.25. The nonlinearity of $y_1 \oplus y_2$ is 6 and bias is 0.125. Table 4 shows that bias of the linear approximation of $y_i \oplus y_{i+1}$ has significant value 0.25 for addition modulo 2^n and *Slash* modulo 2^n but bias is negligible 0.0625 in *Nmix* modulo 2^n. Therefore, *Nmix* is cryptographically stronger than addition modulo 2^n. Recently, *Slash* [19] function is used to prevent crossword puzzle attack [18] on stream cipher NLS [14]. The function modular *Slash* is nonlinear, reversible and has a strong resistance against linear cryptanalysis. However the Boolean functions like modular addition, *Slash* have the demerit that the bias of XOR of consecutive bit positions in the output is held constant at $\frac{1}{4}$. The proposed function *Nmix* eliminates above disadvantage.

Di erential Cryptanalysis of *Nmix*: In our proposed scheme, sequence mixing method using nonlinear function offers differential resistance. But the sequence mixing which is done by XOR operator, does not provide any differential resistance as always $\Delta y = \Delta x$, which is independent of the sequence. In the proposed scheme nonlinearity exists only in the sequence mixing so differential resistance of the scheme is same as that of mixing part. Next we calculate the bias of linear approximation of the difference term. Assuming that

Table 5. Comparison of Bias of Best Linear Approximation of Δy_i

Mixing	Bias of best linear Approx. of				
by	Δy_0	Δy_1	Δy_2	Δy_3	Δy_4
Addition modulo 2^n	0.5	0.25	0.1875	0.1719	0.1680
Slash modulo 2^n	0.5	0.25	0.125	0.0625	0.0313
Nmix modulo 2^n	0.5	0.25	0.125	0.0625	0.0313

$Y = (y_{n-1} \, y_{n-2}...y_0)$ is an n-bit MAC, $R = (r_{n-1} \, r_{n-2}...r_0)$ is the key dependent sequence inputs to the non linear operator, $X = (x_{n-1} \, x_{n-2}...x_0)$ is the another n-bit input such that $Y = F(X, R)$ and c_i represents the carry from the ith level. If $Y' = (y'_{n-1} \, y'_{n-2} \cdots y'_0)$ be the another n-bit MAC, $R = (r_{n-1} \, r_{n-2} \, ...r_0)$ be the key dependent sequence inputs to the nonlinear operator, $X' = (x'_{n-1} \, x'_{n-2} \cdots x'_0)$ be the other input such that $Y' = F(X', R)$ and c'_i represents the carry from the ith level. Then $\Delta y_i = (y_i \oplus y'_i) = \Delta x_i \oplus \Delta c_{i-1}$, where $\Delta x_i = x_i \oplus x'_i$ and $\Delta c_{i-1} = c_{i-1} \oplus c'_{i-1}$ Therefore sequence mixing using nonlinear operator offers differential resistance as the probability distribution of Δy_i for given Δx_i is identical to the probability distribution of Δc_{i-1}. From equation (2) it can be shown that

$$\Delta c_{i-1} = x_{i-2}x_{i-1} \oplus x'_{i-2}x'_{i-1} \bigoplus_{j=0}^{i-1} r_j(x_j \oplus x'_j) \qquad (20)$$

It is found from Table 5 that bias of best linear approximation of Δy_i is also decreases exponentially. But in case of addition modulo 2^n, rate of decrease of bias relatively flat compared to *Nmix* modulo 2^n. From (20), it can be shown that $\Delta y_i = \Delta x_i \oplus x_{i-2}x_{i-1} \oplus x'_{i-2}x'_{i-1} \bigoplus_{j=0}^{i-1} r_j \Delta x_j$, where $\Delta y_i = y_i \oplus y'_i$ and $\Delta x_i = x_i \oplus x'_i$, X, X' are the two different inputs to the function and corresponding outputs are Y, Y' for a fixed R and $0 \le i < n$. So it is observed that the probability of a particular output difference ΔY occurs given a particular input difference ΔX is function of all x_i and x'_i for a fixed R. The probability $Pr(\Delta Y|\Delta X)$ is always much less than 1. Therefore the proposed function provides differential resistance.

The following section describes the performance of the proposed scheme as a hashing algorithm.

6   Evaluation of the Proposed Scheme

In this section, we discuss the computational cost of the proposed scheme as well as the conventional scheme (first MAC then ECC). The proposed MAC algorithm is also evaluated against the metrics: (i) Bit-variance test and (ii) Entropy test proposed in [10].

6.1   Computational Cost

In our MAC generation scheme, total computational cost is equal to the computation cost of a systematic RS encoder with programmable generator polynomial and *Nmix* function. The systematic RS encoder [2] requires $2tN_m$ number of $GF(2^n)$ multiplication and $2tN_m$ number of $GF(2^n)$ addition, where N_m is the total number of message symbols in the code word, t is the error correction capability of the code and n is the size of each symbol. From Table 2 it can be shown that for *Nmix*, computational cost is $2t(5n - 7)$ number of XOR operation and $2t(3n - 5)$ number of AND operation. Computational cost of proposed MAC verification scheme consists of computational cost of *I-Nmix* and a systematic RS decoder with programmable generator polynomial. Computational cost of *I-Nmix* is same as that of *Nmix* and is equal to $2t(5n - 7)$ number of XOR operation and $2t(3n - 5)$ number of AND operation. It has been shown in [4] that for decoding RS code with programmable generator polynomial require extra four Galois field multipliers and two registers of size same as that of symbol size. Therefore, computational cost of the stated RS decoder is equal to computational cost of a non programmable RS decoder and $2(N_m + N_c)$ number of $GF(2^n)$ multiplication, where N_m is the number of message symbols in the code word and N_c is the code word length in symbols.

In case of conventional scheme, first MAC is computed then ECC is computed over message and MAC. In sender, the total computational cost is equal to computational cost of MAC generator and RS encoder. If any HMAC algorithm is used to compute MAC then it mainly requires two hash operations. If SHA-1 is used then for each 512-bit message block round operation is processed 80 times. Each round operation performs four addition modulo 2^{32}, two circular right shift and one logical operation. In the receiver, computational is sum of the computational cost due to RS decoder and MAC generator. Therefore, the computational cost of the integrated ECC-MAC is much less than the computational cost of conventional scheme.

6.2   Evaluation of Our Scheme as a Hash Function

1. Bit Variance Test: Bit variance test shows the impact on the MAC bits by changing the input message bits. Bits of an input message are changed and the corresponding MACs (for each changed input) are calculated for a fixed secret key. Then the difference between the original MAC (corresponding to the original message) and the changed MACs are calculated. Finally, the average probability of 1 and 0 are calculated from all the differences of MACs. For this test, it is difficult to check for all possible bit changes on the input message. Therefore, only changes involving 1 bit and 2 bits have been considered.

Table 6. Result of Bit Variance Test

Message	Probability of change for the variation of							
	One message bit and mixing by				Two message bits and mixing by			
	XOR		Nmix		XOR		Nmix	
	, 0	, 1	, 0	, 1	, 0	, 1	, 0	, 1
1	0.499	0.500	0.501	0.498	0.498	0.501	0.501	0.498
2	0.499	0.500	0.503	0.496	0.498	0.501	0.499	0.500
3	0.499	0.500	0.499	0.500	0.498	0.501	0.505	0.494

Cellular Automata based RS encoder [20] with some modification in the algorithm, is used for our experiment with symbol size 40 bits, message length 10000 bits, and generated MAC length 320 bits. The experiments were performed for three different messages. Results are given in Table 6. It shows that for both the mixing function XOR and *Nmix* the condition $p_0 \approx p_1 = 0.5$ is satisfied, where p_0 and p_1 are the average probability of 0 and 1.

2. Entropy Test: Entropy is a measure of uncertainty. The entropy is maximum when all the MACs are equally likely. Entropy test addresses the question about the actual probability to find a message with given MAC or two messages with the same MAC. Since, it is infeasible to calculate the probability of the individual MACs , an approximate entropy assessment method is used.

Approximate Entropy: Approximate entropy is a measure of the logarithmic frequency with which blocks of length i that are close together remain close together for blocks augmented by one position. By comparing the actual frequency of groups of digits to their expected frequency, approximate entropy of the sequence is determined which is a measure of it's randomness. A random sequence should have equal number of all possible groups. A small value of approximate entropy implies strong regularity. For this test, it is difficult to check for all possible groups. Therefore, only 2 bytes block has been considered.

Approximate Entropy Assessment Method: Assume the MAC is composed of blocks where the length of each block is 1 byte. By taking all possible combinations of byte pairs, a set of 16 bits numbers $(0 - 65535)$ are obtained. For a large number of MAC if the frequencies of these numbers $(0 - 65535)$ are equal, then the approximate entropy of the 16 bit long sub sequence is maximum and the value of this entropy is 16. For approximate entropy calculation we took 260796 samples from the produced MACs with each samples of length 2-byte. The calculated approximate entropy for 16 bits subsequence is 15.8001, which is slightly less than maximum entropy 16.

7   Conclusions

In this correspondence, we have proposed a MAC algorithm based on RS code having t-symbol error correcting capability. In our proposed MAC generation algorithm, we have used a function *Nmix* for mixing the sequence with the error correcting check symbols. The proposed scheme is shown to be secure even if same pad is used for more than one MAC generation. Also the proposed MAC is found to be a good choice for Keyed-Hash technique and has been evaluated successfully for Bit-Variance and Entropy test. The proposed function can be used effectively as a key mixing function in hardware based block ciphers.

References

1. Rothaus, O.S.: On "Bent" Functions. Journal of Combinatorial Theory 20(A), 300–305 (1976)
2. Lin, S., Costello, D.J.: Error control coding: Fundamentals and Applications. Prentice-Hall, Englewood Cliffs (1983)

3. Mceliece, R.J., Swanson, L.: Decoder Error Probability for Reed-Solomon Codes. IEEE Transaction on Information Theory IT-32(5), 701–703 (1986)
4. Shayan, Y.R., Le-Ngoc, T.: Decoding Reed-Solomon Codes Generated by any Generator Polynomial. Electronics Letters 25(18), 1223–1224 (1989)
5. Ohtal, K., Matsui, M.: Differential attack on Message Authentication Codes. In: Stinson, D.R. (ed.) CRYPTO 1993. LNCS, vol. 773, pp. 200–211. Springer, Heidelberg (1994)
6. Krawczyk, H.: LFSR-based Hasing and Authentication. In: Desmedt, Y.G. (ed.) CRYPTO 1994. LNCS, vol. 839, pp. 129–139. Springer, Heidelberg (1994)
7. Bakhtiari, S., Safavi-Naini, R., Pieprzyk, J.: Cryptographic Hash Functions: A Survey. Technical Report 95-09. Department of Computer Science, University of Wollongong (1995),
   http://www.citeseer.ist.psu.edu/bkhtiari95cryptographic.html
8. Bellare, M., Canettiy, R., Krawczykz, H.: Keying Hash Functions for Message Authentication. In: Koblitz, N. (ed.) CRYPTO 1996. LNCS, vol. 1109, pp. 1–15. Springer, Heidelberg (1996)
9. Preneel, B.: Cryptanalysis of Message Authentication Code. In: Okamoto, E. (ed.) ISW 1997. LNCS, vol. 1396, pp. 55–65. Springer, Heidelberg (1998)
10. Karras, D.A., Zorkadis, V.: A Novel Suite for Evaluation One-Way Hash Functions for Electronic Commerce Applications. In: Proc. of 26th EUROMICRO 2000, Netherlands, pp. 464–468 (2000)
11. Menezes, A., van Oorschot, P., Vanstone, S.: Handbook of Applied Cryptography, 5th edn. CRC Press, Boca Raton (2001)
12. Lam, C.C.Y., Gong, G., Vanstone, S.: Message Authentication Codes with Error Correcting Capabilities. In: Deng, R.H., Qing, S., Bao, F., Zhou, J. (eds.) ICICS 2002. LNCS, vol. 2513, pp. 354–366. Springer, Heidelberg (2002)
13. Sarkar, P., Mitra, S.: Construction of Nonlinear Resilient Boolean Functions Using "Small" Affine functions. IEEE Transactions on Information Theory 50(9), 2185–2193 (2004)
14. Rose, G., Hawkes, P., Paddon, M., De Vries, M.W.: Primitive specification for nls (2005), http://www.ecrypt.eu.org/stream/nls.html
15. Liu, Y., Boncelet, C.G.: The CRC-NTMAC for Noisy Messages Authentication. IEEE Transaction on Information Forensics and Security 1(4), 517–523 (2006)
16. Liu, Y., Boncelet, C.G.: The BCH-NTMAC for Noisy Messages Authentication. In: Proceedings of CISS (2006)
17. Contini, S., Yin, Y.L.: Forgery and Partial Key-Recovery Attacks on HMAC and NMAC Using Hash Collisions. In: Lai, X., Chen, K. (eds.) ASIACRYPT 2006. LNCS, vol. 4284, pp. 37–53. Springer, Heidelberg (2006)
18. Cho, J.Y., Pieprzyk, J.: Crossword Puzzle Attack on NLS. In: Biham, E., Youssef, A.M. (eds.) SAC 2006. LNCS, vol. 4356, pp. 249–265. Springer, Heidelberg (2007)
19. Bhattacharya, D., Mukhopadhyay, D., Saha, D., Roy Chowdhury, D.: Strengthening NLS against Crossword Puzzle Attack. In: Pieprzyk, J., Ghodosi, H., Dawson, E. (eds.) ACISP 2007. LNCS, vol. 4586, pp. 29–44. Springer, Heidelberg (2007)
20. Bhaumik, J., Roy Chowdhury, D., Chakrabarti, I.: An Improved Double Byte Error Correcting Code using Cellular Automata. In: Umeo, H., Morishita, S., Nishinari, K., Komatsuzaki, T., Bandini, S. (eds.) ACRI 2008. LNCS, vol. 5191, pp. 463–470. Springer, Heidelberg (2008)

Appendix

A. Proof of the *Nmix* Properties

Theorem 1. The function G is the inverse function of F.

Proof: If X, Y and R be three n-bit data such that $Y = F(X, R)$ and function G is defined as $X = G(Y, R)$, then G is the inverse function of F. From the definition of F, bitwise expressions of Y are as follows

$$y_0 = x_0 \oplus r_0$$
$$y_1 = x_1 \oplus r_1 \oplus x_0 r_0$$
$$y_2 = x_2 \oplus r_2 \oplus x_1 r_1 \oplus x_0 r_0 \oplus x_0 x_1 \oplus r_0 r_1$$

similarly it can be shown that

$$y_{n-1} = x_{n-1} \oplus r_{n-1} \oplus x_0 r_0 \oplus \ldots \oplus x_{n-3} x_{n-2} \oplus r_{n-3} r_{n-2}$$

Let $P = G(Y, R)$, where $P = (p_{n-1} \ldots p_0)$ is an n-bit number. From the definition of G, the bitwise expressions of P after simplification are given below

$$p_0 = y_0 \oplus r_0 = x_0 \oplus r_0 \oplus r_0 = x_0$$
$$p_1 = y_1 \oplus r_1 \oplus p_0 r_0 = x_1 \oplus r_1 \oplus x_0 r_0 \oplus r_1 \oplus x_0 r_0 = x_1$$
$$p_2 = y_2 \oplus r_2 \oplus p_1 r_1 \oplus p_0 r_0 \oplus p_0 p_1 \oplus r_0 r_1 = x_2$$

similarly it can be shown that

$$p_{n-1} = y_{n-1} \oplus r_{n-1} \oplus \ldots \oplus y_{n-3} y_{n-2} \oplus r_{n-3} r_{n-2} = x_{n-1}$$

Since, $p_i = x_i$ for all $0 \leq i \leq n-1$ therefore G is the inverse function of F.

Theorem 2. The function F does not hold associative law, i.e. $F(F(X, Y), Z) \neq F(X, F(Y, Z))$, where X, Y and Z are three n-bit numbers.

Proof: Let A and B be the two n-bit numbers such that $A = F(F(X, Y), Z)$ and $B = F(X, F(Y, Z))$. From the definition of F, bitwise expressions of A are as follows

$$a_0 = x_0 \oplus y_0 \oplus z_0$$
$$a_1 = x_1 \oplus y_1 \oplus z_1 \oplus x_0 y_0 \oplus y_0 z_0 \oplus x_0 z_0$$
$$a_2 = x_2 \oplus y_2 \oplus z_2 \oplus x_1 y_1 \oplus y_1 z_1 \oplus z_1 x_1 \oplus x_0 y_0 \oplus \ldots \oplus x_0 y_1 \oplus x_1 y_0 \oplus z_1 (x_0 y_0 \oplus z_0)$$

similarly it can be shown that

$$a_{n-1} = x_{n-1} \oplus y_{n-1} \oplus z_{n-1} \oplus \ldots \oplus z_{n-2} (x_{n-3} x_{n-4} \oplus y_{n-3} y_{n-4})$$

Similarly bitwise expression of B can be written as

$$b_0 = x_0 \oplus y_0 \oplus z_0$$
$$b_1 = x_1 \oplus y_1 \oplus z_1 \oplus x_0 y_0 \oplus y_0 z_0 \oplus z_0 x_0$$
$$b_2 = x_2 \oplus y_2 \oplus z_2 \oplus x_1 y_1 \oplus y_1 z_1 \oplus z_1 x_1 \oplus x_0 y_0 \oplus \ldots \oplus y_0 z_1 \oplus y_1 z_0 \oplus x_1 (y_0 z_0 \oplus x_0)$$

similarly it can be shown that

$$b_{n-1} = x_{n-1} \oplus y_{n-1} \oplus z_{n-1} \oplus \ldots \oplus x_{n-2} (y_{n-3} y_{n-4} \oplus z_{n-3} z_{n-4})$$

From the bit level expressions of A and B, it is observed that $a_0 = b_0$, $a_1 = b_1$ but $a_i \neq b_i$ for all $2 \leq i < n$. Hence, F does not follow associative property.

Theorem 3. Output difference (XOR) of the function F is not equal to input difference (XOR) when single input changes, i.e. $F(X, R) \oplus F(Y, R) \neq X \oplus Y$.

Proof: Assume $X = (x_{n-1} \ x_{n-2} \ ... \ x_0)$, $Y = (y_{n-1} \ y_{n-2} \ ... \ y_0)$, $R = (r_{n-1} \ r_{n-2} \ ... \ r_0)$, $U = (u_{n-1} \ u_{n-2} \ ... \ u_0)$ and $V = (v_{n-1} \ v_{n-2} \ ... \ v_0)$ be the five n-bit numbers, such that $U = F(X, R)$ and $V = F(Y, R)$, then one need to prove $U \oplus V \neq X \oplus Y$.

According to the definition of nonlinear function F, the bitwise expressions of $U \oplus V$ are as follows

$$u_0 \oplus v_0 = x_0 \oplus y_0$$
$$u_1 \oplus v_1 = (x_1 \oplus y_1) \oplus r_0(x_0 \oplus y_0)$$
$$u_2 \oplus v_2 = (x_2 \oplus y_2) \oplus r_1(x_1 \oplus y_1) \oplus r_0(x_0 \oplus r_0) \oplus (x_0 x_1 \oplus y_0 y_1)$$

Similarly it can be shown that

$$u_{n-1} \oplus v_{n-1} = x_{n-1} \oplus y_{n-1} \oplus \ ... \ \oplus (x_{n-2} x_{n-3} \oplus y_{n-2} y_{n-3})$$

Hence, it is proved that $U \oplus V \neq X \oplus Y$.

Also it can be shown that

Theorem 4. If X, Y and R are the three n-bit numbers then

$$F(F(X, R), F(Y, R)) \neq F(X, Y).$$

Proof: Let $X = (x_{n-1} \ x_{n-2} \ ... \ x_0)$, $Y = (y_{n-1} \ y_{n-2} \ ... \ y_0)$, $R = (r_{n-1} \ r_{n-2} \ ... \ r_0)$, $U = (u_{n-1} \ u_{n-2} \ ... \ u_0)$, $V = (v_{n-1} \ v_{n-2} \ ... \ v_0)$, $W = (w_{n-1} \ w_{n-2} \ ... \ w_0)$ and $P = (p_{n-1} \ p_{n-2} \ ... \ p_0)$ be the seven n-bit numbers, such that $U = F(X, R)$, $V = F(Y, R)$, $P = F(U, V)$ and $Q = F(X, Y)$, then it is required to prove that $P \neq Q$.

Representing P at bit level and after simplification we get

$$p_0 = u_0 \oplus v_0 = x_0 \oplus y_0$$
$$p_1 = u_1 \oplus v_1 \oplus u_0 v_0 = x_1 \oplus y_1 \oplus x_0 y_0 \oplus r_0$$
$$p_2 = u_2 \oplus v_2 \oplus u_1 v_1 \oplus u_0 v_0 \oplus u_1 u_0 \oplus v_1 v_0$$
$$\text{or } p_2 = x_2 \oplus y_2 \oplus x_1 y_1 \oplus x_0 y_0 \oplus \ ... \ \oplus r_0 r_1 (x_0 \oplus y_0)$$

similarly it can be shown that

$$p_{n-1} = x_{n-1} \oplus y_{n-1} \oplus \ ... \ \oplus r_{n-3} r_{n-4} (x_{n-3} x_{n-4} \oplus y_{n-3} y_{n-4})$$

From the definition of F, bitwise expressions of Q are as follows

$$q_0 = x_0 \oplus y_0$$
$$q_1 = x_1 \oplus y_1 \oplus x_0 y_0$$
$$q_2 = x_2 \oplus y_2 \oplus x_1 y_1 \oplus x_0 y_0 \oplus x_0 x_1 \oplus y_0 y_1$$

similarly it can be shown that

$$q_{n-1} = x_{n-1} \oplus y_{n-1} \oplus \ ... \ \oplus x_{i-2} x_{i-1} \oplus y_{n-2} y_{n-1}$$

It is noted that $p_0 = q_0$ but $p_i \neq q_i$, for all $1 \leq i < n$. Hence, it is proved that $F(F(X, R), F(Y, R)) \neq F(X, Y)$

Theorem 5. Keeping one input fixed of the two input function F, modulo-2 addition of three outputs for three different inputs is not equal to output of the function F when input is modulo-2 addition of three individual inputs.

i.e. $F(X, R) \oplus F(Y, R) \oplus F(Z, R) \neq F((X \oplus Y \oplus Z), R)$.

Proof: Assume $X = (x_{n-1} \ x_{n-2} \ \dots \ x_0)$, $Y = (y_{n-1} \ y_{n-2} \ \dots \ y_0)$, $Z = (z_{n-1} \ z_{n-2} \ \dots \ z_0)$, $R = (r_{n-1} \ r_{n-2} \ \dots \ r_0)$, $U = (u_{n-1} \ u_{n-2} \ \dots \ u_0)$, $V = (v_{n-1} \ v_{n-2} \ \dots \ v_0)$ and $W = (w_{n-1} \ w_{n-2} \ \dots \ w_0)$ be the seven $n-$bit numbers, such that $U = F(X, R)$, $V = F(Y, R)$, $W = F(Z, R)$ then the theorem says that $F(X, R) \oplus F(Y, R) \oplus F(Z, R) \neq F((X \oplus Y \oplus Z), R)$. Assuming that $A = U \oplus V \oplus W$ and $B = F((X \oplus Y \oplus Z), R)$, then the bitwise expressions of A are as follows

$a_0 = (x_0 \oplus y_0 \oplus z_0) \oplus r_0$

$a_1 = (x_1 \oplus y_1 \oplus z_1) \oplus r_1 \oplus r_0(x_0 \oplus y_0 \oplus z_0)$

$a_2 = (x_2 \oplus y_2 \oplus z_2) \oplus r_2 \oplus \ \dots \ \oplus r_0 r_1 \oplus (x_0 x_1 \oplus y_0 y_1 \oplus z_0 z_1)$

Similarly it can be shown that

$a_{n-1} = x_{n-1} \oplus y_{n-1} \oplus z_{n-1} \oplus \dots \oplus r_{n-2} r_{n-3} \oplus (x_{n-2} x_{n-3} \oplus y_{n-2} y_{n-3} \oplus z_{n-2} z_{n-3})$

The bitwise expressions of B are given below

$b_0 = (x_0 \oplus y_0 \oplus z_0) \oplus r_0$

$b_1 = (x_1 \oplus y_1 \oplus z_1) \oplus r_1 \oplus r_0(x_0 \oplus y_0 \oplus z_0)$

$b_2 = (x_2 \oplus y_2 \oplus z_2) \oplus r_2 \oplus \ \dots \ \oplus r_0 r_1 \oplus (x_0 \oplus y_0 \oplus z_0)(x_1 \oplus y_1 \oplus z_1)$

Similarly it can be shown that

$b_{n-1} = x_{n-1} \oplus y_{n-1} \oplus z_{n-1} \oplus \dots \oplus (x_{n-3} \oplus y_{n-3} \oplus z_{n-3})(x_{n-2} \oplus y_{n-2} \oplus z_{n-2})$

From the bitwise expressions of A and B, it is observed that $a_0 = b_0$ and $a_1 = b_1$ but $a_i \neq b_i$ for $2 \leq i < n$. Hence it is proved that $F(X, R) \oplus F(Y, R) \oplus F(Z, R) \neq F((X \oplus Y \oplus Z), R)$. Also it can be shown that

Theorem 6. If X, Y, Z and R are the four n-bit numbers then
$F(F(F(X, R), F(Y, R)), F(Z, R)) \neq F(F(F(X, Y), Z), R)$

Proof: Let $P = (p_{n-1} \dots p_0)$ and $Q = (q_{n-1} \dots q_0)$ be the two $n-$ bit numbers such that $P = F(F(F(X, R), F(Y, R)), F(Z, R))$ and $Q = F(F(F(X, Y), Z), R)$. From the definition of F, the bitwise expressions of P are given below

$p_0 = x_0 \oplus y_0 \oplus z_0 \oplus r_0$

$p_1 = x_1 \oplus y_1 \oplus z_1 \oplus r_1 \oplus r_0(x_0 \oplus y_0 \oplus z_0) \oplus x_0 y_0 \oplus y_0 z_0 \oplus z_0 x_0$

$p_2 = x_2 \oplus y_2 \oplus z_2 \oplus \ \dots \ \oplus r_0(x_1 \oplus y_1 \oplus x_1 y_0 \oplus x_0 y_1 \oplus x_0 y_0 \oplus x_1 z_0 \oplus y_1 z_0)$

similarly it can be shown that

$p_{n-1} = x_{n-1} \oplus y_{n-1} \oplus z_{n-1} \oplus \ \dots \ \oplus r_{n-3} z_{n-3}(x_{n-4} x_{n-5} \oplus y_{n-4} y_{n-5})$

Similarly bitwise expressions of Q are

$q_0 = x_0 \oplus y_0 \oplus z_0 \oplus k_0$

$q_1 = x_1 \oplus y_1 \oplus z_1 \oplus r_1 \oplus r_0(x_0 \oplus y_0 \oplus z_0) \oplus x_0 y_0 \oplus y_0 z_0 \oplus z_0 x_0$

$q_2 = x_2 \oplus y_2 \oplus z_2 \oplus \ \dots \ \oplus r_0(x_0 \oplus y_0 \oplus z_0)$

similarly it can be shown that

$$q_{n-1} = x_{n-1} \oplus y_{n-1} \oplus z_{n-1} \oplus \cdots \oplus r_{n-2}z_{n-3}(x_{n-4}x_{n-5} \oplus y_{n-4}y_{n-5})$$

From the bitwise expressions of P and Q, it is observed that $p_0 = q_0$, $p_1 = q_1$ but $p_i = q_i$ for all $2 \leq i < n$. Hence, it is proved that $F(F(F(X, R), F(Y, R)), F(Z, R)) \neq F(F(F(X, Y), Z), R)$.

B. Logic Diagram of *Nmix* and *I-Nmix*

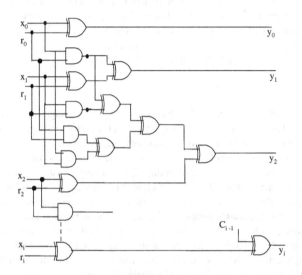

Fig. 4. Logic Diagram for *Nmix*

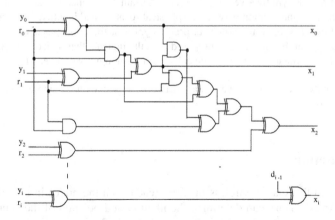

Fig. 5. Logic Diagram for *I-Nmix*

Optimizing Pseudonym Updation in Vehicular Ad-Hoc Networks

Brijesh Kumar Chaurasia[1,*], Shekhar Verma[2], G. S. Tomar[3], and Ajith Abraham[4]

[1,2] Indian Institute of Information Technology-Allahabad,
Deoghat, Jhalwa, Allahabad – 211012, India
[3] Vikrant Institute of Technology and Management, Indore, India
Center of Excellence for Quantifiable Quality of Service
[4] Norwegian University of Science and Technology, Trondheim, Norway
bkchaurasia@iiita.ac.in, sverma@iiita.ac.in, gstomar@ieee.org,
ajith.abraham@ieee.org

Abstract. A vehicle can be tracked by monitoring the messages broadcast from it. The broadcast by a source contains its current identity and also allows estimation of its location by receivers. This mapping between the physical entity and the estimated location through the communication broadcast is a threat to privacy. A vehicle can preserve its anonymity by being indistinguishable in the neighborhood crowd through continual change of identity and by hiding among its neighbors. This paper addresses the challenges in providing anonymity to a moving vehicle that uses a temporary identity for transmission and continually changes this pseudonym. As a vehicle moves on a road, its neighbors change in accordance to its relative speed with neighboring vehicles. The nature and size of the neighborhood changes the effective crowd provided by the vehicles constituting this neighborhood. Since, all neighboring vehicles do not contribute to the anonymity; the degree of anonymity is reduced. The work focuses on updation of pseudonym by a vehicle in order to sustain or enhance its anonymity by decorrelating the relation between its physical location and identity. A heuristic that allows a vehicle to switch its pseudonym at a time and place where the anonymity can be enhanced is proposed. Results indicate that updating pseudonyms in accordance to the heuristic enhances the anonymity of a vehicle.

Keywords: Anonymity, vehicular networks, pseudonyms, anonymity set (key words).

1 Introduction

Transmission in the shared wireless medium reaches all the nodes in the communication range. An adversary can determine the identity and position of the source vehicle from the contents of the communication packets [1, 2]. Its position can further be confirmed by gauging the position of the vehicle from the signal strength [3]. Using

---

* Corresponding author.

M.L. Gavrilova et al. (Eds.): Trans. on Comput. Sci. IV, LNCS 5430, pp. 136–148, 2009.
© Springer-Verlag Berlin Heidelberg 2009

this information, the physical vehicle and its communication identity can be traced and related [1, 4]. Thus, location tracking through eavesdropping of source transmission and physical observation can breach the location privacy of the user. This can be used to disclose personal data of a user and would potentially dissuade a user from joining and reaping benefits from such networks [2].

To obtain and sustain anonymity, a temporal identity, pseudonym, is used for communication. Pseudonyms allow a vehicle to interact with other vehicles anonymously. Pseudonyms are ephemeral and distinct pseudonyms hide their relation from each other and to the user's identity [5]. To preserve privacy, a pseudonym system must prevent credential forgeability and disallow usage of false pseudonym by a user. Moreover, the transaction of obtaining and the process of switching pseudonyms should not reveal the identity of the user or link pseudonyms to each other. Continually changing pseudonyms conceal the real identity of a vehicle by de-linking the source of signals to its original identity [6]. But, the relation between a communicating vehicle and its estimated location can reveal the identity of a vehicle. This vehicle can, then, be physically traced and switching pseudonyms would be meaningless [7]. A vehicle can be under sustained observation and transmissions at different intervals of time with the same pseudonym can reveal the relation between physical vehicle and its current pseudonym if the vehicle is relatively isolated in a crowd. This relation can be established even when pseudonyms are updated when the time interval between transmission prior to and after the updation is short [8]. There is, moreover, one more challenge that needs to be addressed. When a vehicle under observation moves from one cluster and enters another cluster and changes its pseudonym, it can be spotted with high probability as soon as it transmits. This can happen if the number of vehicles from the previous cluster to the current cluster is small and the pseudonyms of vehicles belonging to current cluster are known a priori. The anonymity of the vehicle under observation is limited by the number of vehicles that join the current cluster from the previous cluster [9, 10].

Existing solutions address the problem of randomizing the location based relation between pseudonyms and physical identity through pseudonyms update at a specific time [11] or at pre-determined locations known as MIX-Zones [12]. Continuous transmission before and after an identity switch can be used by an adversary or observer to link pseudonyms through the message contents and signal properties. A random silent period technique [13] in which a node does not transmit for a random period during update of identifiers excludes the possibility of forging this relation. However, the location privacy provided by these solutions is limited by tracking methods that leverage the predictability of the movement of vehicles to correlate their locations before and after the switch [14]. The increase in the size of the MIX-Zone and silence time period mitigate the possibility of any relation formation [12, 15]. The formation of any such relationships based on the predictability of node movement and signal transmission can be diminished further by increasing the frequency of pseudonym switch. However, the switching time and the frequency of switching can be limited by routing [16] and other network needs [17]. To strike a balance, a vehicle should switch as soon as possible after such change is warranted by anonymity requirements. In this work, we focus on the problem of diminishing the possibility of forging a relationship between vehicle identity and its transmissions by determining the conditions that maximize anonymity during an identity switch.

The rest of the paper is organized as follows. Section 2 describes the problem along with a measure of anonymity for a moving vehicle, section 3 gives the proposed heuristic with analytical analysis of anonymity in section 4. The simulation and results are given in section 5; section 6 concludes the work.

2 Problem Formulation and Analysis

2.1 Measuring Anonymity

We assume that a vehicle is under sustained physical observation and all communication emanating from a source (with the same pseudonym) in a region can be listened to by the adversary. The adversaries can also share their observations to obtain a rough estimation of the zone of the presence of communicating vehicle. This zone Z is the anonymity zone. Then, level of anonymity of a vehicle is the inability of the adversary to pinpoint a vehicle as the source of the communication in the set of vehicles V (anonymity set) in the region estimated from the communication. This anonymity set $V \subseteq V_{total}$ with V_{total} being the total number of vehicles in Z. The cardinality of the anonymity set is the measure of the anonymity of a vehicle in the set.

If a vehicle V_i is the source of transmission, then the probability p_i that the vehicle V_i under observation is the target,

$$p_i = P_r(V_i = V), \ \forall i \in Z \text{ and } \sum p_i = 1$$

The entropy is defined as [18]

$$H(p) = -\sum_{i=1}^{V} p_i \log_2 p_i$$

The anonymity of a given vehicle is maximized when all the vehicles are equally likely to be the potential target (source of communication). Under this uniform distribution, the probability p_i that the vehicle V_i under observation is the target becomes

$$p_i = \frac{1}{V} \text{ for all the vehicles}$$

Following the definition of level of anonymity given in [19], we have,

$$A_l = 1 - 1/|V|$$

The population of a zone is dynamic with vehicles joining and leaving a cluster. Let there be a cluster of vehicles (set of initial vehicles $V_{initial}$) at time instant t_i. Some vehicles are communicating while others are silent. At time, $t_i + \Delta t$, a few other vehicles join this cluster. Some of these vehicles had been transmitting just prior to joining the cluster. Some are silent. Let the target vehicle V_i be one of the vehicles in the set of late entrants, V_{late}, in the cluster.

The level of anonymity of a target vehicle is dependent on the size of the crowd indistinguishable from the target vehicle and not the total number of vehicles in the zone Z. The vehicles that stay with the target vehicle when it joins or leaves a cluster determine the level of anonymity enjoyed by a target vehicle.

Following conditions may arise.

Condition 1: Some vehicles in the set V_{late} had communicated immediately prior to joining the cluster. Once these vehicles join the cluster (time $t \geq t_i + \Delta t$), one of the vehicles of the set V_{late} again communicates without a change in its pseudonym. In this case, the anonymity set $V_{c(late)}$ is equal to the number of vehicles who entered cluster and had communicated just prior to entering the cluster.

$$A_l = 1 - \frac{1}{|V_{c(late)}|}, \qquad V_{c(late)} \subseteq V_{late}$$

When a vehicle moves from one cluster to another without changing its pseudonym, its anonymity set is the number of vehicles that are common (move with the vehicle) through different clusters. For example, if some vehicles from cluster $|_1$ join cluster $|_2$ and a few vehicles from $|_2$ join $|_|$, then, the anonymity set for a target vehicle that moved from $|_1| \quad |_2| \quad |_| \quad | \quad | \quad | \quad |_n$ would be $|_1 \cap |_2 \cap |_| \cap$ $| \cap |_n$ and $A_l = 1 - \frac{1}{||_1 \cap |_2 \cap |_| \cap \cap |_n|}$. Thus, the anonymity set may be very small even though a large number of vehicles are present in Z.

Condition 2: All the vehicles in the set V_{late} are silent for a random period before joining the cluster. Communication is received from a source with a pseudonym not used before in the ongoing communication emanating from the cluster. In this case, the anonymity set is the set of all vehicles silent just prior to this communication. If the number of different communication (with different pseudonyms) emanating from the cluster at time t was $V_{c(|ilent)}$, then the anonymity level is

$$A_l = 1 - \frac{1}{|V_{c(late)}| \ |V_{|ilent}|}, V_{c(|ilent)} \subseteq V_{initial}$$

If all the vehicles in the set $V_{initial}$ were communicating, then the anonymity set reduces to the vehicles that have just joined (assuming in this case that pseudonym switch is preceded by a silence period). The anonymity level is

$$A_l = 1 - \frac{1}{|V_{c(late)}|}$$

Consequently, for a target vehicle under observation by an adversary or group of adversaries, the anonymity is maximized when the cardinality of the set is more than k (known as k-anonymity) and all the vehicles in the zone of anonymity have equal probability of being the target. The anonymity level becomes ($A_l = 1 \ \forall |V| \geq k$).

The target is hidden in a crowd of k vehicles in the zone of uncertainty around the target, this enables anonymity even when the time of communication, extended position and pseudonym of a source are known.

3 Heuristic for Pseudonym Updation

The level of anonymity is a function of the cardinality of the anonymity set. Achieving k anonymity is tantamount to increasing the number of vehicles in the intersection set close to k. The proposed heuristic aims to achieve this objective by changing its pseudonym such that the size of the anonymity set becomes sufficiently large to hide the vehicle in the crowd of its neighboring vehicles. Moreover, this change process itself should not expose the vehicle. The heuristic identifies two cases.

Case1: To maximize its anonymity, a moving vehicle V_i continually observes the number of vehicles in its vicinity Z that are communicating.

After an updation, a vehicle does not change its pseudonym for a short period (order of mill seconds) which is fixed. After this period, pseudonym is updated to enhance its effective crowd cover. If sufficient time has elapsed since V_i had from the previous to the current pseudonym or the number of vehicles in the neighborhood from the last transmission becomes less than k; updation in pseudonym is imperative. The change is effected as soon as the number of vehicles that are transmitting becomes more than the critical mass, k. Till such time, the vehicle remains silent. If the vehicle has to transact with an RSU (Road Side Unit) [1] to obtain a pseudonym, it may obtain it a priori and update its identity when the aforesaid condition is satisfied. It can be further observed that the silence period can be before or after the identity change. Hence, if the pseudonym change is immediately warranted; the change must be followed by a time lag before next transmission is done.

Case 2: The above condition of critical mass of the anonymity zone can be relaxed if vehicles are able to observe all the vehicles in their vicinity (using radar). In this case, a pseudonym switch can be performed when the total number of vehicles (silent and communicating) is at least equal to k. All the other conditions remain identical to Case 1.

In general, if the vehicle continues to transmit without change in pseudonym, the cardinality progressively becomes smaller and ultimately, the adversary would be able to map the vehicle to its pseudonym. Thus, if a vehicle is able to monitor the traffic in its neighborhood, it can update its pseudonyms to remain hidden in a crowd of effective size. However, if none of vehicles in the neighborhood are communicating, the vehicle may not be able to decide upon updation. The actual effective size cannot be gauged by the vehicle itself as it knows only of the existence of the vehicles that are communicating. When a vehicle can sense the communication and observe the vehicles in is proximity physically, then, it can measure the effective size of the neighborhood and take decision of pseudonym updation to maximize its anonymity with minimum number of updations.

4 Anonymity Analysis

4.1 System Model

VANETs (Vehicular Ad-hoc Networks) are characterized by a highly dynamic topology with vehicles moving at high speed in restricted geographical strait jackets (highways). When vehicles move on a road, they lateral motion is very restricted and the motion is unidirectional except at the junctions. A vehicle moving on the road in a particular direction can move at different speeds and also pause. Since, the speed of a vehicle can be variable; vehicles may overtake one another without any restriction. Since the transmission range of any vehicle is more than the total width of the road, this sideways motion for vehicle overtaking etc. has no effect on communication and can therefore be neglected. At the junctions or crossroads, the vehicle has a choice of taking one of options. At any junction, new vehicles may enter and continue on the road. Thus, if we consider a single unidirectional road or highway, then vehicles may enter the road at different junction points. A junction is also an exit point where vehicles from may depart from the road or continue their onward journey on the road. In the present model, a departed vehicle does not reenter or participate. Each vehicle on the road is either continually transmitting periodically, aperiodically or is silent. The aim is to find the distribution of the vehicle population on the road when the vehicles move from one end of the highway to the other end to estimate the size of the anonymity set of a target vehicle. To determine the anonymity set, the system model of the road with vehicle mobility is taken from [20].

4.2 Road Model and Input Traffic

A road with multiple unidirectional lanes is considered. The vehicles move in a single direction with different speeds and multiplicity of the lanes allows vehicles to overtake each other without any restriction in the number of lanes. The road has S segments of D meters each. The road length is $S.D$ meters. Vehicles can enter and exit at the end points of a segment and there is no waiting period or queue required to enter the road. There are two end points of the road and there is no exit point at the start of the initial segment or entry at the end of the last segment. Vehicles arrive at the beginning of a segment follow a Poisson distribution p_1 ( ) and travel towards the end point independently of other existing vehicles on the road. The arrival rate at the $(k|)^{tl}$ segment at $(k)^{tl}$ point is λ_1 with the departure rate at the $(|)^{tl}$ point being $|_l$ $(\lambda_1 = 0 \; for \; k = 0 \; and \; |_| \; for \; | = |)$. Once it enters the road at an entry point, it cannot exit from the same point i.e. every vehicle must traverse at least one segment as soon as it enters the road. Hence, this system can be modeled as an $| \; /G/ \; |$ queue [21]. This means that the vehicles can be seen as arriving on the road in accordance with a Poisson process. An arriving vehicle is admitted in the road and starts traversing on the road without any waiting period (on the side of the road). It is assumed that no vehicle has to wait at the side of the road to enter the road. Once on the road, a vehicle cannot exit from the same junction and must traverse at least one segment before it can depart at one of the junctions. The time which a vehicle spends on the road is assumed to be independent general random variable with a distribution function G [21].

The vehicles travel in one direction with variable velocity. The velocity of a vehicle is assumed to be piecewise constant i.e. a vehicle moves with a constant speed for a time period and then changes its speed [20]. The velocity of a vehicle $|_i$ in during time periods follows a normal distribution with mean speed $|$ and variance $|^2||$ $(|,|^2)$. The time durations t_i form i.i.d. random variables with exponential distribution with distribution parameter $^1|_|$. The distance covered in a time duration t_i is $d_i = |_i t_i$ and the total distance covered in i time periods is $T|_i = | \; d_i = |_i t_i$.

The vehicles transmit as they move along the road. Depending on the conditions on the road and other needs, they may transmit. In this simulation, it assumed that the vehicles transmit with Poisson distribution with mean transmission rate as ρ_i.

The uncertainty zone Z of a vehicle is the number of vehicles within its broadcast range. If the target vehicle can be any of the vehicles in the zone Z, then number of vehicles in Z would constitute the anonymity set. However, since a global adversary can observe vehicles during an extended period of time over a large length of the road, hence, as discussed in section 2, the actual size of the anonymity set would depend on the number of vehicles communicating before they join the zone and after they leave Z.

4.3 Change in Cardinality of the Anonymity Set

The effective size of anonymity set Z changes in accordance with communication emanating from different locations and location of the vehicle under observation at that instant of time. There is a group G_1 of vehicles at time instant t_i with some vehicles in the group actively transmitting. After a time duration $t_i + \Delta t$, n_1 vehicles of this group join another group G_2 with n_2 vehicles to form a group G_{2c}. If there is a transmission from the group with a pseudonym used by a source at time instant t_i in G_1, then, the cardinality of anonymity set reduces to n_1 i.e. $|G_1 \cap G_{2c}|$ from ($n_1 +$ n_2) where the total number of vehicles and the vehicles starting from the initial segment can be obtained. The transmissions from the vehicles are ignored by assuming that all the vehicles under consideration are transmitting.

If $n_1 \geq k$, then the target vehicle may not change its pseudonym, however, if $n_1 < k$, then, it is imperative for a vehicle $V_i \in G_1 \cap G_{2c}$ to change its pseudonym to increase its anonymity set to $|G_{2c}|$ before any further signal transmission. This process continues as a vehicle moves along the road.

5 Simulation and Results

A road of S segments is considered. The vehicles arrive at the start of each segment with a Poisson rate λ and their speeds are normally distributed. The vehicles travel along the road as per the mobility model and transmit in accordance to a Poisson distribution. The simulation is run independently multiple times and various statistics like the density of vehicles at different times and distances from the respective start segment is collected.

The total length of the road is taken as 18 km with segments of 3 km each. It is assumed that six segments would sufficient to observe the change in the nature of neighborhood of a vehicle [20]. The input traffic can enter from the junctions $A,..., F$ and exit from $B...G$. The vehicle mean arrival rates are taken as $\lambda = 0.7$ with departure rates as $\delta = 0.1$. The time period for constant velocity is exponentially distributed with mean 1, 2 and 3 seconds and the velocities are normal variates with mean μ (15 and 30 ms^{-1}) and σ (2 ms^{-1}). The mean transmission rate of a vehicle is taken as $\rho_i = 0.5$ [20].

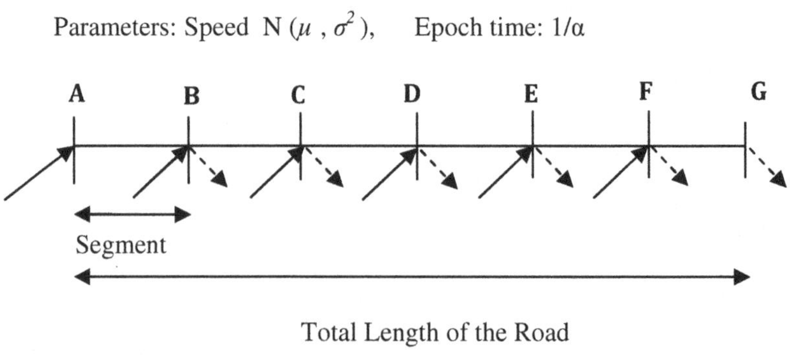

Parameters: Speed N (μ, σ^2),   Epoch time: $1/\alpha$

Fig. 1. Road Model

Fig.1 depicts the number of vehicles with distances. Since vehicles enter at different junctions, the number of vehicles increases with distance. The total number of vehicles at different distance becomes sparse at higher speeds ($\mu = 30\ ms^{-1}$) but interestingly, higher deviation ($\sigma = 2\ ms^{-1}$) at these speeds results in more stable population of vehicles on the road. This might result in a stable cluster size but to determine whether is neighborhood itself is stable; the number of vehicles that stay with the vehicle under observation needs to be traced. To determine the number of vehicles around a vehicle of interest, a vehicle from the initial segment is considered. As this vehicle travels towards the destination, some vehicles form a part of the cluster around this vehicle. The size of the cluster and the neighborhood is a function of the transmission range and the speed of different vehicles. In the present study, we consider that the vehicles have a fixed transmission ranges of 100 and 500 *meter* radius and observe the cluster size around the vehicle for low and very high speeds ($\mu = 15$ and $30\ ms^{-1}$) and variations in speed ($\sigma = 2\ ms^{-1}$). To study the effective size of the anonymity set or entropy, the number of vehicles in the neighborhood cluster that contribute to effective entropy is determined. The scenarios that arise are as follows.

Initially, when the vehicle of interest is silent, all the vehicles around it contribute to its entropy which is effectively infinity. When this vehicle starts transmitting, its entropy becomes finite and becomes equal to the number of vehicles in its transmission radius. The third case is arises when this vehicle is intermittently transmitting and its neighbors change due to speed variations, departure of vehicles from the road and new vehicles are come within its range of transmission. Depending on number of vehicles from the old neighborhood, their transmission pattern with or without pseudonym updation; number of fresh vehicles in the neighborhood and their transmission with or without pseudonym change; the entropy is determined. For example, in a changed neighborhood with n_1 old neighbors and n_2 new neighbors, the vehicle of interest and its old neighbors transmit without pseudonym updation, then for the attacker, anonymity set has only n_1 vehicles reducing the effective entropy. If n_1 is small, a pseudonym updation would useful but for a large n_1 pseudonym updation would be futile and unnecessarily deplete the pseudonym pool.

The effect of speed, frequency of transmission and transmission range on entropy priori (E_{BU}) and posterior ($E_{|\ U}$) to pseudonym updation are depicted in Fig 2 and 3.

Fig 2a illustrates the effect of pseudonym updation on entropy that for a low speed vehicle ($\mu = 15\ ms^{-1}$) with variation ($\sigma = 2\ ms^{-1}$) and transmission range of 100 meters at an interval of 2 minutes. Initially, the vehicle of interest was the only transmitting vehicle and pseudonym updation did not have any effect on entropy. In the 2nd minute, however, $|_{||}$ became significantly larger than $|_{||}$. In some portions of the road, 5th to 7th minute, the vehicle had the same set of neighbors remitting without change in pseudonym. This practically reduced the entropy to zero. In the 8th to 10th minute, the vehicle was without neighbors, hence no crowd to hide in. As the vehicle sped towards its final destination, most of vehicles departed and the entropy was low and did not change with pseudonym updation. For the same conditions, when the transmission range increased to 200 meters, the entropy increased significantly as the neighborhood increased. However, the nature of change in entropy before (E_{BU}) and after ($E_{|\ U}$) pseudonym updation did not vary.

As the speed of the vehicle of interest increased, the neighborhood became sparse and the effective entropy dropped (Fig. 3a and 3b). Interestingly, in most of cases,

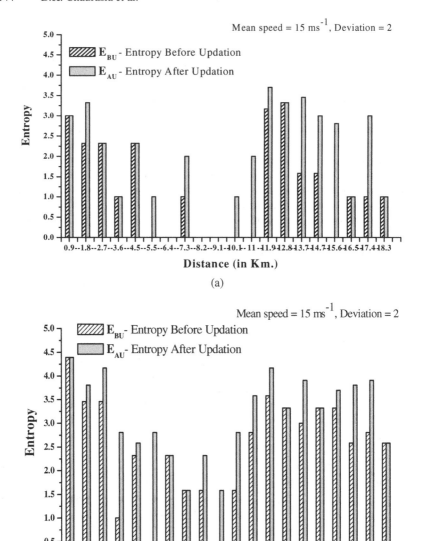

Fig. 2. (a) Entropy of the Vehicle of Interest (Transmission range =100 m). (b) Entropy of the Vehicle of Interest (Transmission range =200 m).

E_{BU} was equal to E_{AU} as the probability of transmission was not changed. It was also observed that the vehicles with similar high speeds formed a neighborhood that remained unchanged except in the initial and final phase of the vehicle's journey from initial to final segment.

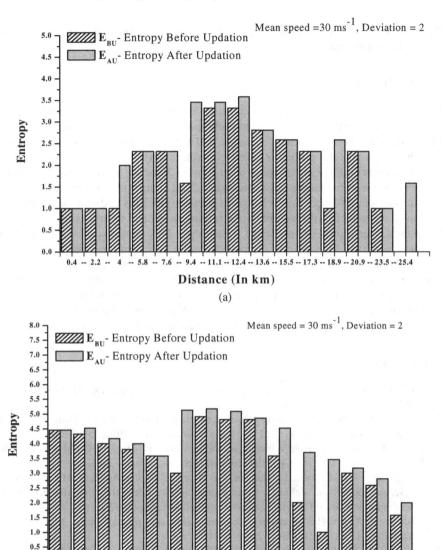

Fig. 3. (a) Entropy of the Vehicle of Interest (Transmission range =100 m). (b) Entropy of the Vehicle of Interest (Transmission range =500 m).

To increase the effective entropy, the transmission range of the vehicle was increased to 500 meters. The effective entropy increased significantly. Moreover, with the increase in transmission range, the neighborhood not only increased but also became varied. Thus, updation had increased effect on entropy especially when the neighborhood became sparse. In most of such cases, (E_{BU}) became much larger than

(E_{BU}). However, in most of the cases, the entropy was large and a change in pseudonym was not warranted.

6 Conclusion

The paper dwelt on the issue of maximization of anonymity of a vehicle through enhancement of the effective crowd size around the vehicle. The transmissions of the vehicle prior to becoming a part of a zone and the other communications emanating from the zone make the probability distribution non uniform. This entails that all the vehicles present in the zone of anonymity do not contribute to the effective entropy. In accordance with the number of vehicles observed along with a vehicle and the need for transmission, a vehicle, may change its pseudonym. This updation dissociates the relation of the vehicle with its a previous neighborhood and makes its indistinguishable in the larger crowd by increasing its entropy. This confirms the efficacy of the proposed heuristics for updating the pseudonym at specified time and place when a minimum critical mass of neighbor vehicles is present for maximization of anonymity with minimum updation frequency. This would reduce the communication required for acquiring pseudonyms and the related possibility of tracking during this process of acquisition. Further, adhoc dynamic zones for pseudonym updation also reduces the possibility of tracking and the cost involved in setting up of such zones.

References

1. Raya, M., Hubaux, J.-P.: The Security of Vehicular Ad Hoc Networks. In: Proceedings of SASN 2005, pp. 11–21 (2005)
2. Raya, M., Hubaux, J.-P.: Securing vehicular ad hoc networks. Journal of Computer Security, Special Issue on Security of Ad Hoc and Sensor Networks 15(1), 39–68 (2007)
3. Dotzer, F.: Privacy issues in vehicular ad hoc networks. In: Danezis, G., Martin, D. (eds.) PET 2005. LNCS, vol. 3856, pp. 197–209. Springer, Heidelberg (2006)
4. Papadimitratos, P., Buttyan, L., Hubaux, J.-P., Kargl, F., Kung, A., Raya, M.: Architecture for Secure and Private Vehicular Communications. In: International Conference on ITS Telecommunications (ITST 2007), Sophia Antipolis, France (2007)
5. Andreas, P., Marit, H.: Anonymity, unobservability, and pseudonymity: A proposal for terminology, Draft, v0.21, HBCC 2004 (2004)
6. Gerlach, M., Guttler, F.: Privacy in VANETs using Changing Pseudonyms - Ideal and Real. In: Proceedings of 65th Vehicular Technology Conference VTC 2007-Spring, pp. 2521–2525 (2007)
7. Kewei, S., Yong, X., Weisong, S., Loren, S., Tao, Z.: Adaptive Privacy-Preserving Authentication in Vehicular Networks. In: Proceedings of IEEE International Workshop on Vehicle Communication and Applications (2006)
8. Sampigethaya, K., Li, M., Huang, L., Poovendran, R.: AMOEBA: Robust Location Privacy Scheme for VANET. IEEE JSAC 25(8), 1569–1589 (2007)
9. Jinyuan, S., Chi, Z., Yuguang, F.: An id-based framework achieving privacy and non-repudiation in Vehicular ad hoc networks. In: Military Communications Conference, MILCOM 2007. IEEE, Los Alamitos (2007)
10. Emanuel, F., Festag, A., Baldessari, R., Aguiar, R.: Support of Anonymity in VANETs - Putting Pseudonymity into Practice. In: IEEE Wireless Communications and Networking Conference (WCNC) (2007)

11. Li, M., Sampigethaya, K., Huang, L., Poovendran, R.: Swing & swap: user-centric approaches towards maximizing location privacy. In: WPES 2006, Proceedings of the 5th ACM workshop on Privacy in electronic society, pp. 19–27 (2006)
12. Freudiger, J., Raya, M., Felegyhazi, M., Papadimitratos, P., Hubaux, J.-P.: Mix-Zones for Location Privacy in Vehicular Networks. In: ACM Workshop on Wireless Networking for Intelligent Transportation Systems (WiN-ITS 2007), Vancouver (2007)
13. Bettstetter, C., Resta, G., Santi, P.: The node distribution of the random waypoint mobility model for wireless ad hoc networks. IEEE Trans. on Mobile Computing 2(3), 257–269 (2003)
14. Huang, L., Matsuura, K., Yamane, H., Sezaki, K.: Silent cascade: Enhancing location privacy without communication qoS degradation. In: Clark, J.A., Paige, R.F., Polack, F.A.C., Brooke, P.J. (eds.) SPC 2006. LNCS, vol. 3934, pp. 165–180. Springer, Heidelberg (2006)
15. Berthold, O., Federrath, H., Köpsell, S.: Web mIXes: A system for anonymous and unobservable internet access. In: Federrath, H. (ed.) Designing Privacy Enhancing Technologies. LNCS, vol. 2009, pp. 115–129. Springer, Heidelberg (2001)
16. Sampigethaya, K., Huang, L., Li, M., Poovendran, R., Sezaki, K.: CARAVAN: Providing location privacy for VANET. WPES 2006. In: Proc. of Embedded Security in Cars (ESCAR) (2005)
17. Gruteser, M., Grunwald, D.: Anonymous usage of location-based services through spatial and temporal cloaking. In: Proc. of ACM MobiSys., pp. 31–42 (2003)
18. Samarati, P., Sweeney, L.: Protecting privacy when disclosing information: k-anonymity and its enforcement through generalization and suppression, Tech. Report SRI-CSL-98-04, CS Lab, SRI International (1998)
19. Wu, X., Elisa, B.: An Analysis Study on Zone-Based Anonymous Communication in Mobile Ad Hoc Networks. IEEE Trans. On Dependable and Secure Computing 4(4), 252–264 (2007)
20. Khabazian, M., Ali, M.K.: Generalized Performance Modeling of Vehicular Ad Hoc Networks (VANETs). In: ISCC 2007, pp. 51–56 (2007)
21. Trivedi, K.S.: Probability and Statistics with Reliability, Queuing, and Computer Science Applications, 2nd edn. John Wiley & Sons, Chichester (2002)

Biographies

Brijesh Kumar Chaurasia is persuing his Ph.D. from Indian Institute of Information Technology, Allahabad, India in Privacy in Ad hoc Networks. He is received his M. Tech. degree from D.A.V.V., Indore, India. His research interest area is Security in infrastructureless Networks.

Shekhar Verma received his Ph.D. from IT, BHU, Varanasi, India in Computer Networks. He is Associate Professor at Indian Institute of Technology, Allahabad, India. His research interest area is Computer Networks, Data Aggregation in Wireless Sensor Networks, Networks Security.

Geetam Singh Tomar received his Ph. D. degree in electronics Engineering from R.G.P.V. Bhopal. He is presently Director, Vikrant Institute of Technology & Management, Indore, India. His research work is air interface for cellular and mobile ad-hoc networks, Antenna design and fabrication, sensors and sensor networks and underwater communication.

Ajith Abraham received his Ph.D. degree in Computer Science from Monash University, Australia. Currently works in Norwegian University of Science and Technology and also holds an Adjunct Professor appointment in Jinan University, China and Dalian Maritime University, China. He works in a multidisciplinary environment involving computational intelligence, network security, sensor networks, e-commerce, Web intelligence, Web services, computational grids, data mining and applied to various real world problems.

Security Analysis of Role Based Access Control Models Using Colored Petri Nets and CPNtools

Hind Rakkay and Hanifa Boucheneb

École Polytechnique de Montréal, Québec, Canada
hind.rakkay@polymtl.ca, hanifa.boucheneb@polymtl.ca

Abstract. Several advanced Role based access control (RBAC) models have been developed supporting specific features (i.e.: role hierarchy, separation of duty) to achieve high flexibility. However, integrating additional features also increases their design complexity, and consequently the opportunity for mistakes that may cause information to flow to inappropriate destinations. In this paper, we present a formal technique to model and analyze RBAC using Colored Petri nets (CP-nets) and CP-Ntools[1] for editing and analyzing CP-nets. Our purpose is to elaborate a CP-net model which describes generic access control structures based on an RBAC policy. The resulting CP-net model can be then composed with different context-specific aspects depending on the application. A significant benefit of CP-nets and, particularly, CPNtools is to provide a graphical representation and an analysis framework that can be used by security administrators to understand why some permissions are granted or not and to detect whether security constraints are violated.

Keywords: RBAC, Colored Petri nets, CPNtools, security formal verification.

1 Introduction

A security policy consists of specific rules that regulates the nature and the context of actions being performed throughout a system. Security models are used to specify the design and to verify the correctness of systems according to specific policies. In analyzing a security model, all possible events must be considered to ensure conformance of a security policy with respect to its implementation. It is then very important to have a mechanism and a corresponding tool to help software developers or system administrators understand and articulate the security model and associated policies. If security administrators can automatically check the security of their systems, security will be improved from the beginning of the design process.

A comprehensive survey of the various access control policies, models and mechanisms is also provided by Samarati and di Vimercati [1]. In this paper, we are concerned with this issue in case of Role-Based Access control (RBAC) [2] models. RBAC models are widely used in the security community, as a basic

---

[1] http://wiki.daimi.au.dk/cpntools

M.L. Gavrilova et al. (Eds.): Trans. on Comput. Sci. IV, LNCS 5430, pp. 149–176, 2009.
© Springer-Verlag Berlin Heidelberg 2009

authorization service mechanism, to express access control rules. With RBAC policy, an organization maps its specific structure, roles and permissions through the RBAC model. The advantage of using roles is several. They simplify authorization administration, so that a security administrator only needs to revoke and assign new roles to a user when changing his job function. RBAC is also policy neutral and can support various security policy objectives as least privilege, static and dynamic separation of duty constraints [3].

However, many problems with role-based security policy analysis automation still require more studies [4]. A compliant RBAC design will contain a set of components selected from the following: 1. Core RBAC, 2. Hierarchical RBAC, 3. Static Separation of Duty (SSD) Relations, and 4. Dynamic Separation of Duties (DSD) Relations. Although these security features certainly increase the expressiveness of an RBAC policy, they also increase its design complexity, and consequently the opportunity for mistakes that may cause information to flow to inappropriate destinations.

To address this issue, we are motivated in exploring the use of CP-nets to contribute to the representation of RBAC models, to the specification of an RBAC policy, and to the validation of both the security model and security policy. CP-nets offer hierarchical descriptions, and are supported by various simulation tools such as CPNtools used in this study. CPNtools is a graphical ML-based tool for editing and analyzing CP-nets. In this tool, the different parts of a CP-net model are constructed in different CP-net pages (modules) to handle large specifications. This helps using CP-net hierarchy constructs that enable the designer to break the complexity of the modeled system into different layers with different abstraction levels [5].

Our purpose then is to elaborate a hierarchical CP-net model which describes generic access control structures based on an RBAC policy. The resulting CP-net model can be then composed with any given application, also organized as one or multiple modules. In this way, RBAC aspects can be reused across different applications with similar access control requirements.

In this paper, we first provide a general CP-net model that expresses most access control aspects with respect to RBAC policy requirements. Then, we associate the application design elements to the resulting graphical representation. Finally, we use CP-nets reachability analysis in order to check whether the access control requirements have been adequately addressed in the design. Also, reference [6] is an interesting research about formalization of RBAC models by means of CP-nets, however, the authors do not provide systematic guidelines to help in modeling RBAC specification using CPNtools and do not show how to model-check correctness properties. We then provide here an in-depth specification using CPNtools to ensure efficient management of authorizations, better flexibility and particularly a lower complexity of constraint representation.

In the next section, we present relevant background on Petri net formalism and provide an introduction to RBAC models. Section 3 reviews related work. The colored Petri-net model of RBAC is detailed in Section 4, with a small example of its use. Section 5 presents the reachability analysis for consistency verification of RBAC Policy. Section 6 provides a Workflow example. Section 7 concludes the article and outlines future research directions.

2   Preliminaries

This section introduces some basic notions and notations to be used in the following sections.

2.1   Basic Concepts of Petri Net

Petri nets, or place-transition nets, are classical models of concurrency, nondeterminism, and control flow, first proposed by Carl Adam Petri in 1962 [7]. The classical Petri net is a directed bipartite graph with two node types called places and transitions. The nodes are connected via directed arcs. Connections between two nodes of the same type are not allowed. Places are represented by circles and transitions by rectangles. Places of Petri nets usually represent states or resources in the system while transitions model the activities of the system. At any time a place contains zero of more tokens, drawn as black dots. The arcs may be labelled with an integer weight. Unlabelled arcs are assumed to have a weight equal to 1.

Definition 1 (Petri net)
A PN is a tuple $(P, T, Pre, Post, M_0)$:

- P is a finite set of places,
- T is a finite set of transitions ($P \cap T = \emptyset$),
- Pre: $P \quad T \to \mathbb{N}$ is the input incidence function
- $Post$: $P \quad T \to \mathbb{N}$ is the output incidence function.
- M_0 is the initial marking indicating which tokens are present initially in the net, $P \to \mathbb{N}$. The marking of the net indicates which tokens are present in places.

A place p is called an input place of a transition t iff there exists a directed arc from p to t. Place p is called an output place of transition t iff there exists a directed arc from t to p. The Petri net dynamics is given by firing enabled transitions, whose occurrence corresponds to a state change of the system modeled by the net. A transition t is firable only if enabled for a marking M such as $\forall p \in P, M(p) \geq Pre(p, t)$, i.e. there are enough tokens available in the input places. When a transition t fires, it removes tokens from its input places and adds some at all of its output places. Tokens removed / added are specified respectively in Pre(p,t) and Post(p,t). The new reachable marking M is computed as follows: $\forall p \in P, M(p) = M(p) - Pre(p, t) + Post(p, t)$

2.2   Colored Petri Net

Colored Petri Nets introduced by Jensen [8] extend Petri nets by allowing tokens to be associated with colors. Each place is associated with a color set that specifies all the legitimate colors of the place. A marking is the set of colored tokens that reside in all Petri net places. A transition is enabled if all input places of the transition have a specified required set of colored tokens in them. The firing of an enabled transition causes the removal of specified colored tokens from the input places and the creation of specified colored tokens in output places. The behavior of the CP-net may be variable depending on which tokens are consumed and produced when a transition fires at the same Petri net marking.

Definition 2. Multi-sets and Power set

- Let A be a set. A multi-set over A is a function $F : A \rightarrow \mathbb{N}$ which associates with each element of A, an integer number. It is represented by the formal sum: $\sum_{a \in A} F(a) \bullet a$, where $F(a)$ is the occurrence number of a in F. Let A be a set, F_1 and F_2 two multi-sets over A. Operators $+, -, \leq, =$ on multi-sets are defined as usual:
  - $F_1 + F_2 = \sum_{a \in A}(F_1(a) + F_2(a)) \bullet a$.
  - $F_1 \leq F_2$ iff, $(\forall a \in A, (F_1(a) \leq F_2(a)))$.
  - $F_1 = F_2$ iff, $(\forall a \in A, (F_1(a) = F_2(a)))$.
  - If $F_1 \leq F_2$ then $F_2 - F_1 = \sum_{a \in A}(F_2(a) - F_1(a)) \bullet a$.

  We denote by A_{MS} the set of all multi-sets over A, and by 0 the empty multi-set.
- Let A be a set. The power set (or powerset) of A, written $PowerSet(A)$ or 2^A, is the set of all subsets of A including the empty set.

Definition 3 (Colored Petri net)
A CP-net is a tuple $(\Delta, P, T, Pre, Post, C, G, E, M_0)$:

- Δ is a finite set of types, called color sets. Each color set is finite.
- $C : P \rightarrow PowerSet(\Delta)$. $C(p)$ is a finite set which specifies the set of allowed values (or colors) for any token of place p. Let CT be the set of all possible colored tokens, i.e.: $CT = \{(p, c) | p \in P \wedge c \in C(p)\}$.
- G is a guard function, mapping each transition to an expression of boolean type. All variables in G must have types that belongs to Δ, i.e.: $\forall t \in T :$ $[Type(G(t)) = B \wedge Type(Var(G(t))) \subseteq \Delta], B = \{true, false\}$.
- E is an expression function, mapping each arc into an expression which must be of type $C(p)_{MS}$ (multi-set over $C(p)$) where p is a place belonging to a given arc. All variables in such expressions must also be of $C(p)$ type (evaluation of the arc expressions indicate what token is to be taken from the transition's input place as well as what token is to be placed in the output place), i.e.: $\forall a \in A : [Type(E(a)) = C(p(a))_{MS} \wedge Type(Var(E(a))) \subseteq \Delta]$.
- M_0 is the initial marking, $M_0 \in (CT)_{MS}$

"A CP-net model is a description of the modeled system, and it can be used as a specification of a system that we want to build or as a presentation of a system that we want to explain to other people, or ourselves. By creating a model we can investigate a new system before we construct it. This is an obvious advantage, in particular for systems where design errors may jeopardize security or be expensive to correct. CP-net also allow the modeling of complex systems and data flows. Furthermore, the behavior of a CP-net model can be analyzed, either by means of simulation or by means of more formal analysis methods" [9].

We refer interested readers to [5] that gives an interesting introduction to the CP-net modelling language and illustrates how construction, simulation, state space analysis, performance analysis and visualisation are supported by CPNtools.

2.3   RBAC Introduction and Features

The NIST (National Institute of Standards and Technology) group proposes the standardization of the RBAC model [2]. The proposed NIST standard presents a RBAC reference model based on four components: Core RBAC, Hierarchical RBAC, Static Separation of Duty Relations and Dynamic Separation of Duty Relations, to permit vendors to partially implement RBAC features in their products.

Core RBAC embodies the essential features of RBAC. It consists of the following sets: **Users**, a user is a human being or a process within a system, **Roles**, a role is a collection of permissions associated with a certain job function within an organization, **Permissions**, a permission is an access mode that can be exercised on a particular object in the system, and **Sessions**, a user establishes a session during which he activates a subset of the roles assigned to him. Each user can activate multiple sessions; however, each session is associated with only one user. The operations that a user can perform in a session depend on the roles activated in that session and on the permissions associated with those roles. Core RBAC supports the specification of:

- $PA : Roles \rightarrow Permissions$ is the permission-role assignment relation, that assigns to roles the permissions needed to complete their jobs;
- $UA : Users \rightarrow Roles$ is the user-role assignment relation, that assigns users to roles;
- $user : Sessions \rightarrow Users$ assigns each session to a single user;
- $role : Sessions \rightarrow 2^{R \ le}$ assigns each session to a set of roles;

Fig. 1 is a classic view of the RBAC model, showing the relationships among permissions on operations and objects, and the sets of roles that have permissions for them.

The RBAC model also provides administrators with the ability of adding other features such as Role Hierarchy (RH), Role/User Cardinality (RC/UC), Static Separation of Duty (SSD), and Dynamic Separation of Duties (DSD) relations.

Hierarchical RBAC adds constraints to Core RBAC for supporting role hierarchies. Role hierarchy is a partial ordering on the set of roles. If one role inherits another and a user is authorized for the inheriting role, then that user becomes also authorized for the inherited role. Formally, we write $RH \subseteq Roles \quad Roles$ is a partially ordered role hierarchy (written $\leq$). If $r_j \leq r_i$, $r_i, r_j \in Roles$ then r_i inherits the permissions of r_j. In such a case, r_i is a senior role and r_j a junior role.

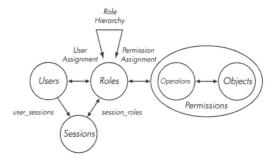

Fig. 1. The RBAC model

Role cardinality is a role attribute that restricts the number of users for which a role may be authorized. Whereas, user cardinality restricts the number of roles for which a user may be authorized.

SSD relations are necessary to prevent conflicts of interest that arise when a user gains permissions associated with conflicting roles (roles which cannot be assigned to the same user). If two roles have a *SSD* relationship, then no user may be authorized for both roles. If two roles have *DSD* relationship, then a user may be authorized for both roles, but that user may not have both roles active at the same time (in the same session or different sessions).

RBAC has been widely researched and extended by several researches [10, 11, 12]. One such interesting extension is the Generalized Temporal Role Based Access Control (GTRBAC) model [12]. The GTRBAC model provides a generalized mechanism to express diverse set of fine-grained temporal constraints in order to meet dynamic access control requirements of an enterprize. The model also offers an event-based mechanism for providing context based access control policies. In particular, GTRBAC distinguishes between four states of a role *Assign, Enable, Disable* and *Active*.

When a user logs into system, the system assigns him the roles he is authorized to assume. The disabled state indicates that the role cannot be used in any user session, i.e., a user cannot acquire the permissions associated with the role. A role in the disabled state can be enabled. The enabled state indicates that users who are authorized to use the role at the time of the request may activate the role. Subsequently, when a user activates the role, the state of the role becomes active, which implies that there is at least one user who has activated the role. Once in the active state, reactivation of the role does not change its state. When a role is in the active state, upon deactivation, the role changes to the enabled state. A role in the enabled or active state changes to the disabled state if a disabling event occurs.

From a design perspective, this distinction between roles is adopted to describe interactions patterns that take place when events on roles occur, such as assigning a role to a user, de-assigning a role from a user, enabling a role, disabling a role, activating and de-activating a role). In a first step, we consider only some constraints of GTRBAC without including time. However, in a subsequent work, we intend to extend our proposition in order to support temporal constraints by using timed tokens.

For more details about GTRBAC, we refer interested readers to [12] for a more thorough review of the model.

2.4   RBAC Consistency Rules

A policy is a set of rules that defines the expected behavior of the system employing that policy. The system is said to be "in conformance" with the underlying policy if each of its state can be deduced from the set of rules/axioms comprising the policy. An inconsistent state or erratic system behavior can be attributed to a potential flaw in the policy specification. This flaw may be caused by the inconsistency in the policy itself, or by its incompleteness. An inconsistent policy is the one in which two or more rules from a given set of rules comprising the policy contradict each other. Incompleteness implies that the given set of rules defining the policy is not sufficient to capture all states of the system. In this context, security verification can be stated as the process of proving that the properties or rules specified in a security policy are enforced in the information system. In [6], a set of consistency rules are proposed which are major extensions of consistency rules defined in [13]. This extended set of rules allows modeling of various constraints of RBAC with an event-based approach. This set of rules mainly cover the cardinality, inheritance and separation of duty.

2.4.1   Cardinality Constraints

- *Authorization Role Cardinality* (RC): The number of authorized users for any role does not exceed the authorization cardinality of that role.
- *Authorization User Cardinality* (UC): The number of roles authorized for any user does not exceed the maximum number of roles the user is entitled to acquire.
- *User Activation Cardinality* (UAC): The number of roles activated by any user u does not exceed the maximum number of roles the user is entitled to activate at any time.
- *Role Activation Cardinality* (RAC): The number of users who have activated a role r in their ongoing sessions does not exceed the role activation cardinality.

2.4.2   Role Hierarchy Constraints

- If a role r_1 inherits role r_2 and both roles are distinct, then r_2 cannot inherit r_1.
- Any two distinct roles assigned to the same user do not inherit (directly or indirectly) one another.

2.4.3 Separation of Duties Constraints

- Any two roles assigned for same user are not in static separation of duties.
- There is no role in static separation of duties with itself.
- The static separation of duties relation is symmetric.
- If a role (directly or indirectly) inherits another role and the inherited role is in static separation of duties with a third role, then the inheriting is in static separation of duties with the third role.
- If a role inherits another role, then the assignment time conflicting set of users of the inherited role is a subset of the assignment time conflicting set of users of the inheriting role.
- Only one user from a set of assignment time conflicting users of role r can be assigned role r.
- If two distinct roles r_1 and r_2 with $r_2 \leq r_1$, have some common assignment time conflicting set of users, then only one user from the common set can be assigned any of the two roles r_1 and r_2 and not both.
- The active role set of any user is a subset of his/her authorized roles.
- Any two roles in dynamic separation of duties do not both belong to the active role set of any user.
- The dynamic separation of duties and static separation of duties are disjoint.
- There is no role in dynamic separation of duties with itself.
- The dynamic separation of duties relation is symmetric.
- If a role inherits a junior role, then the activation time conflicting set of users of the inherited role is a subset of the activation time conflicting set of users of the inheriting role.
- Role r cannot be concurrently activated by users u_1 and u_2, if these users are activation time conflicting for role r.

3 Related Work

In the past years, Petri nets use has become much easier with the availability of high quality environments and tools. According to many researchers [14], Petri Nets (PN) are the only formal techniques able to be used for structural modeling and a wide range of qualitative and quantitative analysis. Petri net has been used for verification of security requirements [15], for specification of workflows [16], and for security analysis of security policies including Discretionary Access Control (DAC) policies [17], Mandatory Access Control (MAC) policies [9, 18, 19, 20, 21, 22, 23, 24] and also Role-Based access control policies [6, 25].

Formal descriptions of access control models are important for explaining and comparing models, for proving properties about models, and for attempts at validating implementations of the models. Using Petri net formalism allows one to visually depict the model through its graphical representation and to analyze its behavior through its rich set of analysis techniques. The topology of a system is an important source of information especially for analyzing authorization flows. Several researches show that Petri net based policy specification and analysis framework present many advantages to overcome some limitations of DAC and MAC security models which focus on access control and are generally static.

Knorr [17] uses Petri nets to make dynamic access control in workflow systems. Instead of using a global static access control matrix to grant subjects rights to data items for the whole system, he proposes assigning a local matrix to each transition to grant rights to subjects (that will execute the transition) only to data being consumed or produced by the transition. When a transition is enabled, subjects will have only the access rights (specified by the access control matrix) which are needed for the execution of this transition. The objective is to realize *the need-to-know* paradigm.

In a subsequent work [20], Knorr shows how to use Petri nets in order to analyze the information flow in a workflow system where authorizations are granted based on Bell-LaPadula's model [26]. The analysis approach consists of constructing the reachability graph augmented with the object security levels. During the analysis, the objects are assigned all possible security levels in order to enumerate all model states. Also Varadharajan [18] proposes an extended Petri net formalism called Information Flow Security net (IFS) to provide a way of modeling information flow security policies expressed through the Petri net structure. This model was reviewed by Juopperi in [19] to show how the security properties of an IFS net can be inspected indirectly by constructing a Predicate/transition Petri net (PrT-nets) [27]. Later, Juszczyszy [21] proposes another security model called Secure Colored Petri Net (SCPN) derived from the IFS net to give a better and more compact representation to efficiently analyze information flows.

Jiang *and al.* [23] also propose a different way to make a system security analysis under Bell-LaPadula's model by using CP-nets. The analysis is based on the reachability graph exploration in order to verify some security attributes, such as the access temporal relations, the objects reachability when subject accesses them, hidden security holes due to the dynamic security level, and the indirect reasoning of confidential information flow between different objects.

Zhang *and al.* [9] present an approach for modeling Chinese Wall Policy [28] using CP-nets. In a subsequent work, Zhang *and al.* [24] also use CP-nets to systematically analyze the information flow under the strict integrity policy like Biba's model [29].

In [22], we propose to use timed colored Petri net with security notions to both express time constraints on information (availability) and specify a wide range of information flow security requirements (through multilevel security policies such as Bell-LaPadula) in a decentralized way. To analyze the resulting model, we also develop an approach that abstracts its generally infinite state space (because of time density) into a graph preserving its reachable markings and traces. The graph obtained is finite if and only if the model is bounded and allows verifying security properties such as confidentiality, integrity, information flow and information availability using a subset of CTL^2 formalism.

---

[2] Computation-tree Logic.

Petri net is not limited to systems with DAC and MAC policies. In fact, in recent years, the importance of Role-Based access control has been widely investigated. Some works focus on Petri nets for representation of workflows with RBAC as a security mechanism to grant authorizations [30,31], while other researches aim at using Petri net frameworks to formalize RBAC administration models [32].

Atluri and Huang [30] use color-timed Petri nets to implement a workflow authorization model. They use Petri nets to ensure synchronization between authorization flow and the workflow such as subjects gain access on the required objects only during the execution of the specific task. Each task is also specified with a time interval during which the task must be executed. However, SoD constraints are modeled in a complicated manner and their model lack to the notion of role hierarchy. In [31], Atluri and Huang's work [30] has been refined to present a role-based authorization model using CP-net formalism. Authors in [31] propose to associate legitimate roles with each task so that only members of the legitimate roles can be authorized to perform the task. However, they create a place for each role, whereas all roles could be grouped in a unique place and distinguished by colors.

Shafiq *and al.* [6] present a verification framework using Colored Petri nets based on GTRBAC. They only consider some interesting constraints without including explicitly the temporal dimension. Moreover, the authors do not use any tool and do not take advantage of the high modeling power of Colored Petri nets to represent e.g. user-role assignment and seniority relationships.

In his thesis research, Shin [33] extends RBAC and composes an advanced access control scheme for trusted operating systems called E-RBAC. He also proposes a CP-net framework with security considerations for a formal specification of E-RBAC. With the CP-net formalism, Shin shows how to formally specify the extended access control system, to simulate and verify security-related properties by CPNtools as an automated tool. This work shows that using CP-nets helps security administration of the extended access control system.

On the other hand, there is a considerable work to specify or verify RBAC model such as using ALLOY [34], Z language [35], first-order linear temporal logic (LTL) [36] and the description logic language $ALCQ$ [37].

Zao *and al.* [34] propose to employ ALLOY [38], a lightweight formal modeling system developed in MIT, to verify internal consistencies of RBAC schema. They do not make distinction between Static and Dynamic SoD. In [35], Chunyang *and al.* present a formal state-based verifiable RBAC model described with Z language, in which the state-transition functions are specified formally. Z language is based on ZF set theory and first-order predicate logic [39]. The authors show how to specify and verify the consistency of a formal RBAC system with theorem proving using Z/EVES [40], a modeling and analysis tool supporting Z specifications. However, using mathematical induction requires a strong mathematical knowledge which is always a drawback of induction. In [36], Drouineaud *and al.* show how to express a simple RBAC security policy using first-order linear temporal logic (LTL)[3] in the theorem prover Isabelle/HOL [41], in order to check constraints of separation of duty. However, their LTL-based description does not handle role hierarchies and sessions.

Authors in [37] propose a formalization of RBAC by a description logic language called $ALCQ$ [42]. They demonstrate how to make access control decision and perform RBAC functions via the description logic reasoner RACER. However, consistency conditions on the RBAC functions cannot be expressed by this logic language.

Knorr and Weidner introduce a *SoD* model based on the Peti net workflow. Their model is analyzed by a logic program [43]. *SoD* rules, Petri net based workflow specification, and organizational facts are all represented as facts in Prolog. The administrator has to put great effort to enumerate all the possible facts in terms of the user and task pairs that would violate the *SoD* constraints in an organization. Representing everything as a predicate in a logic program would make it a tiny job for the administrator to specify workflow, organizational structure, roles, user-role assignments, and *SoD* rules in a logic program. Such languages are too complex for administrators to determine whether a set of constraints really expresses the desired safety requirements properly.

In general, formal logic-based approaches assume a strong mathematical background which makes them difficult to use and understand. Moreover, any first-order logic is generally undecidable.

Other researchers have used constraint formalisms based on graphs (Jaeger *and al.* [44], Neumann *and al.* [45], Nyanchama *and al.* [46], Koch [47]). Although these approaches are easier to understand than formal logic-based approaches, they are primarily static in nature and do not adequately take into account various authorization related RBAC events that can be allowed in a system nondeterministically.

Here, we present a technique to model and analyze RBAC models using CP-nets. We aim to elaborate a CP-net model which describes generic access control structures based on an RBAC policy and that can be then composed with different context-specific aspects depending on the application. Unlike previous works, our main contribution is that we exploit CP-net's modeling power, we provide systematic guidelines to help in modeling RBAC specification using CP-net and we also show how to model-check correctness properties using reachability analysis in CPNtools.

Our approach consists then of three tasks as follows: RBAC representation using CP-nets, RBAC general constraints specification and finally, RBAC model and constraint verification within an application.

4   Modeling RBAC in Terms of CP-Nets

Petri nets can be considered to have sufficient abstraction level to allow the management of the authorizations and the properties related to it. It allows

---

[3] Linear Temporal Logic.

expressing all elements constituting an RBAC model, i.e.: subjects, objects, actions, roles. Petri nets as a support of modeling offers also a support for better managing the specification of an RBAC security policy, its update, in addition to capture dynamic properties of the model, in particular authorization flows.

Here, we represent the RBAC model using CPNtools. In our approach, the definitions related to constraint expressions are incorporated with corresponding components in CP-nets representation.

Furthermore, the adopted modeling assumptions take into account basic event expressions used by the GTRBAC constraint specification language, i.e. *Assign a role to a user*, *De-Assign a role from a user*, *Enable a role*, *Disable a role*, *Activate* and *De-Activate a role*.

4.1   Net Structure and Declarations

In this section, the RBAC model is described using CP-nets. The net structure of the CP-net model consists of seven modules (pages). The top level of the model is the RBAC model, shown in Fig. 2. There are six main functional areas represented by means of substitution transitions and connected by shared places. In this way, each main functional area is modeled by an appropriately named sub-module: *Assign*, *De-Assign*, *Enable*, *Disable*, *Activate* and *De-Activate* respectively. In the following, we elaborate the elements of a CP-net within the context of RBAC.

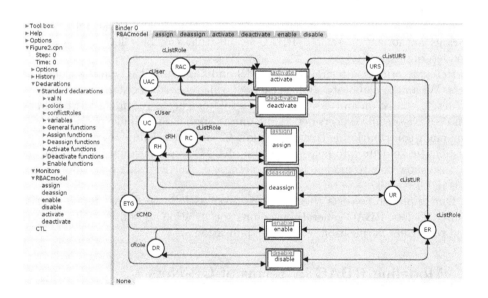

Fig. 2. CP-net representation of the RBAC model

4.1.1   Color sets

Fig. 3 summarizes the color and variable declarations used for the RBAC model. In our modeling of the RBAC model, we choose to represent sets of Users, Roles and Sessions as colors *cUser*, *cRole* and *cSession* respectively. The other color sets are composed from the basic ones. We list below the important ones:

- Color *cRH* defines the role hierarchy relation by specifying for each role, the list of its junior roles represented by *cListRole*, a list of roles.
- Color *cUR* is used to represent for each user the list of roles he is authorized to assume.
- Color *cSR* represents a role in an active state within a session.
- Color *cURS* is used to represent for each user, the set of roles activated within sessions modeled as a list of color *cSR*.
- Commands are composed of atomic fields includng *cUser*, *cRole* and *cSession*. For instance, an assign command *"assign(user, role)"* can be viewed as a tuple *(assign, user, role)*. The same thing for the other commands *(de-assign, user, role)*, *(enable, role)*, *(disable, role)*, *(activate,user, role, session)* and *(deactivate, user, role, session)*. To generalize, we use color *cCommand* to represent the set of commands to execute in the model defined as Color *cCMD*.

```
▼RBACmodel.cpn
    Step: 0
    Time: 0
  ► Options
  ► History
  ▼ Declarations
    ▼ Standard declarations
      ▼ val N=10 ;
      ▼ colors
        ▼ colset INT = int with 0..N;
        ▼ colset cUser = index u with 0..N;
        ▼ colset cRole = index r with 0..N;
        ▼ colset cSession=index s with 0..N;
        ▼ colset cCommande = with assign | deassign | enable | disable | activate | deactivate;
        ▼ colset cListRole=list cRole;
        ▼ colset cRH = product cRole * cListRole;
        ▼ colset cConflictRole = list cRH;
        ▼ colset cUR = product cUser * cListRole;
        ▼ colset cListUR= list cUR;
        ▼ colset cSR= product cRole * cSession;
        ▼ colset cListSessionRole = list cSR;
        ▼ colset cURS = product cUser * cListSessionRole;
        ▼ colset cListURS= list cURS;
        ▼ colset cCMD= product cCommande * cUser * cRole * cSession;
      ▼ variables
        ▼ var ry:cRole;
        ▼ var uz: cUser;
        ▼ var sx : cSession;
        ▼ var n:INT;
        ► var listry
        ▼ var listER: cListRole;
        ▼ var listRC, listRAC:cListRole;
        ▼ var listUR:cListUR;
        ▼ var listURS : cListURS;
```

Fig. 3. Color sets and variables used in the RBAC CP-net

We use variables of the defined color sets as inscriptions for arcs of the CP-net. For instance, u_z, r_y, s_x respectively of type $cUser$, $cRole$ and $cSession$.

Also, based on these color sets, we define the following tokens:

- $<p, u>$ is a *user token* where p is the place to which it belongs and $u \in cUser$.
- $<p, r>$ is a *role token* in place p with $r \in cRole$.
- $<p, r, listr>$ expresses *role hierarchy relations* expressed by $listr$. All junior roles that may be associated with a role r are memorized in the role colored list $listr$ (including r).
- $<p, u, r>$ is a *user-role assignment* token. It indicates a role in an assigned state.
- $<p, u, r, s>$ is a *user-role session activation* token. It indicates that session s is being activated by user u who assumes role r.
- $<p, cmd, u, r, s>$ is a *command* token of color $cCMD$.

4.1.2 Places P

As shown in Fig. 2, the RBAC page comprises ten places and six substitution transitions. The places are used to capture the state information for modeling different constraints. The initial marking of the places is set depending on the context of the application.

Place ETG (*Event token generator*) stores command tokens for user-role assignment and de-assignment, role enabling and disabling, role activation and de-activation. For any transition to get enabled, there must be a corresponding token in the place ETG which acts as a transition firing controller to analyze all possible system states against a given command list. Place ETG can be an output place of another page. The ETG initially contains a finite number of command tokens and will be eventually executed randomly. Places RC (*Role Cardinality*), UC (*User Cardinality*), RAC (*Role Activation cardinality*) and UAC (*User Activation cardinality*) are used to mainly cover various cardinality constraints.

- Place RC contains a list of role tokens ($C(RC) = cListRole$) to enforce role cardinality constraint, i.e., to limit the number of users which can be authorized for a given role. If there are k tokens of color r_y in RC and no user is assigned role r_y, then role r_y can be assigned to at most k users. RC initially contains a list of role tokens. For example, $<RC,[r_0,r_0,r_0,r_1,r_1]>$ means that roles r_0 and r_1 can respectively be assigned to at most 3 and 2 users.

- Place UC, typed by color set $cUser$, helps to enforce assignment user cardinality constraint, i.e., to limit the number of roles for which a given user can be authorized. If there are m tokens of color u_z in UC and u_z is not yet authorized for any role, then user u_z can be authorized for at most m roles. Place UC initially contains a multi-set of user tokens. For example, $3<UC,u_0> + 2<UC,u_1>$ means that users u_0 and u_1 are respectively authorized for at most 3 and 2 roles.

- Place RAC as place RC stores a list of role tokens. It enforces activation role cardinality constraint, i.e., limits the number of concurrent activations of a given role. If there are l tokens of color r_y in RAC, then at most l more copies

Fig. 4. Role hierarchy representation

of role r_y can be activated concurrently. Its initial marking is a multi-set of role tokens.

- Place UAC stores tokens of type $cUser$ to enforce activation user cardinality constraint, i.e., limits the number of concurrent activations of roles for a given user. If there are j tokens $<UAC,u_z>$, then user u_z can make j more activations concurrently. These activations may involve activating same role multiple times or multiple roles for any number of times provided that the total number of such concurrent activations of roles by user u_z do not exceed the user activation cardinality j. This place is initially marked by a multi-set of user tokens.

As we already mentioned, GTRBAC distinguishes among various states of a role: assigned, disabled, enabled and active states. Therefore, places UR (*User Role Assignment/Authorization*), DR (*Disabled Roles*), ER (*Enabled Roles*) and URS (*User Role Session activation*) are used to capture these states respectively.

- Place UR contains a list of roles in assign state. A token $<UR, u_z, listRole>$ means that a user u_z is authorized for all roles specified in the list of role tokens.
- Place DR can only store role tokens ($C(DR) = cRole$) in disable state. Initially, all roles are disabled.
- Place ER stores a list of role tokens. A list $[r_1,r_2]$ in ER implies that roles r_1 and r_2 are in enabled state.
- Place URS stores a list of users who established a session by activating a set of roles. Each token $<URS,u_z, listSessionRole>$ implies that user u_z is assuming roles specified in the list of role tokens according to the session of each one.

Finally, we represent the role hierarchy by the place RH (*Role Hierarchy*). This place contains tokens of color ($C(RH) = cRH$) to show existing role hierarchy relations. Role hierarchy relations of Fig. 4 are represented as follows: $<RH,r_0,listr_0> + <RH,r_1,listr_1> + <RH, r_2, listr_2> + <RH, r_3, listr_3> + <RH, r_4, listr_4>$ where $listr_0 = [r_0..r_4]$, $listr_1 = [r_1]$, $listr_2 = [r_2..r_4]$, $listr_3 = [r_3]$, $listr_4 = [r_4]$.

4.1.3 Arcs, arc Expression and Guards

We use arcs, arc expressions and guards functions to model constraints including cardinality, *SoD* and inheritance constraints as discussed in section 2.4. In Table 1, we first present the general functions and guards used in CP-net modeling of RBAC and as an example, those used in defining user-role assignment.

Table 1. Functions and guards used in defining consistency properties for RBAC

$exist\_role(r_y,\ listRole)$	evaluates true if $r_y \in$ listRole
$exist\_user(uz,\ listUR)$	evaluates true if u_z is assigned a role
$exist\_role\_session(ry,\ sx,\ listSR)$	evaluates true if r_y is active in session s_x
$get\_conflict\_roleset(ry,\ listConflict)$	returns the set of roles that conflict with r_y
$get\_role\_list(uz,\ listUR)$	returns the roles assigned to u_z
$get\_session\_list(uz,\ listURS)$	returns the set of active (in a session) roles of user u_z
$add\_session\_role(ry,\ sx,\ listSR)$	adds a role newly activated (in a session) to listSR
$remove\_role\_session(ry,\ sx,\ listSR)$	removes a role being deactivated from listSR
$removeUR(uz,\ listUR)$	removes a user from the list of authorized users
$removeURS(uz,\ listURS)$	removes a user from the list of active users
$role\_cardinality(listRC,\ listry)$	denotes the authorization cardinality of each role of listry
$user\_cardinality(uz,\ listry,\ listUR)$	denotes the authorization cardinality of user u_z for each role of listry
$direct\_conflict\_role\_assign(ry,\ listRole)$	evaluates true if r_y is not in static SoD (for user-role assignment) with at least a role of listRole
$indirect\_conflict\_role\_assign(listry,\ listRole)$	evaluates true if at least one role from listry is not in static SoD (for user-role assignment) with any role of listRole
$user\_role\_assignment(uz,\ ry,\ listry,\ listUR)$	evaluates true if u_z can be authorized to role r_y without any assignment conflict with his/her current assigned roles
$new\_assignment(uz,\ ry,\ listry,\ listUR)$	updates u_z's list of assigned roles by adding r_y and its junior roles
$update\_role\_cardinality(uz,\ listRC,\ listUR,\ listry)$	updates the number of roles that u_z is entitled to acquire eventually

4.1.4 Transitions

Transitions represent the following components: *User-role assignment/deassignment, Role enabling/disabling, Role activation/deactivation*. Therefore, the proposed CP-net consists of six hierarchically related pages. In Fig. 5, we show the subpage of transition "assign". Input and output places were assigned to the synonyms shown in the top-level CP-net. In CPNtools, some places are identified as port places because they constitute the interface through which a module exchanges tokens with other modules. Port places are recognized by rectangular port-type tags positioned next to them specifying whether the port place is an input (In), output (Out) or input/output (I/O) port.

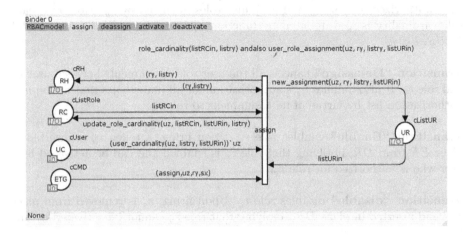

Fig. 5. CP-net construction for user-role assignment

This transition assigns user $u_z \in cUser$ to role r_y by the command $<ETG,$ $assign, u_z, r_y, s_x>$. It may occur at any time whenever all conditions are satisfied. Thus, transition "*assign*" gets enabled if:

- there is an assign command token in place ETG,
- there are n user tokens $<UC, u_z>$ to respect the authorization user cardinality constraint. The number of user tokens n is given by the function *user_cardinality(uz, listry, listUR)*. If the user u_z has an empty assigned role list or no role of those listed by $listr_y$ then the firing will consume "Size $listr_y$". Otherwise the user cardinality will be adjusted by consuming just necessary tokens to assign new roles.
- the guard function *role_cardinality(listRC, listr_y)*, which expresses authorization role cardinality constraint, is satisfied. This function ensures to assign roles memorized in $listr_y$ with respect to their cardinalities contained in place RC.
- the guard function *user_role_assignment(uz, ry, listUR)* is satisfied. This function expresses two conditions in order to validate a user-role assignment. First, user u_z should not already have role r_y in his assigned role list. Also, if u_z is already assigned some roles, we have to be sure that r_y is in static *SoD* with all these roles. This verification is executed by functions *direct_con ict_role_assign(ry, listRole)* and *indirect_con ict_role_assign(listry, listRole)* to avoid that conflicting roles be directly or indirectly (via inheritance) assigned to the same user. *listRole* is the list of conflict roles and is part of the initial specification which is naturally given by the designer. Consequently, a user u_z cannot be assigned role r_y as long as he is assigned a conflicting role r.

Upon firing, the transition "*assign*" inserts a set of tokens in the place UR computed by function *new_assignment(uz, ry, listry, listUR)*. Consequently, user

u_z is authorized for role r_y and all junior roles inherited by r_y. Moreover, each role cardinality is also updated by function *update_role_cardinality(uz, listRC, listUR, listry)*.

Transition "De-assign" cancels all the user role assignments between user u_z and role r_y. It also nullifies u_z's authorization for all junior roles that are on u_z's authorization list by virtue of its assignment to role r_y.

Transition "Enable" enables role r_y. Upon firing, a token r_y is inserted in place ER from DR, implying that role r_y is enabled and can be activated by a user who is authorized for role r_y.

Transition "disable" disables role r_y. Upon firing, r_y is removed from place ER and inserted in place DR, implying that role r_y cannot be activated by any user.

Transition "activate" establishes an active session between user u_z and role r_y. The role is active immediately after firing transition. Then it can be deactivated in any moment upon receiving a deactivate command.

Transition "deactivate" deactivates role r_y from the an active session between user u_z and role r_y.

Although we modeled RBAC with respect to all set of consistency rules, our objective is to express and prove whether we may reach an undesirable state, indicating some potential flaw in the initial specification or weakness in policy specification with respect to the set of consistency properties for the system. So for a given initial state and a set of security policies specified by authorization rules, analysis requires determining all the reachable authorization states. This, known as the *safety problem*, first identified in Harrison *and al.* [48], specifically can be stated as the following question: "Is there a reachable state in which a particular subject possesses a particular privilege for a specific object?". For this purpose, we propose to use reachability analysis to model-checking an RBAC policy.

5   Reachability Analysis for Consistency Verification of RBAC Policy

A state space analysis is an analysis of all possible occurrence paths in the model (represented in the occurrence graph). As we are concerned with security problems that can result from flaws inherent in the security model specification, a lot of information on the properties of the model (and thus on the correctness of an RBAC model) can be gained from the occurrence graph. State space analysis provides some insights on possible configurations.

To illustrate the use of the occurrence graph for security policy verification, let consider the following example taken from [6] and depicted in Fig. 6. There

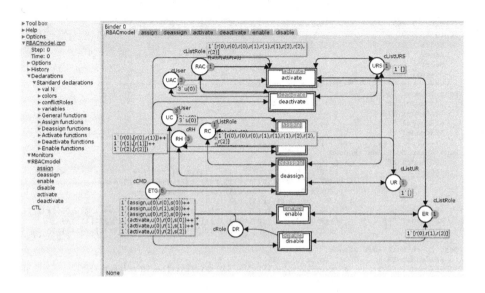

Fig. 6. Example of CP-net representation of an RBAC system

are three roles r_0, r_1, and r_2 and a single user u_0. As an initial specification, we have:

- r_1 is a junior role to r_0 ($r_1 \leq r_0$ and $r_1 \neq r_0$).
- r_1 and r_2 are assignment conflicting roles, i.e., r_1 and r_2 cannot be assigned to the same user implying that roles r_1 and r_2 cannot be activated by the same user concurrently.
- Each role can be assigned to at most 3 users.
- Each role can be activated by at most 3 users.
- User u_0 can be assigned at most 3 roles.
- User u_0 can activate at most 3 roles.

This initial specification is expressed through the CPN model as shown in Fig. 6. Next to each place, there is an inscription which determines the initial marking of the place. For example, the inscription (in the green box) on the left side of the place RH consists of three tokens (of color cRH) representing the role hierarchy. The total number of tokens is represented in the green circle. The ++ and ' are operators that allow for the construction of a multi-set consisting of token colors. The argument on the left of the operator ' is a positive integer which specifies the number of appearances of the argument provided on the right of the operator. The operator ++ takes two multi-sets as arguments and returns their union (sum). The initial marking of place RC consists of one token with the color $cListRole$. Place UR is also marked with one token (an empty list) of type $cListRole$. Place DR has no inscription (i.e. no tokens) because we consider that all roles are initially in enabled state.

Fig. 7 shows the standard report generated for the state space analysis of the described example.

```
Statistics
---------------------------------------------------------------------
  State Space
     Nodes:  13
     Arcs:   13
     Secs:   0
     Status: Full
---------------------- Boundedness Properties-----------------------
  Best Integer Bounds    Upper     Lower
      RBACmodel'ER 1         1          1
      RBACmodel'ETG 1        6          2
      RBACmodel'RC 1         1          1
      RBACmodel'RH 1         3          3
      .........................................
  Best Upper Multi-set Bounds
      RBACmodel'ER 1      1`[r(0),r(1),r(2)]
      RBACmodel'RC 1      1`[r(0),r(0),r(0),r(1),r(1),r(1),r(2),r(2),r(2)]++
                          1`[r(0),r(0),r(0),r(1),r(1),r(1),r(2),r(2),r(2)] ++
                          1`[r(0),r(0),r(0),r(1),r(1),r(1),r(2),r(2),r(2)] ++
                          1`[r(0),r(0),r(1),r(1),r(2),r(2),r(2)]
      RBACmodel'UR 1      1`[]++ 1`[(u(0),[r(0),r(1)])]++ 1`[(u(0),[r(1)])]++ 1`[(u(0),[r(2)])]
      RBACmodel'URS 1     1`[]++ 1`[(u(0),[(r(0),s(0))])]++ 1`[(u(0),[(r(1),s(1))])]++
                          1`[(u(0),[(r(1),s(1)),(r(0),s(0))])]++ 1`[(u(0),[(r(2),s(2))])]
      .........................................
  Best Lower Multi-set Bounds
      RBACmodel'ER 1      1`[r(0),r(1),r(2)]
      RBACmodel'RH 1      1`(r(0),[r(0),r(1)]) ++ 1`(r(1),[r(1)])++ 1`(r(2),[r(2)])
      RBACmodel'UC 1      1`u(0)
      RBACmodel'UR 1      empty
      RBACmodel'URS 1     empty
      .........................................
-----------------------Home Properties------------------------------
  Home Markings : None
-----------------------Liveness Properties--------------------------
  Dead Markings : [7,8,11,12,13]
  Dead Transition Instances
      deactivate'deactivate1 1
      deassign'deassign1 1
      disable'disable1 1
      enable'enable 1
  Live Transition Instances : None
-----------------------Fairness Properties--------------------------
      No infinite occurrence sequences.
```

Fig. 7. The state space analysis standard report for the CP-net of Figure 6

The report contains a lot of useful information about the behavioral properties of the CP-net model. The report is excellent for locating errors and constitute a necessary input source, for correctly expressing the required correctness properties. For the described example, CPNtools generates a full state space of 13 nodes and 13 arcs. We observe the absence of home markings and the absence of live transitions instances. There are no infinite occurrence sequences and the graph terminates in one of the 5 dead markings, with node numbers that are easily found by the provided state space exploration functions. For our example, as r_1 and r_2 are considered to be in SoD (static and dynamic), it will be then interesting to check the following rules :

- Any two roles assigned for the same user are not in static separation of duties.
- Any two roles in dynamic separation of duties do not both belong to the active role set of any user.
- The active role set of any user is a subset of his/her authorized roles.

For this purpose, we use *con icting_role_assignset* and *con icting_role_activeset* as value identifiers which bind each role to a list of its conflicting roles. In the present case, we declare *val con icting_role_assignset* $= [(r(1), [r(2)]), (r(2), [r(1)])]$ and *val con icting_role_activeset* $= [(r(1), [r(2)]), (r(2), [r(1)])]$. Consequently, according to the precedent rules, we have:

- u_0 should not be assigned r_1 and r_2 at the same time.
- u_0 cannot activate r_1 and r_2 concurrently.
- each role activated by u_0 must be in his authorized role list.

The ML-functions used in the model checking of these rules are summarized in Table 2. Function *SearchNodes* is used to detect the marking (s) right after the occurrence of a particular event.

Therefore, to check if all reachable states are consistent with respect to these policy specifications, we use the following ML-functions illustrated in Fig. 8.

Function *assigned_roles* returns the list of authorized roles for each subject. Each element of this list refers to roles authorized for subject u_0 in each reachable state. Whereas function *active_roles* returns a list where each element refers to roles being activated by u_0 within a session. The last function *authorized_roles* is applied on each reachable state to check if a role in an active state is among authorized roles. The function returns true if this condition is satisfied in all reachable state, false otherwise. Therefore, we can say that all reachable states do not show any violation with the initial specifications.

In case a rule does not hold, it is possible to look up for the causes of the problem by e.g closely examining the states not satisfying the rule and the paths

Table 2. State space querying functions

Function description	Use
Mark. <PageName>' <PlaceName> N M	Returns the set of tokens positioned in place <PlaceName> of the Nth instance of page <PageName> in the marking M.
SearchNodes (<search area>, <predicate function>, <search limit>, <evaluation function>, <start value>, <combination function>)	Traverses the nodes of the part of the occurrence graph specified in <search area>. At each node the calculation specified by <evaluation function> is performed and the results of these calculations are combined as specified by <combination function> to form the final result. The <predicate function> maps each node into a boolean value and selects only those nodes, which evaluate to true. We use the value *EntireGraph* for <search area> to denote the set of all nodes in the occurrence graph and the value *NoLimit* for <search limit> to continue searching for all nodes, for which the predicate function evaluates to true.
List.nth(l,n)	Returns the *nth* element in list l, where $0 \leq n <$ length l.

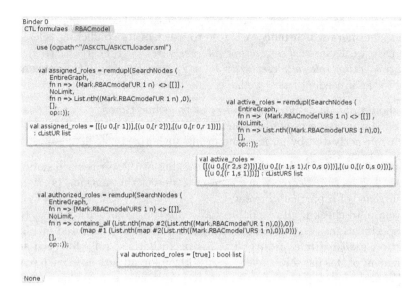

Fig. 8. Model-checking some RBAC consistency rules

leading to these states. This will give insight to locate the source of the problem. It might be the case that some properties derived from the informal specification are not correctly expressed. Then the properties should be changed and the new ones checked [49]. When a colored net is obtained, with most properties satisfied, further analysis can be carried out, leading to possible changes in the specification.

6 Workflow Example

As a basic authorization service mechanism, RBAC is used in various computing environments for access control model. To give an idea how our approach can be used in a real system, we propose a Workflow example taken from [30, 31]. As shown in Fig. 9, this workflow deals with the selection of research papers for a conference. The approach consists of:

A - Derive security key features from the description of the Worfklow, and then transform all this into colored Petri net elements to be expressed in the CP-net based RBAC model.

B - Create a CP-net description of the Workflow.

C - Combine models A and B into a single integrated CP-net model such that only legitimate users are authorized to perform tasks in the Workflow. The RBAC model will be represented on top of the Workflow.

Let apply this approach to the workflow example. This workflow consists of four tasks. Each one must be performed by specific roles. First, an assistant

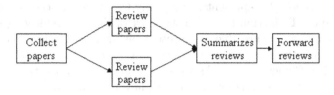

Fig. 9. The workflow example representing the paper reviewing process

collects papers from authors and distributes each of them to two selected reviewers. Each paper is then reviewed by two different reviewers. The conference chair summarizes the review results of each paper from the two reviewers. Finally, the assistant forwards the review result of a paper to its author.

Assistant, reviewer, and conference chair are roles assigned to related tasks. Fig. 10 shows an existing role hierarchy between these roles.

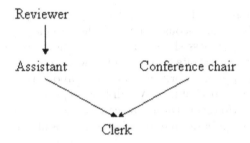

Fig. 10. The role hierarchy

The selection process must obey to some security constraints which are four dynamic *SoD* constraints [31]:

C1: A paper cannot be reviewed by the one who has collected it.
C2: A paper must be reviewed by two different individuals.
C3: The review result of a paper should be summarized by a person different than its reviewers.
C4: The review result of a paper should be forwarded to its author by the one who has originally collected it.

The CP-net based workflow model is shown in Fig. 11. It is represented in an independent page. In addition to role hierarchies, cardinality constraints, we also take into account all *SoD* constraints specific to the workflow. There are four users who are assigned to each role as follows :

- Assistant : u(0)
- Reviewer : u(1), u(2), u(3)
- Conference chair : u(4)

Transitions t_1 and t_2 represent respectively the start and the end of the task collecting paper. Transition t_2 is also the start of the task reviewing paper. Using CP-net features, we are able to represent task-role assignment. For example, transition t_1 has the guard function *assist_review(r(0),r(1),listURSin)*. Transition t_1 fires if a Reviewer or an Assistant is available, as an active role in place *URS*, to collect papers. Whereas in [31], a place is created for each role and the task-role assignment relationship is modeled by specifying this place as the input place of the transition that represents the start of the corresponding task. Firing of transition t_1 produces the same user-role token in both places *Pcollect* and Pd. Constraints C1 and C2 are both verified directly by the guard function of the transition t_2, i.e. *reviewer(r(0), userRole, listURSin)*. This function is true if there are two different users assigned to the reviewer role. Both users must be different from "userRole" color which has collected the paper. Constraint C3 is satisfied by the guard *chair(r(2), rev1, rev2, listURSin)*. This guard ensures that the chair conference is not one of the reviewers. Finally, constraint C4 is satisfied by the place Pd specified as the output place of transition t_1 and the input place of t_4.

Security analysis is done by adopting the occurrence graph to guarantee the absence of ambiguities and inconsistencies in the specification. In the context of this example, the correctness should be verified against both standard rules of RBAC and security constraints specific to the workflow.

Note that in the present work, we care only about the authorization for a role/user to perform a specific task. We did not represent data and their movements among tasks. However, Data flow can be regarded as a subordinate flow to the control flow [31]. Data are created, accessed, and deleted during the executions of tasks.

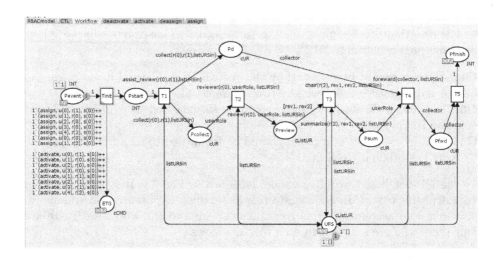

Fig. 11. CP-net representation of the paper review process

7   Conclusion

The explicit CP-Nets' description of security models could provide a solid foundation for security analysis. This approach can be used in the design phase in order to rule out inconsistencies and undesirable properties of RBAC policies early. Developers can use CP-Nets to trace and control the path and timing of each individual token in the net. CPNtools also includes the timed extension of CPNs, which can capture and simulate a systems temporal behavior. The time concept is based on the notion of a global clock that represents model time, not actual physical time. A token can optionally be declared as a timed token, which carries a time stamp through simulation. Clearly, we can extend our proposition in order to support temporal constraints by using timed tokens. Thus, the next step of the current work is to use the time-stamped tokens to govern the availability of roles and handling of user-role assignment/activation.

In this paper, we proposed a standard description of an RBAC including most features (Hierarchical RBAC, Static Separation of Duty (SSD) Relations and Dynamic Separation of Duties (DSD)). However, RBAC is often implemented as combinations of Core RBAC with one or more of the remaining features. Using CP-Nets, some components in the CP-net model could be deactivated if the features are missing without major changes.

References

1. Samarati, P., di Vimercati, S.d.C.: Access control: Policies, models, and mechanisms. In: Focardi, R., Gorrieri, R. (eds.) FOSAD 2000. LNCS, vol. 2171, pp. 137–196. Springer, Heidelberg (2001)
2. Sandhu, R.S., Coyne, E.J., Feinstein, H.L., Youman, C.E.: Role-based access control models. Computer 29(2), 38–47 (1996)
3. Ferraiolo, D.F., Sandhu, R., Gavrila, S., Kuhn, D.R., Chandramouli, R.: Proposed NIST standard for role-based access control. ACM Trans. Inf. Syst. Secur. 4(3), 224–274 (2001)
4. Barkley, J.F., Cincotta, A.V., Ferraiolo, D.F., Gavrila, S., Kuhn, D.R.: Role based access control for the world wide web. In: Proc. 20th NIST-NCSC National Information Systems Security Conference, pp. 331–340 (1997), http://citeseer.ist.psu.edu/101918.html
5. Jensen, K., Kristensen, L.M., Wells, L.: Coloured petri nets and CPN tools for modelling and validation of concurrent systems. STTT 9(3-4), 213–254 (2007)
6. Shafiq, B., Masood, A., Joshi, J., Ghafoor, A.: A role-based access control policy verification framework for real-time systems. In: WORDS 2005: Proceedings of the 10th IEEE International Workshop on Object-Oriented Real-Time Dependable Systems, pp. 13–20. IEEE Computer Society, Washington (2005), http://dx.doi.org/10.1109/WORDS.2005.11
7. Petri, C.A.: Kommunikation mit automaten. Ph.D. thesis, Institut für instrumentelle Mathematik, Bonn (1962)
8. Jensen, K.: Coloured Petri Nets. Basic Concepts, Analysis Methods and Practical Use (1997) Three Volumes

9. Zhang, Z.L., Hong, F., Liao, J.G.: Modeling chinese wall policy using colored petri nets. In: CIT 2006: Proceedings of the Sixth IEEE International Conference on Computer and Information Technology, p. 162. IEEE Computer Society, Washington (2006), http://dx.doi.org/10.1109/CIT.2006.123

10. Bertino, E., Bonatti, P.A., Ferrari, E.: TRBAC: A temporal role-based access control model. ACM Trans. Inf. Syst. Secur. 4(3), 191–233 (2001), doi:10.1145/501978.501979

11. Ahn, G.J., Hu, H.: Towards realizing a formal RBAC model in real systems. In: SACMAT 2007: Proceedings of the 12th ACM symposium on Access control models and technologies, pp. 215–224. ACM, New York (2007), http://doi.acm.org/10.1145/1266840.1266875

12. Joshi, J., Bertino, E., Latif, U., Ghafoor, A.: A generalized temporal role-based access control model. IEEE Transactions on Knowledge and Data Engineering 17(1), 4–23 (2005), doi:10.1109/TKDE.2005.1

13. Gavrila, S.I., Barkley, J.F.: Formal specification for role based access control user/role and role/role relationship management. In: RBAC 1998: Proceedings of the third ACM workshop on Role-based access control, pp. 81–90. ACM, New York (1998), http://doi.acm.org/10.1145/286884.286902

14. Li, J., Fan, Y., Zhou, M.: Performance modeling and analysis of workflow. IEEE Transactions on Systems, Man and Cybernetics, Part A 34(2), 229–242 (2004), doi:10.1109/TSMCA.2003.819490

15. Ahmed, T., Tripathi, A.R.: Static verification of security requirements in role based CSCW systems. In: SACMAT 2003: Proceedings of the eighth ACM symposium on Access control models and technologies, pp. 196–203. ACM, New York (2003), http://doi.acm.org/10.1145/775412.775438

16. Van der Aalst, W.: The application of petri nets to workflow management. The Journal of Circuits, Systems and Computers 8(1), 21–66 (1998)

17. Knorr, K.: Dynamic access control through petri net workflows. In: ACSAC 2000: Proceedings of the 16th Annual Computer Security Applications Conference, p. 159. IEEE Computer Society, Washington (2000)

18. Varadharajan, V.: Hook-up property for information flow secure nets. In: Proceedings of Computer Security Foundations Workshop IV, pp. 154–175 (1991), doi:10.1109/CSFW.1991.151582

19. Juopperi, J.: PrT-net based analysis of information flow security nets. Research Report A34, Helsinki University of Technology, Department of Computer Science and Engineering, Digital Systems Laboratory, Espoo, Finland (1995)

20. Knorr, K.: Multilevel security and information flow in petri net workflows. Tech. rep. In: Proceedings of the 9th International Conference on Telecommunication Systems - Modeling and Analysis, Special Session on Security Aspects of Telecommunication Systems (2001)

21. Juszczyszyn, K.: Verifying enterprise's mandatory access control policies with coloured petri nets. In: WETICE 2003: Proceedings of the Twelfth International Workshop on Enabling Technologies, p. 184. IEEE Computer Society, Washington (2003)

22. Rakkay, H., Boucheneb, H.: Timed secure colored petri net based analysis of information flow. Annals of Telecommunications (2006)

23. Jiang, Y., Lin, C., Yin, H., Tan, Z.: Security analysis of mandatory access control model. In: IEEE International Conference on Systems, Man and Cybernetics, 2004, vol. 6, pp. 5013–5018 (2004), doi:10.1109/ICSMC.2004.1400987

24. Zhang, Z.L., Hong, F., Xiao, H.J.: Verification of strict integrity policy via petri nets. In: ICSNC 2006: Proceedings of the International Conference on Systems and Networks Communication, p. 23. IEEE Computer Society, Washington (2006), http://dx.doi.org/10.1109/ICSNC.2006.76

25. Rakkay, H., Boucheneb, H.: Using timed colored petri net to formalize temporal role based access control policies. In: Proceedings of the 7th International Conference on New Technologies of Distributed Systems, Marrakesh, Morocco (2007)

26. Bell, D.E., LaPadula, L.J.: Secure computer systems: Mathematical foundations. Tech. Rep. MTR-2547, MITRE Corporation, Bedford (1973)

27. Genrich, H.J.: Predicate/transition nets. In: Brauer, W., Reisig, W., Rozenberg, G. (eds.) APN 1986. LNCS, vol. 254, pp. 207–247. Springer, Heidelberg (1987)

28. Brewer, D.D.F., Nash, D.M.J.: The chinese wall security policy. sp 00, 206 (1989), http://doi.ieeecomputersociety.org/10.1109/SECPRI.1989.36295

29. Biba, K.J.: Integrity considerations for secure computer systems. Tech. Rep. MTR-3153, MITRE Corporation, Bedford (1977)

30. Atluri, V., kuang Huang, W.: An authorization model for workflows. In: Martella, G., Kurth, H., Montolivo, E., Bertino, E. (eds.) ESORICS 1996. LNCS, vol. 1146, pp. 44–64. Springer, Heidelberg (1996)

31. Yi, Z., Yong, Z., Weinong, W.: Modeling and analyzing of workflow authorization management. J. Netw. Syst. Manage. 12(4), 507–535 (2004), http://dx.doi.org/10.1007/s10922-004-0674-3

32. Wedde, H.F., Lischka, M.: Modular authorization and administration. ACM Trans. Inf. Syst. Secur. 7(3), 363–391 (2004), http://doi.acm.org/10.1145/1015040.1015042

33. Shin, W.: An extension of role based access control for trusted operating systems and its coloured petri net model. Ph.D. thesis, Gwangju Institute of Science and Technology, Korea (2005)

34. Zao, J., Wee, H., Chu, J., Jackson, D.: RBAC schema verification using lightweight formal model and constraint analysis (2002), http://alloy.mit.edu/community/node/221

35. Yuan, C., He, Y., He, J., Zhou, Z.: A verifiable formal specification for RBAC model with constraints of separation of duty. In: Lipmaa, H., Yung, M., Lin, D. (eds.) Inscrypt 2006. LNCS, vol. 4318, pp. 196–210. Springer, Heidelberg (2006)

36. Drouineaud, M., Bortin, M., Torrini, P., Sohr, K.: A first step towards formal verification of security policy properties for RBAC. In: QSIC 2004: Proceedings of the Quality Software, Fourth International Conference, pp. 60–67. IEEE Computer Society, Washington (2004), http://dx.doi.org/10.1109/QSIC.2004.2

37. Zhao, C., Heilili, N., Liu, S., Lin, Z.: Representation and reasoning on RBAC: A description logic approach. In: Van Hung, D., Wirsing, M. (eds.) ICTAC 2005. LNCS, vol. 3722, pp. 381–393. Springer, Heidelberg (2005)

38. Jackson, D.: Alloy: a lightweight object modelling notation. ACM Trans. Softw. Eng. Methodol. 11(2), 256–290 (2002), http://doi.acm.org/10.1145/505145.505149

39. Spivey, J.M.: The Z notation: a reference manual. Prentice Hall International (UK) Ltd., Hertfordshire (1992)

40. Canada, O.: Z/EVES version 1.5: An overview. In: Hutter, D., Traverso, P. (eds.) FM-Trends 1998. LNCS, vol. 1641, pp. 367–376. Springer, Heidelberg (1999)

41. Brucker, A.D., Rittinger, F., Wol, B., ludwigs-universitat Freiburg, A.: HOL-Z 2.0: A proof environment for Z-specifications. Journal of Universal Computer Science 9, 152–172 (2002)

42. Lenzerini, M.: A uniform framework for concept definitions in description logics. Journal of Artificial Intelligence Research 6, 87–110 (1997)
43. Knorr, K., Weidner, H.: Analyzing separation of duties in petri net workflows. In: Gorodetski, V.I., Skormin, V.A., Popyack, L.J. (eds.) MMM-ACNS 2001. LNCS, vol. 2052, pp. 102–114. Springer, Heidelberg (2001)
44. Jaeger, T., Tidswell, J.E.: Practical safety in flexible access control models. ACM Trans. Inf. Syst. Secur. 4(2), 158–190 (2001),
http://doi.acm.org/10.1145/501963.501966
45. Neumann, G., Strembeck, M.: An approach to engineer and enforce context constraints in an RBAC environment. In: SACMAT 2003: Proceedings of the eighth ACM symposium on Access control models and technologies, pp. 65–79. ACM, New York (2003), http://doi.acm.org/10.1145/775412.775421
46. Nyanchama, M., Osborn, S.: The role graph model and conflict of interest. ACM Trans. Inf. Syst. Secur. 2(1), 3–33 (1999),
http://doi.acm.org/10.1145/300830.300832
47. Koch, M., Mancini, L.V., Parisi-Presicce, F.: A graph-based formalism for RBAC. ACM Trans. Inf. Syst. Secur. 5(3), 332–365 (2002),
http://doi.acm.org/10.1145/545186.545191
48. Harrison, M.A., Ruzzo, W.L., Ullman, J.D.: Protection in operating systems. Commun. ACM 19(8), 461–471 (1976), http://doi.acm.org/10.1145/360303.360333
49. Choppy, C., Petrucci, L., Reggio, G.: Designing coloured petri net models: a method. In: Proceedings of the 8th Workshop and Tutorial on Practical Use of Coloured Petri Nets and the CPN Tools Aarhus, Denmark, pp. 22–24 (2007)

Role Based Access Control with Spatiotemporal Context for Mobile Applications

Subhendu Aich[1], Samrat Mondal[1], Shamik Sural[1], and Arun Kumar Majumdar[2]

[1] School of Information Technology
[2] Department of Computer Science and Engineering
Indian Institute of Technology, Kharagpur, India
`{subhendu@sit,samratm@sit,shamik@cse,akmj@cse}.iitkgp.ernet.in`

Abstract. Role based access control (RBAC) is an established paradigm in resource protection. However, with the proliferation of mobile computing, it is being frequently observed that the RBAC access decision is directly influenced by the spatiotemporal context of both the subjects and the objects in the system. Currently, there are only a few models (STRBAC, GSTRBAC) in place which specify spatiotemporal security policy on top of the classical RBAC. In this paper we propose a complete RBAC model in spatiotemporal domain based on the idea of spatiotemporal extent. The concept of spatiotemporal role extent and spatiotemporal permission extent introduced here enables our model to specify granular spatiotemporal access control policies not specifiable in the existing approaches. Our model is also powerful enough to incorporate classical role hierarchy and other useful RBAC policies including Role based Separation of Duty and Permission based Separation of Duty in spatiotemporal domain.

Healthcare is an area in which information security is of utmost importance. The risk of personal medical data leakage is especially high in mobile healthcare applications. As a proof of concept, we have implemented the proposed spatiotemporal access control method in a mobile telemedicine system.

Keywords: Spatiotemporal domain, Role extent, Permission extent, Spatiotemporal SOD and Telemedicine.

1 Introduction

Role Based Access Control (RBAC) model is capable of expressing a wide range of important access control policies. This includes mandatory access control policies and discretionary access control policies as well as the Principle of Least Privilege and the well-known Separation of Duty (SOD) based policies. Another main advantage of RBAC model compared to other authorization models is the ease of system administration and convenience in authorization information management [16,17]. But it is observed that the security requirements for a significant number of recent applications include access request context in a way which is not expressible through user's membership in role alone. The resource access decision for a protected system quite often depends on contextual information like user location, access time, object type, etc. A number of computer resource access policies deal with the spatial and temporal

M.L. Gavrilova et al. (Eds.): Trans. on Comput. Sci. IV, LNCS 5430, pp. 177–199, 2009.
© Springer-Verlag Berlin Heidelberg 2009

information of both the user requesting the resource as well as the resource being protected. We make the idea clear with real world examples. Suppose a college authority has set an access policy like "Students are allowed to download bulk data from the Internet only at night" or system administration of an organization wants "The DB backup operation to be fired from a computer with *hostname* DB admin only". The classical RBAC model [17] needs an extension in spatiotemporal domain to handle such requirements. Over the last few years, several enhanced models have been proposed [5], [7], [10] to incorporate context based requirements in RBAC. These models successfully extend RBAC in either spatial or temporal domain.

A spatiotemporal access policy depends simultaneously on both the spatial and the temporal (termed as spatiotemporal) information of either the subject or the object or both. Examples of such a policy in a medical application could be "the doctors should be able to view the full Electronic Patient Record (EPR) from his clinic and during the visiting hours only" or "the role of helping nurse should be available during the daily check up time inside the doctor's office only". In this paper, we propose a model to extend RBAC in such a spatiotemporal domain. In a typical access request, a user activates a suitable role where the required permission to access the requested object is available. So in classical RBAC, role and permission are important logical entities through which a user ultimately gains the access to an object. In spatiotemporal domain, roles and permissions are available only in predefined spatiotemporal extents. The objective of expressing a variety of spatiotemporal access policies is achieved through the notion of spatiotemporal role extent and spatiotemporal permission extent. A user in our model gets a required access to a requested object only when the appropriate role is spatiotemporally available to him and the requisite permission is spatiotemporally available to that role. This is called role availability and permission availability. In the proposed model, we describe a procedure to judge whether a user belongs to a spatiotemporal extent or not. The current position of an object in the system may change with time. That is why, apart from the user context, the access control mechanism also considers the current location of the object for access mediation. The model is capable of specifying flexible spatiotemporal access policies at a more granular level then the existing models.

We feel that along with the development of new access control models, it is equally important to make their practical implementation in real life applications. For this purpose, we have applied our model in a telemedicine system developed by our group. The health information of a patient can be stored or transmitted electronically, in paper form or through oral communication. Telemedicine applications facilitate the use of electronic media for exchanging medical information among healthcare professionals. In the year of 2006, the Commonwealth Fund International Health Policy Survey [18], conducted in seven selected countries reported that at least one out of four primary care physicians use electronic medical record regularly for practice. The figure is as high as 90% in the United Kingdom, Netherlands and New Zealand.

Typically a telemedicine application is accessible through PCs and laptops connected in a wired LAN. One important and well-known fact about doctors is that they travel a lot. In case of emergency, they may need to respond from their home even at night. Handheld devices enable the doctors to access a telemedicine application over a wireless network. Equipped with such devices, they can access patient information, diagnostic results, important medical references, drug information, etc., as and when required. A qualitative study [12] conducted among a set of doctors in the United States concludes that doctors expect handheld computers to become more useful, and most seem to be keen on leveraging their use. This paper makes the following unique contributions:

- ☐ An Enhanced Spatiotemporal Role Based Access Control Model (ESTARBAC) is proposed. The concepts of role extent and permission extent are used to define the spatiotemporal access control policies.
- ☐ A set of access control algorithms is introduced for evaluating various access requests along with an analysis of their complexity.
- ☐ The model has been implemented in a real life telemedicine application supporting access from mobile devices.

In the next section, we discuss relevant related work in the field of spatiotemporal authorization in RBAC. Section 3 describes the complete model. Several access control algorithms are presented in Section 4. In Section 5 spatiotemporal separation of duty principles are illustrated. The proposed model is compared with other contemporary spatiotemporal access control models in Section 6. An example application in a hospital environment is discussed in Section 7. Section 8 is devoted to spatiotemporal access control in mobile telemedicine. Finally, we conclude in Section 9 along with a discussion on scope for future extensions.

2   Related Work

The idea of resource access control based on space or time is not particularly recent. Covington et al. [6] stressed the need for incorporating user context in RBAC access decision. The Generalized RBAC (GRBAC) model proposed by them uses two special kinds of role - *Environment role* to capture favorable system state and *Object role* to capture required object properties. A first concrete RBAC model capable of handling system time, named as Temporal RBAC (TRBAC), was proposed by Bertino et al. [5]. TRBAC introduces the idea of role enabling and role disabling based on temporal constraints. Only enabled role is made available for user activation. The Generalized TRBAC (GTRBAC) model by Joshi et al. [10] formally extends the TRBAC model with Role Hierarchy, SOD constraints and several other time dependent constraints. To provide a location based access control service for wireless networks, Hansen and Oleshchuk proposed the Spatial RBAC (SRBAC) model [9]. The location model in SRBAC considers only non overlapping locations. A location aware RBAC model (LRBAC) has been proposed by Ray et al. [13], which considers overlapped location model. But a user position in LRBAC is a single location and not multiple locations. Damiani et al. have proposed GEO: RBAC [7] where space is modeled on Geographical Information System (GIS) standards. In GEO:RBAC, roles are instantiated from predefined role schemas. Each role instance has one single spatial extent associated with it. None of the above models discussed so far, however, consider the combined impact of location and time in access decision.

One of the well-known authorization models capable of handling spatiotemporal information was suggested by Atluri and Chun [3]. This model, known as GeoSpatial

Authorization System (GSAS), enforces resource protection based on the geo-temporal attributes of the data being requested and the spatiotemporal context of the user making the request. GSAS is primarily intended for protecting satellite imagery. The model restricts the specification of policies on the geo-temporal attribute of the image data only, and it does not introduce the concept of role based access in the model. The Environment role defined in GRBAC can be extended for capturing both location and time. But in most of the applications, the Environment role set would be enormously large. As a result, the core management advantage in RBAC Administration is compromised. Ray and Toahchoodee have considered the interaction of location and time contexts with the classical RBAC components [14]. They have formalized a spatiotemporal RBAC model, called STRBAC. Here spatiotemporal constraints are expressed on role activation, user-role assignment, role-permission assignment and role hierarchy. Two separate concepts, called role enabling and role allocation, guide the spatiotemporal role in STRBAC.

Another approach for specification and verification of spatiotemporal RBAC access policy has been proposed by Samuel et al. [15]. This model, known as GSTRBAC, is essentially built on top of the GTRBAC model [10], and it incorporates spatiotemporal access control through role enabling (disabling) using both spatial and temporal constraints. According to GSTRBAC, all the permissions available to the role can be executed whenever and wherever the role is enabled. But the model completely ignores the spatiotemporal nature of the RBAC permission. For example, the basic employee role can be invoked by a person working in an organization in the morning session as well as in the afternoon session. But the online attendance is permitted through employee role only in the morning session and not in the afternoon session. We have recently developed a spatiotemporal RBAC model [2] called STARBAC. It is a simple model based on propositional logic. Various spatiotemporal commands are used for granting or denying access. It explores the syntax and semantics of typical logical operations (command conjunction and command disjunction) on spatiotemporal commands. It has been shown with various examples that the typical logical operations are useful in specifying real world access control requirements. However, STARBAC does not include separation of duty and access control evaluation process. In this paper, we enhance the capabilities of STARBAC in an improved model named as Enhanced Spatiotemporal Role Based Access Control (ESTARBAC). A detailed comparison of the proposed model with other existing models is given in Section 6.

3   Proposed Model

In this section, the core components of ESTARBAC are defined. The formalization starts with the representation of time and location as used in the model. Based on that, the idea of spatiotemporal extent is elaborated. Then the standard access control components, i.e., User, Objects, Operations, Permissions, Roles and Sessions are defined along with the spatiotemporal access components *RoleExtents* and *PermExtents*. This is followed by a discussion on role extent activation and spatiotemporal access control monitor in the model.

3.1 Time, Space and Spatiotemporal Extent

A **time instant** is defined as the fundamental time unit in the ESTARBAC model which uniquely represents one single clock tick for the system. The amount of time represented by a time instant is fixed and theoretically it could be arbitrarily small. The time instants are inherently ordered. One instant always comes before or after another time instant. The set of all time instants with defined clock tick is countably infinite. The set of time instants can, therefore, be perceived as the set of natural numbers. STARBAC uses *periodic expressions* for specifying authorization based on periodic timings [4]. A periodic time instance can be expressed as a tuple $<[begin, end], P>$, where P is a periodic expression denoting an infinite set of time instants and $[begin, end]$ is a scope denoted by a lower and an upper bound that are imposed on instants in P. For example, *Every Monday, First day of every month in the year of 2008*, etc. In ESTARBAC, every interval time is considered through the inclusion of the set **Intervals**. It contains all the interval elements which participate in at least one spatiotemporal policy specification for the system. The set of all time instants corresponding to one periodic expression can be derived. The following mapping returns the set of time instants corresponding to an interval element.

$$\text{Instants : Intervals} \rightarrow 2 \quad \text{where N is the set of real numbers.}$$

- **Overlapping Intervals**: two interval elements T_i and T_j are said to be overlapping if and only if $Instants(T_i) \cap Instants(T_j) \neq \phi$

The granular point for referencing space in our model is a **physical point** p_i. The set of all the physical points for the system is E where $E = \{p_1, p_2, p_3, ..., p_m\}$. A **logical location** L_j is defined as a collection of physical points in the system, i.e., $L_j = \{p_{j1}, p_{j2}, p_{j3}, ..., p_{jk}\}$, a subset of E [7]. Each location for the system identifies different places of interest (classroom, office, etc.). Depending on the application context, the mapping of a physical point into a fixed logical location may be nontrivial. In a typical PC based access environment, the source IP of user computer can be treated as a physical point where different subnets serve the purpose of different logical locations. But in a mobile environment, the mapping may not be that simple. We later show how this can be done in a given mobile application.

The set of all logical locations defined for the system is named as **Locations**.

- **Location Overlapping**: Two location elements L_i and L_j are said to be overlapping if there are common physical points between them, i.e., $L_i \cap L_j \neq \phi$
- **Location Containment**: Location L_i is contained within location L_j if all the physical points of L_i are physical points of L_j, i.e., $L_i \subseteq L_j$.

A spatiotemporal extent refers to an entity having both spatial and temporal characteristics. It is represented as: $<l,t>$ where l is an element of *Locations* and t is an element of *Intervals*. Basically, in spatiotemporal domain, the existence of the spatiotemporal entity is confined in a spatiotemporal zone represented by the corresponding extent. The following operations are allowed over spatiotemporal extents:

- Temporal Containment: $is\_contained_t(<l_1,t_1>,<l_2,t_2>) \equiv Instants(t_1) \subseteq Instants(t_2)$
- Spatial Containment: $is\_contained_l(<l_1,t_1>,<l_2,t_2>) \equiv l_1 \subseteq l_2$
- Spatiotemporal Containment:

  $is\_contained_{lt}(<l_1,t_1>,<l_2,t_2>) \equiv (l_1 \subseteq l_2) \wedge (Instants(t_1) \subseteq Instants(t_2))$
- Spatiotemporal Overlap:

  $is\_overlapping_{lt}(<l_1,t_1>,<l_2,t_2>) \equiv (l_1 \cap l_2 \neq \phi) \wedge (Instants(t_1) \cap Instants(t_2) \neq \phi)$

3.2 Users, Objects and Operations

A user in ESTARBAC represents a human being or an agent acting on behalf of a human. The user, after getting authenticated by the system, represents a principal of the system. The set of all users in the system is **Users**. Unlike classical RBAC, a user could be mobile in nature. The anywhere, anytime accessibility allows a user to request a resource from different locations and at different times. The assumption is that a mobile agent with limited processing capability is attached with the user device. Every time the user makes an access request, the agent sends the current request time and the user device position along with the request. The agent is taken to be a trusted entity and the time it takes to send the request is negligible compared to the clock tick of the system. Since locations can overlap with each other, the current position of a user can belong to multiple locations. The following relation expresses the current association of *Users* with *Locations*.

$$UserLocations \subseteq Users \times Locations$$

Consistent with earlier access control models, object is an entity that contains or receives information [8]. The set of all objects in our model is **Objects**. ESTARBAC assumes the accessed object to be either static or mobile and the location of the object during the request is also considered influential in access decision. Such situations arise in the access control requirements of many organizations. For example, consider the following requirement in an institute network administration - *"During the summer vacation, all the websites hosted from the systems in Server room 5 are not accessible by the users outside the campus. The websites are only available on the intranet"*. The relation given below expresses the current association of Objects with Locations.

$$ObjLocations \subseteq Objects \times Locations$$

An operation is an executable image of a program which, upon invocation, executes some functions for the user. Each operation is applicable to a single object or a set of objects. The set of all operations is **Operations**.

3.3 Roles and RoleExtents

A role in the RBAC model describes the unit of job function or the responsibility and authority conferred to the member of that role in the system [17]. The set of all roles defined for the system is **Roles**. Unlike the classical model, a role in the proposed model is available only in predefined places at specific time intervals. A user can activate a role if and only if the role is spatiotemporally available to him. In spatiotemporal domain, the available extents of a role are specified through the elements of

RoleExtents. A role extent combines both the spatiotemporal extents and classical organizational responsibility. The set *RoleExtents* is derived from the sets *Roles*, *Locations* and *Intervals*. A single role can be available in various spatiotemporal zones. Therefore, one role can be associated with multiple role extents. We define the following functions which return the different components of a role extent *re*.

$$re \in RoleExtents$$
$$RERole : RoleExtents \rightarrow Roles$$
$$RELoc : RoleExtents \rightarrow Locations$$
$$RETime : RoleExtents \rightarrow Intervals$$
$$Extent(re) = <RELoc(re), RETime(re)>$$

Apart from this, the assignment of users to roles is done through the following relation:

$$UserRoles \subseteq Users \times Roles$$

3.4 Permissions, PermExtents and Permission Execution

Permission is an approval to perform an operation on one or more RBAC protected objects [8]. The set **Permissions** is derived from the sets *Objects* and *Operations* as follows:

$$Permissions \subseteq 2^{Operations} \times 2^{Objects}$$

The objects and operations associated with permission are obtained through the following relations:

$$PermObs \subseteq Permissions \times Objects$$
$$PermOps \subseteq Permissions \times Operations$$

The assignment of roles to permission is obtained through the following relation:

$$RolePerms \subseteq Roles \times Permissions$$

An object in our model is dynamic in nature and the logical location of the object may change with time. To spatially constrain the mobile objects accessed through permission, each permission specifies the allowable locations for objects represented by the following relation:

$$PermLocs \subseteq Permissions \times Locations$$

Permission execution is allowed from designated places and durations only. An example in medical application is *"An emergency alarm can be raised from the operation theater during the operation hours only, whereas the alarm can be raised from the ICU anytime of the day"*. Like role extent, the model proposes the concept of permission extent, which combines the spatiotemporal extent and the organizational capability conferred to that permission. A permission assigned to a role can be executed through it only when the permission is spatiotemporally available to that role. Permission can be executed from various spatiotemporal zones. Therefore, a permission can be associated with multiple permission extents. However, it may be noted that, when the extent of a permission is disjoint form the extent of the role to which the permission is assigned to, the user is not given access. The set **PermExtents** is derived from the sets *Permissions*, *Locations* and *Intervals*. We define the following functions which return the different components of a permission extent *pe*.

$$pe \in PermExtents$$
$$PEPerm : PermExtents \rightarrow Permissions$$
$$PELoc : PermExtents \rightarrow Locations$$
$$PETime : PermExtents \rightarrow Intervals$$
$$Extent(pe) = <PELoc(pe), PETime(pe)>$$

3.5 Sessions and Spatiotemporal Role Extent Activation

Typically, users establish sessions during which they may activate a subset of the roles they belong to and execute permissions available in these sessions. The set of all active sessions in the system is **Sessions**. Each session is associated with one single user which does not change over time. Each session in our model is also assumed to be dynamic (since the session user could be mobile). The roles and permissions available to a session user are supposed to change during the session lifetime.

$$SessionUser : Sessions \rightarrow Users$$
$$SessionRoles \subseteq Sessions \times Roles$$
$$SessionPerms \subseteq Sessions \times Permissions$$

In the proposed model, a role gets activated in a session due to one suitable spatiotemporal role extent. Apart from user's membership in the role, the session user needs to spatiotemporally belong to that role extent for successful activation. The following predicate checks if a role extent *re* can be activated in session *s*:

$\forall s \in Sessions \forall re \in RoleExtents[((SessionUser(s),RERole(re)) \in UserRoles \land (SessionUser(s),RELoc(re)) \in UserLocations \land ActivationTime \in Instants(RETime(re)) \Rightarrow can\_be\_activated(re,s)]$

Whether a permission is allowed to be executed in a session is checked by the following predicate:

$(s,p) \in SessionPerms \Leftrightarrow \exists r \in Roles, \exists pe \in PermExtents[(s,r) \in SessionRoles \land (r,p) \in RolePerms \land (SessionUser(s),PELoc(pe)) \in UserLocations \land ExecutionTime \in Instants(PETime(pe)) \land PEPerm(pe)=p]$

Table 1. Predicates and their Semantics

No.	Predicate	Semantics
1	is_contained$_t$(st_1, st_2)	Checks if extent st_1 temporally belongs to extent st_2
2	is_contained$_l$(st_1, st_2)	Checks if extent st_1 spatially belongs to extent st_2
3	is_contained$_{st}$(st_1, st_2)	Checks if extent st_1 spatiotemporally belongs to extent st_2
4	is_overlapping(st_1, st_2)	Checks if extent st_1 overlaps with extent st_2
5	can_be_activated(re,s)	Checks if a role extent re can be activated in session s
6	is_allowed(u,op,o)	Checks if a user u is allowed to do operation op on the object o

The important predicates used in the definitions are summarized in Table 1 and the complete ESTARBAC model is shown in Figure 1. Here the black ellipses represent existing RBAC components and the gray ellipses represent newly proposed components in ESTARBAC. Single directional and bi-directional arrows respectively represent one-to-many and many-to-many relationships between the components.

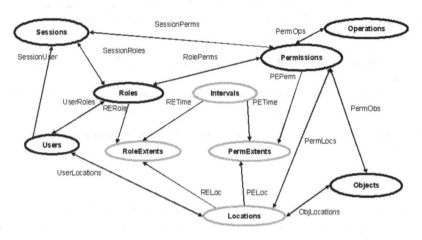

Fig. 1. Proposed ESTARBAC Model

3.6 Access Control Monitor

Every user access request is typically mediated by a reference monitor. The reference monitor either allows or denies the request based on the spatiotemporal roles currently active in that session. The question being asked is of the form 'Is a user *u* permitted to do the operation *op* on the object *o*?'. Along with any authorization request, comes the current user location and access time information. We define a predicate *is_allowed* to answer the access control request.

$is\_allowed(u,op,o) \Leftrightarrow \exists s \in Sessions, \exists p \in Permissions, \exists l \in Locations[SessionUser(s)=u \wedge (p,o) \in PermObs \wedge (p,op) \in PermOps \wedge (s,p) \in SessionPerms \wedge (o,l) \in ObjLocations \wedge (p,l) \in PermLocs]$

If there is no suitable role currently active for the user, the request is denied. If a suitable role can be activated, the user needs to activate it first and then raise the request.

4 Access Control Algorithms

In this section, a set of algorithms is defined to handle user requests for role activation and accessing a protected object. Initially, Algorithm 1 and Algorithm 2 are used for finding suitable role and permission extents respectively. Then, two other algorithms are used to process activation request and access request. *Process_ActivationRequest* (Algorithm 3) handles user request for role activation and *Process_AccessRequest* (Algorithm 4) processes the user request for accessing a protected object. Table 2 gives a listing of the data structures used in the access control algorithms.

Given the context of a user and a spatiotemporal extent (either associated with a role or a permission), the function *st_belongs* evaluates if the user context satisfies the extent or not. Using *st_belongs*, the function *suitable_roleextent* (Algorithm 1) returns suitable extent of a given role for a specified user context. During the phase of initialization of the access control system, the static data set (components 1-10 in Table 2) is populated from the underlying policy repository. Each active (currently logged in) user in the application has an associated context structure stored in the system. A user context has the following fields:

− *coordinate:* The current location value of the user collected during the user request
− *refreshTime:* The last time when the user coordinate value was refreshed in the system

Apart from that, a session object stores the following information about an active user session:

− *sessionid:* the unique session id
− *userid:* the application id of the session user
− *roles:* it returns the set of roles currently activated in the session
− *perms:* it returns the set of permissions currently available in the session for execution

Table 2. Data Structures used in the Access Control Algorithms

Sl No.	Data Set	Description
1	Users	Set of users in the system
2	Roles	Set of spatiotemporal roles in the system
3	Operations	Set of operations allowed in the system
4	UserRoles	Set of relations between users and corresponding roles
5	RoleExtents	For each role, RoleExtents[*rid*] returns the set of spatiotemporal extents associated with *rid*
6	RolePerms	For each role, RolePerms[*rid*] returns the set of permissions associated with *rid*
7	PermExtents	For each permission, PermExtents[*pid*] returns the spatiotemporal extents associated with *pid*
8	PermObs	Set of relations between permissions and objects
9	PermOps	Set of relations between permissions and operations
10	Objects	Set of spatiotemporally protected objects
11	Sessions	For each active session, Sessions[*sid*] returns the session object
12	Contexts	For each active user, Contexts[*uid*] returns the current context

---

Algorithm 1. suitable_roleextent
1: Input: *rid*, *uid*, *ctx*
2: if (*uid*, *rid*) ∉ *UserRoles* then
3:     return null;
4: end if
5: for each *re* ∈ *RoleExtents*[*rid*] do
6:     if *st_belongs*(*re*,*ctx*) then
7:         return *re*;
8:     end if
9: end for
10: return *null*;

Both the context and the session objects are updated periodically in the algorithm. These two types of objects are stored in dynamic data set (components 11-12 in Table 2). The input to the two access control functions is an object of type *Request*. A request can be either a role activation request or a resource access request and each type is processed separately. A request contains the following fields:

- *userid:* application id of the user which initiates the request.
- *roles:* in case of an activation request, it returns the set of roles requested for activation.
- *object:* in case of an access request, it gives the object requested for access.
- *op:* in case of an access request, it gives the mode of access to the requested object.
- *sessionid:* in case of an access request, it returns the current session id of the request.
- *coordinate:* the current location value of the requesting user collected during the request

---

Algorithm 2. suitable_permextent
1: Input: *pid*, *ctx*
2: for each *pe* ∈ *PermExtents*[*pid*] do
3:     if *st_belongs*(*pe*,*ctx*) then
4:         return *pe*;
5:     end if
6: end for
7: return *null*;

Similar functionality is provided by *suitable_permextent* (Algorithm 2) for a given permission and a given user context. Thus, *st_belongs* does the evaluation in both spatial and temporal dimensions. There is a well defined algorithm which checks if a time instant belongs to a periodic expression or not [5]. Evaluating whether a physical point belongs to a logical location depends on the definition of the logical location in a specific application. During a new session initiation (such as at the time of user login), a role activation request is raised to the access control system. The request is handled by the function *Process_ActivationRequest* (Algorithm 3). The function returns an activation success only when all the requested roles are activated. At first, if the required user context is not available in *Contexts*, a new user context is created (lines 2-6). The context coordinate is updated from the request values and a new session is created for the user (lines 7-8). Using *suitable_roleextent*, the for loop in lines 9-16 activates the requested roles in the new session. A subset of the permissions corresponding to the activated roles is included in the new session using the *suitable_permextent* (the for loop in lines 17-22). Finally, in line 23, the updated context values and the new session are stored in dynamic data set.

Algorithm 3. Process_ActivationRequest
1: Input Request: *req*
2: if (*Contexts*[*req.userid*]==*null*) then
3:      *ctx* = new *Context*();
4: else
5:      *ctx* = *Contexts*[*req.userid*];
6: end if
7: *ctx.coordinate* = *req.coordinate*;
8: *s* = new *Session*(*req.userid*); *tempset* = ϕ;
9: for each *rid*∈ *req.roles* do
10:     *re* = *suitable_roleextent*(*rid*,*req.userid*,*ctx*);
11:     if (*re* == *null*) then
12:        return "Activation Failure";
13:     else
14:        *s.roles* = *s.roles* ∪{*rid*}; *tempset* = *tempset* ∪*RolePerms*[*rid*];
15:     end if
16: end for
17: for each *pid*∈ *tempset* do
18:     *pe* = *suitable_permextent*(*pid*,*ctx*);
19:     if (*pe* ≠ *null*) then
20:        *s.perms* = *s.perms*∪{*pid*};
21:     end if
22: end for
23: *Sessions*[*s.sessionid*]=*s*;*ctx.refreshTime*=*servertime*;*Contexts*[*req.userid*]=*ctx*;
24: return "Activation Success";

The resource access request is handled by *Process_AccessRequest* (Algorithm 4). The function is dictated by a system defined parameter called *refreshinterval*. The request is granted by default if the requested object is not a spatiotemporally protected object (lines 2-4). Otherwise, in lines 5-6, the session object and the user context corresponding to the access request are fetched. The algorithm does not refresh the user context at each and every access request (the *if clause* in line 7). The refreshing is done if the last refresh time is older than the *refreshinterval*. If the context is refreshed then the roles in that session are reactivated and the permissions corresponding to the reactivated roles are also rechecked for suitable extent availability (lines 7-24). The next for loop in lines 25-29 checks if there is a suitable session permission which grants the requested object (*req.object*) in the requested mode (*req.op*). Line 11 and line 17 ensure that the spatiotemporal user context (*ctx*) satisfies both the role extent and the permission extent. Therefore, if a user is granted an access request, then the context certainly satisfies one of the activated roles and the corresponding permissions. The user context can be perceived as a point in the intersection of matching role extent and matching permission extent.

Algorithm 4. Process_AccessRequest
```
1: Input Request: req
2: if (req.object   Objects) then
3:    return "granted"
4: end if
5: s = Sessions[req.sessionid];
6: ctx = Contexts[req.userid];
7: if servertime - ctx.refreshTime    refreshinterval then
8:    roleids = s.roles; ctx.coordinate = req.coordinate;
9:    s.roles = φ; s.perms = φ, tempset = φ;
10:   for each rid ∈ roleids do
11:       re = suitable_roleextent(rid,req.userid,ctx);
12:       if (re ≠ null) then
13:           s.roles = s.roles∪{rid};tempset = tempset∪RolePerms[rid];
14:       end if
15:   end for
16:   for each pid ∈ tempset do
17:       pe = suitable_permextent(pid,ctx);
18:       if (pe ≠ null) then
19:             s.perms = s.perms∪{pid};
20:       end if
21:   end for
22:   ctx.refreshTime = servertime;
23:   Sessions[s.sessionid] = s;Contexts[req.userid] = ctx;
24: end if
25: for each pid ∈ perms do
26:     if (pid,req.object)∈ PermObs∧(pid, req.op) ∈ PermOps then
27:         return "granted";
28:     end if
29: end for
30: return "denied";
```

Let the number of different spatiotemporal extents associated with a single role is upper bounded by a parameter K_{RE} and the number of different spatiotemporal extents of a single permission has an upper bound K_{PE}. During role activation, the for loop in lines 10-15 is executed at most $|R|$ times where R denotes the set of application roles. The union operation of the permission subsets in line 13 has complexity of $O(|P|)$ where P is the set of application permissions. The for loop in lines 16-21 is executed at most $|P|$ times. The time complexity of the algorithm during role activation is therefore, $O(|R|K_{RE} + |R||P|+|P|K_{PE})$. Following a similar argument, if the user context is refreshed in the function *Process_AccessRequest*, the algorithm has total time complexity of $O(|R|K_{RE} + |R||P| + |P|K_{PE})$. If the context is not refreshed, the algorithm complexity is $O(|P|)$ (due to the for loop in lines 25-29). Permissions are recomputed once in each refresh interval. Thus, if there are K access requests from the same user within the refresh interval, only the first request will take longer time while processing of the rest K-1 requests will be fast (as there is no permission computation). It is a trade off between response time and correctness of the access control algorithm.

5   SOD in Spatiotemporal Domain

Separation of Duty (SOD) is an important property in computer security that reduces the chances of fraud by involving more than one user to complete a sensitive task. Ahn et al. [1] specified different types of SOD properties in standard RBAC model using a constraint specification language. The basic idea is to apply mutual exclusion of roles among the users and mutual exclusion of permissions to the roles to distribute sensitive jobs among more than one person in the organization. The different kinds of SOD properties specifiable in ESTARBAC are discussed here in detail. The predicates used have been listed in Table 1.

5.1   Conflicting Spatiotemporal Extents

A set of mutually exclusive roles forms a conflicting role set *CR*. The meaning of conflicting role set is that in a session, a user should not be allowed to activate more than one role from *CR*. Analogous to the idea of conflicting roles, a set of conflicting permissions (*CP*) contains sensitive permissions. In a single session, the session user should not be allowed to execute more than one permission from *CP*. Some of the well known situations in an organization where conflicting permission or conflicting role is relevant, are *applying for a leave and granting a leave, initiating a payment and authorizing a payment,* and *the roles supervisor and subordinate.* In spatiotemporal domain, roles and permissions are available in spatiotemporal extents. So, conflict can be detected between two role extents (or two permission extents) based on spatiotemporal overlapping. The set *CRe* consists of all conflicting role extent pairs. A similar conflict set *CPe* also exists for permission extent pairs.

– **Conflicting role extents CRe**:

$(re_1, re_2) \in CRe \Leftrightarrow [RERole(re_1) \in CR \wedge RERole(re_2) \in CR \wedge is\_overlapping(Extent(re_1), Extent(re_2)) \wedge RERole(re_1) \neq RERole(re_2)]$

– **Conflicting permission extents CPe**:

$(pe_1, pe_2) \in CPe \Leftrightarrow [PEPerm(pe_1) \in CP \wedge PEPerm(pe_2) \in CP \wedge is\_overlapping(Extent(pe_1), Extent(pe_2)) \wedge PEPerm(pe_1) \neq PEPerm(pe_2)]$

5.2   Role Based SOD

In spatiotemporal domain, different versions of SOD can be defined based on the *CRe* set:

– *RSOD$_1$*: Conflicting roles should not have overlapping spatiotemporal extents. This is a restriction imposed on **role extent assignment**. This SOD property is expressed by the notation $RSOD_1$ where $RSOD_1(CRe)$: $CRe=\phi$. A weaker version of $RSOD_1$, called $RSOD_{1st}$ enforces the same restriction in a particular spatiotemporal zone.

$RSOD_{1st}(L,T,CRe)$: $\neg\exists(re_1,re_2)\in CRe[is\_overlapping(Extent(re_1),(L,T))$ $\wedge$ $is\_overlapping(Extent(re_2),(L,T))]$

- $RSOD_2$: If a pair of conflicting roles have been assigned to a single user, the role pair should not overlap spatiotemporally. This is also a restriction imposed on **role extent assignment**. It is expressed by the notation $RSOD_2$ where $RSOD_2(CRe)$: $\exists u_1\in Users, \exists r_1,\ r_2\ \in Roles[(\{(u_1,r_1),(u_1,r_2)\}\subseteq\ UserRoles\wedge r_1\neq r_2)$ $\Rightarrow \neg\exists(re_1,re_2)\in CRe(RERole(re_1)=r_1\wedge RERole(re_2)=r_2)]$

- $RSOD_3$: If two conflicting roles have overlapping spatiotemporal activation zone, the roles should not be assigned to a single user. This is a restriction imposed on **user to role assignment**. The intended SOD is expressed by the notation $RSOD_3$ where

  $(re_1,re_2)\in CRe\Rightarrow \forall u\in Users(\{(u,RERole(re_1)),(u,RERole(re_2))\}\ UserRoles)$

5.3 Permission Based SOD

In spatiotemporal domain useful variations of SOD can be derived on the CPe set:

- $PSOD_1$: Conflicting permissions should not have any overlapping spatiotemporal extents. This is a very strong restriction imposed on **permission extent assignment**. This SOD property is expressed by the notation $PSOD_1$ where $PSOD_1(CPe)$: $CPe=\phi$. A weaker version of $PSOD_1$, called $PSOD_{1st}$ enforces the same restriction in a particular spatiotemporal zone.

  $PSOD_{1st}(L,T,CPe)$: $\neg\exists(pe_1,pe_2)\in CPe[is\_overlapping(Extent(pe_1),(L,T))$ $\wedge$ $is\_overlapping(Extent(pe_2),(L,T))]$

- $PSOD_2$: If two conflicting permissions are already assigned to a single role, they should not have overlapping extent. This is also a restriction imposed on **permission extent assignment**. This SOD property is expressed by the notation $PSOD_2$ where

  $PSOD_2(CPe)$: $\exists r_1\in Roles,\ \exists p_1,\ p_2\ \in Permissions[(\{(r_1,p_1),(r_1,p_2)\}\subseteq\ Role\text{-}Perms\wedge p_1\neq p_2)\Rightarrow \neg\exists(pe_1,pe_2)\in CPe(PEPerm(pe_1)=p_1\wedge PEPerm(pe_2)=p_2)]$

- $PSOD_3$: If two conflicting permissions have overlapping spatiotemporal extents, these two permissions should not be assigned to a single role. This is a restriction imposed on **role to permission** assignment.

  $(pe_1,pe_2)\in CPe\Rightarrow \forall r\in Roles(\{(r,PEPerm(pe_1)),(r,PEPerm(pe_2))\}\ RolePerms)$

5.4 Dynamic SOD

In the pervious subsections, the SOD constraints are enforced during the role and permission assignment and applicable to the administrative model of ESTARBAC. The notion of conflicting role extents (and permission extents) is fundamentally true in all stages of access control. Such restrictions, based on the idea of overlapping spatiotemporal extent, can be enforced during the conflicting role activation or conflicting permission execution at run time. This is the core idea of dynamic SOD constraints in ESTARBAC. A detailed discussion on this topic is beyond the scope of this paper.

6 Comparison of ESTARBAC with Contemporary Models

In spatiotemporal domain, to the best of our knowledge, only STRBAC model [14] and STARBAC model [2] come close to our approach. Here we point out the differences of the proposed model over them.

- The functions *RoleEnableLoc*(*r*) and *RoleEnableDur*(*r*) used in STRBAC separately specify the sets of locations and the sets of durations for enabling role *r*. But these location and duration elements are not related with each other. In ESTARBAC, *RoleExtents* achieves it by associating a role with a (location, interval) pair. This enables the proposed model to specify granular spatiotemporal access policy and makes it more expressive than STRBAC. For example, if an institute policy is "*During weekdays faculty members should be able to access resources from their office computers in college and on weekends the resources are available from their home computers*", it can be specified in our model by introducing two separate elements in *RoleExtents*, i.e., (faculty, weekdays, office) and (faculty, weekend, home). Such a granular resource access policy is difficult to express in the STRBAC model. Similar to role extent, the proposed model introduces *PermExtents* which enables it to specify more granular permission based access control policy than STRBAC.
- In STRBAC, two separate ideas concerning role namely, *role allocation* and *role enabling* are introduced. A user can activate a role only on those places and time where a role can be both allocated as well as enabled. A user would not be able to activate the role at any other place and time where and when a role can be allocated but not enabled (or vice versa). Therefore, the individual relevance of role allocation and role enabling is not clear. In our model, user is assigned to roles statically like the standard RBAC [17]. The role availability for role activation in a session solely depends on spatiotemporal role extents. The proposed model stays close to classical RBAC and achieves the spatiotemporal activation through *RoleExtents*. To summarize, the idea of role availability achieves the intended spatiotemporal access and clears the confusion between role allocation and role enabling in STRBAC.
- In STRBAC, the idea of user session is not included directly in actual access control (*PermUserAcquire*(*u, o, p, d, l*)). In our model, the access control question is answered explicitly in terms of user session.
- Spatiotemporal overlapping is considered in ESTARBAC model (*UserLocations* is a many to many relation). But STRBAC does not allow overlapping locations.

Our proposed model extends the basic model STARBAC [2] and aims for a better formalization. ESTARBAC improves over STARBAC in the following ways:

- The core idea of STARBAC is the spatiotemporal aspect of role in RBAC. However, in real life, RBAC permissions can also be spatiotemporal in nature. The proposed approach takes spatiotemporal permission into account.
- ESTARBAC includes concrete access control evaluation algorithms which evaluate whether a particular access can actually be granted on a resource at a given spatiotemporal point. It has also been applied in a real world application.

- STARBAC is computationally simpler model expressed in propositional logic. ESTARBAC, on the other hand, is represented in predicate logic.
- Separation of Duty, though mentioned in STARBAC, was not implemented in detail. It has been considered in ESTARBAC.

7 An Example Application

In this section we explain how ESTARBAC can be implemented in a model situation. It may be noted that this is not a real life application. Actual implementation of ESTARBAC in a telemedicine system is depicted in the next section. Figure 2 shows the basic layout of a typical hospital. The medical information of a patient admitted in this hospital is stored electronically (Electronic patient record or EPR). The doctors, while moving around inside the hospital premises, access the required EPR through their PDA. Here, we discuss a brief spatiotemporal policy based on our model for preventing unauthorized access of EPR. An example of classical role based policy concerning the doctor's use of EPR is as follows:

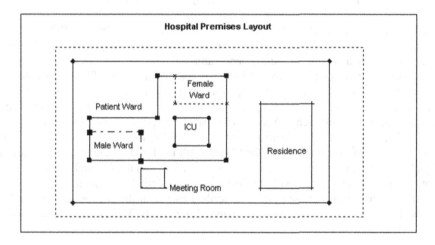

Fig. 2. A Simplified Layout of a Hospital

$Roles = \{Doc, PD, Dod, SC\}$
$Objects = \{Medication, EPR\}$
$Operations = \{Prescribe, ViewFull, ViewPrivacyPreserved\}$
$PermObs = \{(p_1, Medication),(p_2, EPR),(p_3,EPR)\}$
$PermOps = \{(p_1,Prescribe),(p_2,ViewFull),(p_3,ViewPrivacyPreserved)\}$
$Permissions =$
$\{PrescribeMedication(p_1),ViewFullEPR(p_2),ViewPrivacyPreservedEPR(p_3)\}$
$RolePerms = \{(Doc, p_1), (PD, p_2), (Dod, p_3), (SC, p_3)\}$

Doc is the basic role for the doctors. Doc is allowed to prescribe patient medication, i.e., p_1. A typical EPR can be viewed by the doctors in two different modes. In p_2, the complete EPR is exposed whereas in p_3, only part of the EPR is revealed in such a way so that patient privacy is not compromised. The primary doctor PD, is mainly responsible for the admitted patients and he can access p_2. The Doctor on duty Dod role is assumed by the doctor currently in charge of Intensive Care Unit (ICU) and he can access p_2. The Specialist Consultant SC external to the hospital can only execute p_3. The conflicting permission set CP is composed of p_2 and p_3. The following time intervals are crucial from the point of spatiotemporal access control:

$Intervals = \{Anytime, Visitinghour, Meetingtime\}$

As evident from the connotation, '$Anytime$' refers to always. '$Visitinghour$' refers to a fixed time of the day when the hospital PDs use to visit the ward patients. A spatiotemporal RBAC policy is defined based on the above classical RBAC policy.

$RolePerms = RolePerms \cup (PD, p_3)$

$RoleExtents = \{re_1 : (Doc, PatientWard, Anytime), re_2 : (PD, PatientWard, Visitinghour), re_3 : (PD, Residence, Anytime), re_4 : (PD, Meetingroom, Meetingtime), re_5 : (SC, Meetingroom, Meetingtime), re_6 : (Dod, ICU, Anytime)\}$

$PermExtents = \{pe_1 : (P_1, PatientWard, Anytime), pe_2 : (p_2, PatientWard, Anytime), pe_3 : (p_3, Residence, Anytime), pe_4 : (p_3, Meetingroom, Meetingtime)\}$

Inside the patient ward, the basic Doc role is available anytime but the PD role is spatiotemporally available during visiting hours only, i.e., re_2 of the policy. The PD role is spatiotemporally available in the residence area anytime, i.e., re_3. Hence, a PD would be able to see the full EPR during patient visit whereas a partial EPR is accessible to a PD from residence. This is a useful spatiotemporal policy for preserving patient privacy in the hospital. A spatiotemporal permission hierarchy (STPH) is constructed from the basic PH hierarchy. According to spatiotemporal permission inheritance in our model, PD would be able to prescribe medication during his ward visit but not from residence or meeting room. The PDs consult the hired specialists only on a fixed day of each week referred to here as $Meetingtime$. So, both the PD and the SC roles are spatiotemporally available inside the meeting room during the Meetingtime, i.e., re_4, re_5. In the classical role based policy described earlier in the section, a PD is able to see the full EPR in the presence of the external specialists. This is not desirable for patient privacy.

8   Instantiation of ESTARBAC in Mobile Telemedicine

In this section, we show how the proposed ESTARBAC model can be instantiated in a healthcare application. Individual health information maintained in a healthcare organization is considered as the personal data of the concerned patient. Special attention needs to be paid before sharing medial data with other parties. Typically, healthcare data contain important information about the past and the present physical and mental condition of the concerned patient. The health information therefore is highly sensitive in nature and should not be disclosed without taking consent from the subject of information. On the other hand, there is a need for sharing the personal medical record among group of healthcare professionals for timely treatment of the patient. Apart from that, private patient data need to be disclosed in a few other specific situations, e.g., for research purposes, for quality assurance and compliance checking as well as for public benefit. Sufficient assurance should be provided to the patient that the personal data is handled carefully and it would not fall in the wrong hand. We first introduce the security requirement and then show the applicability of ESTARBAC.

8.1 Security Requirements in Telemedicine

The healthcare organizations must acquire trust of public with the protection of their private medical data. The privacy of personal health information is a well debated issue and an interesting research topic. In United States, the Health Information Portability and Accountability Act (HIPAA) direct the requirement for protecting the *individually identifiable health information* called Protected Health Information (PHI). The HIPAA security and privacy rule, released by Department of Human and Social Services (DHSS), sets up generic standards to be followed by all the involved healthcare entities called *covered entities*. Broadly, the HIPAA *privacy rule* defines and limits the circumstances where PHI needs to be disclosed by the covered entities. The rule also directs the covered entities to develop and implement access control policies that limit the use and disclosure of the PHI to the minimum necessary for the specific purpose.

8.2 Overview of iMedik – A Web Enabled Telemedicine Application

We now describe iMedik - a web enabled telemedicine application developed at IIT Kharagpur, India. iMedik carries out several important tasks including patient information management, doctors' appointment scheduling and online patient medical report maintenance. It allows storage and access of different kinds of patient data including text, image, graphics, audio and video. The application follows a multi-tier architecture [11] realized using .NET web application development framework. Microsoft SQL server is used as the database. The other layers are hosted in Internet Information Service (IIS) running in Microsoft Windows Server 2003. The business logic code is written in *C#* and published as a remote object through IIS. The presentation layer pages (.aspx files) call the business layer methods using .NET remoting. The patient records can be accessed and manipulated through the business logic code only. The core functionality (filling up different kinds of patient forms, accessing patient list, reading test results, etc.) is grouped into different methods and exposed as a .NET remote object in IIS environment.

One of the important features of iMedik is that the application can be accessed by handheld devices. iMedik has been successfully tested with various mobile phones including HP iPAQ rw6828, Blackberry 8800 and Compaq iPAQ 3760. Out of these various models used for experimentation, Blackberry 8800 has got a unique feature that it is a GPS enabled phone. Therefore, the physical location of the device can be easily and reliably extracted. In the implemented system, the remote methods are spatiotemporally protected from unauthorized access through Blackberry devices. Each business method call (an underlying .NET remote call) is either a telemedicine resource access request or an application role activation request. The calls from Blackberry devices are intercepted and forwarded based on the spatiotemporal policy specified for the application.

8.3 Architecture of the Access Control System

Figure 3 shows the detailed functional architecture of the spatiotemporal access control system. A request for business level method is raised by the client code (.aspx files) residing in the presentation layer of the application. The remote call is intercepted and passed for authorization check to the **Central Controller** (CC). There is a single copy of the Central Controller residing in the system memory. During instantiation, CC initializes the internal **static data set** (static policy data) from policy DB. XML has evolved as the de facto standard for policy specification [19]. It is also extensible and easy to read. Therefore, XML is a natural choice for ESTARBAC policy specification. Here, **Policy Loader** handles the job of processing and loading the XML policy data into the system in proper format. A part of the data set stored in the system reflects the current state of the authorization system. This **dynamic data set** contains information about active user context and active sessions. It may change with time. Depending on the spatiotemporal access decision, the remote call is either forwarded to the intended object or a program level exception is raised and returned to the client. The security console is primarily aimed to edit the spatiotemporal access policy for the system. It also displays the current state of authorization based on the access log maintained by the system.

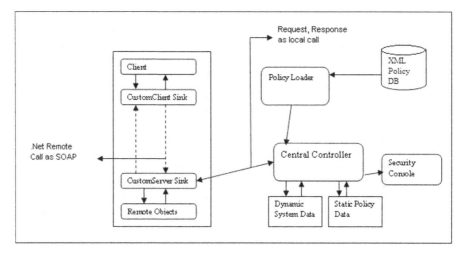

Fig. 3. Access Control System Architecture

The access control system is implemented in three separate modules. Each component of the proposed ESTARBAC model (shown in Fig. 1) is designed as a separate class and inherited from a basic class called *Entity*. All the entity classes are packed into a separate dynamic linked library (Windows .dll component) and called by CC. The second module is access control module. It encapsulates different classes critical for the functioning of the access control system. The Central Controller initializes the whole access control system, processes incoming request, and responds back the access decision. It serves as the Access Control Monitor of the system. The Policy Loader handles the detail security policy loading job. Policy loading is initiated by the Central

Controller. The third module is security console. This has been developed as a separate executable tool for editing the policy data. This tool can also read the access control log and present the current access status of the system in a user friendly manner.

8.4 System Integration

The access control system is plugged into iMedik as a separate dll component. The remote calls are intercepted in both client side and server side using the facility of .NET sink classes. In the presentation layer, a custom sink called CustomClientSink is written which is responsible for augmenting the current user context with each and every remote call to the business layer. In the business logic layer, a customized sink called CustomServerSink is added. The server sink intercepts any remote call to the business methods and passes the user request to the CC. The request and response between server sink and CC are realized as local function call. We need to make few changes in the core application code in the presentation layer aspx files for integration.

8.5 Collection of Context Values in iMedik

In iMedik, user level access control uses the following important credentials: userid, password, role and http sessionid. Apart from these usual security parameters, the proposed access control mechanism acquires the access time and the current user location from the application. Collecting request access time is straightforward. Since access control is launched in IIS, during processing a user request, the absolute time of the hosting IIS environment is fetched. This is taken as a fair approximation of the current resource access time. In *C#* .NET, the *System.DateTime* class provides required API for processing system time. On the other hand, the current user location value requires reasonable assumption for the system. Two different strategies have been tried to pick up the GPS coordinates from the blackberry phone. In the first strategy, the proprietary java script (blackberry.location java script calls) are embedded within the iMedik web pages which is supposed to capture the device during any iMedik resource access. In another strategy, a separate agent running in the Blackberry phone periodically refreshes the location values to the iMedik server using TCP connection. Unfortunately, the first strategy did not work for us while the second strategy worked successfully.

9 Conclusion and Future Work

In this paper, we have suggested an approach to incorporate spatiotemporal access context in standard RBAC decision model. All the components of the model except location and time are logically developed from the classical RBAC components. The concept of spatiotemporal access is introduced in the form of role extent and permission extent which is simple to understand and expressive in terms of specifying combined space time based security policy. The model has been implemented in a real-life telemedicine application supporting access from mobile devices. Access control mechanisms can be incorporated in the system with minimal changes to the existing code. In future, we intend to elaborate the usefulness of spatiotemporal role and permission extent in detail with analysis and more practical examples. At the same time, we would like to develop a framework for specifying useful spatiotemporal access policies based on the proposed model. The current concept of spatial constraint on mobile objects can be extended to make the model applicable in providing access control in peer-to-peer interactions. The work may also be further enhanced by considering access restriction depending on spatial or temporal access history. Role hierarchy along with associated spatiotemporal constraints can be included making the model even more flexible.

Acknowledgements

This work is partially supported by a research grant from the Department of Science and Technology, Government of India, under Grant No. SR/S3/EECE/ 082/2007. The authors would like to thank the anonymous reviewers for their constructive suggestions for improving the quality of the paper.

References

1. Ahn, G., Sandhu, R.: Role-Based Authorization Constraints Specification. ACM Transactions on Information and System Security 3(4), 207–226 (2000)
2. Aich, S., Sural, S., Majumdar, A.K.: STARBAC: Spatiotemporal Role Based Access Control. In: Meersman, R., Tari, Z. (eds.) OTM 2007, Part II. LNCS, vol. 4804, pp. 1567–1582. Springer, Heidelberg (2007)
3. Atluri, V., Chun, S.A.: A Geotemporal Role-based Authorisation System. International Journal of Information and Computer Security 1(1/2), 143–168 (2007)
4. Bertino, E., Bettini, C., Ferrari, E., Samarati, P.: An Access Control Model Supporting Periodicity Constraints and Temporal Reasoning. ACM Transactions on Database Systems 23(3), 231–285 (1998)
5. Bertino, E., Bonatti, P.A., Ferrari, E.: TRBAC: A Temporal Role-Based Access Control Model. ACM Transactions on Information and System Security 4(3), 191–223 (2001)
6. Covington, M.V., Long, W., Srinivasan, S., Dey, A.K., Ahamad, M., Abowd, G.D.: Securing Context-aware Applications using Environment Roles. In: Proceedings of ACM Symposium on Access Control Models and Technologies, pp. 10–20 (2001)
7. Damiani, M.L., Bertino, E., Catania, B., Perlasca, P.: GEO-RBAC: A Spatially Aware RBAC. ACM Transactions on Information and System Security 10(1) Article 2, (February 2007)
8. Ferraiolo, D.F., Sandhu, R., Gavrila, S., Kuhn, D.R., Chandramouli, R.: Proposed NIST Standard for Role-based Access Control. ACM Transactions on Information and System Security 4(3), 224–274 (2001)
9. Hansen, F., Oleshchuk, V.: Spatial Role-Based Access Control Model for Wireless Networks. In: Proceedings of IEEE Vehicular Technology Conference, pp. 2093–2097 (2003)
10. Joshi, J.B.D., Bertino, E., Latif, U., Ghafoor, A.: A Generalized Temporal Role based Access Control Model. IEEE Transactions on Knowledge and Data Engineering 17(1), 4–23 (2005)
11. Maji, A.K.: Vulnerability Analysis of a Multi-tier Architecture for Web-based Services with Application to Tele-healthcare, MS Thesis, IIT Kharagpur, India (2008)
12. McAlearney, A.S., Schweikhart, S.B., Medow, M.A.: Doctors' Experience with Handheld Computers in Clinical Practice: Qualitative Study. British Medical Journal 328, 1–5 (2004)

13. Ray, I., Kumar, M., Yu, L.: LRBAC: A Location-Aware Role-Based Access Control Model. In: Proceedings of International Conference on Information Systems Security, pp. 147–161 (2006)
14. Ray, I., Toahchoodee, M.: A Spatio-Temporal Role-Based Access Control Model. In: Proceedings of 21st Annual IFIP WG 11.3 Working Conference on Data and Applications Security (2007)
15. Samuel, A., Ghafoor, A., Bertino, E.: A Framework for Specification and Verification of Generalized Spatio-Temporal Role based Access Control Model, CERIAS Tech Report 2007-08, Purdue University, West Lafayette, IN 47907-2086.
16. Sandhu, R.: Role Activation Hierarchies. In: Proceedings of ACM Workshop on Role-Based Access, pp. 33–40 (1998)
17. Sandhu, R., Coyne, E.J., Feinstein, H.L., Youman, C.E.: Role-Based Access Control Models. IEEE Computer 29(2), 38–47 (1996)
18. Schoen, C., Osborn, R., Huynh, P.T., Doty, M., Peugh, J., Zapert, K.: On the Front Lines of Care: Primary Care Doctors' Office Systems, Experiences, and Views in Seven Countries. Health Affairs 25(3), 555–571 (2006)
19. XML - http://www.w3c.org/XML/

A Method for Estimation of the Success Probability of an Intrusion Process by Considering the Temporal Aspects of the Attacker Behavior

Jaafar Almasizadeh and Mohammad Abdollahi Azgomi

Department of Computer Engineering,
Iran University of Science and Technology, Tehran, Iran
j_almasi@comp.iust.ac.ir, azgomi@iust.ac.ir

Abstract. The aim is to propose a new approach for stochastic modeling of an intrusion process and quantitative evaluation of the probability of the attacker success. In many situations of security analysis, it is necessary to obtain the probabilities of success for attackers in an intrusion process. In the proposed method, the intrusion process is considered as elementary attack phases. In each atomic phase the attacker and the system interact and this interaction can transfer the current system state to a secure or failure state. Intrusion process modeling is done by a semi-Markov chain (SMC). The distribution functions assigned to the SMC transitions are a linear combination of some uniform distributions. These mixture distributions represent the time distribution of the attacker or the system in the transient states. In order to evaluate the security measure, the SMC is converted into a discrete-time Markov chain (DTMC) and then the resulting DTMC is analyzed and the probability of the attacker success is computed based on mathematical theorems. The desired security measure is evaluated with respect to the temporal aspects of the attacker behavior.

Keywords: Security, attacker, system, modeling, evaluation, intrusion process, semi-Markov chain (SMC), discrete-time Markov chain (DTMC).

1 Introduction

The increasing growth of successful attacks and intrusions into computer systems has taught us that it is not practical to build a perfect secure system. Hence, it is important to be able to quantitatively evaluate the security level of systems. In this paper an efficient method for stochastic modeling and quantifying the security of computer systems and networks is presented. The proposed method is simple and general. It has a stochastic nature and therefore is suitable for describing the dynamic attacker behavior.

Most of the research on security analysis has pointed out the system security from a qualitative point of view. Nowadays, it is accepted that security is a quality of service measure of computer and communication systems. However, as the best of our knowledge, only few works have considered the security assessment in a quantitative manner.

M.L. Gavrilova et al. (Eds.): Trans. on Comput. Sci. IV, LNCS 5430, pp. 200–214, 2009.
© Springer-Verlag Berlin Heidelberg 2009

There is an important difference between dependability evaluation and security analysis. In dependability modeling and evaluation, the faults which cause failure, have unintentional and stochastic nature; while as stated in [14] in security analysis it is required to assume that the failures are caused by human intent, resulting in security failures that are definitely correlated, that depend in subtle ways on system state, and that attackers learn over time.

Thus, to quantify the security of the systems, it is necessary to consider the behaviors of the attacker and the system over time. For this purpose, we utilize stochastic modeling techniques. First, we present a state transition model for describing the dynamic interactions between the attacker and the system. After parameterization and the assignment the distribution functions to the transitions of the model, we obtain a stochastic model. As will be explained, the underlying stochastic model will be a semi-Markov chain (SMC). The presented method considers the intrusion process as a series of sequential steps of attacks. An attacker initiates the intrusion process with a basic level of privilege and advances to the security target, step by step. However, at each step, he may be detected by the system and therefore the intrusion process is thwarted. Based on this scenario, the probability of the attacker success is computed. This probability is a numerical measure for the security level provided by the system.

In many situations of security analysis, it is necessary to obtain the probabilities of success for the attackers. These probabilities can be used directly as desired security measures or indirectly as inputs to the security models for evaluating the other security measures.

The rest of this paper is organized as follows. In section 2, related work on quantifying security is described. In section 3, our proposed approach for intrusion process modeling is discussed and then it is explained how to model and to evaluate intrusion process by the model. In section 4, our method is demonstrated by a case study. Finally, section 5 represents the conclusions of the paper and outlines the future work.

2 Related Work

As the best of our knowledge, in few publications, state-based stochastic models, like Markovian models or Petri nets, have been used as useful and feasible tools for security evaluation. The following is a brief introduction of the related work.

In [10] as a first step towards security quantification the similarities between reliability and security from the perspective of evaluating measures of operational security of systems is discussed. In [15] a quantitative model to measure known UNIX security vulnerabilities using a privilege graph is presented, which is then transformed into a Markov chain. The model allows for the characterization of operational security expressed as the mean effort to security failure. In [7] a quantitative analysis of attacker behavior based on empirical data collected from intrusion experiments is presented. A typical attacker behavior comprises of three phases: the learning phase, the standard attack phase and the innovative attack phase.

In [6] an approach for quantifying security of systems using colored Petri nets is presented. The unified security and dependability framework covers not only breaches caused by users and non-users, but also traditional dependability failures. In [16] a method for probabilistic validation of an intrusion-tolerant replication system is described. It uses a hierarchical stochastic activity network model to validate the intrusion tolerant system. In [14] a survey on the existing model-based system dependability evaluation techniques is provided, and methods for extending them for security evaluation are summarized.

In [17], game theory is suggested as a method for modeling and computing the probabilities of expected behavior of attackers in a quantitative stochastic model of security. In [18, 19] the use of stochastic modeling technique as a suitable method for assessing the trustworthiness of a system, regardless of whether the failure cause is intentional or not is presented. By viewing the system states as elements in a stochastic game and modeling attacks as transitions between the states of system, the probabilities of expected attacker behavior can be computed. The proposed game model is based on a reward- and cost concept. In [11, 25] security is considered as a quality of service attribute and an approach to quantify the security attributes of intrusion tolerant systems using stochastic modeling techniques is presented.

In [10, 14] a new model for estimating the time to compromise a system component that is visible to an attacker is proposed. The model provides an estimate of the expected value of the time-to-compromise as a function of known and visible vulnerabilities, and attacker skill level. In [22] a flexible extensible model for computer attacks is presented and showed that how it can be used in security applications such as vulnerability analysis, intrusion detection and attack generation. In [21, 23], some illustrations on how probabilistic modeling can be used in an integrated validation procedure and successfully bring insight and feedback on a design is presented. It allows comparing different algorithms, features, or infrastructures.

In [12], quantitative threat modeling method is presented, which quantifies security threats by calculating the total severity weights of relevant attack paths for commercial-off-the-shelf systems. Comparing to the existing approaches, this method is sensitive to an organization's business value priorities and information technology environment. In [2], the authors use a special operational semantics for predicting quantitative measures on systems describing cryptographic protocols. They also consider a possible attacker. The transitions of the system carry enhanced labels. Rates to transitions are assigned by only looking at these labels and then by mapping transition systems to Markov chains and performance of systems are evaluated, using standard tools. In [9] some empirical analysis based on the data collected from the honeypot platforms deployed on the Internet and some preliminary modeling studies aimed at fulfilling such objectives are presented.

3 The Proposed Stochastic Model

In this section we present the method for estimation of the success probability of the attackers. The proposed method is based on the presented concepts and ideas used in [11, 14, 17, 24]. In the following subsections, we will first mention the contributions of this work. Then, we will present the underlying assumptions and the graphical representation of the model. Finally, the model will be parameterized and solved.

3.1 Contributions

As stated earlier for security quantification an appropriate notion of time must be considered. It is necessary to evaluate the security measures based on the temporal aspects of the attacker and the system's actions. In most the existing approaches [6, 8, 12, 20, 22] the concept of time is not considered at all and, therefore, they cannot obtain the quantitative security measures. Also, a main problem in [2, 8, 15, 17, 18, 19] is that the assigned time distribution to transitions of the models is assumed to be exponential. As investigated and stated in [9, 10, 11, 16, 25], this assumption may not be appropriate in many situations of attack process. In contrast to the accidental failure situation, the attacker and the system behavior will be gradually changed over time. We utilize non-exponential distribution functions for describing the temporal aspects of the attacker and the system behavior. As will be seen these distributions are a linear combination of some uniform distributions. Additionally, as stated in [14], just as appropriate fault models are critical to dependability evaluation, an appropriate attacker model is critical to quantitative security evaluation. However, most of the existing approaches do not provide a suitable attacker model. For example, in [11, 18, 25] the attacker behavior is modeled by only two transitions. A security model needs to include more detailed attacker behavior. For this purpose, we present an appropriate and detailed model for describing the attacker behavior.

In summary, a detailed state transition model for analyzing intrusion process is proposed and parameterized by assigning the distribution functions to the transitions of the model. Also, the proposed model is a mathematical model which makes it appropriate for analytic computation of the security measures.

3.2 The Model Assumptions

Each intrusion process into a system can be modeled as a series of elementary attack phases that gradually transfer the system from a secure initial state to a security failure final state. In order to evaluate the security of a system, it is necessary to consider the actions of the attacker as well as the reactions of the system to the attacker's actions. Therefore, we must consider the interaction between the attacker and the system in each attack phase of the attack process.

If the attacker successfully passes the current phase, then the system security state will be changed; that is, the attacker will be transferred to the next step provided that he passes the current step successfully. Also, each atomic step of the intrusion process, changes the attacker's capabilities. In the other words, at each attack phase the attacker affects on system state until system will finally go to the security failure state. On the other hand, system can detect and undo the intermediate steps of the intrusion process and transfers its state into a secure state.

It is assumed that the intrusion process will not be repeated; that is, the attacker's actions have two results at each step: success or failure. In our method, any intrusion process can be modeled and analyzed; it is sufficient to analyze the intrusion process exactly in order to determine sequential attack steps. Then, the interactions between the attacker and the system are modeled and with respect to the attacker and the system's abilities and the probability of the attacker success in the intrusion process is computed. This measure specifies a quantitative indicator for the security level of the system.

3.3   The Model Representation

As stated before, it is necessary to model the interactions between the attacker and the system. Due to the uncertainty in the attacker behavior and even that of the system, it is necessary to use stochastic modeling approaches to capture the complexities of the temporal aspects of the interactions between the attacker and the system. To an attacker with an incomplete knowledge of the system, there is uncertainty as to the effects of the attack and to the system designer/owner/operator, there is uncertainty as to the type, frequency, intensity and the duration of the attack, and even as to whether a particular attack would result in a security breach[11]. Therefore, we describe the events that change the state of the model, probabilistically. Note that these events are caused by the attacker or the system. For doing so, we present a state transition model and transform this abstract model to a stochastic model by assigning the time distributions to it.

Determining the appropriate level of detail/abstraction in an attacker model is very important, and depends on the scope and purpose of the model [14]. The state transition model has two absorbing states and the rest of its states are transient. These two absorbing states represent the success and failure situations of the intrusion process. The transient states represent the sequential steps of the intrusion process. Note that the attacker's or the system's activities are implicitly defined in the transitions of the model. The general state transition model is depicted in Fig. 1.

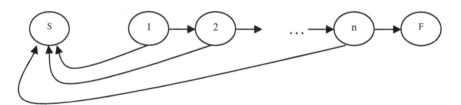

Fig. 1. The General stochastic model for analyzing an intrusion process

In Fig. 1, in each intermediate phase of the intrusion process, the attacker proceeds towards the security target or he may be detected before doing any suitable action. It is assumed that the attacker never retreats voluntarily and only moves towards the final target, unless he is stopped by the system; that is, we only consider the normal situations in which the attacker and the system interact. Note that the attacker will succeed if he is able to exploit the vulnerabilities before the system detect and remove the vulnerabilities.

The intermediate states of the model represent the different levels of privilege that currently the attacker holds. The states S and F are absorbing states: This means, if the model is entered to these states, then it stays there forever. Our problem is to characterize the probabilities of the entrance to one of the two absorbing states. If the model is finally entered the absorbing state F, then the attacker has succeeded in the intrusion activity and if it is entered the absorbing state S, the attacker has failed in the intrusion activity. It should be noted that we consider the intrusion processes for which there is a nonzero probability of the success for the attacker. So, if there is no way for the attacker in order to reach the security target, such an attack process is regarded as a secure attack process and therefore is not an attack process of interest.

The proposed model can be used for quantifying any attack process. For this purpose, two unique characteristics of the attack process must be specified: the number of the elementary attack phases of the attack process and the nature of the interactions between the attacker and the system in each attack phase. With respect to these two factors, we analyze an intrusion process and determine the number of attack phases and the nature of each attack phase.

In this work, we restrict the presented concepts to the modeling approaches. To our knowledge, there is no rigorous theoretical fundamental in the area of the quantitative security evaluation at present. First of all, it is necessary to develop a method for capturing the attacker and the system behavior. So, here, our focus is on developing concepts for presenting a suitable modeling approach for describing the dynamic interactions between the attacker and the system. Additionally, empirical methods are too time-consuming and too inaccurate. It is for these reasons that we leave the experimental work for the future work.

There are many attack paths in the real-world. Note that an intrusion process shows an attack path. Therefore, we only analyze an intrusion process in each modeling process. Thus, it is necessary to construct a suitable model for describing each intrusion process.

3.4 The Model Parameterization

The attacker must spend some time to pass an attack phase of the attack process. This time can be suitably described by a nonnegative continuous random variable. Since this variable indicates time, it must be nonnegative and continuous. Assume that an attack phase is started in zero time and completed at time $a \leq x \leq b$. Thus the initial time interval of the attacker is defined as $|a, b|$, where a and b can be considered to be any nonnegative real values:

$$0 \leq a \leq b \leq | \tag{1}$$

We expect the successful completion of an attack phase within this specified time. The time to the next attack phase would have this entire time interval of values as possible values. Let X be the continuous random variable indicating the attacker's needed time for the intrusion activities. This assumption about the attacker behavior is formally expressed as follows:

$$P(a \leq X \leq b) = 1 \tag{2}$$

On the other hand, the system needs some time to detect the attack effects. There is always a nonzero probability that the system detects the attacker's actions before the attack phase is completed by the attacker. So, the suitable initial time interval for the system' actions is defined to be time interval $|0, b|$. We expect the successful detection of an attack phase within this specified time. Let Y be the continuous random variable indicating the system's needed time for the prevention and detection activities. This assumption about the system behavior is formally expressed as follows:

$$P(0 \leq Y \leq b) = 1 \tag{3}$$

In order to define the mixture distribution functions, two principal factors must be considered: attacker skill level and system's abilities in the intrusion prevention and detection. We consider the typical attacker as a representative of all the probable attackers against the system. In the other word, the range of the expected attacker behavior must cover the behavior of all the categories of the attackers. Also, in each attack phase we consider all possible methods for exploiting the vulnerabilities. These complexities of the attacker behavior are suitably specified by a mixture distribution function.

Therefore, we define an initial time interval for the attacker (the system) so that the instant of activity completion of the attacker (the system) will be some point of this interval. Now, In order to carefully specify the complexities of the temporal aspects of the interactions between the attacker and the system, we divide each of these initial time intervals of the attacker and the system into some subintervals.

Now, with respect to the above assumptions, we want to define the distribution functions of the transitions of the model. The desired distribution functions are a linear combination of some uniform distributions. Formally, the mixture distribution function is written as follows:

$$F_X(t) = \sum_{i=1}^{n} p_i F_{X_i}(t), \quad \sum_{i=1}^{n} p_i = 1 \tag{4}$$

where the distribution function $F_X(t)$ is the mixture distribution function of each transition of the model and is a linear combination of some uniform distribution functions $F_{X_i}(t)$. p_i is the corresponding weight of the distribution function $F_{X_i}(t)$ and shows the probability that the attacker (the system) behavior will be described by this distribution. Every uniform distribution function $F_{X_i}(t)$ is also defined over interval (a_i, b_i). Let X_i be a continuous random variable. It is said that X_i is uniformly distributed over interval (a_i, b_i) , if its distribution function is given by

$$F_{X_i}(t) = P(X_i \leq t) = \begin{cases} 0 & t < a_i \\ \dfrac{t - a_i}{b_i - a_i} & a_i \leq t < b_i \\ 1 & b_i \leq t \end{cases} \tag{5}$$

and its density function is given by

$$f(x_i) = \begin{cases} \dfrac{1}{b_i - a_i} & a_i < x_i < b_i \\ 0 & otherwise \end{cases} \tag{6}$$

To obtain a reliable estimation of the security measure, it is important to suitably determine the time intervals over which the uniform distribution functions are defined.

Note that, since the time distributions of the transitions of the model are not exponential and the future behavior of the model is completely characterized by the current state, the underlying stochastic model will be an SMC. To completely specify the SMC, the distribution time of each transition of it must be defined.

We believe that by describing the temporal aspects of the attacker and the system behavior, it is possible to capture the complexities of the interactions between the attacker and the system. We must consider all the probable options of the attacker and the system in each attack phase. Thus, such complexities in the attacker and the system behavior are described by defining a mixture distribution function. Depending on the nature of each attack phase and the attacker skill level, the suitable initial time interval is defined for the attacker. Similarly, depending on the nature of each attack phase the existing security mechanisms, the suitable initial time interval is defined for the system. With regard to the type of the intrusion process and by tuning the parameters of the mixture distribution functions appropriately, the different situations of the interactions between the attacker and the system are described. The starting point and the length of an interval characterize the attacker skill level and system's capability. Hence, a more experienced attacker and a more robust system have a smaller time interval as well as a smaller starting point. If each of the attacker's (the system's) actions is described by a uniform distribution, then the overall attacker (system) behavior is expected to be described well by a linear combination of these uniform distributions.

Since, the knowledge of the attacker and the system is gradually increased; therefore we can assume that the random variable related to each attack phase has the increasing failure rate situation. In such conditions, the probability of the attacker success and the probability of the detection of the attacker by the system increased with time and this is matched with our intuition of the attacker and the system behaviors. Note that the uniform distribution is an increasing failure rate distribution. It can be verified with respect to the following equation [24]:

$$r_X(t) = \frac{f_X(t)}{1 - F_X(t)} \tag{7}$$

where $F_X(t)$ and $f_X(t)$ are the distribution and density functions of the uniform random variable X, respectively. Since, the uniform distribution is an increasing failure rate distribution; it is simple to show that a linear combination of these distributions is also a distribution with increasing failure rate situation.

To summarize, the reasons for the use of the mixture distribution of the uniform distributions are as follows. It is an increasing failure rate distribution. Additionally, its parameters can be estimated suitably and arbitrarily. Also, it describes the stochastic and uncertain nature of the attacker behavior and the system suitably. Finally, based on the selected time intervals, the attacker skill level and robustness of the system can be determined by the modeler.

3.5 The Model Solution

In this section, we present an interesting method for evaluating the security measure. As stated earlier, our desired security measure is the probability of the attacker success. We want to evaluate the probability of the typical attacker success in an intrusion process by considering the temporal aspects of the attacker and the system behavior. In the terminology of an SMC, it means that the SMC will finally be absorbed in the absorbing state while its current state is a transient state.

We note that the SMC eventually will enter an absorbing state from any transient state. It means the attacker may compromise the security of the system with different levels of privilege. Thus, we need to compute the probabilities of the transitions from each transient state to the absorbing states. Therefore, all levels of privilege must be considered. If an SMC is seen only at discrete instants at which state transitions occur, the resulting chain is a DTMC. The DTMC is completely described by its transition probability matrix. Thus, the first step of the evaluation processes it to construct the transition probability matrix of the DTMC.

Let X be the continuous random variable indicating the attacker's needed time for the intrusion activities and Y be the continuous random variable indicating the system's needed time for the prevention and detection activities in each phase. Therefore, the transition probability related to the attacker's actions can be expressed as $P(X < Y)$ (the situation the attacker acts before the system) and the transition probability related to the system's actions can be expressed as $P(X < Y)$ (the situation the system acts before the attacker). Since the resulting matrix is a stochastic matrix, it is clear that the sum of the probabilities of the outgoing transitions of each state will be unity:

$$P(X < Y) + P(X > Y) = 1 \tag{8}$$

Note that X and Y are a linear combination of some uniform distribution functions. Assume that the mixture distribution function of the transition of the attacker is defined as follows:

$$F_X(t) = \sum_{i=1}^{n} p_i F_{X_i}(t), \quad \sum_{i=1}^{n} p_i = 1 \tag{9}$$

and the mixture distribution function of the transition of the system is also defined as follows:

$$G_Y(t) = \sum_{i=1}^{m} q_i F_{Y_i}(t), \quad \sum_{i=1}^{m} q_i = 1 \tag{10}$$

The desired probabilities are calculated by the theorem of total probability. For this purpose, we use the following integral:

$$P(X < Y) = \int_{-\infty}^{\infty} P(X < Y | Y = t) f_y(t) \, dt \tag{11}$$

where $P(X < t)$ $(F_X(t))$ is the distribution function of the random variable X and $f_Y(t)$ is the density function of the random variable Y. After substitution and simplification, we compute the above integral as follows:

$$P(X < Y) = \int_{-\infty}^{\infty} \left(\sum_{i=1}^{n} p_i F_{X_i}(t) \right) \left(\sum_{i=1}^{m} q_i f_{Y_i}(t) \right) dt = \sum_{i=1,j=1}^{n,m} (p_i q_j) \int_{0}^{b} F_{X_i}(t) f_{Y_j}(t) \, dt \tag{12}$$

As a result, for computing the probability of $P(X < Y)$, it is necessary to evaluate mn of such integrals. Suppose that the interval (a_i, b_i) be one of the intervals of the attacker and the interval (l_j, d_j) be one of the intervals of the system. All the different arrangements between the time intervals must be considered and based on theses arrangements, the desired integral is obtained. It is clear that there are three different situations:

1. The time intervals do not overlap with each other. In this situation if $b_i \leq \mathsf{l}_j$ then

$$P(X_i < Y_j) = 1 \tag{13}$$

and if $d_j \leq a_i$ then

$$P(X_i < Y_j) = 0 \tag{14}$$

2. One of the time intervals covers another time interval completely. In this situation, if we have $\mathsf{l}_j \leq \mathsf{l}_i \leq \mathsf{l}_{\mathsf{l}} \leq d_{\mathsf{l}}$, then the desired integral becomes as follows:

$$P(X_i < Y_j) = \int_{a_i}^{b_i} \frac{t - a_i}{b_i - a_i} \Bigg| \frac{1}{d_j - \mathsf{l}_j} dt + \int_{b_i}^{\mathsf{l}_j} \frac{1}{d_j - \mathsf{l}_j} dt = \frac{b_i - a_i + |(d_j - b_i)}{|(d_j - \mathsf{l}_j)} \tag{15}$$

and if we have $\mathsf{l}_j \leq \mathsf{l}_i \leq \mathsf{l}_{\mathsf{l}} \leq d_{\mathsf{l}}$, then the above integral becomes as follows:

$$P(X_i < Y_j) = \int_{c_j}^{\mathsf{l}_j} \frac{t - a_i}{b_i - a_i} \Bigg| \frac{1}{d_j - \mathsf{l}_j} dt = \frac{d_j + \mathsf{l}_j - |a_i}{|(b_i - a_i)} \tag{16}$$

3. The time intervals overlap with each other partially. In this situation, if we have $a_i \leq \mathsf{l}_j \leq b_i \leq d_j$, then the above integral becomes as follows:

$$\begin{aligned}
P(X_i < Y_j) &= \int_{c}^{b} \frac{t - a_i}{b_i - a_i} \Bigg| \frac{1}{d_j - \mathsf{l}_j} dt + \int_{b}^{\mathsf{l}_j} \frac{1}{d_j - \mathsf{l}_j} dt \\
&= \frac{(b_i - \mathsf{l}_j)(b_i + \mathsf{l}_j - |a_i) + |(d_j - b_i)(b_i - a_i)}{|(b_i - a_i)(d_j - \mathsf{l}_j)}
\end{aligned} \tag{17}$$

and if we have $\mathsf{l}_j \leq a_i \leq d_j \leq b_i$, then the above integral becomes as follows:

$$P(X_i < Y_j) = \int_{a}^{\mathsf{l}} \frac{t - a_i}{b_i - a_i} \Bigg| \frac{1}{d_j - \mathsf{l}_j} dt = \frac{(d_j - a_i)^2}{|(b_i - a_i)(d_j - \mathsf{l}_j)} \tag{18}$$

Now, with respect to the above equations, the transition probability matrix of the DTMC is obtained. The resulting matrix can be rearranged as:

$$P(t) = [p_{ij}(t)] \quad P = \begin{vmatrix} T & A \\ 0 & I \end{vmatrix} \tag{19}$$

where submatrix T represents the transition probabilities between the transient states and submatrix A represents the transition probabilities from the transient states to the absorbing states. Matrix I is identity matrix. Now, we define matrix H as follows [24]:

$$H = \left[h_{ij}\right] = (I - T)^{-1}A \tag{20}$$

where h_{ij} denotes the probability that the DTMC starting with a transient state i finally get in an absorbing state j. Each row of the matrix H has two values that represent the transition probabilities from the current transient state to the absorbing states S and F. Since we apply the stochastic modeling approaches, then the resulting measure is a relative security measure. We need a reliable estimation of the measure. In fact, the security measure characterizes the expected behavior of the attacker.

4 Case Study: DNS Spoofing Attack

4.1 The Attack Modeling

In this attack, which is named DNS Spoofing attack, the domain address sent by the user (victim) to the DNS server is intercepted by the attacker and is translated to a fake IP address and then it will be sent back to the user. Based on this scenario, the user trusts to the attacker and establishes a TCP connection with the attacker. Finally, the attacker discloses the confidential data of the user or issue special commands to the user by exploiting of this connection. We assume that the attacker has not direct access to the network and cannot sniff packets. We can describe the steps that an attacker needs to perform as follows:

- At step (1), the attacker after accessing to a machine in the local network, installs a suitable program like *DNSSpoof* on the machine. It is assumed that the attacker steals a password of an authorized user for the access to the local machine.
- At step (2), the attacker intercepts the DNS query packet of the user in order to translate the domain address to a fake IP address. Then, the attacker sends this fake IP address for the user instead of the DNS IP address and pretends to be the DNS.
- At step (3), the user trusts to the attacker and establishes a TCP connection with him. The victim is now in a situation where it believes that a TCP connection has been established with a trusted agent (DNS). However, the attacker has a one-way connection with the victim and issue commands to the target or steals the confidential data. The confidential data are disclosed by the attacker using this connection.

In Fig. 2, the intrusion process modeling by the SMC is presented. This model has three transient states and two absorbing states. Note that the attacker's privileges are represented by the transient states of the SMC and the attacker or the system's actions are represented by the transitions between the states. At each step, if the system decides to close the connection to the attacker after it detected the attacker's pre-attack actions, then it is returned to the secure state.

4.2 The Model Evaluation

In this study, our main purpose is to present a method for modeling and evaluation rather than exact parameterization of the model. In the other words, here, our primary

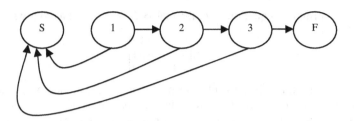

Fig. 2. The DNS spoofing attack modeling

focus is on developing a methodology for quantitative analysis of the security measure of a system rather than accurate model assessment. Therefore, only the good guessed values are used to demonstrate how the proposed model can be used to obtain quantitative measures.

Now, we obtain the security measure with respect to the above model. As stated earlier, an SMC is completely specified by the time distributions of its transitions. The mixture distribution functions assigned to the SMC transitions are defined over the proposed time intervals as indicated in Table 1. For simplicity, we divide each initial interval of the attacker and the system into two subintervals.

Table 1. The Time intervals and their corresponding weights

Transition	The Time intervals and the corresponding weights			
$\mid_{12}$	$\mid\mid 0,50\mid$	0.4	$\mid 50,80\mid$	0.6
$\mid_{2\mid}$	$\mid 10,\mid 0\mid$	0.5	$\mid\mid 0,60\mid$	0.5
$\mid_{\mid\mid}$	$\mid 5,10\mid$	0.7	$\mid 10,30\mid$	0.3
$\mid_{1\mid}$	$\mid 0,\mid 0\mid$	0.8	$\mid\mid 0,80\mid$	0.2
$\mid_{2\mid}$	$\mid 0,40\mid$	0.4	$\mid 40,60\mid$	0.6
$\mid_{\mid\mid}$	$\mid 0,\mid 0\mid$	0.5	$\mid\mid 0,30\mid$	0.5

It is assumed that the time unit used in this example is hour. The proposed time intervals represent the situations that both the attacker and the system act normally.

By using the defined time intervals and their corresponding weights we construct the mixture distribution functions. Now, based on the equations (12, 13, 14, 15, 16, 17, 18), the entries of the transition probability matrix of the DTMC are calculated as:

$$P_{12} = P(X_1 < Y_1) = 0.3\mid, \qquad P_{2\mid} = P(X_2 < Y_2) = 0.55, \qquad P_{\mid\mid} = P(X_\mid < Y_\mid) = 0.31$$

Now, based on these values, the matrices T (the transition probabilities between the transient states) and A (the transition probabilities from the transient states to the absorbing states) are constructed as:

$$T = \begin{bmatrix} 0 & 0.63 & 0 \\ 0 & 0 & 0.45 \\ 0 & 0 & 0 \end{bmatrix}, \quad A = \begin{bmatrix} 0.3\mid & 0 \\ 0.55 & 0 \\ 0.31 & 0.69 \end{bmatrix}$$

Finally, according to equation (20), the matrix H is obtained as follows:

$$H = \begin{bmatrix} 0.81 & 0.19 \\ 0.66 & 0.34 \\ 0.31 & 0.69 \end{bmatrix}$$

The above matrix, H, gives us full information about the model. Note that there are three transient states in this SMC. Hence, three probabilities of success can be defined and calculated with respect to the attacker's capabilities. Here, h_{ij} denotes the probability that the SMC starting with a transient state i finally get in an absorbing state j. For example, if the intrusion process is started in transient state 1, it will complete successfully with probability 0.19 and it will fail with probability 0.81 and so on.

5 Conclusions and Future Work

This paper introduces a new approach for the intrusion process modeling and the evaluation of the probability of the attacker success. In the proposed method, an intrusion process is divided into some elementary attack phases. At each phase, the probability of the attacker success is computed. The interactions between the attacker and the system are displayed by an SMC. Then the SMC is converted into a DTMC and by analyzing the resulting DTMC, the security measure can be obtained. We believe that this approach can help one estimate the probability of the attacker success more careful. So far, this measure has been computed based on the user's intuition. The major novelty of this paper is the assumption that the time distribution assigned to the transitions between states of the model is a mixture distribution of some uniform distribution.

One of the goals of our future work is to concentrate on obtaining some new security measures such as steady-state security measures (i.e., the long-run proportion of time the model spends in the security failure or the mean time to first security failure). For these purposes, we must extend the proposed model.

Also, it is useful to investigate the rest of distribution functions such as normal or hypoexponential for estimating the behavior of the attacker. These distributions or a mixture distribution of them may be a better estimator for the intrusion process modeling.

As another future work, one can extend the proposed model. It is necessary to consider the complexities of the attack scenarios. The attacker may reach to the security target through different attack paths. Considering these aspects of the attacker behaviors, give rise to a more exact method for quantification of security measures.

For evaluating real-world intrusion process, it is necessary to validate the presented ideas against the real attack data. This will require extended and time-consuming work.

References

1. Avizienis, A., Laprie, J.-C., Randell, B., Landwehr, C.: Basic Concepts and Taxonomy of Dependable and Secure Computing. IEEE Transaction on Dependable and Secure Computing 1 (2004)

2. Bodei, C., Curti, M., Degano, P.: A Quantitative Study of Two Attacks. In: Proc. of the 2nd International Workshop on Security Issues with Petri Nets and other Computational Models (WISP 2004). Electronic Notes in Theoretical Computer Science, vol. 121, pp. 65–85. Elsevier, Amsterdam (2005)
3. Cao, Y., Sun, H., Trivedi, K.S., Han, J.: System Availability With Non-Exponentially Distributed Outages. IEEE Transaction on Reliability 51(2) (2002)
4. Bolch, G., Greiner, S., de Meer, H., Trivedi, K.S.: Queueing Networks and Markov Chains: Modeling and Performance Evaluation with Computer Science Application, 2nd edn. John Wiley & Sons, Chichester (2006)
5. Go eva-Popstojanova, K., et al.: Characterizing Intrusion Tolerant Systems Using a State Transition Model. In: DARPA Information Survivability Conference and Exposition (DISCEX II), vol. 2, pp. 211–221 (2001)
6. Houmb, S.H., Sallahammar, K.: Modeling System Integrity of a Security Critical Using Coloured Petri Nets. In: Proc. of the 1st International Conference on Safety and Security Engineering, Rome, Italy, June 13-15 (2005)
7. Jonsson, E., Olovsson, T.: A Quantitative Model of the Security Intrusion Process Based on Attacker Behavior. IEEE Trans. of Software Engineering 23(4), 235–245 (1997)
8. Jonsson, E.: Towards an Integrated Conceptual Model of Security and Dependability. In: Proc. of the First International Conference on Availability, Reliability and Security (AReS) (2006)
9. Kaâniche, M., Alata, E., Nicomette, V., Deswarte, Y., Dacier, M.: Empirical Analysis and Statistical Modelling of Attack Processes Based on Honeypots. In: Proc. of Workshop on Empirical Evaluation of Dependability and Security (WEEDS 2006), Philadelphia, USA, June 25–28 (2006)
10. Littlewood, B., et al.: Towards Operational Measures of Computer Security. Journal of Computer Security 2, 211–229 (1993)
11. Madan, B.B., Goseva-Popstojanova, K., Vaidyanathan, K., Trivedi, K.S.: A Method for Modeling and Quantifying the Security Attributes of Intrusion Tolerant Systems. Performance Evaluation 56 (2004)
12. Malhotra, S., Bhattacharya, S., Ghosh, S.K.: A Vulnerability and Exploit Independent Approach for Attack Path Prediction. In: Proc. of IEEE 8th International Conference on Computer and Information Technology Workshops (2008)
13. McQueen, M.A., Boyer, W.F., Flynn, M.A., Beitel, G.A.: Time-to-Compromise Model for Cyber Risk Reduction Estimation. In: Proc. of Quality of Protection Workshop (2005)
14. Nicol, D.M., Sanders, W.H., Trivedi, K.S.: Model-Based Evaluation: From Dependability to Security. IEEE Trans. on Dependable and Secure Computing 1(1), 48–65 (2004)
15. Ortalo, R., et al.: Experiments with Quantitative Evaluation Tools for Monitoring Operational Security. IEEE Transaction on Software Engineering 25(5) (1999)
16. Sallhamar, K.: Stochastic Models for Combined Security and Dependability Evaluation. Ph.D. Thesis, Norwegian University of Science and Technology (2007)
17. Sallhammar, K., Knapskog, S.J.: Using Game Theory in Stochastic Models for Quantifying Security. In: Proc. of the 9th Nordic Workshop on Secure IT-Systems (NordSec 2004), Espoo, Finland, November 4-5 (2004)
18. Sallhammar, K., Helvik, B.E., Knapskog, S.J.: On Stochastic Modeling for Integrated Security and Dependability Evaluation. Journal of Networks 1(5) (2006)
19. Sallhammar, K., Knapskog, S.J., Helvik: Using Stochastic Game Theory to Compute the Expected Behavior of Attackers. In: Proc. of the 2005 International Symposium on Applications and the Internet Workshops (Saint 2005) (2005)

20. Shahriari, H.R., Makarem, M.S., Sirjani, M., Jalili, R., Movaghar, A.: Modeling and Verification of Complex Network Attacks Using an Actor-Based Language. In: Proc. the 11th International CSI Computer Conference (CSICC 2006), January 24-26 (2006)
21. Singh, S., Cukier, M., Sanders, W.: Probabilistic Validation of an Intrusion-Tolerant Replication System. In: Proc. of the 2003 International Conference on Dependable Systems and Networks (DSN 2003) (2001)
22. Steven, J., Templeton, K.L.: A Requires/Provides Model for Computer Attacks. In: Proc. of the 2000 Workshop on New Security Paradigms, Ballycotton, County Cork, Ireland, pp. 31–38 (2001)
23. Stevens, F., Courtney, T., Singh, S., Agbaria, A., Meyer, J.F., Sanders, W.H., Pal, P.: Model-Based Validation of an Intrusion-Tolerant Information System. In: Proc. of the 23rd Symposium on Reliable Distributed Systems (SRDS 2004), Florianpolis, Brazil (October 2004)
24. Trivedi, K.S.: Probability and Statistics with Reliability, Queuing, and Computer Science Applications, 2nd edn. John Wiley & Sons, Chichester (2001)
25. Wang, D., Madan, B., Trivedi, K.S.: Security Analysis of SITAR Intrusion-Tolerant System. In: Proc. ACM Workshop on Survivable and Self-Regenerative Systems (2003)

A Hardware Architecture for Integrated-Security Services

Fábio Dacêncio Pereira[1] and Edward David Moreno Ordonez[1,2]

[1] University of São Paulo-USP, Polytechnic School, São Paulo, SP, Brazil
[2] State University of Amazonas-UEA, Manaus, AM, Brazil
fabio.dacencio@poli.usp.br, edwdavid@gmail.com

Abstract. There are numerous techniques, methods and tools to promote the security of a digital system, however, each day the mechanisms of attack evolve
and are integrated, creating separate spheres of combined attacks. In this context, this paper presents an embedded security system (into a SoC system) that
has as main goal an integration of the security services. It reaches an improved
performance and prevents malicious attacks on systems and networks. The SoC
prioritizes the implementation of dedicated functions in hardware as cryptographic algorithms, communication interfaces, among others. In our prototype,
initially, the flow control functions and settings are running in software. This
article shows the architecture, functionality and performance of the system developed, and we discuss a real implementation in FPGA.

Keywords: Embedded System, Integrated Security Services, FPGA Performance and System-on-Chip.

1 Introduction

Researches on security systems have focused typically on creating new services or
improving the performance and reliability of a single technique, algorithm or mechanism. The approaches that aim some integration among several security mechanisms
have focused usually on a specific strategic application, since the systematic approach
to integrate security systems requires an analysis of relations among the data.

In this context, we like to intend to describe not only an integration model for security services, but also provide mechanisms to implement it in hardware and software,
and we will focus on requirements as transparency, performance and productivity.

The research on security systems integration (SSI) may be noted since 70'. The concern in become a security technical set in a single integrated system is of paramount
importance, since the possible fragility of a security service may be offset by other.

Commercially, network devices and software of security have the challenge to create this integration. The greatest difficulty is for establishing a common strategy for
innumerable devices, tools and techniques of information security.

The study of this integration is not new. The first research about this integration
appeared in 1975, and it was proposed by David Elliott Bell and Len LaPadula and it
is known as the Bell-LaPadula model [1]. This model was intended to create classes

M.L. Gavrilova et al. (Eds.): Trans. on Comput. Sci. IV, LNCS 5430, pp. 215–229, 2009.

of access control for the DoD's systems. After this pioneer model, many techniques to integrate security systems were developed [1-3].

The current models of SSI determine the relationship between a specific set of security mechanisms which exchange information for preventing or treat system's anomaly.

The current models propose solutions under a specific set of services disregarding the existence of other [4-8]. The most of those models has been used UML techniques to represent the features, functionality and methodology.

So, this paper proposes a special architecture and describes the functionalities of an Embedded System of SSI. It was implemented in FPGA of the Virtex kind. The different modules dedicated to security as AES, RSA, HASH, among others, were implemented. It is important note that the performance statistics (runtime related to circuit delays) and physical area of implementation in hardware are presented and discussed.

This paper is organized in 10 sections. The description, methodology and objectives of embedded system are in section 3, whereas section 2 is dedicated to related works. In section 4 has a better description of our proposed system, while section 5 emphasizes at libraries dedicated to security services. The section 6 shows the description of the services layer, and Soc Configuration Interface appears in section 7. Some results of implementation are provided in section 8 and section 9 ends with some conclusions.

2 Related Works

The integration of security services is a necessity since the attacks techniques are using the integration to increase the strength and efficiency of the attacks. Some works have solutions to integrate a specific set for security services set and they are bringing protection to the system.

The model proposed by Nimal Nissanke [8] focused on the protection of three pillars: secret information, user identification and access control mechanisms. The current models have mainly focused on services integration of access control and intrusion detection, they created a prevention system and dynamic protection.

Kim, in your work [25], affirms that Conventional security systems provide the functions like intrusion detection, intrusion prevention and VPN individually, leading to management inconvenience and high cost. To solve these problems, attention has been paid on the integrated security engine integrating and providing intrusion detection, intrusion prevention and VPN. This work introduces a security framework that allows secure networking by mounting integrated security engine to the network nodes like router or switch. The solution was tested and validated in Cisco Router 2620 and 3620. The results were not discussed in paper.

The main concept discussed by Zilys [5] in your paper involves representation through objects graphs that represent security services. From this concept may be a link among security events. The concept, which is formulated, enables strategic control of integrated security systems (ISS) considering from the influence-reaction parameter point. Reaction strategy algorithm selection allows minimizing reaction time to danger influence and maximizing efficiency of security system. The author does not explore the different possibilities of constructing security objects. The paper presents only a basic form that could be further explored.

Jonsson [7] proposed a model defines security and dependability characteristics in terms of a system's interaction with its environment via the system boundaries and attempts to clarify the relation between malicious environmental influence, e.g. attacks, and the service delivered by the system. The model is intended to help reasoning about security and dependability and to provide an overall means for finding and applying fundamental defense mechanisms. Since the model is high-level and conceptual it must be interpreted into each specific sub-area of security/dependability to be practically useful.

The model propose by Jonsson is a suggested an integrated conceptual model of security and dependability. The model is aimed at improving the understanding of the basic concepts and their interrelation.

The model categorizes system attributes into input, internal and output attributes, whether from the traditional security domain or the traditional dependability domain. It should be helpful for reasoning about security, so that effective defence methods can be developed and tangible results with respect to security/dependability performance can result. Furthermore, the model is intended for use for the development of security metrics. Did not find this model applied in a case study specific.

One more recent proposal of Hassan Rasheed [18] proved the integration of services as, intrusion detection, access control and the author specifies how to respond to intrusion detection. Along this same line other researchers have proposed similar works. Security devices, as the CISCO ASA family also demonstrated the integration of these services.

The differential of our proposed system with those related works is that our approach tries to explore a universe of greater security services and the union of features and functionality in an integration layer.

The main contribution of this work when compared with other listed earlier is that in addition to presenting a model different are also described mechanisms and an architecture capable of linking various security services into a single structure.

3 Embedded Security Services

This section shows descriptions and our methodology and main objectives related to our embedded system which should contain security services.

The embedded system of SSI proposed can be divided into cores in hardware and software libraries that collaborate among themselves for supporting the specifications of an integrated security system.

The proposed system use security services as asymmetric and symmetric encryption, hash functions, IDS, firewall and audit aspects. These services can do tasks for cooperating among them through a Security Services Integrated Layer (SSIL).

The main function of the SSIL is unifying the security services so that an application would have access to them through a common database and a specific set of methods. The advantages can be summarized mainly by transparency access to security data, productivity, and robustness and achieved performance.

The technology and methodology adopted in developing this project have direct impact on the viability, power consumption, area, complexity, flexibility and other factors related to the final application. In this context, we have studied three models: dedicated hardware, embedded software and a hybrid model:

- Dedicated Hardware: Initially was adopted that all modules and functionality would be described and implemented in hardware. The modules for processing and control should be able to run operations with a high level of abstraction and complexity. This proposal was discarded because it would lead to creation of hardware with a high power and area consumption. Besides it is being unwieldy and difficult to do updates.
- Embedded Software: This proposal adds flexibility to the system for allowing the creation of specific security libraries and implementation of robust operations. The use of embedded software allows the creation of interface functions as USB, RS232, Ethernet, SVGA, graphics displays, among others. The disadvantages of this model are in low performance in complex functions implementation as encryption and data compression when compared with hardware solutions.
- Hybrid Architecture: This model supports the integration into a single system, hardware and embedded software. So, by using an interface for communication could be made that hardware and software have interactions, extracting the benefits offered by both.

To classify the services that would be implemented in hardware and software we have adopted the following methodology. In first version, the system was described in embedded software and it is executed by the PowerPC which is embedded in a FPGA Virtex.

After, we have created some libraries with the function of time calculation and instructions counting (timer.h and InstC.h). These were used to detect code sentence and instructions sets that consume high processing time.

Based on these results optimizations were performed at the level of software, but the main contribution was the competence for detecting the system functions that could be implemented in hardware. The result of this technique can be seen in section 8 on the final performance of our system. In the sequence we present the organization in layers of our embedded system.

The final architecture is composed of dedicated cores and embedded software that implements the system's control. The software runs under the Linux operating system version 2.6.0, and this distribution was dedicated and compiled for the PowerPC processor 405.

Using a Linux distribution allows the embedded software makes use of the advantages of an OS as described in [14]: scheduling process, semaphores, file system, memory access control, among others. These characteristics make this architecture a good choice for our project. Fig. 1 describes the organization of our embedded system.

As can be seen in Fig. 1, the system's features are divided into two categories: (i) high performance functions which are implemented in dedicated hardware (cores) and (ii) control functions, data structures and flow process, that are implemented in embedded software. In this case the C language was adopted as the best performance to native applications.

The PowerPC physically present into the FPGA Virtex [15] is responsible for running the embedded software including the security functions, flow control and operating system installed, which were also implemented in this project.

At the highest level of abstraction is the Security Services Integrated Layer (SSIL). The main function of this layer is ignore the existence of different security services, and spread the use of the system's features.

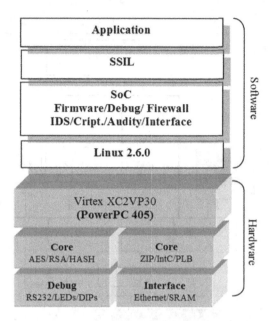

Fig. 1. Organization of embedded system in SoC

4 Top-Level Architecture

The project's architecture is composed of dedicated cores that communicate among them with the PowerPC processor through controlled buses (PLB). Fig. 2 shows how the embedded system proposed is organized, highlighting the main cores and software stored in memory of 512 Mbytes RAM.

We have projected a preliminary version of this system by using the XUPV2P platform which consists of a FPGA Virtex 2 Pro (XCV2P30) and peripherals of Input and Output, where there are the interfaces used as Ethernet, memory SRAM, RS232, Leds and Switches. In the sequence has the description of the cores use.

Xilinx PLB EMAC 10/100
This cores defines the Ethernet protocol layers, where can set a MAC address, allowing the communication through a conventional network. Thus, the embedded security system presents as a device to network.

Xilinx MCMP
To control the access was necessary to include the module MCMP (Multi-Controle Memory Port) which is the interface between the SRAM memory of 512 Mbytes and the PowerPC processor.

Xilinx IntC
IntC (Xilinx Interrupt Control) is responsible by interruptions control allowing different modules can interrupt the flow of the main program (PowerPC Processor), for

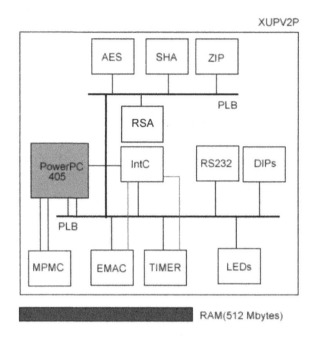

Fig. 2. Top-level architecture

treatment of an event. Currently the timer module and EMAC generate interruptions that are treated as dedicated routines for PowerPC.

Xilinx Timer
Timer used by cores and PowerPC to create and define time scales.

Xilinx PLB
The integration of the PowerPC with dedicated cores is achieved through a common bus, called the PLB (Processor Local Bus). To control the access to bus there is an access arbiter, avoiding conflicts and information collisions.

Debug Interface
Primitive interfaces of the debugging and configuration are used only at the development stage, validation and prototyping processes.

- 4 DIP Swtiches
- 4 Leds
- 1 RS232 serial interface (integration with the PC): transfer rate 9,600 bps, without parity control.

The system debugging is important, especially at the development stage and validation to reduce the design time and minimize the occurrence of errors not foreseen during the project specification.

Symmetric Encryption
Dedicated component that has exclusive function of cipher and decipher the information by using symmetric encryption algorithm, AES (Advanced Encryption Standard). In our project, the AES module can be configured to blocks from 128, 192 and 256 bits. It is important to note that the operation modes, the generation of cryptographic keys and padding control are implemented by software.

Asymmetric Encryption
The module of asymmetric cryptography uses the RSA algorithm that is prepared to encrypt information using keys of 512 and 1024 bits. Later will be implemented a version of 2048 bits. Again the control of vector of clear text and encrypted, keys generation and padding control are implemented in embedded software.

Hash Functions
The hash function initially implemented in system uses the MD5 and SHA-2 algorithms. Even knowing the fragility of the MD5 algorithm compared to the number of collisions detected [19], many applications have adopted. So was implemented and inserted in this project. The flow control is done by software.

Binary Compression
The compression algorithms are used in system as a complement of the embedded application. We adopted the algorithms Shannon-Fano and Huffman [12]. They have a good compression rate to generic applications. There are some algorithms for specific applications as audio and video that can achieve higher compression rates for these specific cases.

In the proposed architecture are implemented in hardware the specific modules for security, compression and the communication interface. The control flow of the data capture to the hard core drive was implemented in software and runned by the PowerPC embedded, this feature adds greater flexibility for security system. The PLB Bus facilitates the addition of new security services. Thus the system can be adapted and updated for different needs.

5 Dedicated Security Libraries

The libraries in software are of critical importance to the viability of the project, since they make use of cores of interface and security for running the functions that require performance. Next, we present a brief feature's description of the main libraries created:

- crypto.h: invokes the functions and parameters for the encryption algorithms based initially in AES and RSA, where can generate key, Subkey, set the mode of operation, encrypt, decipher, among others.
- firewall.h: functions and parameters to insert, delete, alter, and select information in rules table.
- ids.h: allows operations to insert, delete, alter, select anomaly patterns in specific table.
- hash.h: implements operations related to hash functions MD5, SHA-1 and SHA-2.

- audit.h: functions of creation of logs and failures debugging.
- zip.h: data compression (huffman and shannon fano)
- hashtable.h: allocates structure in memory and implements manipulation functions and selection. This is used by other libraries to create customized tables.
- xml.h: contains a parser to that the information generated by the security system can be accessed by other systems through the XML format.
- ciss.h: describes functions for creating of the SSIL, described in the next section.
- http.h: implements the HTTP protocol for access to Soc Configuration Interface.
- server.h: primitive of a web server for access to Soc Configuration Interface.

These libraries are used by embedded application and SSIL to create an environment of personal security.

6 Security Services Integration Layer (SSIL)

The Security Services Integration Layer (SSIL) describes a mechanism to store information on security system, in pursuit of different devices, techniques and tools share relevant information.

The SSIL will attend a universe of devices, tools and algorithms that exist and that still will be created. This is possible only if have a dynamic structure that allows customize their characteristics, maintaining the information integrity.

All information relating to system security or network that can be considered vital can be stored locally for each security service, and this can generate an event and register in SSIL frame. The storage structure (frame) is shown in Fig. 3 and is described in the sequence:

- Package ID: identifies a single package; field with auto-increment.
- Application ID (2 bytes): This field stores the application ID that generated the notification.
- Service Type (1 byte): classifies the security service type that detected the anomaly.
- Anomaly Level: quantifies and specifies the depth of anomaly.
- Reference ID: reporting reference number (more details on anomaly identified).
- Register Number (1 byte): sequential number indicating the number of notifications made by a particular application on an anomaly identified.
- IP / MAC (10 bytes): register the IP number and MAC address of the creator of notification
- Permission (4 bits): Set the access level
- Remote access (4 bits): allows or not remote access to notification.
- Data (100 bytes): information on notification.

All and any anomaly of system identified by some of security services must be formatted according as structure shown in Fig. 3. This structure contains sufficient information to a security policy adopted a decision consistent in regarding indications of possibles anomalys.

The Decision-making after the identification of an anomaly is the responsibility of the application that uses the SSIL. For the initial tests was adopted a simplified model of integrated services based on the security structure published in 2007 by NIS-SANKE [8].

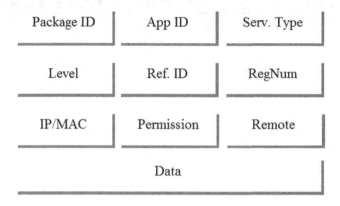

Fig. 3. SSIL Frame

This structure aims to prioritize the network access control. That is, the sum of deficiencies identified by the system can lead to blockage of access. Thus, devices of a network that make anomalies will be blocked.

The system will be able to deny access to network without necessarily knowing where or what security services identified the anomaly.

Specific information about any anomaly may be necessary for the decision. This information can be accessed through the Reference ID that has the function to point the index or code to locate the anomaly generated by a specific security service.

Our security model is simplified and implements the decision based on IP field and anomaly level. The level is defined with the values of 1 to 5 for gravity anomaly identified. In this case, we decided that an accumulation of 12 points on the same network device leads a blockage of service. The appropriate decision about these values deserves more attention and research, but it is not the focus on this phase of our project. Thus, regardless of who generated the notifications, the device network will be blocked.

It is important to note that more sophisticated and specific rules can be created easily if supported the structure (frame) of SSIL, as shown in Fig. 3.

7 SoC Configuration Interface

The SoC Configuration Interface is important to system, because through a friendly interface the user can configure the main modules of the system as the dedicated cores and routines of the overall functioning of the system.

The Interface, implemented in HTML + Javascript, allows the access by a conventional network computers, only the IP mapping pre-defined (198.162.0.1: 8008) in a browser. Fig. 4 shows the Soc Configuration Interface version 1.3. The Interface is not the focus of this article and will not be explored in detail.

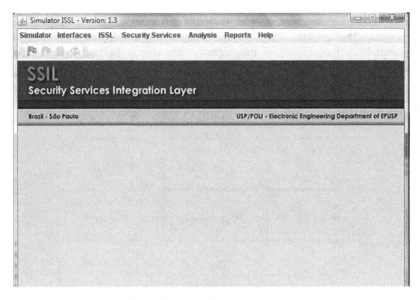

Fig. 4. SSIL Configuration Interface

8   Statistics of Occupation and Performance

The performance and occupation are important factors to evaluate the proposed system. The performance of the embedded system varies depending of the application implemented. In this section, we describe the fully implemented version in embedded software and the hybrid version.

Initially, we present results of the fully software implementation for highlighting the critical performance points (see table 1).

The times recorded were made after the execution of each service on a load of 1MB storing information in memory.

For a detailed review of performance results, in software, described in table 3, it is evident the need to dedicated cores in hardware in pursuit of optimizing the overall processing system.

In this context, the table 2 shows the modules implemented in hardware (VHDL description). The impact of this implementation can be viewed in the following sections.

Table 1. Runtime of some security services in software

Services	Runtime(ms)
AES	753
RSA	8582
SHA-1	638
SHA-2	787
MD5	523
Huffman	1014
Shannon-Fano	938

In this analysis was considered the total time of propagation of the system including all modules described. Information on occupation were evaluated by the number of slices and the total percentage in relation to selected FPGA (see table 2).

8.1 Analysis of Spatial Resources

The table 2 presents the results generated after synthesis and routing of the cores of the system, We show the numbers of SLICES consumed by each module and of the all system.

As can be seen between the security cores, the RSA algorithm consumed the largest area (already expected) given its complexity and difficulty of implementation in hardware [17].

Table 2. Occupancy Statistics in FPGA

Core	Slices	Occupation
AES	810	3%
RSA1024	3929	13%
SHA-2	1974	6%
MD5	1225	4%
Shanon	2407	8%
Debug Interface	10765	35%
Total	25391	84%

The total area consumed can not be considered the sum of areas of each core since the statistical data presented represent the occupation of each module specific (as data generated by the synthesis process) and does not consider the logic consumed, for example the integration / interconnection of them.

The total occupancy was 84% of the FPGA. Unable to enter simultaneously some modules as RSA 512 and 1024 bits, well as the data compression algorithms, Shannon-Fano and Huffman.

Thus, at this stage of the project, the statistical data of total occupation FPGA are only made in 1024-bit RSA algorithms and Shannon-Fano.

8.2 Analysis of Propagation Time

The performance analysis supports mainly in propoagation time of each module and the system propagation time. Table 3 presents statistical data performance. The time unit is the nanoseconds (ns).

When looking table 3 note that the propagation time of the complete system is approximately 8.4 ns, this indicates that the external clock can be a maximum value of 119 MHz.

Considering the device and system complexity the maximum frequency is satisfactory. The propagation time of each module dedicated shows again that the RSA has the largest delay. In this case, the RSA algorithm 1024 and the Shannon-Fano was implemented in this full version of the system.

Table 3. Performance Statistics

IP Core	Propagation Time	Frequency (Max.)
AES	8,8495 ns	113 MHz
RSA1024	9,3458 ns	47 MHz
SHA-2	6,3694 ns	157 MHz
MD5	7,4627 ns	134 MHz
Shanon	8,2645 ns	121 MHz
Debug Interface	8,6206 ns	116 MHz
Total	8,4033 ns	119 MHz

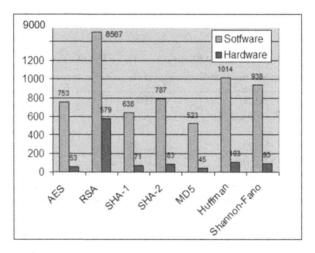

Fig. 5. Impact of the dedicates cores

The frequency for the PowerPC is 300MHz, so the performance implementation in software is associated with this frequency. It is important to note that the Soc Configuration Interface is described in software consuming part of DDR memory SRAM (external) and processing time of the PowerPC.

8.3   The Impact of Adding Dedicated Cores

The performance difference between the version fully in software and the hybrid version can be measured in Fig. 5.

As can be noticed the hybrid version promotes a more effective and efficient processing. The average optimization was of 12.3 times in performance of the proposed system.

8.4   Comparison with Other Dedicated Cores

There are many cryptographic cores and compression of data. The table 4 presents data from implementations works related. In a comparison would be ideal important that all cores were implemented the same device and synthesized by the same software. Even with these differences is possible compare the proposed project, based on the number of Slices and Frequency Acquired.

Table 4. Comparison with related works

Algorithm	Version	FPGA Device	Occupation	Frequency
AES	SSIL	VC2VP30	810 Slices	113 MHz
	[22]	XC2V4000	753 Slices	118 MHz
RSA	SSIL	VC2VP30	3929 Slices	47 MHz
	[20]	XC40250XV	2902 Slices	31 MHz
SHA-2	SSIL	VC2VP30	1974 Slices	157 MHz
	[23]	VC2VP30	1667 Slices	141 Mhz
MD5	SSIL	VC2VP30	1225 Slices	134 MHz
	[21]	XC2V4000	1057 Slices	78 MHz
Huffman	SSIL	VC2VP30	2407 Slices	121 MHz
	[24]	EP20k100E	4160 LEs	173 MHz

In reviewing the information you can see that the system developed a good track record regarding occupation and performance. The focus of this project is not conceive of color to compete with the best implementations, but providing an environment for testing of integrated services and security.

The biggest difference was found on the RSA algorithm. This difference may be explained by different techniques adopted in implementation. The version implemented by Mazzeo [20] is based on the Montgomery algorithm, the version already implemented this project uses conventional multiplier. Most of the slices are consumed for the implementation of large multiplier justifying the difference more pronounced.

9 Conclusions

This work presented a specialized embedded System of Integrated Security Services. We propose and discuss the architecture, features and performance when it is projected in a FPGA Virtex.

The main objectives of the project have been achieved. The security services were created and we have a prototype of the embedded platform which offers integration among different security services. Our embedded system offers transparent and user-friendly provided to the user, productivity and greater involvement of the security mechanisms of the present system.

The robustness of the system generated a concern about the performance that it could achieve. As the performance data and area may be noted that the system has reached a good performance level.

The performance of dedicated security cores can be compared to the best published implementations of algorithms AES [9], SHA [11], MD5 [10]. A new systematic search is being conducted to find better solutions to implementation of algorithms compression and RSA in hardware [13].

In the near future, it would be interesting work on the following issues: The proposed system can be expanded with the addition of new modules for security, as new encryption algorithms.

It is evident that the insertion of new services directly to performance and involve mainly in the area occupied. As future work aims to study the possibility reconfigure the device to facilitate the customization for specific applications and verify the impact of reconfiguration in security applications.

The system was developed on the platform XUPV2P by the availability, but it would be very important test in the most robust platforms such as a FPGA Virtex 5.

Finally, it would be very important to create a Soc Configuration Interface with greater resources and assessment.

References

1. Bell, D.E., Lapadula L.: Secure Computer System: Unified Exposition and Multics Interpretation. Technical Report MTR-2997 Rev. 1, MITRE Corporation, Bedford, MA (1975)
2. Baker, M.P.: Integrated security system. In: Proceedings International Carnahan Conference on Security Technology (1989)
3. Okamoto, E.: Proposal for integrated security systems. In: Proceedings of the Second International Conference on Systems Integration ICSI 1992 (1992)
4. Ferraiolo, D.F., Sandhu, R., Gavrila, S., Kuhn, D.R., Chandramouli, R.: Proposed NIST standard for role-based access control. ACM Transactions on Information and System Security 4(3), 224–274 (2001)
5. Zilys, M., Valinevicius, A., Eidukas, D.: Optimizing strategic control of integrated security systems. In: 26th International Conference on Information Technology Interfaces (2004)
6. Ghindici, D., Grimaud, G., Simplot-Ryl, I., Liu, Y., Traore, I.: Integrated Security Verification and Validation: Case Study. In: IEEE Conference on Local Computer Networks (2006)
7. Jonsson, E.: Towards an integrated conceptual model of security and dependability, Availability, Reliability and Security. In: ARES 2006 (2006)
8. Nissanke, N.: An Integrated Security Model for Component–Based Systems. In: IEEE Conference Emerging Technologies & Factory Automation, ETFA (2007)
9. Zambreno, J., Nguyen, D., Choudhary, A.: Exploring Area/Delay Tradeoffs in an AES FPGA Implementation, Department of Electrical and Computer Engineering Northwestern University (2004)
10. Deepakumara, J., Heys, H.M., Venkatesan, R.: FPGA implementation of MD5 hash algorithm. In: Emerging VLSI Technologies and Architectures. IEEE Computer Society, Los Alamitos (2006)
11. McEvoy, R.P., Crowe, F.M., Murphy, C.C., Marnane, W.P.: Optimisation of the SHA-2 family of hash functions on FPGAs. In: Emerging VLSI Technologies and Architectures. IEEE Computer Society, Los Alamitos (2006)
12. Brian Connell, J.: A huffman-shannon-fano code. In: Proceedings of the IEEE, pp. 1046–1047 (July 1973)
13. Michalski, A., Buell, D.: A Scalable Architecture for RSA Cryptography on Large FPGAs, Field-Programmable Custom Computing Machines. In: FCCM 14th Annual IEEE Symposium (2006)
14. Monta Vista Embedded Linux Software, http://www.mvista.com/
15. Xilinx Document, PowerPC 405 Processor Block Reference Guide, Embedded Development Kit, document: ug018 (2008)
16. den Boer, B., Bosselaers, A.: Collisions for the compression function of MD-5. In: Helleseth, T. (ed.) EUROCRYPT 1993. LNCS, vol. 765, pp. 293–304. Springer, Heidelberg (1994)

17. Fry, J., Langhammer, M.: RSA & Public Key Cryptography in FPGAs, Altera document (2005)
18. Rasheed, H., Randy, Y.C., Chow: An Information Model for Security Integration. In: 11th IEEE International Workshop on Future Trends of Distributed Computing Systems (FTDCS 2007) (2007)
19. Sasaki, Y., Wang, L., Ohta, K., Kunihiro, N.: Security of MD5 challenge and response: Extension of APOP password recovery attack. In: Malkin, T.G. (ed.) CT-RSA 2008. LNCS, vol. 4964, pp. 1–18. Springer, Heidelberg (2008)
20. Mazzeo, A., Romano, L., Saggese, G.P.: FPGA-based Implementation of a serial RSA processor. In: Proceedings of the Design, Automation and Test in Europe Conference and Exhibition (DATE) (2003)
21. Järvinen, K., Tommiska, M., Skyttä, J.: Hardware Implementation Analysis of the MD5 Hash Algorithm. In: Proceedings of the 38th Hawaii International Conference on System Sciences (2005)
22. Zambreno, J., Nguyen, D., Choudhary, A.: Exploring area/Delay tradeoffs in an AES FPGA implementation. In: Becker, J., Platzner, M., Vernalde, S. (eds.) FPL 2004. LNCS, vol. 3203, pp. 575–585. Springer, Heidelberg (2004)
23. Chaves, R., Kuzmanov, G., Sousa, L., Vassiliadis, S.: Improving SHA-2 Hardware Implementations. LNCS. Springer, Heidelberg (2006)
24. Zeng, G., Ito, H.: Efficient Test Data Decompression for System-on-a-Chip Using an Embedded FPGA Core. In: Proceedings of the 18th IEEE International Symposium on Defect and Fault Tolerance in VLSI Systems (DFT) (2003)
25. Kim, J.: Design and implementation of integrated security engine for secure networking. In: IEEE Advanced Communication Technology (2004)

Evaluating Resistance of MCML Technology to Power Analysis Attacks Using a Simulation-Based Methodology

Francesco Regazzoni[1], Thomas Eisenbarth[2], Axel Poschmann[2],
Johann Großschädl[3], Frank Gurkaynak[4], Marco Macchetti[5,*], Zeynep Toprak[6],
Laura Pozzi[7], Christof Paar[2], Yusuf Leblebici[6], and Paolo Ienne[8]

[1] ALaRI – University of Lugano, Lugano, Switzerland
`regazzoni@alari.ch`
[2] Horst Görtz Institute for IT Security, Bochum, Germany
`{eisenbarth,poschmann,cpaar}@crypto.rub.de`
[3] University of Bristol, Department of Computer Science, Bristol, UK
`johann@cs.bris.ac.uk`
[4] Swiss Federal Institute of Technology – ETH, Zurich, Switzerland
`kgf@ee.ethz.ch`
[5] Nagracard SA, Cheseaux-sur-Lausanne, Switzerland
`Marco.Macchetti@nagra.com`
[6] School of Engineering – EPFL, Lausanne, Switzerland
`{zeynep.toprak,yusuf.leblebici}@epfl.ch`
[7] Faculty of Informatics – University of Lugano, Lugano, Switzerland
`laura.pozzi@unisi.ch`
[8] School of Computer and Communication Sciences – EPFL, Lausanne, Switzerland
`Paolo.Ienne@epfl.ch`

Abstract. This paper explores the resistance of MOS Current Mode Logic (MCML) against attacks based on the observation of the power consumption. Circuits implemented in MCML, in fact, have unique characteristics both in terms of power consumption and the dependency of the power profile from the input signal pattern. Therefore, MCML is suitable to protect cryptographic hardware from Differential Power Analysis and similar side-channel attacks.

In order to demonstrate the effectiveness of different logic styles against power analysis attacks, two full cores implementing the AES algorithm were realized and implemented with CMOS and MCML technology, and a set of different types of attack was performed using power traces derived from SPICE-level simulations. Although all keys were discovered for CMOS, MCML traces did not presents characteristic that can lead to a successful attack.

1 Introduction

During the past ten years, a number of new techniques for attacking implementations of cryptographic algorithms have been discovered. These techniques

---

* This work was done while at C.E. Consulting (Altran Group) Milan, Italy.

M.L. Gavrilova et al. (Eds.): Trans. on Comput. Sci. IV, LNCS 5430, pp. 230–243, 2009.
© Springer-Verlag Berlin Heidelberg 2009

exploit information leaking from a device (e.g., a smart card) while data is being processed. The term *side-channel attacks* summarizes all possible ways of collecting the leaked information: power consumption, timing, and electromagnetic emission are possible examples [MOP07]. Side-channel attacks which exploit the power consumed by a device were reported for the first time in 1999 by Kocher et al [KJJ99]. The power consumption of a device strongly depends on the data being processed, thus leaks information about the secret key. Among the different types of power-based attacks available in literature, the most common are *Simple Power Analysis (SPA)* and *differential power analysis (DPA)*. The latter and its powerful variant called *correlation power analysis (CPA)* are of particular interest since they do not require specific knowledge about the implementation of the target device to be effective.

In this paper we present a design flow that enables the evaluation of Power Analysis Attack resistance and using it we demonstrate the robustness of a special logic style, namely MOS Current Mode Logic (MCML), against such attacks, considering in particular SPA and CPA. Previous papers on this subject just argued robustness qualitatively or required hardware manufacturing to prove it. Contrary to past works, we evaluate the robustness of MCML *with real attacks* and *without the need for manufacturing prototypes*. To achieve this result, we developed a design flow and a SPICE-level simulation environment derived from the one presented by Bucci at al. [BGLT04], that allows collection of power traces in reasonable time, thus enabling a more direct experimental study of the resistance of complex blocks, such as entire cryptographic cores. As a result, our traces are much closer to the circuit real behavior than those obtained simulating only small portion of a core. A clear advantage of the proposed simulation-based evaluation is that in this way it is easy and thus possible to iterate the design flow to investigate further points of optimization before the fabrication of the real chip.

The remainder of this paper is organized as follows: Section 2 discusses related work, Section 3 overviews the AES algorithm, and Section 4 describes MCML technology. The design flow, including simulation-based power analysis, is explained in Section 5, and simulation results are presented in Section 6. Finally, conclusions are drawn in Section 7.

2   Background and Related Work

Side-channel cryptanalysis has emerged as a serious threat for smart cards and other types of embedded systems performing cryptographic operations. It was demonstrated in a number of publications that side-channel attacks are an extremely powerful and practical tool for breaking unprotected (or insufficiently protected) implementations of cryptosystems. These attacks exploit the fact that the execution of a cryptographic algorithm on a physical device leaks information about sensitive data (e.g., secret keys) involved in the computations. Many sources of side-channel information have been discovered in recent years, including the power consumption and timing characteristics of a cryptographic algorithm [Koc96, KJJ99], as well as deliberately introduced computational faults

[BS97]. *Simple Power Analysis (SPA)* uses the leaked information from a single computation, while *Differential Power Analysis (DPA)* utilizes statistical methods to evaluate the information observed from multiple computations [KJJ99]. Currently, there exists no perfect protection against DPA attacks. However, by applying appropriate countermeasures, it is possible to make the attacker's task more difficult and expensive.

A multitude of so-called *DPA-resistant logic styles* have been proposed during the past five years. The idea behind these logic styles is to tackle the problem of side-channel leakage at its actual root, namely at the hardware level. The power consumption of circuits realized with DPA-resistant logic cells is uniform and, in the ideal case, independent of the processed data and the performed operations. The first concrete implementation of a DPA-resistant logic style was reported by Tiri et al. in 2002 [TAV02]. Their *Sense Amplifier Based Logic (SABL)* combines the concepts of dual-rail logic and pre-charge logic [MOP07]. SABL cells have a constant power consumption, provided that they are designed and implemented in a carefully balanced way. All SABL cells of a circuit are connected to the clock signal and become pre-charged simultaneously, which causes very high current peaks. Furthermore, SABL cells require at least twice as much silicon area as conventional CMOS cells and suffer also from high delay. Besides the logic cells, also the wires connecting these cells must be routed in a special balanced way to achieve a uniform power profile.

The present work improves on the results of our previous work [RBE+07] in several substantial ways. Below is a list of the main differences along with a brief explanation.

- The custom design flow for MCML has been completed. Thus, it is now possible to start from the same HDL netlist for both CMOS and MCML, rather than completely design by hand the netlist for the latter case.
- The simulation flow has been extended in order to support a back-end design phase. This task, particularly challenging for MCML technology, has been carried out for all analyzed circuits. Net parasitics have been extracted into *SPEF* files and back-annotated on the netlists. Although this increased the simulation time, results mimic more closely the actual behaviour of the fabricated device.
- Full cryptographic cores (implementations of the AES block cipher algorithm) have been considered as targets of the attacks. This has surely a negative impact on simulation speed, but is representative of a typical real attack. This step was made possible by the level of maturity reached in the simulation flow.

Additionally, note that post-processing and stimuli writing procedures have been fully automated, the same has been done for the simulation and attack routines that have also been extended to support Simple Power Analysis attacks.

3   Overview of the AES Algorithm

In this section we provide an overview of the Rijndael (AES [IoSTN01]) algorithm and some highlights on its possible implementation, focusing on the two that we used.

The Rijndael algorithm implements a block cipher for symmetric key cryptography, supports a key size of 128, 192 and 256 bits, and allows for a block size of 128 bits. Every block is represented using 32-bit words. The number of words that compose the input block is equal to 4, while the length of the key can be a sequence of 128, 192 and 256 bits, and can take the values 4, 6, or 8, which reflects the number of words the key is composed by.

The algorithm works on a two dimensional representation of the input block called state, that is initialized to the input data block and holds the intermediate result during the cipher and decipher process, and ultimately holds the final result when the process is completed. All the transformations of the algorithm are grouped in a single function called round. The round is iterated a specific number of times that depends on the key size; specifically, for a key length equal to 128, 192 or 256 the number of rounds is equal to 10, 12 and 14, respectively.

The encryption process starts by copying the input block into the state array, followed by the first key addition. In the encryption process, the round function is composed by four different transformations. *ShiftRows* cyclically shifts to left the bytes in the last three rows of the state with different offsets. *SubBytes (or S-box)* operates independently on each byte of the state and is composed by the multiplicative inverse in the finite field $GF(2^8)$ followed by an affine transformation over $GF(2)$. *MixColumns* multiplies modulo $x^4 + 1$ the columns of the state by the polynomial $\{03\}x^3 + \{01\}x^2 + \{01\}x + \{02\}$. *AddRoundKey* adds the round key to the state. To generate all the needed round keys, the AES algorithm takes the secret key k and performs the expansion routine to generate a total of Nb   (Nr + 1) words. The round transformations are cyclically executed at every round: all the Nr rounds are identical with the exception of the final round, which does not include the *MixColumns* transformation.

Decryption is similar to the encryption process and uses the same basic transformations, but inverted. The key schedule is identical to the one described for the encryption process but starts with the last round key.

Many alternatives are available when implementing an AES core, the choice among them being driven by application constraints and by performance, area, and power trade-offs. Our goal is to estimate the level of robustness given by the MCML technology with respect to the CMOS one, thus instead of attacking a single implementation of the block cipher, for each of the two attacks we considered a different core, selected to perform this evaluation in the best possible conditions for the adversary. The two considered AES implementation have a datapath of 128 and 32 respectively. In the first core considered, a single register of 128 bit is used to store the result of the first key addition and the results of the rounds computation, and the key is unrolled *on the   y*, while ciphering the data. The latter has a number of 32-bit registers that are used to store the result of each transformation inside the round, with the only exception of the shift rows. In this implementation, all the round keys are computed before starting ciphering.

4   Design of DPA-Resistant Functional Units Using MCML Gates

The circuit-level implementation of DPA-resistant logic gates requires systematic use of circuit techniques that (i) have significantly reduced power supply current levels, (ii) do not produce prominent current spikes or fluctuations during the switching events, and (iii) do not exhibit a significant input pattern-dependence with respect to current drawn from the power supply [TV03]. It is worth noting that the classical CMOS logic gates do not fare particularly well in any of these categories, and therefore, are not considered to be a good choice for DPA-resistance, in general. Standard CMOS digital gates are notorious for generating sharp and input-pattern dependent current pulses (also referred to as delta-I noise [GR99, AAE02]) due to charging and discharging of the gate's parasitic capacitances and fan-out.

Due to the differential and current steering nature of the its logic style, Current Mode Logic (CML) reduces the generated switching noise by about two orders of magnitude [TAY+05, MKA92]. The low delta-I noise generation makes the CML style an excellent candidate for DPA-resistant logic gate design.

In detail, a MOS Current Mode Logic (MCML) gate consists of a tail current source, a current steering logic core, and a differential load, as shown for the simplest MCML gate, the MCML buffer, in Figure 1. The operation of MCML circuits is based on the principle of re-directing (or switching) the current of a constant current source through a fully differential network of input transistors, and utilizing the reduced-swing voltage drop on a pair of complementary load devices as the output. A logic inversion without additional delay is possible by simply exchanging the differential terminals. The operation principle already suggests that the power consumption is static (the circuit must dissipate the same amount of current continuously) regardless of the switching activity and fan-out conditions. True differential operation of the circuit with small output voltage swing ensures fast switching times. Note that the propagation delay is proportional to the output swing, and independent of the power supply voltage. Other advantages include better noise immunity compared to classical CMOS logic circuits, and significantly less switching noise.

The supply current fluctuation in MCML gates is typically 5% of the nominal tail current during switching events. Figure 2 shows the simulated current variation of an MCML buffer for a fan-out of 5. MCML circuits are also more robust against common-mode fluctuations (power supply noise) due to their inherent common-mode rejection as a result of full differential signaling property.

From the DPA-resistance point-of-view, it can be seen that the supply-current variation of the MCML gate will remain significantly smaller during switching events, compared to that of a conventional CMOS gate. At the same time, the magnitude of the supply-current variation is largely independent of the applied

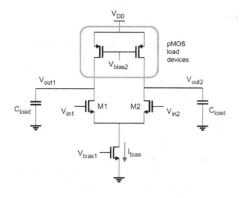

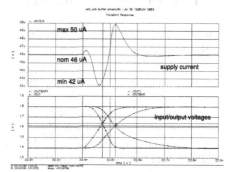

Fig. 1. Schematic of an MCML buffer (or MCML inverter, depending on the output signal definition)

Fig. 2. Simulated gate delay and supply current fluctuation of an MCML buffer for a fan-out of 5

input vector, as well as of the fan-out load capacitance. The amount of static current dissipation can be reduced dramatically while preserving all of the advantages concerning the DPA-resistance, at a lower speed, when the transistor sizing is done to satisfy modest speed constraints (e.g., a typical switching speed of 400MHz). It was shown [TAY+05] that the peak current fluctuation of the classical CMOS realization is in the order of 28mA, while the current fluctuation of the MCML version remains confined to a narrow band of about 0.5mA, around the constant value of 11.5mA. A more detailed analysis was performed by modelling also the measurement set-up: a probing instrument having a low-pass filter characteristic and the filtered output was monitored. As expected, the design based on CMOS logic still shows large variations (400μA peak), sufficient to be distinguished quite easily. On the other hand, the maximum current fluctuation in the MCML-based design remains below 25μA, further increasing DPA-resistance of the security-critical block.

Besides being beneficial from the security point of view, usage of the MCML technology also poses additional constraints while designing secure devices. The main drawbacks regard the area requirements, MCML gates are generally 1.5 to 2 times larger than their CMOS counterparts. The power consumption is also higher, particularly for low operating frequencies, where the constant power consumption of the MCML gates does not offset the dynamic switching power of the CMOS gates. In particular, this increased consumption can adversely affect the current budget in power-constrained devices such as smart cards or cryptographic tokens. When low power is a design constraint, it may become necessary to isolate the areas of the design which are critical from the point of view of security and implement them using MCML gates, the rest of the circuit being realized using standard CMOS libraries. This approach obviously increases the complexity of the back-end design phase, as it introduces the need to deal with multiple technology libraries.

5   Design and Simulation Flow

The robustness of a hardware implementation of a block cipher against power analysis attacks can be evaluated by means of circuit simulation at different stages of the design flow. The decisive proof is obtained when the actual fabricated microchip is attacked using high frequency probes and an oscilloscope; nonetheless, *mounting an attack using the current traces obtained from transistor-level simulation can be useful to get a good approximation of the actual level of Power Analysis resistance, and an indication of possible sources of weakness.*

The simulation techniques used by designers for this robustness evaluation are typically divided in two groups: at the *analog level* or at the *logic level* [MOP07]; the first provides higher precision, while the second is faster. A common way of achieving the best of two worlds, i.e., precise results while keeping the simulation speed high, is to divide the circuit into blocks and simulate at the SPICE level only the parts under analysis. Although this approach provides results with good approximation, the problem with limiting the simulation to only parts of the circuit is that one eliminates the contribution of the algorithmic noise to the power consumption (the noise produced by all components of the circuit that are not targeted by the attack hypothesis). The only way to obtain a more realistic situation is to simulate the entire core, but this raises two main challenges: the required simulation time and the capability of the simulation flow to handle complex designs automatically. Indeed, automation is of capital importance: while it might be possible to manually adapt a small portion of a cryptographic core, it is certainly not so for a complex design.

To achieve both goals of fast simulation time and high accuracy, we developed an automated flow based on existing tools and described in the following. The actual design flow presents some differences for the two cases of CMOS and MCML; even though the RTL description of the core is the same, the flow of generating the netlist and the extraction of parasitic is different for the two considered technologies.

In the CMOS case, an HDL description of each of the cores under attack has been synthesized using Synopsys Design Compiler on the UMC $0.18\mu m$ process. Placing and routing phases are carried out using Cadence Design Systems SoC Encounter, and a parasitic information file is produced along with the verilog netlist of the circuit. These are used together with the SPICE models of the technology cells to run a transistor level simulation using Synopsys Nanosim. The employed transistor models are the BSIM3 p-MOS and n-MOS models.

In the MCML case, the standard ASIC design flow has been extended by introducing a complete library with views for transistor level simulation (schematic), schematic capture (symbol), synthesis (lib), placement and routing (abstract), and physical design (layout). It is worthwhile here to discuss the way in which this library has been built and under which aspects the extended flow is different from the standard CMOS flow; for a more comprehensive discussion the reader is referred toas the work of Badel at al. [BGI+08].

We first describe the process of the MCML logic cell generation. Generally speaking, the logic function implemented by an MCML differential cell is given by the network of nMOS transistors (e.g. M1 and M2 in Figure 1); thus, as a first step, a basic set of nMOS networks (called footprints) has been created. Since the speed characteristics of the cell are adversely impacted by the number of levels of nMOS transistors in the footprint, a limit of 3 levels was considered. The basic set comprises 19 different footprints, which by exhaustive search have been found to be sufficient to implement all functions that can be mapped to 3-level MCML gates. Starting from the set of footprints, we can explore all different ways of assigning logic inputs to the transistor gates; 63 unique functions with 1 to 7 input variables are produced in this way, as well as 45 redundant functions, whose cell realizations present different electrical characteristics. Thus, a total of 108 standard cell templates are obtained. As a last step, we exploit a property of the differential cells for which a switching of the differential (input or output) pins results in a complementation of the associated boolean variable. We extensively apply this transformation and obtain a total of 4660 differential cells describing different logic functions that make up the core of the dedicated technology library.

In a typical design flow, different realizations of the same logic cells characterized by different driving strengths are usually needed; in the MCML case, switching speed is directly proportional to the amount of static current injected by the current source. Thus, by simply scaling the footprints of the cells we easily obtain such variants that will be added to obtain a rich and versatile cell library.

A second important process is the generation of a so-called fat library, in addition to the fully differential library. The two libraries share the same cell footprints and electrical characteristics, but the former contains single-ended (non differential) variants of the cells; this library is the one actually used during the synthesis and place&route phases. The reason is that modern place&route tools treat differential wires as different variables, which are thus routed in the layout in different ways; as a result the differential pair will typically undergo different noise contributions, and will suffer from mismatches in the capacitive loads. When the place&route phase has ended, the fully differential library is used for the layout phase; the single-ended cells are replaced by the differential ones (with zero impact on the footprint) and the single-ended wires are cut into pairs of wires which are thus (by-design) always side by side in the chip layout. Of course to render this step seamless, the cell input/output pins must be designed in an opportune way so that connections with the differential wires are easily introduced; an exact description of this achievement can be found in the work of Badel et al [BGI+08]. The result of the full process is an extended design flow, ranging from RTL design to layout, that can be used to design fully-differential MCML digital circuits with enforced differential routing. We use the output of the place and route phase along with the MCML technology SPICE models to run transistor level simulations of the full circuit.

As already mentioned, analog simulation can be done on netlists produced by different stages of the design flow. A first possibility is to use the current traces obtained from a post-synthesis power simulation. This approach allows evaluation of circuit DPA resistance at a very early stage. However, the current traces obtained are rather inaccurate, because the contribution to the power consumption of the wire loads and parasitics is not considered. Depending on the attack point, such a consumption can have a significant effect on the side-channel resistance. Therefore, going one step further, and using the outputs of place&route tool for simulation, allows us to obtain power traces that are much more realistic.

In our work, we have decided to run accurate transistor-level simulations of the post-place&route netlist, at very high timing resolution (about 10ps) and with no additional noise coming from the measurement device or the environment. From one point of view, this is a best-case condition for an attacker; on the other side there are certainly some physical effects that cannot be correctly modeled, for instance crosstalk between adjacent nets or variations in the manufacturing process. A worthwhile-mentioning advantage of simulations is that in this way it is also possible to iterate the design flow to investigate further points of optimization.

We would like to underline that simulation results of Nanosim are comparable to those of SPICE (when Nanosim is set to run with full capabilities), but the simulation process requires significantly less time to be carried out. This is beneficial not only because the number of possible design iterations is greatly increased, but also because it enables simulation and verification of the robustness of complex designs such as an entire cryptographic core. Results obtained by simulating only a small portion of a core can miss a correct simulation of algorithmic noise as well as correct wire loads and parasitics, while simulation results of an entire cryptographic core are much closer to the real behavior of the circuit.

6   Resistance against Power Analysis

In this section we describe the attacks we mounted on the CMOS and MCML implementations of AES core and we compare the results. In this work we focused on attacks based on the analysis of the power consumption, and in particular in the two powerful ones: Simple Power Analysis (SPA) and Differential Power Analysis (DPA).

In an SPA, an attacker measures the power consumed by a device while performing cryptographic operations and, by observing the traces, deduces information produced either by the *Hamming weight leakage* or by the *transition current leakage*. Both of them are justified by the fact that the amount of current is directly proportional to the Hamming weight of the processed data, hence it can be derived. DPA attacks, on the other hand, are more effective than SPA attacks, but also more difficult to mount. A typical DPA attack consists of four steps: At first, an intermediate key dependent result is selected as the target, then the attacker encrypts (decrypts) a certain number of known plaintexts (ciphertexts) and measures the corresponding power consumption traces. Subsequently, hypothetical intermediate values are calculated based on a key guess and they are used as input of a selection function. This function is used to partition the power traces into sets, depending on the values of the intermediate results. The difference of means of the two sets is then calculated and a peak is clearly visible for the right key hypothesis in correspondence to the time frame where the information is leaked.

An improvement with respect to DPA attack, called *correlation power analysis* (*CPA*), was discussed in [BCO04]. It hypothesizes the Hamming weight or the distance of Hamming of the targeted register and evaluate the hypothesis statistically. Usually CPA shows better results than the original DPA because it uses hypotheses based on multiple bits rather than the single bit typical of DPA. The statistical correlation $\rho_{(P(t),\ )}$ between the power traces $P_n(t)$ and the hypothesis H is a normalized value between $-1 \leq \rho \leq 1$ where $\rho = 1$ ($\rho = -1$) means that the variables $P(t)$ and H are perfectly correlated (anti-correlated) and $\rho = 0$ means there is no correlation at all. The strongest correlation corresponds to the right key hypothesis.

Mounting the Attacks

Using the simulation flow described in Section 5, we obtained the power traces for attaking the AES algorithm described in Section 3. It is important to notice the differences between the simulated and the real attack. In a real environment, an attacker has to collect a huge number of traces in order to filter out the noise. In fact, when power consumption of any device is measured, the collected traces include noise, both thermal and algorithmic, the latter is produced by other components of the device. Since it is an uncorrelated normally distributed random variable, the noise can be filtered out by increasing the number of traces. The simulation environment we used is partially noise free: only algorithmic noise is present into the traces. Furthermore, the simulation was performed with a very high resolution both for the current ($1\mu A$) and the time ($10ps$), which is the best possible condition for an attacker.

To evaluate the resistance against the power based attacks, we considered the two most powerful univariate ones: the Simple Power Analysis Attack, and the powerful variant of Differential Power Analysis based on correlation. This decision is coherent with the goal of the paper: we aim to provide a realistic evaluation of Power Analysis resistance by means of simulation for MCML and CMOS rather then attack a specific implementation of a cryptographic algorithm. Since none of the considered logic styles offer masking schemes, practically there would not be any benefit in considering attacks of higher order. We thus concentrate on the SPA and CPA and we selected for each of the attacks a core that would represent the best possible situation for the attacker and we realized each of the two cores using both of the technologies. For the same reason, we decided to use as attack point a register, since is well known in literature that this is the easiest point for mounting an attack (because the signals are synchronized by the clock)[MOP07].

The first evaluation was done performing a Simple Power Analysis attack: in the target core of this attack, the output of the first key addition is stored into a register. As depicted in Figure 3, our SPA attack targeted that register. Coherently with the purpose of this paper, with this attack we are interested in

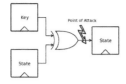
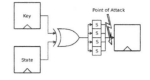

Fig. 3. Point of attack for SPA   **Fig. 4.** Point of attack for CPA

verifying if the MCML logic, that is fully differential, is sufficient to protect the circuit rather then the robustness of a specific implementation under test.

The attack was performed bit by bit. After the application of a reset signal, that sets all flip-flops in the register to zero, we applied a plaintext in which all bits were set to logical 0. The result of the xor of this input with the secret key was then stored in the register and the power consumption in this point was measured. A second measure was performed as the first, with the only difference that one bit of the input plaintext was changed from 0 to 1. The two traces obtained for CMOS are plotted in Figure 5, that present the two measure overlapped. As is possible to see, the trace corresponding to the plaintext with the bit set to 1 has a higher power consumption with respect to the same situation when the plaintext is 0. This clearly indicated that the value of the secret key in corrispondence to this specific bit is 0. By iterating this procedure for all the bits of the key, it is possible to reconstruct all the correct values of the secret key by simply looking at the difference between the reference power trace with the plaintext all zero and the one with a bit set to 1 in corrispondence to the target bit of the key.

The same attack was perfomed on the same AES core implemented using MCML technology. As can be seen from Figure 6, the two traces corresponding to the plaintext 0 and the plaintext with the target bit set to 1 are completely overlapped and thus is impossible to derive the value of the key bit.

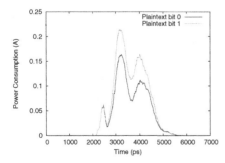
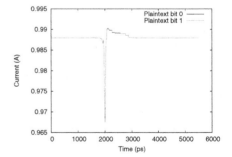

Fig. 5. SPA on CMOS: the power consumption traces clearly indicate the value of the target key bit

Fig. 6. SPA on MCML: the power traces are completely overlapped, thus not distinguishable

A second evaluation of the MCML resistance was done mounting a CPA. For this purpose we used a 32 bit datapath AES core, and we targeted the register that stores the output of 4 S-boxes, as depicted in Figure 4. To mount the attack, we used a selection function based on the Hamming weight of one byte of the target register. It is important to notice that 24 bits are not part of the hypothesis, thus they are contributing as algorithmic noise. This makes our attack more difficult with respect to a situation where only a single S-box is considered, but the problem can be easily solved by increasing the number of collected traces.

Repeated attacks performed by ciphering 600 random plaintexts were computed both for CMOS and MCML technology. In all these cases our attacks on the CMOS logic were always successful. The differential trace of the correct key (plotted in black) is the one that clearly shows the highest value for the correlation, thus it is clearly distinguishable from the other ones, as can be seen from Figure 7 (hypotheses based on the Hamming weight of the register), where the correlation value of $\rho_{(P(t),\ )} = 1$ clearly indicates the guessed key was the correct one.

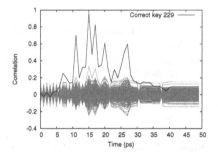 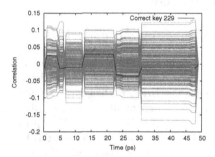

Fig. 7. CPA on CMOS technology   **Fig. 8.** CPA on MCML technology

As for the SPA, the same CPA attack was performed on the same core implemented using MCML technology. In this case the situation is completely different: in all the experiments in fact, no keys were found. An example of CPA attack on MCML technology is plotted in Figure 8. As can be seen, the black line representing the correct key is not distinguishable from the remaining differential traces that are plotted in gray. Additionally, it can be noticed that, for all the key guess, the maximum absolute value for the correlation is about 0.17. It is important to notice that in an attack mounted on a real device, this values are so small that they are very likely to be completely overshadowed by the noise of the measurement set-up, making the attack more difficult. Once again, we stress the fact that the attacks were mounted within a simulation environment, thus in an ideal condition for an attacker, both in terms of sampling rate accuracy and absence of noise.

7   Conclusions

In this paper we introduced a simulation-based methodology for evaluating the resistance of cryptographic circuits to power analysis attacks. We used our methodology to evaluate the MCML technology as a possible counter measure against Side Channel Attacks based on Power Analysis, and demonstrated the robustness of MCML against the SPA and against the powerful variant of DPA based on correlation.

Contrary to previous papers on this subject, we did not argue robustness just qualitatively, but with real attacks. Furthermore, since our approach is based on SPICE-level simulations, it does not rely on the manufacturing of prototypes, which allows a more direct experimental study of Power Analysis-resistance.

Our results show that the power traces obtained by simulating two full cores, implementing the AES algorithm and realized in MCML, are very difficult to attack, as opposed to a CMOS implementation for which the same attacks were always successful.

References

[AAE02]   Anis, M., Allam, M., Elmasry, M.: Impact of technology scaling on CMOS logic styles. Circuits and Systems II: Analog and Digital Signal Processing, IEEE Transactions on [see also Circuits and Systems II: Express Briefs, IEEE Transactions on] 49(8), 577–588 (2000)

[BCO04]   Brier, É., Clavier, C., Olivier, F.: Correlation power analysis with a leakage model. In: Joye, M., Quisquater, J.-J. (eds.) CHES 2004. LNCS, vol. 3156, pp. 16–29. Springer, Heidelberg (2004)

[BGI+08] Badel, S., Guleyupoglu, E., Inac, O., Martinez, A.P., Vietti, P., Gurkaynak, F., Leblebici, Y.: A Generic Standard Cell Design Methodology for Differential Circuit Styles. In: Design Automation and Test in Europe 2008, pp. 843–848 (2008)

[BGLT04] Bucci, M., Guglielmo, M., Luzzi, R., Trifiletti, A.: A Power Consumption Randomization Countermeasure for DPA-Resistant Cryptographic Processors. In: Macii, E., Paliouras, V., Koufopavlou, O. (eds.) PATMOS 2004. LNCS, vol. 3254, pp. 481–490. Springer, Heidelberg (2004)

[BS97]   Biham, E., Shamir, A.: Differential fault analysis of secret key cryptosystems. In: Kaliski Jr., B.S. (ed.) CRYPTO 1997. LNCS, vol. 1294, pp. 513–525. Springer, Heidelberg (1997)

[GR99]   Gonzalez, J.L., Rubio, A.: Low delta-I noise CMOS circuits based on differential logic and current limiters. Circuits and Systems I: Fundamental Theory and Applications, IEEE Transactions on [see also Circuits and Systems I: Regular Papers, IEEE Transactions on] 46(7), 872–876 (1999)

[IoSTN01] National Institute of Standards and Technology (NIST). Announcing the Advanced Encryption Standard (AES). Federal Information Processing Standards Publication 197 (November 2001)

[KJJ99]   Kocher, P.C., Jaffe, J., Jun, B.: Differential Power Analysis. In: Wiener, M. (ed.) CRYPTO 1999. LNCS, vol. 1666, pp. 388–397. Springer, Heidelberg (1999)

[Koc96]   Kocher, P.C.: Timing Attacks on Implementations of Diffie-Hellman, RSA, DSS, and Other Systems. In: Koblitz, N. (ed.) CRYPTO 1996. LNCS, vol. 1109, pp. 104–113. Springer, Heidelberg (1996)

[MKA92]   Maskai, S.R., Kiaei, S., Allstot, D.J.: Synthesis techniques for CMOS folded source-coupled logic circuits. IEEE Journal of Solid-State Circuits 27(8), 1157–1167 (1992)

[MOP07]   Mangard, S., Oswald, E., Popp, T.: Power Analysis Attacks: Revealing the Secrets of Smart Cards. Advances in Information Security. Springer, Heidelberg (2007)

[RBE+07]   Regazzoni, F., Badel, S., Eisenbarth, T., Gro schädl, J., Poschmann, A., Toprak, Z., Macchetti, M., Pozzi, L., Paar, C., Leblebici, Y., Ienne, P.: A Simulation-Based Methodology for Evaluating the DPA-Resistance of Cryptographic Functional Units with Application to CMOS and MCML Technologies. In: International Symposium on Systems, Architectures, Modeling and Simulation, SAMOS VII (2007)

[TAV02]   Tiri, K., Akmal, M., Verbauwhede, I.M.: A dynamic and differential CMOS logic with signal independent power consumption to withstand differential power analysis on smart cards. In: Proceedings of the 28th European Solid-State Circuits Conference (ESSCIRC 2002), September 2002, pp. 403–406. University of Bologna, Bologna (2002)

[TAY+05]   Toprak, Z., Verma, A., Leblebici, Y., Ienne, P., Paar, C.: Design of Low-Power DPA-Resistant Cryptographic Functional Units. In: Workshop on Cryptographic Advances in Secure Hardware (2005)

[TV03]   Tiri, K., Verbauwhede, I.: Securing encryption algorithms against DPA at the logic level: Next generation smart card technology. In: Walter, C.D., Koc, C.K., Paar, C. (eds.) CHES 2003. LNCS, vol. 2779, pp. 125–136. Springer, Heidelberg (2003)

Putting Trojans on the Horns of a Dilemma: Redundancy for Information Theft Detection

Jedidiah R. Crandall[1], John Brevik[2], Shaozhi Ye[3], Gary Wassermann[3], Daniela A.S. de Oliveira[3], Zhendong Su[3], S. Felix Wu[3], and Frederic T. Chong[4]

[1] Dept. of Computer Science, University of New Mexico
crandall@cs.unm.edu
[2] Dept. of Mathematics and Statistics,
California State University, Long Beach
jbrevik@csulb.edu
[3] Dept. of Computer Science, University of California at Davis
{yeshao,wassermg,oliveira,su,wu}@cs.ucdavis.edu
[4] Dept. of Computer Science,
University of California at Santa Barbara
chong@cs.ucsb.edu

Abstract. Conventional approaches to either information flow security or intrusion detection are not suited to detecting Trojans that steal information such as credit card numbers using advanced cryptovirological and inference channel techniques. We propose a technique based on repeated deterministic replays in a virtual machine to detect the theft of private information. We prove upper bounds on the average amount of information an attacker can steal without being detected, even if they are allowed an arbitrary distribution of visible output states. Our intrusion detection approach is more practical than traditional approaches to information flow security.

We show that it is possible to, for example, bound the average amount of information an attacker can steal from a 53-bit credit card number to less than a bit by sampling only 11 of the 2^{53} possible outputs visible to the attacker, using a two-pronged approach of hypothesis testing and information theory.

Keywords: Intrusion detection, information theft detection, malware analysis, information theory.

1 Introduction

Suppose an attacker installs a Trojan on a system S (*e.g.*, an ATM[1]) to steal confidential information (*e.g.*, a 16-digit or 53-bit credit card number) and transmit it over some channel to the attacker through a low-security output such as the network. Let the confidential information (the high-security input) be A and the low-security output be B. The only way for the attacker who can view B to

---

[1] Note that ATMs often run commodity operating systems and can be susceptible to malicious code attacks, such as the Slammer worm [1].

M.L. Gavrilova et al. (Eds.): Trans. on Comput. Sci. IV, LNCS 5430, pp. 244–262, 2009.

learn information about A is through the mutual information between A and B, written as $I(A; B)$. In this setting the Trojan is the encoder that encodes input A and sends this over a channel where the attacker receives B and decodes it.

We wish to frame a policy that bounds $I(A; B)$, and detect any violations of this policy. There are many difficulties because the attacker can execute arbitrary code on system S and choose an arbitrary distribution of the possible output states for B. Furthermore, for a practical system S we must account for architectural nondeterminism, such as hard drive turbulence, electrical noise, high speed buses, memory scrubbing [2], or user input, and we must also consider the possibility of covert channels. We leave applying existing and new techniques to covert channel analysis as future work, and instead in this paper focus on a general two-pronged approach to bound $I(A; B)$ that could be applied to many different applications where an attacker (or their Trojan) can arbitrarily encode information.

The basic idea is to checkpoint the system and record all nondeterministic events while a transaction executes. Then, possibly in parallel, multiple deterministic replays of the transaction from the checkpoint with varying high inputs can be used to measure the entropy of low outputs. The recording and replaying can be done either by placing the system in a virtual machine or using special hardware. After removing the architectural nondeterminism, we can probabilistically measure the amount of information leaked using Shannon's information theory [3] and hypothesis testing. Figure 1 illustrates our approach.

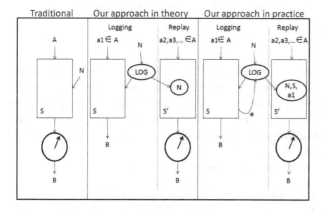

Legend:

A: High-security input

B: Low-security output

N: Architectural nondeterminism

S: System

S': System during replay

: Only possibility of covert channels

Fig. 1. An overview of our approach

For the traditional system S in the first case, measurement of the entropy in the visible output B is confounded by the architectural nondeterminism N. In theory, as illustrated in the second case, we could log all nondeterminism N during the original transaction (where the high input is a_1) and then create a deterministic system S' using deterministic replay of the transaction, then repeatedly vary the input A $(a_2, a_3, ...)$ to obtain a measurement of the mutual information between A and B without the possibility of covert channels.

In practice, we cannot log architectural nondeterminism directly, but we can log nondeterministic events (interrupts and input events to the CPU) and perform deterministic replay. This is illustrated in the third case of Figure 1. There still is no possibility of exploiting covert channels from the original system, but it is possible for entropy to be hidden from us during replay because nondeterministic events can contain both architectural nondeterminism and information that should otherwise be deterministic, such as the original input $a_1 \in A$. For example, the Trojan might mask out the first bit of a_1 and make a request to the hard drive for data far away on the other side of the cylinder if the bit is a 1 or make a request for data closer to the head's current position if the bit is a 0. If we log the timing of this disk request and force it to be the same during repeated replays for $a_2, a_3, \ldots$ then mutual information between A and B is hidden from us during measurement. Fortunately, a very important property of our approach in practice is that covert channels are only possible as channels with timing characteristics involving at least one event in the log file. This could enable a systematic, exhaustive covert channel analysis by directly applying Wray's technique [4] to all events that we log. We leave the details for future work.

A hypothesis test is performed by counting the number of distinct output states for B, assuming an equal distribution. In this paper we will also show that with an attack model where the attacker must pass the hypothesis test with a minimum probability of ρ, the attacker has a very limited amount of additional entropy that can be utilized assuming an arbitrary distribution. Thus the attacker is placed "on the horns of a dilemma" [5] between using an unequal distribution, which lowers their channel capacity, and being detected.

1.1 Contributions

At a high level, the contribution of this paper is an approach that detects information theft by measuring explicitly everything that could have happened. Historically, information flow security mechanisms have suffered from specific problems, such as implicit channels and covert channels, which are caused at their root by the fact that information is a measure of everything that could have possibly happened, not what did happen.

The specific contributions of this paper are:

- A general method to detect information theft based on repeated deterministic replays. Compared to previous approaches, this method allows for more realistic policies where information leakage is bounded rather than strictly forbidden. For example, when passwords are entered one bit of information is leaked about the password file because of the success or failure of logging in, thus information flow cannot be completely contained but if it can be bounded then confidentiality of the password file can be enforced in a practical way.
- A theory of replay-based enforcement of information flow security based on logging nondeterministic events that incorporates the only possibility of covert channels: channels with timing characteristics through the logging

mechanism, where we show that all covert channels must act through mutual information between high-security input A and the log L.

- A probabilistic bound on the mutual information between a high input and low output based on hypothesis testing and assuming an equal distribution of states.
- A bound on the additional mutual information an attacker can gain by using an unequal distribution of states with an attack model that allows the attacker some probability ρ of passing the hypothesis test (and therefore evading detection).

The two bounds calculated with the latter two, ϵ and δ respectively, form a probabilistic bound $\epsilon + \delta$ on the average amount of information that can be leaked to an attacker.

1.2   Applications

We envision many applications of the approach proposed in this paper, including:

- **Malware analysis:** A Trojan that employs cryptovirology [6] and exploits covert channels in commodity operating systems could be placed in a virtual machine and the mutual information between various inputs (*e.g.*, credit card numbers, passwords, personal files) and potential outputs (*e.g.*, the network, the hard drive) could be measured as an analysis of the Trojan's capabilities and purpose.
- **Testing to guide system design:** The basic framework for information flow measurement via repeated deterministic replays presented in this paper could be used to test existing systems for inference and side channels [7,8,9,10].
- **Information "ow security systems:** Researchers have begun to explore the possibility of building systems that enforce information flow security by comparing different outputs for different inputs [11]. We envision a virtualization system that could enforce probabilistic non-interference [12] policies on commodity systems by applying the basic concept of redundancy and using the unwinding theorem [13].
- **Intrusion detection for dedicated systems:** Compared to traditional time-sharing systems, systems such as voting machines and ATMs have well-defined transactions and relatively coarse information flow policies, making our intrusion detection approach to information security directly applicable to such systems.

1.3   Structure of the Rest of the Paper

This paper is structured as follows. After illustrating an example using our implementation of replay-based confidentiality enforcement in Section 2, we formally state our problem and give an overview of the entire approach in Section 3. Then Section 4 explains how to bound the mutual information measured in bits between a high input and low output by some parameter ϵ, using hypothesis testing and assuming an equal distribution of states is used by the attacker for the output. Section 5 shows that we can calculate some caveat δ, based on the equivocation that is forced on the attacker by a probabilistic attack model where they must have a probability ρ of passing this hypothesis test, where δ is the maximum amount of additional mutual information that can be gained by the attacker by violating the assumption that their distribution of states for the output is equal. We review the related work in Section 6 followed by the conclusion and discussion of future work in Section 7.

2   Prototype Implementation and Example

This section gives an example of replay-based detection of information theft Trojans. Our main goal in this example is to demonstrate that information flow detection can be applied in practice for a full system. We chose a simple policy to enforce: that no more than $\epsilon = 2$ bits of a secret input can be written to the hard drive during the transaction. We were able to enforce this policy in a full system implementation that exercised code in all the components, including all of the drivers, the kernel, library code, and applications of a Linux system. We used a deterministic full-system replay virtual machine implementation that is described in another paper [14].

In our example, the user inputs a high input, which is read as a generic block device. This generic block device is handled in the same manner as the hard drive by our VM implementation: interrupts and port input timings are logged and replayed but the data is read deterministically through port input. The input, a random string of 10 characters, after being processed by drivers and kernel services, is delivered to an application which encrypts it using RSA from the OpenSSL libraries [15] and a randomly generated key based on entropy from

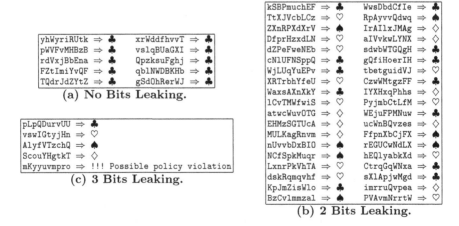

Fig. 2. Results from repeated replays for (a) no bits leaking, (b) 2 bits leaking (allowed by the policy $\epsilon = 2$), and (c) 3 bits leaking (violation of policy). Each replay has an input $\Rightarrow$ output pair where ♣, ♡, ♠, and ◇ represent distinct outputs observed for that experiment.

"/dev/urandom". The output is the MD5 cryptographic checksum of the hard drive change log, which contains only hard drive blocks that have been modified since the last checkpoint.

Figure 2(a) shows the results of 10 replays of the original transaction when no information is leaked to the hard drive. Each entry shows an "input ⇒ output" pair. Because no information leaks in this case, all output states are the same.

Figure 2(b) shows the results of the same experiment when slightly less than 2 bits leak (per 10 characters). In this example two bits are simply masked out and written directly to the hard drive[2]. Figure 2(b) shows that after 38 replays of the transaction only four states have been observed, so that with 99.8% confidence (see Section 4.3) we can reject the null hypothesis and ensure that the policy $\epsilon = 2$ was enforced. Figure 2(c) shows the same experiment with slightly less than 3 bits leaking. After only 5 replays a fifth final state is observed, which signals that the policy $\epsilon = 2$ was probably violated and thus the information flow theft by the Trojan is detected.

3 Definitions and Overview

This section gives the problem definition and an overview of our approach to bounding the amount of information leaked from a high input A to a low output B. The important symbols are listed in Figure 3.

Definitions

$S : A$	B	A nondeterministic system
D		The system specification
N		The nondeterminism for a particular trace
L		The log file of nondeterministic events
$S' : A$	B	S' is a deterministic system, A is the high input, B is the low output

Parameters

ϵ	Number of bits allowed to leak in the policy
c	Constant, shorthand for 2
	Confidence of hypothesis test
ρ	Attack model parameter, probability the attacker needs of passing the hypothesis test
	Caveat, the most entropy the attacker can gain by using an unequal distribution of the states of B
r	The number of replays needed in the hypothesis test for a confidence of at least
q	The proportion of the states in B that the attacker must use as equivocation to pass the hypothesis test

Fig. 3. Legend

---

[2] The actual amount of information leaked is slightly less than two bits since the ASCII representation of possible characters between A and Z or a and z does not have an equiprobable distribution of the last two bits.

3.1   Problem Definition

Through logging and deterministic replay of a system S we have a deterministic system S' that takes a high input A and maps it to a low output B that is visible to the attacker, $i.e.$, $S' : A \rightarrow B$. We wish to bound with high confidence the mutual information $I(A; B)$ by the constant $\epsilon + \delta$, where ϵ is the maximum amount of entropy assuming the attacker uses a uniform distribution of the possible outputs in B and δ is the maximum amount of entropy that can be gained in addition to ϵ by using an arbitrary, possibly non-uniform distribution of B. Part of the attack model is that the attacker must encode the channel so that they have a probability ρ of passing the hypothesis test that assumes a uniform distribution of B. We assume that we know the distribution of confidential input A. ϵ is chosen beforehand and δ is calculated as a caveat added to the test for ϵ.

3.2   Overview of Approach

The first step is to perform r deterministic replays such that, assuming an equal distribution of B, the mutual information $I(A; B)$ is bounded by ϵ. This is done through hypothesis testing as described in Section 4.

The second step, described in Section 5, is to calculate some caveat, so that if the attacker did choose an encoding for the channel from input A to output B (recall that the attacker can view only B, but may install arbitrary malicious code on the system S to encode input A in output B) with an arbitrary distribution but under the constraint that they must have a probability ρ of passing the first step, then—because of the equivocation forced on them—the most additional entropy beyond ϵ bits that they can use to transmit information from A to B is bounded by δ. Thus, with confidence γ, $I(A; B) \leq \epsilon + \delta$. Here ϵ is a parameter and δ is calculated as a caveat based on the distribution of A, ϵ, and the number of replays r.

4   Hypothesis Testing to Bound ϵ

In this section we describe how to perform hypothesis testing of system S' through repeated deterministic replays to enforce a bound of ϵ on the mutual information between high input A and low output B.

4.1   Deterministic Replay in Theory

We want to bound the mutual information between A and B, $I(A; B)$. The entropy (or information) in B can only come from three sources (all defined from the attacker's perspective): D (determinism, or the specification of the system along with all malicious software and configuration), A (confidential data), and N (architectural nondeterminism such as hard drive turbulence or electrical noise [2]). In theory, D, A, and N are independent[3]. Thus, $H(B) = I(B; D) +$

---

[3] The input A that we are interested in is separated out from N by definition, since we assume that it is entered through a special device that distinguishes it as high-security information.

$I(B;A) + I(B;N)$. The term $I(B;D)$ is zero by definition[4] so we can bound $I(B;A)$ to be as small as the arbitrary policy-specific constant ϵ, by bounding $H(B) - I(B;N)$, which is equal to the conditional entropy of B if N be known $H(B|N) = H(B) - I(B;N)$[5].

$$I(B;D) + I(B;A) + I(B;N) = H(B)$$
$$0 + I(B;A) = H(B) - I(B;N)$$
$$I(B;A) = H(B|N)$$

Therefore, if we measure that $H(B|N) \leq \epsilon$, then:

$$I(B;A) \leq \epsilon$$

4.2   Theory vs. Practice

If we replay from a log file L then we are able to measure $H(B) - H(L)$, where $H(L) \leq I(L;D) + I(L;A) + I(L;N)$. This inequality says that the entropy in the log file can only come from three sources: D, A, and N. The deterministic behavior that we did not need to log and replay from the log but did ($I(L;D)$) is chosen nondeterministically, meaning that before the transaction we do not know what determinism will be logged, so this term can be non-zero[6]. Any entropy from the confidential data A that was logged ($I(L;A)$) and then replayed will mask the entropy and can hide a covert channel from us. The last term ($I(L;N)$) is all of the architectural nondeterminism that actually must be logged and replayed for deterministic replay to work correctly. The total entropy in the log $H(L)$ is given as an inequality since logging and replaying what would otherwise have been deterministic causes $I(L;D)$, $I(L;A)$, and $I(L;N)$ to no longer be independent. Now we have:

$$H(B) - H(L) \quad I(B;D) + I(B;A) + I(B;N) - I(L;D)$$
$$-I(L;A) - I(L;N)$$

Under replay, assuming the replay is in fact deterministic with respect to the nondeterminism N, we have the equality $I(L;N) = I(B;N)$. It says that for the replay to work all of the truly nondeterministic events must be in the log.

With logging there is now some imprecision in our policy enforcement:

$$I(B;D) + I(B;A) + I(B;N)$$
$$-I(L;D) - I(L;A) - I(L;N) \leq H(B) - H(L)$$
$$0 + I(B;A) + I(B;N)$$
$$-I(L;D) - I(L;A) - I(L;N) \leq H(B) - H(L)$$
$$I(B;A) - I(L;D) - I(L;A) \quad\quad \leq H(B) - H(L)$$

---

[4] Note that $H(D) = 0$ for a system that behaves as specified, so the information of D, and therefore its mutual information with all other variables, is 0. We take the system S as its own specification, so $H(D) = 0$ is only possible for S' during replay.

[5] Conditional entropy is also sometimes written as $H_N(B)$.

[6] Recall that D is the system specification and is therefore only deterministic when the system S behaves as specified, so that $I(L;D)$ can be non-zero for S' during replay.

Assume that we have measured $H(B) - H(L) \leq \epsilon$, then:

$$I(B;A) \leq \epsilon + (I(L;D) + I(L;A))$$

In other words, for the policy to be enforced it suffices that $I(L;D) + I(L;A) = 0$, which implies that $I(L;D) = 0$ and $I(L;A) = 0$ since entropy cannot be negative. When $I(L;D) \neq 0$ that implies that there is some benign imprecision in our replay due to the fact that we are logging and replaying, explicitly or implicitly, part of the system specification that should be deterministic[7]. When confidential data is logged $I(L;A) \neq 0$, meaning that there is a covert channel from A to B through logged entropy that will be replayed from the log during replay and mutual information between A to B will be hidden from our measurement. Covert channels are a concern because we cannot tell the difference between these two sources of imprecision without a precise information flow analysis to distinguish among $I(L;D)$, $I(L;A)$, and $I(L;N)$, but a specific ordering property of events in the log enables a systematic, exhaustive covert channel analysis because the log file is the only source of covert channels. No high-security input can be transmitted through a covert channel without also being logged as $I(L;A)$, something we plan to explore in future work.

4.3   Measuring $H(B) - H(L)$

We wish to do r replays using the log file L, from the original transaction, and then be able to say that with some probability γ, that at least $c+1$ final system states in B (or c more final states) would have been observed if the policy were violated, meaning more than ϵ bits of entropy has leaked, where $c = 2^\epsilon$. The number of possible final system states may be greater than $c+1$ but we assume the worst case so that we can do hypothesis testing and gain certainty that the policy was enforced. Our alternate hypothesis is that $|B| - |N| \leq 2^\epsilon = c$, thus varying the confidential data will not introduce too many extra final states in B's view and we can say that the policy was enforced.

We assume an equal distribution of possible final states in B for the hypothesis test. If the attacker desires a probability $\rho = 1$ of passing the hypothesis test, i.e., if they want a zero chance of the information flow security violation being detected, then they can not use more states than what ϵ allows. Therefore, the attacker must use an equal distribution of B to maximize $I(A;B)$ since an unequal distribution only decreases the entropy[8]. In the next section, Section 5, we will calculate a caveat δ that is the maximum additional entropy the attacker can gain from an unequal distribution of their coding of B when $\rho < 1$, but for the hypothesis test we assume an equal distribution.

Note that hypothesis testing only gives us confidence that the policy was enforced if we reject the null hypothesis, it does not prove that the policy was

---

[7] Note that for practical implementations this benign imprecision is unavoidable, because of caches and other hardware issues.

[8] For example, for a random variable with two possible output states the maximal entropy is $0.5 \log \frac{1}{0.5} + 0.5 \log \frac{1}{0.5} = 1$ bit, an unequal distribution decreases the entropy, such as $0.3 \log \frac{1}{0.3} + 0.7 \log \frac{1}{0.7} \approx 0.881$ bits.

violated if the null hypothesis is not rejected. The designer of a system based on our technique would have to take great care in defining the set A and varying it randomly, since attacker assumptions need to be accounted for [16]. For our purposes in this paper we assume that the distribution of A that the attacker assumes is known to us, and our bound of $I(A; B) \leq \epsilon + \delta$ is probabilistic and is a bound on the *average* amount of information about A the attacker can learn.

For $\epsilon = 0$ there are two possible final states if a single bit leaks, so the probability is $\gamma = 1 - 2^{-(r-1)}$. With every replay that does not reach a different final state of B from the original trace we cut our uncertainty that the policy was enforced in half, so that our certainty that the policy was enforced asymptotically approaches 1. Only in the special case that $\epsilon = 0$ is the equation for $1 - \gamma$ similar to a geometric distribution, in general the trials are not independent (a trial being whether or not we observe a new state for B), which becomes a factor when $\epsilon \neq 0$ meaning that there are more than two possible states for B.

Non-zero values of ϵ, even if they are small, may be important for some practical policies. For example, if the attacker can determine whether a user entered a valid input or not then that is a leak of one bit of information that the system designers may wish to allow. For practical values of ϵ we have performed a numerical matrix power calculation to determine the number of replays needed to gain 99.9% certainty ($\gamma = 0.999$), shown in Table 1.

Table 1. The number of replays necessary for 99.9% certainty that the policy was enforced

ϵ	$c + 1 = 2^\epsilon + 1$	Number of replays (r)
0	2	11
1	3	15
2	5	39
3	9	78
4	17	161
5	33	338

The numerical method for generating this table is as follows. For the general case that $\epsilon > 0$, we can view the process as a Markov process with $c + 2$ Markov process states (0 being the start state, $c + 1$ being a saturating end state) where being in state j means that j different final system states have been observed (note that a final system state and a Markov state are not the same, just two uses of the same word). Then we assume that more than ϵ bits were leaked, *i.e.*, our null hypothesis is that at least $c + 1$ final states will be observed.

Thus the probability of the Markov process going from state j to state $j + 1$ for each replay is $m_{j,j+1} = \frac{c+1-j}{c+1}$, and the probability of staying in the same state j is $m_{j,j} = 1 - m_{j,j+1}$ when $j \neq c + 1$ and 1 when $j = c + 1$, all other elements being 0. For small values of ϵ a transition probabilities matrix M can be constructed with the elements $m_{i,j}$ forming an upper bidiagonal matrix, where M^k gives the k-step probabilities matrix that we will go from state i to state j in k steps. Then the probability γ that we make it to state $c + 1$ in k steps can be solved numerically by performing the matrix power calculation M^k and γ

will be equal to the upper right corner element $(0, c+1)$ of the upper triangular matrix Q^k. We can choose the minimum $r = k$ where $(M^k)_{0,c+1} > \gamma$.

5   Caveat δ

In this section we show how to calculate the caveat δ, which is the additional amount of entropy in $I(A; B)$ that the attacker can utilize given the constraint that they must pass the hypothesis test with probability ρ. The structure of this calculation is as follows: the attacker must use a proportion q of their state space of B in order to, with probability ρ, pass the hypothesis test that bounds ϵ. This equivocation (mapping multiple inputs from A to the same output states of B), which is forced on the attacker by the hypothesis test, will bound by δ the additional amount of entropy in $I(A; B)$ that can be gained by an arbitrary distribution. This section is structured as follows: first we show how to calculate the probability ρ of passing the hypothesis test for a given value for q, then we solve this equation for a bound for q as a function of ρ since in practice ρ is a policy parameter of the attack model and q is the value we want to calculate, and finally we show how to calculate δ as a function of q.

5.1   Start with ρ as a Function of q

The optimal strategy, in terms of ρ, for an attacker to pass the hypothesis test with probability ρ and $I(A; B) > \epsilon$ is to divide the states of B up into $c + 1$ bins, with a proportion q of these states dedicated to the c bins of size $\frac{q}{c}$ that through equivocation will be allowed by the hypothesis test. The remaining bin of size $1 - q$ is the bin which the attacker is allowed to use for additional entropy beyond ϵ. We assume that $1 - q < \frac{q}{c}$, which holds for appropriate values of ρ, r, and γ. The optimal strategy for the attacker to maximize their entropy is to use some bin smaller than $1 - q$ and not equivocate all the states in the bin. By assuming a bin size of $1 - q$ where the attacker can gain additional entropy, we are covering the worst case for a bin size, and then a worst case entropy for that bin size serves as our bound δ. Thus δ is not a tight bound, *i.e.*, the attacker cannot actually achieve δ bits of additional entropy, but δ serves as a good bound in practice.

Based on our assumption that $1 - q < \frac{q}{c}$, we can calculate the probability ρ that an attacker will pass the hypothesis test using a portion q of their states for B.

$$\rho = q^r + c\left(1 - \frac{q}{c}\right)^r$$

This equation is based on the insight that all r samples for the hypothesis test must come from at most c of the $c+1$ bins. Thus either all must from come the portion q, *or* if any sample comes from the bin of size $1 - q$ then there are c ways of not having sampled one of the $\frac{q}{c}$-sized bins.

5.2   Bound q as a Function of ρ

In practice, we wish to set ρ as a parameter and calculate q. Rather than solving for q, we can bound q as follows. The proof is provided in the appendix.

$$q > \left(\rho - \frac{c^{r+1}}{(c+1)^r} \right)^{1/r}$$

5.3   Calculate δ as a Function of q

We wish to bound the additional entropy the attacker can gain from an unequal distribution of states, $I(A; B) - \epsilon \leq \delta$. By equivocation, in order to pass the hypothesis test with probability ρ, the attacker now can have $n \leq (qH(A))$ states in a bin of size $p \leq 1 - q$ with which to transmit information beyond the ϵ bits allowed by the hypothesis test.

This additional entropy is maximized when $I(A; B) - \epsilon = p \log n - p \log p$ (this is a corollary to Shannon's result on additivity). Note that $q > 0.5$ because we have assumed that $1 - q < \frac{q}{c}$ with $c \geq 1$.

This means that $I(A; B) - \epsilon \leq (1 - q) \log (qH(A)) - (1 - q) \log(1 - q)$, so we can bound $I(A; B) - \epsilon \leq \delta$ by setting $\delta = (1 - q) \log (qH(A)) - (1 - q) \log(1 - q)$.

5.4   Example

Table 2 shows the various stages of the calculation of the caveat for different policy parameter values of ϵ, assuming $\rho = 0.9$ and that the high input A is a credit card number which can be viewed as a 53-bit number so that $H(A) = 53$. It is interesting to note that the caveat δ depends on ρ, $H(A)$, and r, and other than the dependence of r on γ, r is totally independent of ϵ. If a system designer's goal was to drive $I(A; B)$ as close to 0 as possible, for example, they could set $\epsilon = 0$, $r = 161$, and with a very high confidence γ bound $I(A; B)$ to be less than 0.0350100747.

A system designer that wanted to trade some security for better performance while allowing for small leaks that would lead to false positives in other systems might do the following. By setting $\gamma = \rho = 0.69$ and $\epsilon = 4$ we get $r = 64$ and $\delta = 0.185241912$. Thus a single transaction can be parallelized over, e.g., 64 cores of a multicore processor, yet with an assurance of 0.69 a leak of more than 4.2 bits will be detected[9]. In the ATM example, a Trojan could steal more than 4.2 bits of at most 3.22580645 credit card numbers[10] before being detected (in the expected case), and if it steals all 53 bits then it is very likely to be detected on the first try.

Interestingly, if information theft detection is defined in terms of Moskowitz and Kang's short message criterion [17], then the system designer need only set $\epsilon = 0$ and integrate over multiple transactions the product of the maximum number of bits leaked (δ) and the attacker probability of not getting caught, with the former diminishing as ρ, ρ^2, ρ^3, ..., and so on down to zero. This geometric

---

[9] Note that $\epsilon +$ 4.2.

[10] This can be calculated with a geometric series.

Table 2. Example bounds where $H(A) = 53$ and $\rho = 0.9$

ϵ	$c + 1 = 2^\epsilon + 1$	Number of replays (r)	q	δ	$I(A; B) \leq \epsilon + \delta$
0	2	11	0.9904186332	0.5078124405	0.5078124405
1	3	15	0.9926638266	0.3888171917	1.3888171917
2	5	39	0.9972832036	0.1439902071	2.1439902071
3	9	78	0.9986384823	0.0721604367	3.0721604367
4	17	161	0.9993394326	0.0350100747	4.0350100747
5	33	338	0.9996851317	0.0166880219	5.0166880219

series converges at 5.078124405 bits for $\epsilon = 0$ and $\rho = 0.9$. To the best of our knowledge the short message criterion has never been achieved in practice, yet a replay-based approach makes this possible.

5.5   Performance

Any application of information flow security is a tradeoff between security and performance [17]. We did not take any specific performance measurements because this paper proposes a general approach and the performance tradeoff is specific to the particular application, but we will note two important points about performance. First, the replays are trivial to parallelize. Each replay can be executed on a different core of a multicore processor or in its own virtual machine. Second the performance tradeoff can be much better than many traditional approaches such as noise injection [18], because our repeated-deterministic-replay approach operates on the other side of Shannon's equation for the equivocation of a noisy channel.

$$H(A) - H(A|B) = H(B) - H(B|A) \qquad (= I(A; B))$$

Noise injection works on the right side of the equation and increases the noise $H(B|A)$, which can inadvertently increase $H(B)$ so that the trick is to minimize $H(B) - H(B|A)$ to the point where an equivocation $H(A|B)$ is forced on an attacker to get their signal through the noisy channel. Our approach directly forces an equivocation of $H(A|B)$ on the attacker if they want to pass the hypothesis test. For $H(A) \ll H(B)$, which is typical of many common scenarios such as A is a credit card ($H(A) = 53$) and B is all network output (quite possibly $H(B)$ is in the millions or billions), working on the left side of the equivocation equation is orders of magnitude more efficient. Furthermore, noise injection requires that the randomly injected noise be unknown and unpredictable to the attacker, because if they can predict the noise then they can greatly increase their channel capacity [19]. Thus, our intrusion detection approach to information flow security is more practical than traditional approaches.

6   Related Work

We classify related work into four categories: secure information flow, information-theoretic approaches, language-based information flow security, and covert channel analysis.

6.1   Secure Information Flow

TightLip [11] detects application leaks of confidential information by spawning a "doppleganger" process with scrubbed inputs and comparing the output of the application process and the doppleganger process. This allows for low-overhead detection of confidentiality policy breaches for unmodified applications with minor changes to the operating system. Because TightLip focuses on applications with bugs and misconfigurations that leak confidential information it is implemented at the system call level. Our work, in contrast, can be applied to a full system in a virtual machine to bound information leakage for arbitrary malicious code such as a Trojan installed on the system, which is a more challenging problem. Also, when the basic concept of redundancy involves more than two versions of the process or system, the probability of getting the same output by chance is not geometrically distributed because the events of seeing each new output are not independent, which is why our approach is based on hypothesis testing and not simply comparing two versions of the output.

The RIFLE project [20] adds dynamic information flow mechanisms to the Itanium processor. The current implementation of RIFLE is conservative in marking information flow and relies on static analysis to reduce the marking of false information flows. Dynamic information flow systems always require static analysis in practice. Fenton's data mark machine [21,22], for example, cannot support variable data marks and thus in practice would require the compiler to know the security class of every data object at each possible program point so that it can be placed in the appropriate register. Thus, both RIFLE and Fenton's data mark machine rely on static analysis for enforcing information flow security, which has its own set of limitations.

Both Denning [23] and Bishop [24] give a good summary of the challenges of enforcing information flow policies, either statically or dynamically. The common theme is that, for confidentiality policies, what could have happened carries as much information as what did happen (demonstrated by the existence of implicit flows and covert channels). Our approach explicitly goes back to the beginning of a transaction and measures what could have happened.

6.2   Information Theory

Our own work was inspired by the idea of using entropy analysis to both understand and detect malicious software such as worms [25]. The idea of applying the information theory that Shannon [3] developed for the theory of communication to information flow security is not new. What is novel about our work is the observation that entropy can be controlled and measured using checkpointing and deterministic replay, even for commodity systems. A related work on deterministic replay is ReVirt [26], where the purpose of checkpointing and replaying is to analyze intrusions.

Wittbold and Johnson [27] provide a theoretical approach to information flow security and covert channels that is entirely from an information-theoretic perspective. Gray [28] also addresses covert channels with information theory, but observes that, "we need to provide a connection between source code and [the] system model." The architecture we present in this paper provides that connection by replaying the system, thus using the system as its own specification. Gianvecchio and Wang [29] take an entropy-based approach to detecting covert channels on a network. Köpf and Basin [30] develop quantitative, information-theoretic metrics for side-channel attacks.

The work of Browne [31,32,33] is the most relevant to our work in terms of the underlying ideas. The Turing test for information flow [32] represents entropy as uncertainty about the mathematical definition of a system, rather than true uncertainty. This observation is important for covert channel analysis. Another important observation [31] is that noise-effect entropy is not unique. This becomes a problem when a CPU event such as a hard drive request or keyboard interrupt depends on the high input A. Yumerefendi et al. [11] found that many useful applications of confidentiality policy enforcement do not have this problem, and for future work we plan to explore the possibility of branching the log file whenever nondeterministic events differ during replay to build an "entropy tree" and preserve deterministic replay under such a scenario.

6.3   Language-Based Information Flow Security

Language-based information flow security is a well-developed area and we will refer the reader to a survey paper by Sabelfeld and Myers [34]. Here we will only point out some interesting results related to non-interference or practical implementations of information flow policies. JFlow [35] checks information flow of Java programs, mostly statically. A more recent development is the link between information theory and language-based information flow security, including the ability to handle loops [36]. This can allow a static calculation of the rate of information leakage rather than a binary answer about whether information leaks or not. McCamant and Ernst [37] develop a simulation-based proof technique based on the same basic idea as TightLip [11], namely comparing the outputs of a program with access to secret information to the outputs of a version of the program without access to the secret information. More recently, the same authors demonstrate that quantitative information flow can be calculated as a network flow capacity [38].

6.4   Covert Channel Analysis

The "light pink book" [39] in the rainbow series is an excellent resource on the difficulties of designing a systematic covert channel [40,41] analysis. See also McHugh's chapter in the Handbook for the Computer Security Classification of Trusted Systems [42] and Millen's position paper [43]. Kemmerer [44] developed the shared resource matrix methodology to help identify all covert channels as a transitive closure of subjects and their ability to read or modify objects. This methodology has been very successful due to its generality and because it can be applied to different specifications or implementations at every design stage. The limitation of this technique is that it requires all objects to be enumerated, and covert channels often use variables not normally viewed as data objects. A more attractive method for addressing covert channels in our repeated-deterministic-replay approach is due to Wray [4]. Wray's analysis can be applied to any covert channel with timing characteristics.

7 Conclusion

We described an approach to bound the mutual information between high input A and low output B for an arbitrary system S. We showed that, through a two-pronged approach of hypothesis testing and information theory, it is possible to bound $I(A; B)$ even for an attacker with an astronomical number of states and an arbitrary choice for the distribution of those states, assuming the attacker must have some probability ρ of not being detected. We expect that this general approach will lead to more secure systems and more fruitful analysis techniques for a variety of applications.

For future work, because covert channels are only possible through $I(L; A)$, it should be possible to address them exhaustively for real, interesting applications. For example, most nondeterministic events need not depend on A (*i.e.*, there is no reason why a different hard drive block should be requested when a different credit card number is entered), so that any attempt to exploit a covert channel can be detected as a difference in L during replay. We plan to explore this for specific applications in the future.

For some real applications, nondeterminism does depend on high input. If, for example, A is a filename of a file to be accessed then we must still be able to do replay and measure even when the log file will differ. We plan to explore the possibility of building "entropy trees" by branching the log file when nondeterministic events differ during replay, and the issues raised by this.

Acknowledgements

We would like to thank many who provided comments and suggestions on earlier ideas related to this work, including Norm Matloff and Richard Kemmerer. We are also very grateful to the editorial board and the anonymous reviewers of the special issue on Security in Computing. This work was supported by ETRI, Intel, NSF CyberTrust Grant No. 0627749, and US Air Force grant FA9550-07-1-0532.

References

1. Moore, D., Paxson, V., Savage, S., Shannon, C., Staniford, S., Weaver, N.: Inside the Slammer worm. IEEE Security and Privacy 1(4), 33–39 (2003)
2. Sarangi, S.R., Greskamp, B., Torrellas, J.: CADRE: Cycle-Accurate Deterministic Replay for Hardware Debugging. In: DSN 2006: Proceedings of the International Conference on Dependable Systems and Networks (DSN 2006), Washington, DC, USA, pp. 301–312. IEEE Computer Society, Los Alamitos (2006)

3. Shannon, C.E., Weaver, W.: The Mathematical Theory of Communication. University of Illinois Press, Urbana (1949)
4. Wray, J.C.: An analysis of covert timing channels. In: IEEE Symposium on Security and Privacy, pp. 2–7 (1991)
5. General William T. Sherman, as quoted in B. H. Liddell Hart, Strategy, second revised edition
6. Young, A., Yung, M.: Malicious Cryptography: Exposing Cryptovirology. Wiley Publishing, Inc., Chichester (2004)
7. Song, D.X., Wagner, D., Tian, X.: Timing analysis of keystrokes and timing attacks on SSH. In: USENIX Security Symposium 2001 (2001)
8. Kuhn, M.G.: Optical time-domain eavesdropping risks of CRT displays. In: Proceedings of the 2002 IEEE Symposium on Security and Privacy, pp. 3–18 (2002)
9. Kohno, T., Broido, A., Claffy, K.C.: Remote Physical Device Fingerprinting. In: IEEE Symposium on Security and Privacy (May 2005)
10. Wang, Z., Lee, R.B.: New cache designs for thwarting software cache-based side channel attacks. SIGARCH Comput. Archit. News 35(2), 494–505 (2007)
11. Yumerefendi, A., Mickle, B., Cox, L.P.: Tightlip: Keeping applications from spilling the beans. In: Networked Systems Design and Implementation (NSDI) (2007)
12. Goguen, J.A., Meseguer, J.: Security policies and security models. In: IEEE Symposium on Security and Privacy, pp. 11–20 (1982)
13. Goguen, J.A., Meseguer, J.: Unwinding and inference control. In: IEEE Symposium on Security and Privacy, pp. 75–86 (1984)
14. de Oliveira, D.A.S., Crandall, J.R., Wassermann, G., Su, Z., Wu, S.F., Chong, F.T.: ExecRecorder: VM-based full-system replay for attack analysis and system recovery. In: Workshop on Architectural and System Support for Improving Software Dependability, San Jose, CA (October 2006)
15. The OpenSSL Project, http://www.openssl.org/
16. Clarkson, M.R., Myers, A.C., Schneider, F.B.: Belief in information flow. In: CSFW 2005: Proceedings of the 18th IEEE Computer Security Foundations Workshop (CSFW 2005), Washington, DC, USA, pp. 31–45. IEEE Computer Society, Los Alamitos (2005)
17. Moskowitz, I.S., Kang, M.H.: Covert channels - here to stay? In: Compass 1994: 9th Annual Conference on Computer Assurance, Gaithersburg, MD, National Institute of Standards and Technology, pp. 235–244 (1994)
18. Kang, M.H., Moskowitz, I.S.: A pump for rapid, reliable, secure communication. In: CCS 1993: Proceedings of the 1st ACM conference on Computer and Communications Security, pp. 119–129. ACM Press, New York (1993)
19. Costa, M.: Writing on dirty paper (corresp.). IEEE Transactions on Information Theory 29(3), 439–441 (1983)
20. Vachharajani, N., Bridges, M.J., Chang, J., Rangan, R., Ottoni, G., Blome, J.A., Reis, G.A., Vachharajani, M., August, D.I.: RIFLE: An architectural framework for user-centric information-flow security. In: Proceedings of the 37th International Symposium on Microarchitecture (MICRO) (December 2004)
21. Fenton, J.S.: Information protection systems. Ph.D. Thesis, University of Cambridge (1973)
22. Fenton, J.S.: Memoryless subsystems. The Computer Journal 17(2), 143–147 (1974)
23. Denning, D.E.R.: Cryptography and Data Security. Addison-Wesley Longman Publishing Co., Inc., Boston (1982)
24. Bishop, M.: Computer Security: Art and Science, p. 344. Addison-Wesley, Reading (2003)

25. Kumar, A., Paxson, V., Weaver, N.: Exploiting underlying structure for detailed reconstruction of an internet-scale event. In: IMC 2005: Proceedings of the 5th ACM SIGCOMM on Internet measurement. ACM Press, New York (2006)
26. Dunlap, G.W., King, S.T., Cinar, S., Basrai, M.A., Chen, P.M.: ReVirt: Enabling intrusion analysis through virtual-machine logging and replay. SIGOPS Oper. Syst. Rev. 36(SI), 211–224 (2002)
27. Wittbold, J.T., Johnson, D.M.: Information flow in nondeterministic systems. In: IEEE Symposium on Security and Privacy, pp. 144–161 (1990)
28. Gray III, J.W.: Toward a mathematical foundation for information flow security. In: IEEE Symposium on Security and Privacy, pp. 21–35 (1991)
29. Gianvecchio, S., Wang, H.: Detecting covert timing channels: an entropy-based approach. In: CCS 2007: Proceedings of the 14th ACM conference on Computer and Communications Security, pp. 307–316. ACM, New York (2007)
30. Köpf, B., Basin, D.: An information-theoretic model for adaptive side-channel attacks. In: CCS 2007: Proceedings of the 14th ACM conference on Computer and Communications Security, pp. 286–296. ACM, New York (2007)
31. Browne, R.: An entropy conservation law for testing the completeness of covert channel analysis. In: CCS 1994: Proceedings of the 2nd ACM Conference on Computer and Communications Security, pp. 270–281. ACM Press, New York (1994)
32. Browne, R.: The turing test and non-information flow. In: IEEE Symposium on Security and Privacy, pp. 373–388 (1991)
33. Browne, R.: Mode security: An infrastructure for covert channel suppression. In: IEEE Symposium on Security and Privacy, pp. 39–55 (1999)
34. Sabelfeld, A., Myers, A.: Language-based information-flow security. IEEE Journal on Selected Areas in Communications 21(1) (2003)
35. Myers, A.C.: JFlow: Practical mostly-static information flow control. In: POPL 1999: Proceedings of the 24th ACM SIGPLAN-SIGACT Symposium on Principles of Programming Languages. ACM Press, New York (1999)
36. Malacaria, P.: Assessing security threats of looping constructs. In: POPL 2007: Proceedings of the 34th ACM SIGPLAN-SIGACT Symposium on Principles of Programming Languages. ACM Press, New York (2007)
37. McCamant, S., Ernst, M.D.: A simulation-based proof technique for dynamic information flow. In: PLAS 2007: ACM SIGPLAN Workshop on Programming Languages and Analysis for Security, San Diego, California, USA, June 14 (2007)
38. McCamant, S., Ernst, M.D.: Quantitative information flow as network flow capacity. In: Proceedings of the ACM SIGPLAN 2008 Conference on Programming Language Design and Implementation, Tucson, AZ, USA, June 9–11 (2008)
39. Light Pink Book: A guide to understanding covert channel analysis of trusted systems, version 1. NCSC-TG-030, Library No. S-240,572, TCSEC Rainbow Series Library (November 1993)
40. Lampson, B.W.: A note on the confinement problem. Communications of the ACM 16(10), 613–615 (1973)
41. Lipner, S.B.: A comment on the confinement problem. In: SOSP 1975: Proceedings of the fifth ACM Symposium on Operating Systems Principles, pp. 192–196. ACM Press, New York (1975)
42. McHugh, J.: Covert channel analysis (1995)
43. Millen, J.K.: 20 years of covert channel modeling and analysis. In: IEEE Symposium on Security and Privacy, pp. 113–114 (1999)
44. Kemmerer, R.A.: Shared resource matrix methodology: an approach to identifying storage and timing channels. ACM Trans. Comput. Syst. 1(3), 256–277 (1983)

Appendix: Bound q as a Function of ρ

Proposition. Let c and r be positive constants, ρ a real number such that $1 > \rho > \frac{c^r}{(c+1)^{r-1}}$. Then there exists q such that

$$\left(\rho - \frac{c^{r+1}}{(c+1)^r}\right)^{1/r} < q < 1 \text{ and } c\left(1 - \frac{q}{c}\right)^r + q^r = \rho.$$

Proof. Set $f(x) = c\left(1 - \frac{x}{c}\right)^r + x^r$. Then $f'(x) = -r\left(1 - \frac{x}{c}\right)^{r-1} + rx^{r-1}$, so f has exactly one positive critical point x_0 where

$$x_0 = \left(1 - \frac{x_0}{c}\right), \text{ so that } x_0\left(1 + \frac{1}{c}\right) = 1 \text{ and } x_0 = \frac{c}{c+1}.$$

x_0 is a minimum (as one can see by taking the second derivative or simply noting that $f \to \infty$ as $x \to \infty$), and

$$f(x_0) = f(\frac{c}{c+1}) = c\left(1 - \frac{1}{c+1}\right)^r + \left(\frac{c}{c+1}\right)^r =$$

$$(c+1)\left(\frac{c}{c+1}\right)^r = \frac{c^r}{(c+1)^{r-1}}.$$

As $f(x_0) < \rho < 1 < f(1)$ and f is continuous, $f(q) = \rho$ for some q between x_0 and 1. Next, note that $f'(x) < rx^{r-1}$ for all positive x; therefore f grows less slowly than x^r. Thus for $x > x_0$, $f(x) < x^r + f(x_0) - x_0^r$, by the fact that the two sides in the last inequality are equal at $x = x_0$ and the growth-rate observation above. This gives, for $x > x_0$,

$$f(x) < x^r + \frac{c^r}{(c+1)^{r-1}} - \left(\frac{c}{c+1}\right)^r = x^r + \frac{c^r(c+1) - c^r}{(c+1)^r}.$$

In particular, then, for the value q such that $f(q) = \rho$,

$$\rho < q^r + \frac{c^r(c+1) - c^r}{(c+1)^r} \Rightarrow \left(\rho - \frac{c^{r+1}}{(c+1)^r}\right)^{1/r} < q,$$

as desired.

Author Index